DATE DUE

HIGHSMITH #45231

Thematic Guide to Young Adult Literature

Thematic Guide to Young Adult Literature

Alice Trupe

GREENWOOD PRESS
Westport, Connecticut • London

Library of Congress Cataloging-in-Publication Data

Trupe, Alice.
   Thematic guide to young adult literature / Alice Trupe.
      p. cm.
   Includes bibliographical references and index.
   ISBN 0-313-33234-7 (alk. paper)
1. Young adult fiction, American—History and criticism. 2. Young adult
fiction, American—Themes, motives. 3. Teenagers—Books and reading—
United States. 4. Teenagers in literature—Bibliography. 5. Young adult
literature—Bibliography. I. Title.
   PS374.Y57T78   2006
   813.009'928—dc22   2006006174

British Library Cataloguing in Publication Data is available.

Library of Congress Catalog Card Number: 2006006174
ISBN: 0-313-33234-7

First published in 2006

Greenwood Press, 88 Post Road West, Westport, CT 06881
An imprint of Greenwood Publishing Group, Inc.
www.greenwood.com

Printed in the United States of America

The paper used in this book complies with the
Permanent Paper Standard issued by the National
Information Standards Organization (Z39.48–1984).

10 9 8 7 6 5 4 3 2 1

Contents

Preface

Contemporary Young Adult (YA) literature is a comparatively new field, usually dated by scholars to the publication of S. E. Hinton's *The Outsiders* (1967), when the author was seventeen. Hinton had begun writing it two years earlier because she was not interested in the saccharine novels marketed to teen girls. This was the kind of fiction Hinton wanted to read, with characters who were both tough and vulnerable, who faced real social and emotional problems, who had economic worries and life choices to make, in a well-plotted, exciting narrative. The novel remains one of the most popular texts for young adults.

The genre of YA literature has thrived since the 1960s, though critical recognition and scholarly interest has lagged a bit behind the inventiveness of authors in the field. Today's YA literature features more complex plotting and motivation and more moral ambiguity than pre-1960s literature for teens did, and it is more likely to experiment with the novel form. Young readers need not be naive readers. The increasing sophistication of the genre has been recognized with an award specifically for YA literature, the Michael L. Printz Award, and the Young People's Literature category of the National Book Award.

There is a large and rapidly growing body of very good literature for young adult readers today, but with the exception of only a few well-known works, there is no established YA canon, and indeed, some of the best YA works available have been published within the last ten to fifteen years. For anyone new to the field, particularly for someone who wants to select meaningful, high-quality literature for classroom assignment or individual reading recommendations for teens, the wide range of available titles may be daunting. Moreover, except for book reviews, little criticism of contemporary YA literature has yet been published. This book is intended as an introduction to critical discussion of some of the best fiction for young adults. A selected bibliography of secondary sources includes critical works for readers interested in additional critical views. I have not included biographies, brief book reviews, or articles suggesting classroom uses of the literature but have indicated those texts that are of more interest to teachers than students with a parenthetical note.

While the book is organized as a thematic guide, with thirty-two chapters identifying significant themes of particular interest to young adults, critical discussions of the novels comment on form, characterization, point of view, and symbolism as appropriate, in order to provide a balanced critical introduction to each work. Three to eight novels are discussed in each chapter, beginning with a novel dating from the 1960s, 1970s, or early 1980s that may be considered a contemporary classic on the theme and followed by discussion of more recent works chosen to represent a range of variations in treatment of the theme. I am indebted to my daughter Mary Tasillo for sharing her paper on heroes in contemporary YA literature, reprinted here as Chapter 15: Heroism: What Does It Mean to Be a Hero? While this guide is not a comprehensive overview, it includes discussions of more than 150 works. Each chapter ends with lists of additional works on the same theme. Alternative thematic groupings are suggested in the appendix.

One of the issues involved in categorizing YA literature is the meaning of the term "young adult." Some children may be able to read young adult literature at age ten while others may not be ready for the more mature themes dealt with in many novels marketed to young adults. By some definitions, "young adults" include people in their early twenties. For the purposes of this book, I have assumed that the themes will be of interest to young people ranging from about age twelve to age seventeen. Some of the books discussed are appropriate for the younger end of this range while others are not. No attempt has been made to categorize books by age level, however, given the range in maturity of individual readers in the young adult group. A teacher or parent may use discussions of content as a guide to whether a particular text is appropriate for the group or individual reader for whom it is being considered.

Additionally, some of the works discussed may have originally been published for an adult audience but, because of their themes or age of the protagonist, may be widely read by young adults or selected for classroom use. Robert Cormier wrote *The Chocolate War* (1974) without a specifically young adult audience in mind, but his publisher suggested a marketing decision that placed this modern classic squarely in the YA category. Rudolfo Anaya's *Bless Me, Ultima* (1972) and Sandra Cisneros's *The House on Mango Street* (1984) are widely used in high school or middle school curricula.

The themes selected for this book by no means form a comprehensive list. Moreover, while each text under discussion is characterized by a dominant theme, other themes may play an important role as well. Texts selected are, for the most part, novels.

It has been my intention in writing this guide to introduce a wide range of interesting, well-written literary texts to a larger reading audience and to provide a point of departure for critical discussion of those about which little has been written to date.

Abuse, Sexual Violence, and Healing

Are You in the House Alone? by Richard Peck (1976)
Happy Endings Are All Alike by Sandra Scoppettone (1978)
When She Was Good by Norma Fox Mazer (1997)
The Watcher by James Howe (1997)
You Don't Know Me by David Klass (2001)
I Hadn't Meant to Tell You This by Jacqueline Woodson (1994)
I Was a Teenage Fairy by Francesca Lia Block (1998)

Abuse and sexual violence, though sensitive topics, hold special interest for middle school and secondary school readers. Many teens' lives are touched by physical or sexual abuse or by rape, through their own experience or that of a friend. Therefore, it is not surprising that the protagonist or another character in many YA novels may suffer systematic physical, emotional, or sexual abuse at home. In S. E. Hinton's *The Outsiders* (1967; discussed in Chapter 19: Insiders and Outsiders), for instance, the heroic Johnny Cade saves Ponyboy Curtis from death by drowning at the hands of a drunken member of another gang and later rescues small children from a burning abandoned church, but there are no models for heroism in Johnny's life. At home, Johnny has been ignored at best, beaten at worst, and this is simply a fact of life to his friends, who therefore harbor special sympathy for Johnny. In *Tears of a Tiger*, Sharon M. Draper's popular 1994 novel about the impact of a star basketball player's death in an automobile accident caused by alcohol use, one of the victim's friends is known to have an abusive stepfather; this friend believes life is tough, so when horrible things happen, the only thing to do is face them, to "be a man." Thus, routine abuse is accepted as just part of life.

Confronting adult abuse can play a role in the transition from childhood to young adulthood. Children become bigger and more independent, able to earn money and drive; they develop a sense of themselves as individuals apart from their parents; and they form deeper relationships outside the family, relationships that can make it easier for them to end victimization. These factors can also make young adults more vulnerable to sexual assault by those outside the family.

Thus rape also appears in young adult fiction, accurately reflecting its status as a realistic concern for teens, many of whom have been raped or may face rape at a later point in life. In the fiction discussed in this chapter, such violence itself plays a central role or is the catalyst for significant action in the novel. (Both of these subjects are discussed as well in Chapter 7, "Breaking Silence, Speaking Out," in which the focus is on teens' refusal to be abused any longer.)

Treatments of rape in young adult literature of the 1970s, such as Richard Peck's *Are You in the House Alone?* (1976) and Sandra Scoppettone's *Happy Endings Are All Alike* (1978), focused on the social attitudes that made reporting rape difficult. Each novel deals with a teen girl's rape by a teen boy known to her, and each is set in a small town where allegations of rape immediately ignite the rumor mill that brands the victim as promiscuous, provocative, and in some way "asking for it," an attitude that is first displayed by the law enforcement officials who interview the girls in their hospital rooms. Class issues exacerbate the victim Gail's powerlessness to pursue justice after her rape by the son of a leading family in her community in *Are You in the House Alone?* With no witness to her assault, she decides not to press charges, even though she has been stalked and terrorized for weeks before the rape occurs. Her attacker is clearly unbalanced but also seems to have so strong a sense of entitlement that he cannot see anything wrong with his actions. Only a second appalling assault results in his socialite parents' discreet removal of the boy from their community, but no one really knows where he has been sent—to a mental institution or a prep school. The first-person narrative explores Gail's growing fear and her frustration at others' responses after the rape, chiefly the responses of her boyfriend and her best friend, who is the rapist's girlfriend and who believes him to be too much of a gentleman to force sex on anyone. Gail, though victimized, sympathizes with her father, who feels helpless both to protect her and to "get satisfaction" for the crime. Conveying accurate information about the legal, physical, social, and psychological impact of rape was Peck's goal in writing about this sensitive topic ("About the Author," Peck 158).

Happy Endings Are All Alike in contrast, is one of the first novels for young adults to address sexual love between women, and Scoppettone delicately explores the tightrope that the young lovers walk as their relationship develops. Frighteningly, their fulfillment sparks violent impulses in a young man who believes that he can cure Jaret of her attraction to Peggy by initiating her into heterosexual intercourse. Jaret and Peggy not only must work out their own relationship without much information to guide them but also face active hostility from Peggy's older sister and denial from Peggy's father, who is focused on his own grief over his wife's recent death and blames Peggy's homosexuality on her loss. In contrast, the couple are buoyed by sympathy from Jaret's mother but are reluctant to come out to other members of her family. The third-person narrative allows Scoppettone to reveal the feelings of all involved and to explore how family relationships create a context for both girls' attitudes toward coming out and for their handling of the publicity that prosecution of the rapist brings.

As the narrative of the relationship develops, it is punctuated with ominous interludes, the first-person rants of a sixteen-year-old who spies on and then stalks the girls. Filled with hatred and anger, he makes Jaret the scapegoat for all that he believes is wrong in his life and relationships. The girls are oblivious of his hatred, not knowing him personally, and the anonymity of the diary-like chapters spewing his anger create intense suspense as to who he is and what, specifically, he intends, until he rapes Jaret at knifepoint.

After the rape, the two families' reactions to Jaret and Peggy's relationship, and thus the families' functionality, are starkly contrasted. Peggy's family breaks apart, with Peggy sent to a psychiatrist to satisfy her father's rationalization that she is simply going through a phase on her way to maturation and heterosexuality, while Jaret's family members support her decision to seek legal redress. Peggy's commitment to the relationship initially seems unlikely to survive the strain of public knowledge, but in a resolution of their temporary separation, she and Jaret seem headed for continued love, willing to accept "happy moments" if not "happy endings."

Abuse by older family members is the form that violence takes in several novels discussed here. *When She Was Good* (1997), by Norma Fox Mazer, delineates Em Thurkill's persecution by her older sister Pamela as Em gradually frees herself from Pamela's influence after her sudden, unexpected death. As she explores her feelings and deals with her new freedom at age eighteen, Em gradually reveals the circumstances of her past life—lack of friends due to the family's abject poverty, her father's alcoholism, her mother's illness and death, her casual sexual relations with boys, her father's remarriage, escape with Pamela to an apartment in the city, and Pamela's increasing emotional disturbance. Pamela's physical and verbal abuse has nearly squelched Em's spirit. Pamela attempted to destroy Em's very voice, tearing up her notebook for English class, the notebook that enabled Em to express her feelings in beautiful words that shape themselves into poems.

Em's gradual emergence from the grip of demoralizing domination is reflected in her growing ability to silence Pamela's disembodied abusive voice in her head. (She told the undertaker she would like to have the coffin nailed shut, in her fear of Pamela's return to life.) As she realizes that she no longer has to obey any of Pamela's rules for their life together, she starts envisioning possibilities—of having friends, growing flowers and vegetables, holding a steady job. She throws away Pamela's dolls that, like Pamela, seemed to watch her every move; she rediscovers her meager treasures that Pamela has locked up; she stops having nightmares about Pamela and confronts her memory of Pamela's death before her eyes.

When She Was Good follows a structure dictated by the course of Em's release from Pamela's control, including many flashbacks. Beginning with Pamela's death and a brief overview of the unhappy family life they shared with their parents, the novel ends with Em's freedom to remember the best times with her mother, making elderberry jam, preserving the happiness of those moments in the sweetness of the jam that lasts throughout the year and, it is implied, throughout Em's subsequent life. A period of months has elapsed, and Em's transformation is well under way. Em identifies with her mother: both have a capacity for happiness and live in expectancy of it. The strong sense of hope that nourished Em throughout the years of abuse and unhappiness is realized, and her agency is established.

In *The Watcher* (1997), James Howe builds a picture of self-effacing Margaret, who is physically abused by her father. The abuse, in the novel as in real life, is concealed, although hinted at, until the climactic moment when two other teens and a police officer arrive on the scene. Set at the beach, the novel unfolds through scraps of a journal in which Margaret translates the real people she watches and her family members into the characters of fantasy tales. An apparently perfect family is thus transformed into king, queen, prince, and princess in Margaret's fantasy life, while her father becomes the beast and her mother, in complicit silence, becomes the doll. The attractive lifeguard who glimpses Margaret's trouble in her eyes becomes an angel. The journal's language is halting and accurately illustrates writing in process as well as Margaret's troubled mental state.

Short chapters of third-person narrative focus on the people Margaret observes, giving the reader insights into their real lives and relationships, a reality that belies her rose-tinted interpretations of what she sees. The emerging images give the reader three different views of families and of child-parent relationships. The apparently perfect family is troubled by tension between the parents. The lifeguard, Chris, lives in a state of tension, needing to save someone. His own family life was shaped by the drowning of an older brother at age four, before Chris was born; this tragedy left his father a hollow shell. In some ways, his family situation resembles Margaret's: he lives in a private hell, feeling unloved and unable to reach his father or wake love in him. At the climax of the novel, when Margaret's father is holding her head under water, her thoughts reveal how he justifies the abuse, telling her she is bad and worthless, a feeling very similar to what Chris feels. Paradoxically, it is Margaret's one "bad" bold act that brings about her rescue: she has stolen several talismanic beloved objects from the happy family she has observed, including a framed photograph into which she inserts her own photograph, enraging her father. Evan, the boy her age whom she has been imagining as both a prince and her brother, is searching for the thief when loud music draws him to Margaret's house. Glimpsing her desperate situation through the window, Evan seeks out Chris, and together the boys interrupt the violence. At last Chris saves someone from drowning, and in doing so, realizes that it is really his father whom he has been trying to save through all his years of swimming and lifeguarding. A police officer arrives on their heels, drawn like Evan by the arias Margaret's mother listens to at top volume, covertly drawing official attention to her husband's brutality. At the crisis, when finally the reader is allowed to see what has driven "the watcher"—Margaret—to the beach and kept her a silent observer, the reader also sees that Margaret's mother, apparently paralyzed by her husband's violence, has similarly tried to transform unhappy experience into accepted artistic form. Dealing with violent emotion and tragic events, the unnamed opera gives a sort of shape and rationale to the raw events of life.

Another theme emerges in Evan's family life. In addition to the family photo, Margaret has stolen a shawl and a kite, significant gifts that symbolize happiness. Evan's mother wraps the shawl tightly around her to clothe herself in the familial love it represents. The kite was brought to the beach by Evan's father, and when Evan flew it, he brought joy to his seven-year-old sister, as well as to Margaret, who spread her arms as though to fly herself, while she watched from her observation point. Evan's family presents a real, functional alternative to Margaret's and Chris's unhappy lives. Evan's mother tells him that she has learned to see the beauty in imperfect shells. Their family is not perfect but it is nonetheless beautiful. Above all, Howe demonstrates the importance of looking beyond surface appearances to the family dynamics that shape the individual faces that people show to the world. Howe also shows the importance of really paying attention to other people's faces.

You Don't Know Me (2001) by David Klass is probably the funniest book on abuse in print. The physical abuse is described sufficiently to make a compassionate reader wince, but the wry, subversive first-person narrative is very entertaining, especially when Klass focuses on the challenges of dating, maintaining friendship when two young men desire the same young woman, surviving the tortures of math classes, and evading the kindly teacher as skillfully as one evades the authoritarian principal. John, who makes a lot of passing gibes at the father who named him for a toilet and then left, addresses most of the narrative to his mother. "You don't know me," he tells her, because she does not realize that her live-in boyfriend regularly hits him. To be sure, she is so tired from working double shifts at her factory job that she barely notices anything. John observes behavior like an anthropologist: much of his commentary on social relations takes the form of contrast between his school's social norms and those of the fictional Lashasa Palulu, tribal customs made up on the spot to suggest alternatives that would save him from whatever situation he has gotten into, whether it is his friends' attempts to pick up girls at a pet store in the mall or his mother's boyfriend's "whops," "whaps," or beatings with his belt.

Much of John's life, however, revolves around "anti-school," where he takes "anti-math," trying to avoid notice by "Mrs. Moonface" (as he calls the teacher in his internal monologue), so that he may concentrate on the prettiest fourteen-year-old girl he knows, "Glory Hallelujah" (known otherwise as Gloria). The other part of his day that involves him enough for comment is band practice, where he plays the tuba, or rather, the giant frog that masquerades as a tuba plays him, and he observes the contest between "Violent" (Violet) Hayes and her saxophone, which is really a monitor lizard—sometimes the lizard wins, sometimes Violent does, in their efforts to get through various musical pieces, including those composed by their new band director, Mr. Steenwilly. The director is the only adult who ever queries John about marks of abuse.

John's longing for Glory Hallelujah consumes him as he works up his nerve to ask her out. The course of true love fails to run smooth: his friend Bill (who is not a friend, because he also plans to ask Gloria out) stalks the couple on their date; a near-riot breaks out at the basketball game; and Gloria entices him into her family's basement rec room, locks the door, turns up the music loud enough to wake her parents, and begins to strip John, in a manipulative game that she plays with her psychotically protective father. The game ends with John's making a fast getaway through the pet door in the dark, leaving behind his shoes, his only decent jacket, and the sweater that his mother gave him for Christmas two years ago, just ahead of Gloria's father and the police. Gloria may have turned out to be shallow, envious of others' dates or money, and vindictive, but coping with her is nothing compared to surviving in the escalating war at home.

John's stepfather-to-be (identified with typical wry wit as "the man who is not my father") reveals his true profession as a mover of stolen goods when he drags John along to help move hot TVs in the dead of night immediately after the escape from Gloria's father. Thus in one short weekend, not only is it proved that John's mother does not know him but also that John does not know either Gloria or the precariousness of his own future. His mother's visit to a dying aunt turns John's normally danger-filled existence into a nightmare. At school, his exhaustion and fragile mental state betray him into crisis. First, he finds to his horror that he is actually uttering some of his usually silent monologue in math class, and then, in band, the tuba dies—he cannot play it and begins to weep. The first act results in his suspension from school and the latter results in Mr. Steenwilly's heightened awareness of John's problems.

Violet, in contrast with the popular but self-absorbed Gloria, shows a genuine interest in John. A grim crisis comes when he unwarily returns home late from a date with Violet—his drunk stepfather is convinced John is lying and nearly kills him. John's pain and the time required for his recovery are realistically, though briefly, depicted. John felt his mother did not know him, but it is clear that he did not know her when he kept his trouble and trauma from her because her anguish at the hell he has suffered is apparent. She turns the monster out of her home, and the school community, embarrassed at the abuse it has countenanced, reintegrates John at a band concert. Most of the adults who do not know John are petty tyrants or well-meaning but intrusive and mostly ineffectual would-be soul mates. Throughout the novel, John expresses a need to know his father, in fantasies of conversations or meetings with him. It is, ultimately, his father who does not know him and whom John does not know.

Sexual abuse is a delicate subject for young adult novels since explicit unwanted sex may be too unpleasant to keep the reader reading. The novels discussed here deal circumspectly with sexual abuse. Jacqueline Woodson's *I Hadn't Meant to Tell You This* (1994) is a slim, powerful, and haunting novel of a friendship. The narrator is Marie, a comfortably middle-class black twelve-year-old, an athlete, well-dressed, and popular, who finds herself unaccountably drawn to Lena, a poor, raggedly dressed white girl with a secret that she tells Marie: her father is sexually abusing her. Shunned by her friends as an Uncle Tom and forced to defend her friendship to her father, a veteran of the Civil Rights movement, Marie nonetheless makes the choice to befriend Lena and her younger sister, Dion. What the girls share is a painful sense of loss of their mothers. Lena's died of breast cancer, her death likely hastened by lack of money for medical treatment. Marie's mother has walked out, enabled by an inheritance from her parents to travel widely; she sends cryptic poetic messages on postcards from an array of sunny, warm places. Since her mother left, Maria's father has stopped touching her—there are no hugs, no pats to reassure her that she is, indeed, loved, though she and her father get along well. Her own secret is that she writes letters to her mother and buries them in her closet, knowing that her mother won't return and that she, Marie, is losing touch with who her mother is.

Initially, Marie flinches from Lena's secret—that she gets "too much love" from her father—and insists that it cannot be true, that Lena just wants attention, despite Lena's assertion that she really wants to be invisible (she tries to keep people away with her unwashed hair and dingy, semi-buttonless clothes). As Marie's disbelief is overcome, together the girls acknowledge and demonstrate that, given the sad and frightening elements life can hold, racial difference just is not a good reason for not being friends. They even win over Marie's former best friend, Sherry, who sets store by appearance. Throughout their friendship, and after Lena and Dion's departure to an unknown destination, Marie keeps Lena's secret. They have discussed options: Lena tells Marie that a social worker once separated her and Dion from their father but, unfortunately, from each other too by placing them in separate foster families, with the result that they ran away to be together again, rejoining their father because they had nowhere else to go. Now her father moves them every time any-one seems to be getting close to uncovering the secret of their relationship; he has forbidden her friendship with blacks as well, taking the girls away without even giving them an opportunity to say goodbye. Marie wants to kill Lena's father and suggests that Lena herself do so, but the complicated feelings Lena acknowledges— needing to have a father, pointing out that his life, too, has been hard—keep both girls from taking this suggestion seriously. Lena's concern for protecting Dion—she tries to take her everywhere with her and they spend little time in their home—hints at the kind of solution she has in mind: running away. Yet, when she leaves, the reader is left like Marie with an unresolved mystery: did the girls run away? Or has their father simply moved them again?

The relationship is ephemeral; Marie realizes that life can bring hard news about loved ones and that one is often powerless to bring happiness, or even relief from suffering, to people one loves. But Marie is a strong twelve-year-old who has learned that, given the brevity of life and relationships, people's common bond as human beings, no matter their color or class, is worth claiming.

In Francesca Lia Block's *I Was a Teenage Fairy* (1998) little is said of the actual abuse that two child models experience at the hands of a creepy photographer, but Barbie finds her fairy, Mab, because she has been sexually abused. The names res-onate with cultural significance, "Barbie" associated with the doll, "Mab" the wild queen of ancient legend. Mab is a pinkie-sized bad-tempered fairy who calls Barbie's mother the "vile crocodile," refuses to let Barbie perpetually apologize for everything, and gives her the courage, eventually, to stand up for herself. Abused at age eleven, at the time when her father (a psychiatrist, ironically, who shows little affection or concern for his daughter) is withdrawing from the family and her mother tacitly accepts her abuse as the price to be paid for a modeling career, Barbie is thin, famous, and detached from most people and circumstances by age sixteen. At this point she begins to care for an equally famous actor and heartthrob, whose sidekick is the boy model Barbie saw on his way into the photographer's studio immediately after she was abused by the photographer. As Barbie's romance with the actor, Todd, develops, Griffin, the other model, encounters Mab, more or less (he is not quite convinced of her reality, unlike Barbie, who has known her from childhood), and slowly he approaches the brink of suicide, then pulls back in time. Barbie, on the other hand, seems capable of a normal relationship, though she is unwilling to trust Todd entirely. The people she has trusted in the past have hurt her or abandoned her.

However, Todd has put the instrument of her deliverance into her hands. Even when she was first posing, Barbie wanted to take the pictures rather than sit for them, and Todd gives her a camera. She repeatedly promises to capture Mab on film, but she does not follow through on her promise. Finally, however, she uses the camera to photograph the photographer at work and expose his abuse of another small child. Mab has helped her survive her trauma over the years, but at sixteen, Barbie is ready to take a stand not only for herself but for others. She goes on to rename herself Selena Moon, as she claims the life as an artist that makes her happy and leaves behind the mother who betrayed her. All of this takes tremendous strength, and as this strength emerges, Mab, no longer needed, departs. Mab functions as a voice protesting against victimization, ultimately representing the love and support that enables the victims themselves to repudiate responsibility for victimization and to form healthy, mature relationships that foster growth and independence.

ADDITIONAL READING RECOMMENDATIONS

If Beale Street Could Talk by James Baldwin, 1974 (discussed in Guilty or Innocent?)
Chinese Handcuffs by Chris Crutcher, 1987
Bruises by Anke de Vries, 1992; English translation, 1995
Weeping Willow by Ruth White, 1992
Fair Game by Erika Tamar, 1993
Staying Fat for Sarah Byrnes by Chris Crutcher, 1993 (discussed in Beauty's Meaning)
Breath, Eyes, Memory by Edwidge Danticat, 1994
3 NBs of Julian Drew by James M. Deem, 1994
When She Hollers by Cynthia Voigt, 1994
When Jeff Comes Home by Catherine Atkins, 1999
Dreamland by Sarah Dessen, 2000
When Kambia Elaine Flew in from Neptune by Lori Aurelia Williams, 2000
Breathing Underwater by Alex Flinn, 2001
A Step from Heaven by An Na, 2001
Catalyst by Laurie Halse Anderson, 2002 (discussed in Friends Forever?)
America by E. R. Frank, 2002 (discussed in Emotional Problems Confronted)

Accepting Difference

Chernowitz! by Fran Arrick (1981)
Slave Day by Rob Thomas (1997)
Whale Talk by Chris Crutcher (2001)
Seedfolks by Paul Fleischman (1997)
Go and Come Back by Joan Abelove (1998)
From the Notebooks of Melanin Sun by Jacqueline Woodson
(1995)

Changing demographics in the United States, as well as increased interaction with dramatically different cultures half a world away, bring to the fore the need for American teens to understand and tolerate the range of people they may encounter in a multicultural world, whether their differences come from race or ethnicity or religion or language or sexual orientation. Multiculturalism is a well-established curricular component today, yet prejudices persist, erupting occasionally into hate crimes. Both outsiders and insiders must come to terms with prejudice when they encounter it in school and the community. The novels discussed in this chapter show characters in the process of coming to terms with a range of attitudes toward difference.

In *Chernowitz!* (1981), Fran Arrick illustrates how inhumane persecution could escalate to culminate in the Holocaust by showing the impact of one racist bully on a Jewish teen's life. Bob Cherno first encounters Emmett Sundback in ninth grade, and in the next year and a half, he learns what it is like to be ostracized and persecuted simply because he is a Jew, as Emmett systematically turns Bob's friends against him and isolates him socially both in and out of school.

Emmett's persecution begins with trivial questions that Bob finds unsettling, though it is difficult for him to pinpoint just why the questions feel like challenges. The challenges escalate into physical intimidation and school rumors of threats against Bob's home on Halloween. Bob wonders why Emmett has singled him out until the first clear clue to Emmett's anti-Semitism comes with his question "what kind of a name" Bob's last name is, followed by his calling Bob "Chernowitz." The persecution lasts into the beginning of their sophomore year, and escalates to the painting of a swastika on the family car and an attempt to kill the family's cat. It is the car vandalism that turns the tide: Bob's mother insists that the local newspaper be called to photograph the hateful symbol, and the subsequent news story brings kindness and sympathy from the neighbors, showing that Emmett's hatred is anomalous.

Emmett has no difficulty in influencing other teens. At the outset, Bob's former friends, classmates since elementary school, join in the exclusionary "joke" of walking away from him at the bus stop and laughing at him or taking his things and tossing them around, shredding his homework, and performing similar acts of hazing. Bob's best friend Brian at first treats him normally when they are alone, walking to the bus stop, though he joins the gang when they arrive, but eventually Brian avoids Bob altogether and, as the persecution escalates, even calls him "Jew bastard." Bob's shock is so great as to leave him breathless. Months later, when Brian wants to join Bob to race Bob's sailboat, Brian dismisses this incident as a "joke," unable or unwilling to comprehend the impact the epithet has had on Bob. Emmett's influence over them wanes rapidly after the swastika incident.

Bob tries to hide the extent of his persecution from his concerned parents, believing that he must handle this situation himself. At first, he fears that the bullying will become worse if his parents intervene, but as he recognizes the situation for what it is, an overt expression of anti-Semitism, he also wants to protect them from hurt, an increasingly difficult task. Not only do the incidents become more public, but also, because Bob is an only child, his parents cannot help but notice that he no longer hangs out with former friends. Furthermore, they are educators, who initially assume that, as in normal adolescent conflicts, Bob bears equal responsibility with his former friends for the "falling out" that has occurred, so they urge him to participate in neighborhood gatherings, arrange car pooling to soccer practices, and try to get him and Brian out to run mornings with their fathers. These efforts fail to reintegrate Bob with his peers, but over time he loses his fear of the bullying and humiliation, facing the new school year with a resolve that has been strengthened by his parents' intervention with the school to keep him and Emmett from sharing any classes.

Freedom from persecution is not enough to satisfy Bob, though, as he carefully plans revenge, framing his tormentor for theft, but he learns that getting even is not emotionally satisfying. Instead, after discovering that Emmett's father has beaten the boy badly, putting him in the hospital, Bob tries to talk with Emmett, then confesses and tells the whole story to his parents, who insist that he tell the principal all that he has told them. In the ensuing confrontation in the principal's office, it is clear that Bob's act of revenge has changed nothing; all Emmett wants to know is whether his father will find out he has been called into the office again. Emmett's fear of his father's violence has made him the bully that he is, and will remain.

The school's response is more satisfying: realizing how peer group sadism has turned into anti-Semitism, the administration educates the students about prejudice-driven violence by showing films of concentration camp survivors made by their Allied liberators, films that shock and sicken most of the audience. Observing this, as well as Emmett's continued hardened attitude, Bob realizes that the humanity of most of the students far outweighs the nasty bigotry of Emmett and his ilk. Simultaneously, he realizes that nothing he can do will change Emmett. The majority, Arrick indicates, will be free from unreasoning prejudice, even if it takes education to draw attention to its existence, but the tendency to bully will continue when it is nurtured in those who are themselves bullied.

In *Slave Day* (1997), Rob Thomas explores a range of attitudes toward race in Robert E. Lee High School, whose annual fund-raiser features an auction of members of student government and teachers as "slaves" for a day. In brief first-person segments, the novel traces the day of several participants—a black student who calls for a boycott, the (first) black president of student government, a poor white actor whose long hours at a fast-food restaurant prevent his earning the grades he needs for a scholarship, the rigorous no-nonsense teacher who failed the actor and who has lost most of the joie de vivre he had as a young teacher, a white football player, his girlfriend who is tired of him, a computer geek, and the mayor's daughter. These characters illustrate the spectrum of political attitudes toward Slave Day, but the way each experiences the day is determined as much by social status as by political awareness. Throughout this day, however, even the apathetic are brought to reconsider the historical background for the fund-raiser: the student who attempted unsuccessfully to initiate a boycott finds surprising support for a number of guerilla theater episodes, and the black football players quietly resign from the team. Ultimately, all the black students assert their dignity, and, as the activist student predicts at the end of the day, it is likely the school will not sponsor another Slave Day.

Other themes of high school social interaction emerge from the day's events. The teacher and the teen actor he has failed—the student has purchased this teacher for the day—discover a surprising mutual sympathy. The high-powered mayor's daughter finds a use for her computer geek slave's skills and gets him drunk before inviting him to wipe some of her father's business files, only to find that he was not too drunk to keep a copy of the files to establish his own power. A girl resists her boyfriend's pressure for more sexual intimacy than she wants, and he comes to the rescue of another girl who has been drugged by his football teammate so that he can rape her. His girlfriend makes the hard decision to break up with him and choose independent status for the time being, recognizing the hypocrisy of her friends' sympathy as they prepare to compete for the honor of stepping into her place. Thomas, as always, writes with humor, and there is much to laugh at in this exposure of high school politics and social relations, but the overriding theme is a serious one: that each student deserves to be treated with dignity.

In *Whale Talk* (2001), Chris Crutcher's protagonist explicitly investigates what it means to be human. A range of human behaviors and attitudes is depicted, but the novel seems to urge the reader as well as the protagonist to refrain from passing judgment. This is a novel of forgiveness—of forgiving oneself as well as others. There is a lot to forgive: neglect and abuse of small children, the mentally impaired, and women; virulent racism; petty political maneuvering within the school athletic community, responsibility for accidents that result in children's accidental death, stalking, murder.

T. J. Jones, the protagonist and narrator, is a mixed race child of an addict whose neglect in his infancy led to his adoption by a loving couple involved in the child welfare system—his mother as an attorney prosecuting child-abuse cases and his father as a volunteer representative of children in the system. As an adolescent, T. J. still harbors a lot of anger, but after years of therapy, he helps his psychologist work with other, younger children.

T. J. chooses his own crusades—against animal slaughter in the guise of hunting, against football players' bullying of a sweet brain-damaged kid who wants to wear his dead older brother's letter jacket, against guys' beating up the girls they date, against verbal abuse of spouses and children. He mixes it up with the bullies who show up in several of these crusades: the football player Mike Barbour and a recent graduate of the school, football booster and family man Rich Marshall, who has a nasty, abusive temper and a twisted view of reality.

Several intertwining plot lines shape the novel. In the foreground is the development of a swim team at Cutter High by T. J.'s English teacher, Mr. Simet. T. J. has principled objections to team sports—until he sees Chris, the boy who sustained brain damage as a result of early abuse and now suffers bullying, in the water. T. J. realizes that Chris could earn his own letter jacket, so he begins recruiting other potential team members. Though he likes Chris, T. J.'s motive is as much a combative desire to shove Chris's and other misfits' prowess into the faces of the school's athletic elite. And it is decidedly a group of misfits who go out for the swim team—one significantly overweight, one with a prosthetic leg, as well as a very bright nerd, a bodybuilder, and a consistently silent, perpetual outsider. They acquire an assistant coach, a middle-aged homeless man living at the gym where they train. In eastern Washington, it is a long bus ride to every meet, and the intimacy that grows on the bus rides turns them into a team in ways that their competitive swimming does not. Despite members' uneven abilities, Coach Simet and T. J. have negotiated letter requirements that ensure every teammate will earn one, but the political element of high school sports is ruthlessly exposed as members of the athletic council realize they have been manipulated. Ultimately, the decision as to whether the swim team's letter requirements will stand is determined by "single combat," Mike Barbour swimming against his victim, Chris, in a contest that is no contest at all, since Chris has been training all season. Chris and the other misfits all earn their letters. After the season ends, their sense of belonging is so powerful that they form a three-man team for Hoopfest, a basketball competition for pickup teams. If *Whale Talk* exposes the politics of high school football and paints a portrait of football players as bullies, it also shows the really positive impact sports can have on the lives of lonely people when they bond as a team.

The theme of abuse runs through the novel in multiple ways. Like Chris, team member Andy Mott has been abused, and like Chris, he is free from anger, even though he lost a leg. At first surly and apparently aggressively antisocial, Andy proves capable of friendship and of philosophical acceptance of his past. A lot of the mothers in this novel need to be forgiven: T. J.'s biological mother; Chris's, Andy's, and Heidi's mothers; and perhaps the mother of T. J.'s unknown half brother.

A second plot line revolves around Rich Marshall's abuse of his biracial step-daughter, Heidi, whom T. J. first meets at the therapist's. T. J. gradually forms a relationship with the child, so when Marshall's abuse of his wife, Alicia, leads to a restraining order, it is natural for the family to stay temporarily in T. J.'s home. T. J.'s father, a huge, gentle man who spends a lot of time with his motorcycles and can appear frightening, quickly connects with Heidi and proves a strong protector of this foster family as well as of his own when Marshall begins stalking his wife and threatening T. J. Marshall is truly dangerous and, with his volatile emotional state, proves the most striking foil imaginable for T. J.'s dad, a man who has earned true wisdom the hard way, through his responsibility for a fatal accident to a child and the subsequent years of coming to terms with it.

This third plot line reveals the kind of person T. J.'s father is and the kind of impact he has on all the people around him, giving the novel its title. When bleak depression settles on Mr. Jones, he watches videos of whales. The "whale talk" of the title is the unedited communication that travels on and on through the ocean, revealing to each whale who hears it the whole of the communicator's emotional experience and nature. Whales know what it means to be whales, Mr. Jones points out. He himself grew up not knowing much about what it means to be human. In coming to terms with his guilt, in atoning by acting as a child advocate, and in raising T. J. to be humane and tolerant, Mr. Jones demonstrates the best of human nature, though he never quite acknowledges it in himself. He has achieved some measure of self-forgiveness, at least in his final selfless sacrifice of his own life to save Heidi. In his last moments, he says he has saved a child although he killed one; T. J. grieves that he could not tell his father that he has saved two—T. J. as well as Heidi.

Just when the reader thinks this novel has wrapped up all plot elements, another chapter brings one more element of closure to this complex story. Looking for the mother of the child who died all those years ago, T. J. finds her son, the half brother that T. J.'s father never knew about, a man who also likes motorcycles and whales. This brother can partially fill a void in T. J.'s life, and T. J. can share his knowledge of their father's character, filling a void for him in turn. Ultimately, Mr. Jones has "saved" three—sent three children into the world who may be able to share some of his wisdom in their acceptance of others.

A young adult reader may also recognize the need for understanding others in the community, outside of school life. Paul Fleischman's *Seedfolks* (1997) chronicles in thirteen multicultural voices the development of a community garden in a vacant lot in Cleveland. At first distrustful of one another, holding prejudiced negative stereotypes, neighborhood residents become a true community through sharing the gardening space and getting to know each other. The initiative comes from a Vietnamese girl whose father died before she was born; she plants several dried lima beans, hoping to reach his spirit. The elderly Rumanian woman who glimpses Kim's activity from her apartment window is convinced the girl is burying drugs or a gun, until she digs up the beans and then, in chagrin, gently re-covers them. As others recognize the lot's potential and plant their own vegetables and flowers, they gradually nurture a seedling community that reaches fruition with a harvest festival at which these urban farmers share their produce.

Throughout the summer, the garden provides a haven for old and young, a spot of color, a reminder that seeds plus earth plus water plus light bring growth. The earth's rhythms continue when man-made systems shut down: the plants just keep growing when a storm interrupts electric service; a pregnant teen comes to terms with the life that is growing in her uterus against her will. The garden's fresh promise helps the elderly step out of their indoor isolation into hope, restoring peace of mind. The gardeners' shared interest overcomes communication barriers caused by age, cultural, and even language differences, as they share knowledge and join forces to solve problems like watering efficiently. Similarly, they share life knowledge, and before long they band together to pursue a mugger. Those who have been isolated and fearful discover that they are part of a community, despite their differences. In pioneering this gardening project, the group of city residents have become "seedfolks," like one resident's ancestors, who served as her family's "seeds" in the community where three more generations would be born.

The novel ends on a note of hope, as Kim returns to plant a second summer's lima bean crop. Dramatically different perspectives represented in the brief chapters introduce the reader to a highly varied community of immigrant and other voices and illustrate the barriers to mutual understanding that these individuals must overcome in order to be a community, while at the same time attesting to the power of what is green and growing.

Go and Come Back (1998) by Joan Abelove illustrates the challenges of accepting cultural difference through the story of two American anthropologists' study of a Peruvian tribe, told from the perspective of the tribal member Alicia, who learns to accept these strange white women's ways over the course of their yearlong visit. Her voice establishes the cultural perspective of the fictional Isabos from the outset of the novel, for example in her identification of villagers in terms of their kinship to her: she easily identifies her "mother's brother's wife's brother." The tribal people are astounded by the ignorance of the "old white ladies" (in their late twenties) and are angered by their stinginess. Equipped for a lengthy stay, the women fail to share the supplies they have brought, an attitude the villagers do not understand. The village ethic is Feast when you can, and be generous, for on a day when you have no meat, you can count on your friends to share their meat. This attitude toward supply and scarcity is manifested in the villagers' standard of beauty as well: fat is beautiful. Their attitude toward the future marks another significant cultural difference from the white visitors': what comes will be. When death comes, the mourning period is brief, the deceased is buried, and people no longer allude to the death; but no one is left alone—widowers remarry, and everyone has kin.

The Isabos have other, more transient contacts with whites: the trader who travels up and down the river by boat and missionaries from the outside world. Alicia takes in a sickly girl baby from the trader's wife because, in a drunken rage, he has threatened to drown it, convinced it is not his. His behavior is totally incomprehensible to the villagers, who value girls. When the headman boasts to one of the anthropologists that he has seven daughters and one son, she commiserates with him, giving proof of her ignorance. The anthropologists' lack of families puzzles the villages, but they soon find explanations for the women's unmarried state in their lack of manners, lack of generosity, and downright craziness. The women begin truly to learn from the villagers once they have gained respect for their hosts, a change that occurs after the shaman brings quick healing to one of them by coaxing a spirit out of her belly. White missionaries come after the white women have gained a better understanding of the people they are studying, so that they now share the Isabos' judgment that whites are stingy, as the missionaries sit among them eating food they have brought and failing to offer it to any of the tribal people. This is the most important lesson the anthropologists have learned, and they demonstrate how well they have learned it when they give away their possessions on the eve of leaving the village for good.

During the year, the anthropologists have left from time to time for various purposes, and each time the villagers doubted that they would return. Yet the accepted form of farewell is to say, "Go and come back." It is only at the end of their stay that Alicia can say this with sincerity. She realizes how much she has learned from "the old ladies," especially after being given a brief ride in the small plane that will take them away. The opportunity to see her world from the air, to see its smallness in relation to the rest of the region as well as its connectedness, gives her a new perspective on cultural difference.

Attitudes toward same-sex romance are another important element of accepting difference. Jacqueline Woodson's 1995 novel, *From the Notebooks of Melanin Sun*, explores the impact on a teen of learning that his long-single mother is a lesbian. The unusually named Melanin Sun, called Mel by his mother EC, is a thirteen going-on-fourteen-year-old whose solitary ways, concerns about endangered species, and stamp-collecting sometimes draw from his friends the teasing epithet of "faggot." Melanin, however, is pretty sure of his heterosexuality because of the effect the lovely Angie has on him. She slipped him her phone number at the end of the school year, inviting him to call her during the summer, but he is nervous. He needs his mother's advice, and he never minds seeking it because the two of them are very close. While he contemplates broaching the subject, EC gradually reveals to him her involvement with a woman—and not just any woman, but a white woman.

Melanin is bewildered and angry, feeling betrayed in several ways: he cannot believe EC is really a lesbian; he would find her falling in love with anyone threatening because of their closeness as a twosome; he does not feel he can share his own concerns about beginning to date with her; he fears the fallout in his own relationships that is likely to follow upon his friends' and neighbors' knowledge of his mother's sexuality; and he feels his mother's bringing a white woman into his black community is a betrayal of their shared racial pride and identity. Thus, when his mother asks him to open his mind and his heart and try to understand her happiness, Melanin closes his mind and his heart for as long as he can. However, his natural sympathy for victims of prejudice begins to open his mind as he discovers the depth of friends' and neighbors' prejudice against EC's sexuality. When she asks him to make just one day's effort to get to know Kristen, Melanin finds, in spite of himself, that he likes her. In fact, she is a lot like his adored mother, even like him (as shown in her choice of clothing for their first meeting, remarkably similar to his own).

Melanin's concerns about his own developing sexuality complicate his ability to respond to his mother's revelation. As she prepares to reveal her love for Kristen, he at first thinks she is concerned about whether he is indeed a "faggot." Melanin readily admits to himself that his stamp-collecting and journal-keeping are suspect activities, less than all-male.

He writes in his notebooks because he cannot always articulate his thoughts in speech, speaking slowly when he attempts to do so. This has led to his being placed in a "slow" class in the past, a circumstance that brought his mother to the school in protest with lightning speed; in fact, Melanin Sun is gifted rather than the opposite. He is also very clear about his difference from white people. Very dark-skinned himself, he lives in an all-black neighborhood and has no desire to mix with whites. Melanin has the dual challenge, then, of accepting his own differences from others and accepting simultaneously two kinds of difference in his mother's newfound love. "Difference matters," he reflects, even before his mother's revelation. A thoughtful young man and loving son, he rises to the challenge, learning in the process just who his own friends are. The novel's epigraph, a poem by lesbian poet Gerry Gomez Pearlberg about the destruction of amphibian species, emphasizes the need for care, for attention to all the different kinds of life that make the world what it is.

ADDITIONAL READING RECOMMENDATIONS

Summer of My German Soldier by Bette Greene, 1973
Jack by A. M. Homes, 1989
Athletic Shorts: Six Short Stories by Chris Crutcher, 1989
Maniac Magee by Jerry Spinelli, 1990
Children of the River by Linda Crew, 1991
The Day That Elvis Came to Town by Jan Marino, 1991
Necessary Roughness by Marie G. Lee, 1996 (discussed in Insiders and Outsiders)
Danger Zone by David Klass, 1996
Parrot in the Oven: Mi Vida by Victor Martinez, 1996
Walker's Crossing by Phyllis Reynolds Naylor, 1999
Breaking Rank by Kristen D. Randle, 1999
Life Is Funny by E. R. Frank, 2000

Accidents and Adjustments

Winning by Robin Brancato (1977)
Are You Alone on Purpose? by Nancy Werlin (1992)
God of Beer by Garret Keizer (2002)
Whirligig by Paul Fleischman (1998)

Accidents are the leading cause of death among young people, and most teens lose at least one classmate to accident during their school years. Nearly as distressing are the accidents that result in disabling, or the loss of limb or functionality. American teens have a great deal of freedom; too many are given to alcohol or other substance abuse to keep the highways entirely safe, and they are inexperienced drivers; teens engage in challenging and sometimes risky physical sports—and even without these risks in living normal lives, they may face disabling disease. Any of these challenges can change young people's lives dramatically.

Accidents and disabilities impel significant adjustment on the part of victims and their friends and families. The old identity is shattered, and a new identity must be forged. Effects ripple through family and community. An accident may be a crucible for friendships, and those who are disabled because of an accident or disease may find themselves outsiders in groups where they were once insiders. Young people— engaged in developing a sense of identity, in developing new relationships and reconsidering old relationships, in balancing their need for family support and for independence, and in forming goals for the future—will find all these issues altered by the death or disability of someone near to them or by their own disability.

Furthermore, accidental death or the shattering of a talented young person's physical abilities has a poignancy of its own; the subject draws many readers into absorbed empathy. The questions raised by such events involve some of the most fundamental to human experience: Why do things happen as they do? Where is God when tragedy strikes? How can young life be so profligately wasted? Novels that deal with these issues have emotional intensity. Some novels deal with the inadequacy of religion to ameliorate such loss and, not surprisingly, draw the disapproval of those who want conventional answers reaffirmed. Yet some of the best fiction leaves these questions unanswered. The novels discussed here deal with accidental death, disabling sports accidents, and family members' disabilities.

It must be difficult to end a book about a freak football accident that leaves a high school senior a quadriplegic, and Robin Brancato makes a valiant effort at realism rather than sentimentality in *Winning* (1977), but she is not entirely successful. In comparison to today's grittier novels, *Winning* seems a bit saccharine. The novel opens in September, two weeks after Gary G. Madden's accident, when he still hopes to recover from his spinal injury, and ends at New Year's, when he has decided against suicide. Gary's parents, while mildly annoying (his mother, apparently looking for sainthood, wants to do everything for him, as though he were an infant, and his father hides his feelings), seem to have no negative emotions; his girlfriend is faithful and wants to go to college wherever he goes so she can take care of him; he has a friend who visits and a friend who does not; the coaches still care about him and visit him; and a compassionate English teacher begins to overcome her own loss—her husband died in an accident—in befriending him. Gary is quiet about his feelings but eventually begins making small jokes about his condition; his grief and anger seem muted. Playing word games with his teacher, he comes up with "damned raggedy" as an anagram for his name, but he shares this with humor. At the rehab/physical therapy center, he is nicknamed "Superquad" for his cooperativeness and consistent hard work. Thus, his decision to commit suicide, near the end of the novel, seems surprising. He is easily talked into revealing his resolution; he is easily talked out of following through on it; and his teacher attributes it almost entirely to the fever he is suffering from. The reader may suspect that the novel stops short of where Gary's real struggle with grief and anger will begin.

Still, there is no easy happy ending here. Gary and his teammate Jason make gentle fun of the coaches' "win one for the Gipper" rhetoric, but the book is truly about "winning"—though the game to be won is a different, more serious one than Gary suspected when he went out for football. Winning on this playing field takes a deeper commitment and struggle, and success is not measured in scoring the most points— the most conspicuous and quantifiable markers of success. Other serious issues surface. Jason, the teammate who visits, is black, causing some discomfort for this white family. (Billy, the best friend since elementary school, does not visit.) The English teacher speculates on the role of masculine biology in the aggression of football, echoing 1970s feminist rhetoric. Some explanation of Gary's growth as an individual is seen in the tutoring sessions: Gary reflects on *Crime and Punishment* and *Death of a Salesman*, and he writes in a variety of ways, talking into a tape recorder and dictating to his girlfriend Diane or his mother. This kind of intellectual activity has brought many a sufferer to acceptance.

Gary's Superquad status is brought out through other characters who act as foils: Tommy, whose love of speed and danger and alienation from his parents has resulted in numerous accidents; David, who is so quiet and withdrawn that his eventual suicide remains enigmatic; and various other patients whom Gary meets or hears horror stories about from the voluble Tommy. In contrast to these young people, who lack meaningful relationships with others, Gary has everything to live for. But it is questionable whether he would see this without his English teacher, whose widowhood has given her empathy, appreciation of honest appraisals from doctors and others, and the wisdom to nudge others in the right direction when their sympathy prevents them from meeting Gary's needs. It is appropriate that her point of view is the only other one shown besides Gary's, and ultimately this novel reveals the importance of friendship and the potential for real-life mentoring by a caring teacher.

In *Are You Alone on Purpose?* (1992), Nancy Werlin examines the ways in which several people have isolated themselves: Adam, an autistic savant; his twin sister,

Alison, an intelligent, "normal" girl with a love of reading that isolates her from others and who acquires the nickname "Queen Nerd"; Harry, an unpleasant bully who tries to cause pain for all around him who are targets for his anger; and Harry's father, the rabbi, who has never been good at connecting emotionally with people and who now talks daily to his wife, dead from cancer four years earlier. Harry tells Alison that she is on her own planet, and in response she queries whether that is not true of everyone.

Harry and Alison arrive at friendship and then at romance through a coincidence that links their families' fates. When the rabbi refuses to admit the autistic Adam to Hebrew school on the grounds that he lacks the facilities to meet Adam's needs, Adam and Alison's mother explodes in anger and wishes ill upon his son, Harry, who she has learned has picked on her children for several years. Coincidentally, on that day Harry has a diving accident at summer camp, and the rabbi believes the accident is God's judgment on him for refusing Adam his education in Judaism. Consequently, he offers to tutor Adam in his home on Sundays, and Alison accompanies Adam to the weekly classes. Eventually, after treatment and rehabilitation, Harry returns home, confined to a wheelchair. Alison—after questioning whether Harry's accident was indeed a divine punishment and recoiling from the rabbi's belief that Harry was only a pawn in God's plan for reaching him—decides to pay attention to Harry.

Harry's father pays no attention to him. It seems strange to both Harry and Alison that Rabbi Roth is so preoccupied with—even fixated on—Adam, while he is unable to listen to Harry. Sympathy between them grows, as Alison reveals some of her struggles for notice in her own family. She has concluded that her parents love her because she is normal, unlike Adam, and she strives not to make any waves, not even to call attention to herself. Alison and Harry reach out to each other—against Harry's will at first, but Alison is his salvation when he returns to school, interacting with him normally and totally oblivious to the stares of other students, as she always is. As their relationship grows, Alison finds the courage to voice some of her own anger. She explains to her parents how she feels, and, though they do not really understand her feelings, all three begin to work toward better mutual understanding.

Harry, in contrast, begins to overcome the anger that has made him so unpleasant a person. In counseling sessions, a part of his rehabilitation after the accident, Harry eventually reveals that his mother died the day before his birthday. Because Jewish custom requires that she be buried within twenty-four hours, her funeral was on Harry's birthday. He has been at odds with his father ever since, and since his father is reserved, having been able to open up emotionally only with his wife, they have led a life of silences, marked by resentment on Harry's part and bewilderment on his father's.

Adam's autism is clearly the central symbol of human aloneness in this novel. Alison, though more normal, is content with relative isolation from the school's social life. When her long-time best friend Paulina begins pursuing acceptance by the popular kids and abandons Alison, Alison seems to take her defection in stride, perhaps because of her interest in Harry. Additionally, her isolation within the world of math, which she tries to explain to Harry at one point as a rule-governed world one can enter wholly through imaginative power, bears a resemblance to Adam's solitude. In this novel, Harry's accident, which precipitates a number of changes in relationships, ultimately has positive effects. Harry is determined to regain as much control over his life as possible, though the loss of his former athletic ability is a serious blow. The possibilities for connection with others have, however, opened up for everyone but Adam at the end of the novel.

In *God of Beer* (2002), Garret Keizer depicts the danger of mixing alcohol and driving and, more importantly, the community's acceptance of this behavior. There is not much to do in rural northern Vermont, as one student persistently asserts in social studies class, the class when Kyle first suggests that the god of the locals is beer. His assertion is not surprising, considering that his parents' marriage broke up over drinking; drinking is the norm at his peers' weekend parties; and the community accepts the occasional fatal car accident caused by underage drinking. Kyle's brainy friend "Quaker Oats" enthusiastically picks up the idea Kyle has casually tossed out, pushing Kyle and their friend Diana, along with another friend, to develop a class project called the Beer Rebellion, identifying themselves as SUDS, Students Undermining a Drunk Society. Quake is an idealist, with a clear sense of what they will protest and how they will protest it, but their actions are consistently misunderstood and misrepresented.

SUDS has three goals: to promote lowering of the legal drinking age, to heighten other students' knowledge of alcohol, and to make it socially acceptable to decline alcohol. They reason that illegality adds to the social pressure for alcohol consumption, and hence reducing its significance as a symbol of adult fun would reduce drinking's importance in their peers' lives. They plan and carry out three protest actions, but further acts of protest arise spontaneously after Diana's death is caused by the drunken Condor: first, Kyle's friend David, the "slow" young man whom Diana tutored, begins destroying the convenience store's beer supply, and, consequently, at David's court hearing, Quake smashes beer bottles to demonstrate that David's action should be respected as a legitimate protest rather than explained away by humiliating him. The most widespread misinterpretation of all of these actions is that the group is simply agitating for a lowered drinking age, and ultimately they find themselves commemorated for standing up for the right to drink to excess, an irony that they find difficult to accept.

The teens also draw an ironic lesson from David's arrest for destruction of the convenience store's beer supply: the authorities rally to prosecute the violation of property rights, but adults fail to rally over the problem of drinking, taking in stride the occasional death of a teenager as one of the normal dangers of growing up. Adults' acceptance of drinking beer as a badge of manhood is shown in the two offers of beer that Kyle receives at the end of his first day of work in the local factory a couple of months short of his eighteenth birthday, offers that come from his father, along with a group of coworkers, and from his mother. The prominent local memorial to a teen who died earlier in a drunken driving accident is a painting of the deceased, depicted with his car and a beer, on the side of an abandoned barn. The site has become a place for parties, glorifying the incident. A similar memorial is planned for the bridge that Diana crashed into, and it is here that Kyle's anger boils over, sparking David's destruction of the merchant's beer. Kyle is frustrated by the futility of all their actions and the wastefulness of his friend's death, seeing Diana's memory being taken over by self-indulgent mourners and made meaningless by their lack of understanding about what she was trying to change.

Diana's death is, of course, shocking and tragic to everyone, especially since she was not drinking but was attempting to take the drunken Condor home. Condor survives the crash, a hero to most of his classmates because of his painful injuries and his grief over Diana's death. Kyle is not so forgiving, knowing that Condor was probably entirely responsible for the accident. Kyle's grief is intensified because he has loved her and wanted to date her for a long time but has feared risking any change that might harm their long-time friendship. Watching her with Condor just before she leaves the party, he has finally asked her whether she would go out with him and has been rewarded with her invitation to call her. In the course of one short evening, he has gone from jealousy and disgust with Condor to joy and finally to shock and grief. Ironically, he learns when Condor moves away, that Condor was simply making the effort with Diana to be "normal," since his last romance—on the other side of the country—was a gay romance, a discovery that seems to exacerbate the sense of waste.

Issues of class, of pride, and of love for this small Vermont town divide the characters. Kyle's father is a factory worker, his mother a bookkeeper at the factory. He attends parties in expensive homes, and recognizes in a girl's interest her slightly romanticized—or cynical—perception that he is a bit "rough." When the first protest party results in Kyle's arrest, his mother points out that his "preppy" friends will go on with their lives and warns that high school friendships will not outlast the different lives they will lead after graduation. His father, in contrast, accuses him of acting out of "spite," the motive to which he also attributes Kyle's unwillingness to go to college. Kyle is in some ways closer to David than to his other friends. David is struggling to finish high school at age twenty-one but can teach Kyle all sorts of things about the woods when they hunt or camp together. David is likely to stay in Salmon Falls, holding down a blue-collar job and generally being a decent guy. Kyle, too, loves Salmon Falls and wants to stay there, so his reluctance to apply to colleges grows out of deep ambivalence about his future. He understands David better than anyone else does, at least until David and Quake are sentenced to community service together, and Quake sees the challenge to David's pride as he struggles with his learning disability. David's character is sterling, if his ability to do schoolwork is impaired, and one of the most optimistic elements in the novel's ending is his getting a job with the storeowner whose beer he destroyed, because the owner appreciates David's hard work in repairing damages. This novel gives good reasons for identifying the community's god as beer.

When one causes a death, rather than simply witnessing one, a different kind of adjustment is called for. Paul Fleischman's *Whirligig* (1998) explores the need for atonement that follows when one's careless actions have resulted in grave harm to another. Drunk and angry after his humiliation at a party, Brent deliberately loses control of his car. Instead of fulfilling his death wish, his action brings death to an eighteen-year-old woman with everything to live for. When her mother asks Brent to make whirligigs in Lea's memory and place them in the four corners of the United States, handing him a forty-five-day bus pass, she sets in motion a series of events at those four corners. To begin with, Brent is transformed from a shallow, self-centered person obsessed with gaining peer acceptance to a craftsman and seeker of knowledge. His mind opens through travel, and he discovers the joy of knowing the names of constellations, peeks into the interesting lives led by foreign travelers fluent in his own language and knowledgeable about world politics, and experiments in learning to play the harmonica. As Brent is reborn, his creations spin inspiration and change into other lives.

Events are set in motion, and in turn set others in motion; actions beget actions; art survives and memorials survive, and they transform those who see them. Lea's mother specifies the whirligigs because Lea's grandfather made them for her and because Lea was a person who made people smile. The justness of Brent's restitution becomes clear through the stories of others whom he never meets but who nonetheless find special, personal meaning in the whirligigs he constructs. Like Lea, they inspire smiles: in the last episode recounted, an elderly Auschwitz survivor, dying of cancer, tells her granddaughter that those who perished in the camps would not want the survivors to be always serious but would want them to laugh. Brent comes to see the world itself as a whirligig, each part connected and affecting others.

After completing his last whirligig, Brent is drawn into the complex human whirligig of a contradance, signaling his reintegration into the human community, the culmination of his growing contact with others on his journey. Structurally, the book is a whirligig, alternating the straightforward chronology of Brent's journey in third person with first-person narratives by those whose lives are affected by the whirligigs. These chapters show the passage of time and are titled by location. The novel reflects a sense of action, agency, motion in form and style as well as theme, and ultimately is a thing of beauty made of interacting parts.

ADDITIONAL READING RECOMMENDATIONS

I Know What You Did Last Summer by Lois Duncan, 1973

Running Loose, 1983 (discussed in Teammates), and *The Crazy Horse Electric Game*, 1987, by Chris Crutcher

Izzy, Willy-Nilly by Cynthia Voigt, 1986 (discussed in Beauty's Meaning)

Say Goodnight, Gracie by Julie Reece Deaver, 1988

In Lane Three, Alex Archer, 1989, and *Alex in Rome*, 1992, by Tessa Duder

Painting the Black by Carl Deuker, 1993

Tears of a Tiger, 1994, and sequels by Sharon M. Draper

In the Middle of the Night by Robert Cormier, 1995

Necessary Roughness by Marie G. Lee, 1996 (discussed in Insiders and Outsiders)

Heat by Michael Cadnum, 1998

Catalyst by Laurie Halse Anderson, 2002 (discussed in Friends Forever?)

Addressing Addiction

The Contender by Robert Lipsyte (1967)
Fat Kid Rules the World by K. L. Going (2003)
Smack by Melvin Burgess (1996)
Shayla's Double Brown Baby Blues by Lori Aurelia Williams (2001)

Youth is a time for experimentation, and it is tempting to experiment with legal and illegal drugs, especially under peer pressure. Unfortunately, peer pressure seems more often to lead young people into self-destructive behaviors than into healthy and constructive experimentation. Experimentation with addictive substances can dramatically change one's life. Addiction interferes with relationships with friends and family, performance in school and on the job, interest in the opposite sex and in the future. Use of alcohol and illegal drugs can pose problems for friends and family members of addicts, who may feel helpless in the face of the changes they see in their loved ones.

Young people not only experiment with substance abuse but also may be significantly affected by family members' substance abuse. Whether they find themselves complicit in the lies and cover-ups of a codependent household or try to distance themselves from it, they may well feel that they have little control over the day-to-day circumstances of their lives. As maturing individuals separating themselves from their families, though, they make choices, and these choices—as well as the choices made by many of their peers to become addicted—make a significant appearance in fiction for young adults.

The Contender (1967), by Robert Lipsyte, is about a lot of important subjects—the trap of poverty and racist ideologies in 1960s America, the impact of loss and abandonment by a parent, the challenges of friendship in a volatile inner-city environment—but its title is Lipsyte's best cue to its central theme. Alfred Brooks, the protagonist, tests himself, in life as well as in the boxing ring, to determine whether he is truly a contender—someone who can stay the course and struggle against the odds. Abandoned by his father and orphaned by his mother's death, living with his aunt in Harlem, Alfred has given up his early dream of being a successful builder of things with his best friend James, whose early goal was to be an engineer, and has dropped out of school, which seemed futile, his example soon to be followed by James. In the political climate of the 1960s, Alfred feels himself pulled in different directions: by the Black Power advocates speaking on street corners; by the drug-using, law-breaking denizens of the basement clubroom where James is spending his time; by his God-fearing Aunt Pearl.

After refusing to help James's friends, a group of "punks," in their attempt to rob the Jewish grocery where Alfred works and, in consequence, taking a beating from them, Alfred responds to the lure of Donatelli's Gym and the chance to prove himself through discipline and training, maybe even to make big money. As Alfred accepts and even learns to welcome the strain of developing his stamina and speed, he sees less and less of James, who has chosen an addict's life instead of an athlete's life. Alfred learns a lot about himself and the other men he comes to know better as he trains, finding a strength that gives him new self-esteem, allowing him for the first time to compare himself favorably with a suburban middle-class cousin, a college man who aspires to join the Peace Corps. These gains compensate for his realization that he is not cut out for a boxing career, and he proves himself a contender as he plans to go to night school and share his skills with neighborhood kids in a recreation program. After this growth has occurred, James resurfaces in Alfred's life, now helplessly in the grip of his heroin addiction and desperate for money to support his habit. Loyal to James, who has been like a brother to him, Alfred reaches out to support him, promising to help James kick the habit and turn his life around.

Lipsyte frames Alfred's growth with his expression of deep love and concern for his best friend, and this underlines the theme of friendship's obligations and persistence in the face of challenges. All their significant crises of the past, from childhood, have been weathered in each other's company, when the two boys retreated to a tiny cave in the local park, in each case emerging as if in a new birth. After the robbery that sets events in motion in the first chapter, Alfred goes to the cave, emerging as someone who will seek out the gym and a new kind of life. He remembers his grief after his mother's death, when James helped him leave the safety of the cave and move on to a new life with his Aunt Pearl. In the closing incident of the novel, Alfred finds James hiding in the tiny cave, and with a promise of giving even his life's blood to help his friend, he assists James in emerging to seek help in remaking his life without addiction.

Fat Kid Rules the World (2003), by K. L. Going, tells another story of male friendship that ends with the promise of a struggle against drug addiction. Seventeen-year-old Troy, obese and depressed, is contemplating suicide when he is addressed by the punk guitarist Curt in a brief but real moment of personal contact that proves the beginning of an unlikely alliance, which ultimately begins to rescue both from destructive behaviors. This is Troy's narrative, a present-tense story punctuated with the headlines of news stories Troy envisions about life episodes, beginning with "Fat Kid Messes Up," as he contemplates a failed suicide attempt in the subway station, and culminating in "Fat Kid Rules the World," as he starts a concert as drummer for the new band Curt has been trying to pull together, articulating the feeling that he first expressed when he realized that Curt takes him seriously as a friend and prospective fellow musician. The novel successfully reveals the isolation and pain experienced by overweight young people as well as by drug users, along with a surprisingly functional father-son relationship and the reestablishment of a lost relationship with a younger brother.

Troy feels like a failure and a disappointment to his fit and trim military dad and athletic brother; his weight is a barrier to friendship, even with his brother. Curt, a famous character in their high school, appears cool to some peers but a loser to Troy's brother, Dayle. The friendship begins with Troy's feeding Curt and taking him home, where his father's first response is to feed Curt again. As Troy comes to know him, he realizes how precarious an existence Curt leads, always dreaming of a new opportunity, certain he can overcome any obstacle, but in reality nearly homeless, choosing drugs over food, running himself into the ground. The first time he takes Troy along with him on a raid of his alcoholic mother's apartment, Curt grabs some of her prescription drugs, listens to classic rock, then grabs CDs and flees as his mother arrives home.

This is in many ways Troy's story—of a friendship that helps him recognize his own functionality, of a restored relationship with his family, of stepping outside the barrier his weight has placed between him and the world, of pursuing a dream of participating in an exciting world of music where he can be accepted for his performance, not just his looks. However, it is also Curt's story of reaching bottom and recognizing that he must acknowledge his addiction in order to begin coping with it.

Melvin Burgess's *Smack* (1996; titled *Junk* in Great Britain) takes the reader into a 1980s punk world of drug use and "squatting"—simply moving into unused homes and living there—through the experiences, primarily, of two fourteen-year-old runaways, Gemma and Tar. Tar leaves home to escape his father's beatings and his mother's manipulation; both are alcoholics. Gemma just wants her freedom: she cannot accept her parents' restrictions on her life following an all-night stay with Tar. Tar is an open, vulnerable artist at first, but following after Gemma, who wants to live a wild, fast life, he slides into heroin use, and once he has begun, addiction takes a far more powerful hold on him than it ever does on Gemma, even after his two arrests force him off heroin and methadone, the first time in a rehab center, the second in a juvenile detention center. With their friends Lily, Rob, and Sally, they support themselves by stealing, the girls and Rob also through prostitution, in a rough life that Gemma finally walks away from when she discovers she is pregnant at eighteen.

Tar's addiction, with which he still struggles at age nineteen, after incarceration and a failed attempt to live a normal family life with Gemma and their infant daughter, has roots in his parents' alcoholism. Once he experiences the release from pain that the drug brings, he is an addict. Despite his own misery as a teen in a household full of arguments, his mother incapable of doing the housework, his father headed toward loss of his teaching job shortly after Tar's leaving, Tar reproduces much of his father's behavior, frightening himself when he beats Gemma. Addiction is addiction, no matter whether the substance is legal or illegal. This is Tar's tragedy. Other people, especially Richard, the anarchist who takes young runaways under his wing in Bristol and tries to help Tar get off of heroin on his own, mention the shyness, sweetness, and openness that they first noted in him, qualities he has lost, along with his ability to sustain artistic production, once he has allowed heroin to take over his life. Tar has always been a needy child at heart.

Gemma, in contrast, is a rebellious child, as much of a user as any of the addicts with whom she spends her teen years, but always able to step back from the scene and see it for what it is and ultimately able to walk away from it, fortunate enough to have parents who will take her in when she is ready to get clean because she is unwilling to bring an addicted infant into the world. She has watched her friend Lily, on the streets from the age of twelve, turn blue when she was pregnant and using, bear an addicted baby, suffer violence at the hands of her tricks, and begin to lose her hold on reality, and Gemma has called the police to turn in her friends, in the only move she can think of to release them from the prison they have built around themselves. This action gets Lily and Rob and their baby into detox, but it is Tar's second arrest, so he goes to jail.

Tar and Gemma's relationship begins, grows, and finally ends because of dependency. Tar needs her more than she does him at the outset, and she first gives herself to him as a gift, in an attempt to fill his enormous need. Her love for him dates from the beginning of their heroin use; it reaches its climax during his time in prison, when she is pregnant. After his release, when both are clean and there are no barriers to their living an adult life together, she discovers that she no longer responds to him sexually. While this troubles her, it is ultimately his resuming drug use that ends her effort to live with him. Clean herself since she learned she was pregnant, she has been very clear on one point: if Tar uses, he may not live with her and the baby.

Parents' actions are largely irrelevant to these teens' choices and lifestyle. Tar has a truly sad home life to escape, but drug use cannot bring him healing. Gemma's parents have perhaps been stricter than circumstances warranted, at least in calling her employer to end her job, but their actions are not responsible for her tendency to run wild and have a good time, and ultimately she chooses their respectable lifestyle for herself. Rob and Lily have almost no contact with their parents. The older Richard, who functions as a leader and parental figure to the young runaways, and Vonny, who even at sixteen mothers everyone, argue Gemma into contacting her parents, while they try to protect Tar from his mother's manipulation. They all live in a world of young street people, where their former values are reshaped by the need to eat and get high without getting a job.

This is a grimly realistic picture of a seamy way of life; there is no glamorizing of drug use in this novel. The teens lie to themselves, justifying their stealing in the punk argot of the era, claiming that they merely "liberate" food and other goods from capitalists. This is articulated most fully by Lily, who is perhaps the most lost figure of the novel. The anarchist Richard actually has political convictions; he glues doorknobs to interfere with banks' business in a fairly harmless protest typical of the period, according to Burgess's note on squatting in the American edition (which also features a glossary of British slang). The story emerges through first-person chapters representing the perspectives of various characters, some of them headed with punk lyrics. By the end of the novel, it is clear that Gemma has escaped addiction but that Tar still lies to himself and will face the battle every day of his life.

Alcohol addiction can be just as dangerous as illegal drug use. In *Shayla's Double Brown Baby Blues* (2001), Lori Aurelia Williams continues the story of Shayla Dubois and her friend Kambia told in *When Kambia Elaine Flew in from Neptune*. The earlier novel focuses on sexual abuse and Shayla's older sister Tia's relationship with the much older artist Doo-Witty that brings friction into the household and results in Tia's running away from home. The focus of this novel is twofold: Shayla's feelings of displacement and envy when her father, the charming but irresponsible Mr. Anderson Fox, has a new infant daughter whom he dotes on, and her friend Lemm's alcohol addiction. Shayla's friendship with Kambia has played an important role in her life, since the girls she used to hang out with have become interested only in their appearance and their popularity with older boys, boys who ultimately involve them in the violence that accompanies their purchases from drug dealers. But as Kambia's troubled past begins resurfacing and she withdraws from interaction with others, Shayla's new friend Lemm becomes more important to her, and his nearness makes her tingle, at the same time that she is discovering the extent of his alcohol abuse.

Lemm's past life includes enough tragedy to account for his dependency on alcohol to escape his despair. The story in the neighborhood is that his father was responsible for Lemm's younger twin sisters' death because he was drunk when he picked them up from daycare and walked them home. The reality is that Lemm himself was drunk and responsible for his sisters' death. His mother, who, at her husband's insistence, left the children shortly after the twins' birth, fed Lemm alcohol from infancy, sharing her own need of drinking with him, so that he has had a nearly lifelong addiction. When Shayla first meets Lemm, she does not realize how often he is drunk, and Lemm is skilled at diverting attention from himself with superpoliteness to adults, elegant speech, and a steady stream of compliments for older women. Once she happens upon the knowledge, however, Shayla begins to recognize his use of breath mints to cover any odor of alcohol. Learning more about Lemm, she faces one moral dilemma after another as she continues to choose keeping her knowledge to herself rather than exposing Lemm, until matters come to a head when Lemm and two of Shayla's former girlfriends are involved in a shooting incident by an older teen who tries to cheat a drug dealer, a shooting that results in another death of a small child.

Shayla is at an age when she does not confide everything to her mother and grandmother and is especially reluctant to incriminate her friends. As a result, Shayla's grandmother worries that she has been experimenting with alcohol and has gotten mixed up with the wrong crowd. When she fails to expose Lemm and Maya even to the police after they have fled to her home, Maya bleeding from the wound she got from a stray bullet, Shayla comes close to being implicated in the situation she was smart enough to walk away from, when the older boys began urging the younger kids to drink. The seriousness of the situation is borne in on Shayla when Lemm, Maya, and Sheila go to court.

Shayla discovers that the person who best understands her difficulty in determining the right course of action to take with Lemm is her young stepmother, Jada, who identifies herself and Shayla as "fixers," who attempt to solve other people's problems, even ones that they cannot fix. She explains that she had Shayla's stepsister in an effort to fill an empty spot in Shayla's father's life but that, since he is still not ready to be a father, she has the same problem with him that Shayla has: she always wants and needs him to be more than he is, and her continuing disappointment in him breaks her heart and still cannot fill the need she sees in him. While Jada's explanation cannot entirely ease the hurt that Shayla experiences from her father's neglect, it does help her see the limits of her own responsibility to him and to her little stepsister.

As the truth of Lemm's situation becomes known to Shayla's family, her mother and grandmother understand her better, and her grandmother is better able to interpret Shayla's troubling recurrent dream as a vision of the kind of person Shayla is and will be as an adult—a dependable, loving woman whom people will come to when they are in need of help. This recognition is underscored with Kambia's audioletter to Shayla, revealing not only more of her history, which Kambia has begun coming to terms with in therapy at an institution, but also the importance Shayla's friendship continues to have in Kambia's life. Shayla is an exceptionally strong young woman, though her capacity for empathy often leaves her sadder than she would be if she were more self-centered. She is part of a family of strong women, and in their strength they support each other. Though Shayla may have to face the immediate future without her closest friends, Lemm and Kambia, she knows that they are now getting the help that they need, help that is more than she is capable of providing, and that she has the strength she needs to go on by herself.

ADDITIONAL READING RECOMMENDATIONS

Go Ask Alice, Anonymous, 1971

A Teacup Full of Roses by Sharon Bell Mathis, 1972

A Hero Ain't Nothin' but a Sandwich by Alice Childress, 1973 (discussed in Heroism: What Does It Mean to Be a Hero?)

Angel Dust Blues by Todd Strasser, 1984

The Moonlight Man by Paula Fox, 1986

No Kidding by Bruce Brooks, 1989

Painting the Black by Carl Deuker, 1993

Whistle Me Home by Barbara Wersba, 1997 (discussed in Sexual Identity, Sexual Desire)

Rules of the Road by Joan Bauer, 1998 (discussed in Jobs: Assuming Adult Responsibility)

Harley, Like a Person by Cat Bauer, 2000

Born Blue by Han Nolan, 2001

God of Beer by Garret Keizer, 2002 (discussed in Accidents and Adjustments)

Stoner & Spaz by Ron Koertge, 2002 (discussed in Disease and Disability)

Lucy the Giant by Sherri L. Smith, 2002 (discussed in Jobs: Assuming Adult Responsibility)

The Dream Bearer, 2003, and *The Beast,* 2003, by Walter Dean Myers

The Blue Mirror by Kathe Koja, 2004

Animals and the Environment

Dogsong by Gary Paulesen (1985)
Bearstone by Will Hobbs (1989)
Beardance by Will Hobbs (1993)
The Haymeadow by Gary Paulesen (1992)
Tangerine by Edward Bloor (1997)
Straydog by Kathe Koja (2002)

A number of enduring children's classics are animal stories, reflecting young people's love for animals and conveying the life lessons many children learn through relationships with their pets: *Sounder* by William Armstrong, *Where the Red Fern Grows* by Wilson Rawls, *The Black Stallion* by Walter Farley, and *Misty of Chincoteague* and other novels by Marguerite Henry. These novels lay the foundation for enjoyment of fiction with more mature themes in which animals and the environment play a major role. Teens' experiences build on those of childhood, and though, typically, as teens get jobs, learn to drive, start to date, and participate in after-school activities, they may spend less time at home, with a pet as an important friend, a kind of family member, they may still maintain intense relationships with animals as well as develop a more mature understanding of the environment and humans' place in it.

Most of Gary Paulsen's books deal with the natural world in some way. One of his best is *Dogsong* (1985), a coming-of-age story about a fourteen-year-old Inuit youth whose friendship with an elderly man initiates him in knowledge of the old ways, leading him to pursue a quest for a vision. Russel is restless in the tiny government house—a box to keep people in. Each winter morning, he wakes to the sound of villagers' snowmobiles starting up, testimony to the changes in his people's lives. Russel's restlessness is not satisfied by the Christianity that comforts his father, so he sends Russel to Oogruk. Oogruk conveys his knowledge of traditional culture to Russel, sends him out to learn to work with his own dog team and to hunt, and, after Russel has learned what the old man has to bequeath, releases him to pursue his personal quest, a quest that enables Russel to make the transition into manhood.

One of Russel's earliest lessons is the importance of living their heritage, not enshrining it in museums (where tools have become artifacts) or subordinating it to a different culture's values (the villagers' personal songs and dancing were given up because they feared the missionaries' hell). Russel is not just to get a song but to become a song himself. As he learns to work with the dogs, he discovers that his own feeling of being alive is embedded in the life of the sled and the snow and the ice, all part of the same enveloping life, and he finds that often he can trust them, their sense of direction, their awareness of the weather.

Russel's dream run—going away from the village into the north, into the dark and the cold, the wind, the shifting snow—signals his transition into manhood. His extended dream of a man whose successful hunting trip ends in sorrow when he returns home to find his family dead of hunger strengthens Russel and gives him wisdom for the challenges he faces when he finds a pregnant girl near death in the snow. The experiences of the dream and the run intermingle in his mind, giving him a new sense of reality: Russel needs strength, for he must kill a bear with only a lance and the help of the dogs, to keep them all from starving, and then must coax Nancy back into life and a return to the community after delivering her stillborn infant.

Russel's initiatory experience enfolds him in a mystical understanding of the interconnection of life that he expresses in the "Dogsong" with which the novel ends, a deceptively simple song about his identification with the dogs and their interdependency. The entirety of the narrative gives substance to the song, showing the reader how a man's song can be his life.

In *Bearstone* (1989) and *Beardance* (1993), Will Hobbs explores cultural attitudes toward bears, especially grizzlies, through the experiences of an orphaned Ute teen, Cloyd, as he develops a close relationship with an elderly farmer and miner, Walter, and then experiences the closeness to bears that his ancestors knew. Cloyd has hit a lot of dead-ends in his life, and he is angry: his parents are dead; he has not been allowed to substitute herding his grandmother's goats for school; he cannot read well and has been humiliated in school; and he wants to run free in the canyons near his grandmother's Utah home in the summer rather than work for the white farmer in Colorado. On his first day at Walter's, however, he enters a cave where he discovers a small, ancient turquoise grizzly bear in an ancient burial site. Taking this as a sign, he chooses the name Lone Bear for himself, a name he will never share except with one other person, following his people's tradition, and the bearstone becomes an emblem for the strength he will receive from his spirit-helper bear, strength he will be able to share with Walter and eventually with two grizzly cubs that may be the last grizzlies in Colorado. In addition to finding a name for himself, Cloyd embarks on a quest for knowledge of his relationship to the spirit world and the world around him, a quest that will begin in exploration and end in an initiatory dream quest that brings him into manhood. He has three helpers on his journey: Walter, who helps him open up to people; a Native American wildlife biologist, who teaches him bear lore; and his spirit helper, a large male grizzly bear who visits Cloyd in dreams after being killed by a hunter.

Cloyd has grown up knowing his people's past; being sent to work for Walter actually takes him closer to his ancestors, a group of Utes who lived in the Colorado mountains. Much of his time with Walter, as chronicled in *Bearstone*, is spent in overcoming his anger, through hard work and a slowly evolving relationship with the elderly man. One reason for his anger is Walter's friendship with the hunter and tracker Rusty, who has led white hunters to a black bear that they killed near Walter's farm and who later kills a male grizzly in the mountains in a family bow-and-arrow competition. Despite Cloyd's anger, Walter keeps trying to reach him, and eventually their relationship is cemented by a trip to the mountains, where he witnesses the grizzly's death. Cloyd is haunted by a sense of responsibility for the grizzly, since he mentioned the animal to Rusty, not imagining the man would kill an endangered creature. At the end of his first summer with Walter, though, Cloyd chooses responsibility to other people over dedication to the wild, and, as his heart opens to Walter, he leaves the bearstone with him in the hospital to lend Walter strength for recovery. Cloyd's decision to live with Walter enables the old man to keep his independence and his land. Their closeness is sealed when Cloyd shares his secret name.

Staying with Walter, caring for him and doing most of the farm work, Cloyd grows and matures before the events of *Beardance* again take them into the mountains. By this time, Cloyd has participated in his people's beardance, traditionally practiced to lend the Utes' support to the bears as they woke from hibernation and left their dens, and, dancing, he experienced the parting of his spirit from his body, dreaming of bears, especially of the grizzly that Rusty killed. When he helps Walter search for an abandoned Spanish mine at the end of their second summer together, Cloyd meets the Tlingit woman Ursa, a university professor of biology who is helping the Fish and Wildlife Department search for grizzlies, a search sparked largely by Rusty's reported sighting of a female with three cubs. (Rusty appears to have found a conscience.) Ursa acts as a human guide and mentor, sharing much of her knowledge of bears—knowledge from her tribal past, her personal interest in native people's bearlore, and her formal education as a biologist.

After the mother grizzly's sudden death in a rockfall, Cloyd is committed to saving the two surviving cubs, and his commitment takes him on a strange journey into the realm of relationship between bears and humans that his people have told of, in a mythical past when bears became human and humans became bears. His transformation begins when he approaches them in their mother's skin, not wanting to tame them and run the risk of turning them into "nuisance bears." Thus Cloyd becomes a sort of bear-man, fishing for the cubs and foraging with them but never sharing humans' food with them. He teaches them caution about humans, fleeing in real fear when they sight any and keeping them from contact with the old sheepherder whose help he must solicit when they tumble into an old mine tunnel.

After they are pursued by Rusty and caught in an avalanche, an avalanche from which the cubs save Cloyd, sniffing for his presence and rapidly digging him out of the snow, they are all three believed dead. Cloyd's resources dwindle, leading him involuntarily into the kind of hunger and exhaustion that bring the dreams, both sleeping and waking, that demonstrate to Cloyd that the grizzly is his spirit helper. A dream prompts him to the place where he can make a final kill, giving him strength for the journey out of the mountains, a heavy snowfall sends the cubs into hibernation in the den they have dug with Cloyd, and he reemerges into the human land as though into the land of the living, returning to Walter's glad welcome.

The bearstone has changed hands again in this second novel: Walter returns the stone to Cloyd when he reaches the highest point he can climb to in the mountains, grateful for an unexpected chance for this last excursion; Cloyd loses the stone to one of the cubs, who swallows it as he is showing it to them and talking about it; and Rusty retrieves it from the cub's droppings when he is tracking Cloyd and then returns it to Walter. When Cloyd dances the beardance at the farm in the spring, helping his bears wake from their winter sleep and traveling in the spirit to keep them company, he is ready to return the relic to the cave where he found it, now that he has internalized the bear's strength.

Beardance reveals Rusty's true transformation. In Alaska, he has trapped a young male grizzly and secretly driven it back to Colorado so that he may bypass the governmental red tape and introduce it to the wilderness where he shot the older grizzly. Rusty embodies a range of attitudes toward bears, showing a hunter's love for the beast coupled with a desire to kill it. He shows himself capable of growth and change over the course of the two novels. The elderly sheepherder, Sixto Loco, has the reputation of being antagonistic to bears as well as crazy, but he proves surprisingly supportive of Cloyd, leaving him food and supplies in his camp as he takes the herd to winter at a lower altitude. One of the two Fish and Wildlife wardens proves to be antagonistic to the bears, having come from a ranching background; for him, there are good animals and bad animals. His attitude is not shared by his colleague. The most despicable characters are the unseen ones who trash the sheepherder's camp after his departure, for no reason other than drunkenness. The greatest understanding of the bears is shown by Cloyd, Ursa, and Rusty, and thus Hobbs avoids oversimplified stereotypes of native people's attitudes in simple opposition to whites' attitudes.

Gary Paulsen's 1992 novel, *The Haymeadow*, tracks the almost-overnight maturation of young John Barron when he spends the summer alone with six thousand sheep, four border collies, and two horses in a mountain pasture, the "haymeadow." John is fascinated by his heritage of independence and courage from his great-grandfather, who laid claim to 960,000 acres in Wyoming, a ranch subsequently lost—so the story goes—by John's grandfather, a man too kind to hold onto his money. John at fourteen is a natural rider, a good shot, and an experienced sheep rancher who has maintained the herd with his father and two hands for the corporation that now owns Barron land. With his mother long since dead, John lives a spare life: his father, the thirty-five-year-old Cawley, and the elderly Tinckner speak little and live simply, eating most of their meals from cans.

It is Tink's job to mind the herd through the summer in the high country, but when he is diagnosed with cancer, it becomes John's job. His father plans to spend as much time as possible at Tink's bedside because the old man is practically family, and Cawley must run the ranch. John feels a bit desolate when Cawley leaves him to set up camp in the mountains—not knowing what questions he should have asked the taciturn hand and not even sure that Cawley could frame the answers he needs. Within the first few days, John copes with rattlesnakes, skunks, coyotes, a black bear, the dogs' cut paws and broken ribs, and a flash flood that tips the wagon he lives in and scatters most of his supplies along the streambed. His experiences mature him fast.

John's father's taciturnity magically disappears when he arrives several weeks later with supplies, his tongue apparently loosened by his watch over Tink, now on the mend, his cancer contained. He talks throughout the night, relating family and personal history, including his memories of John at birth. Cautiously, he reshapes John's role models as he corrects John's image of his great-grandfather, recounting his ruthlessness and disabusing John of the idea that his grandfather's kindness resulted in financial ruin. John's right to knowledge is part of his rite of passage. Most importantly, though, separation has laid the foundation for a new and richer relationship between father and son, and his father decides to spend more time in the high country. The remaining weeks of the summer will be a time for cementing their new understanding, now that John has entered manhood by taking on adult responsibility.

Tangerine (1997), by Edward Bloor, may be first and foremost an ecological tale, since it is set in a Florida community where upscale new housing developments are sprouting without regard to climate or the land where citrus groves once flourished, but it is also a story of athletics, class difference, and family dynamics. Almost immediately after moving into a new home in Lake Windsor Estates near Tangerine, Florida, Paul Fisher and his family learn that the new homes are built near lignite deposits, and the lignite—a step away from being coal—occasionally catches fire in thunderstorms. The resulting muck fire has to burn itself out because the fire department can do nothing to stop it. Paul's family also learns that daily thunderstorms bring death by lightning at a higher rate than anywhere else in the country. Paul, looking carefully at the land and reflecting on what he sees, realizes that the construction companies have leveled the land artificially, but in reality, the lightning is drawn to high ground: one of their neighbors, considered unlucky by the community, has bought the house on the highest ground, and that house has been struck three times. To combat the muck fires, the homeowners' association arranges to sink deep shafts and pour in water, but the unplanned outcome is the creation of breeding grounds for mosquitoes, and soon all the houses on the street nearest the muck fire are tented by the exterminating company to protect people and pets from their high-powered pesticides.

Another environmental issue, but a mere annoyance compared with other problems, is the mystifying disappearance of expensive koi the homeowners have imported for the community's small drainage lake. Suspecting illicit fishing in the lake, the adults fail to see that their lake is being fished by the native osprey, though Paul observes who the thieves are. Ironically, Paul's father is a civil engineer, but he practices his profession largely oblivious of the environment he lives and works in. When Paul draws his father's attention to the osprey nests on the utility poles along the highway, all that his father says is that someone ought to get rid of the birds because they may cause power outages. Before they moved to Florida, Paul notes, they lived in the same kind of communities in Houston and in Huntsville, Alabama, and the expensive suburbs are interchangeable around the country, irrespective of local conditions.

Paul points out to his mother the waste of the citrus trees, which are simply burned to clear land for more building, but she shrugs it off. His father's blindness to the environment can have more serious consequences, though, as he works for the county, where building permits are issued. The collapse of the school's temporary classroom modules into a sinkhole dramatically brings Mr. Fisher's boss's corruption to public notice, underscoring the rottenness of the new culture that has imposed itself on the landscape. The collapse also affords Paul a second chance to play soccer when he takes the opportunity to attend Tangerine Middle School.

It is another significant irony that Paul, who sees things more realistically than his parents, is legally blind. His mother shamelessly uses his condition to get a tour of the school before the school year begins, claiming that Paul needs to preview his surroundings. But, as Paul keeps pointing out to his parents, he can see quite well with his thick glasses—he is legally blind only without them. His mother's manipulation of school authorities has unexpected consequences for Paul: the principal asks her to fill out an IEP, a guide is assigned to him to help him get around between classes, and he is ineligible for the soccer team because the school has no insurance coverage for athletes with disabilities. Paul is an excellent goalie, though, so when he takes advantage of the transfer to another school, his mother helps him hide the information she volunteered at his first school.

The opportunity to attend Tangerine enables Paul to see and understand another dimension of life in Florida, one that has grown naturally out of the climate and terrain, its agricultural production. When he helps the Cruz family save trees from freezing and learns about developing new breeds of fruit, his suspicion about the climate is confirmed: the weather that interferes with football practice, starts up the muck fire, and opens up sinkholes is just right for growing citrus. The Latino family's meaningful connection with their land forms a sharp contrast to the suburban residents' ignorance of their environment. Paul is open to new experiences and learning about others: he loves the scent of citrus that permeates the air, unlike his friend Joey, who perceives it as a bad smell, associating it with the lower-class culture that he disdains, and unlike his own family, who seem oblivious to the aroma.

What drew his father to Florida is the high-powered state university football teams. Paul's brother, Erik, has been a star placekicker as a junior, and their father is pursuing the "Erik Fisher Football Team" by bringing him to the attention of Florida coaches. Unfortunately, Erik's debut becomes a slapstick back-flop into the mud, making him a laughingstock in the local sports broadcasts and exacerbating Erik's meanness. Another irony of the novel is Mr. Fisher's inability to see Paul for who he is, blinded by his preoccupation with Erik as a football hero. He is equally unable to see Erik for who he is.

Paul's skill as a soccer player is totally overlooked by his father. At Paul's home game at Tangerine, he is amazed to see teammates' family members in the crowd—his parents attend every one of Erik's football games but not his soccer games. Even his mother, a bit more in tune with Paul's sports ability, fails to understand team dynamics, patronizing his female teammates, offering them "encouragement" by telling them how wonderful it is they play with boys, not recognizing these girls are terrific players and include the county's highest scorer. Moreover, she does active harm by getting the local newspaper in to photograph and interview the girls, again demonstrating how little the newly arrived suburbanites understand of the community where they live.

Blind to Paul's abilities, independence, and perception, the Fishers also overlook Erik's sociopathological tendencies. Erik is a bully and a lawbreaker. His offensive cruelty toward Paul's friend Joey, when Joey's brother is electrocuted by lightning during football practice, is the least of his aggressive actions. Erik's criminal behavior finally becomes too blatant for his parents to avoid seeing it: he gets his buddy to hit the oldest Cruz brother on the head, causing a fatal aneurysm, an action that brings in the police. And Mrs. Fisher discovers that her storage locker holds a cache of goods burgled from the exterminator-tented houses.

As these cases of lawlessness are uncovered, Paul finally recovers the memory that has teased at the edges of his memory, like something in his peripheral vision—Erik's causing the severe damage to Paul's eyesight that Erik subsequently attributed to Paul's having stupidly watched the sun during an eclipse, nicknaming him Eclipse Boy. It is clear, in the final analysis, that Paul is the clearest-sighted member of his family, despite their efforts to blur the truth. He acts with courage and intelligence, on an ethical basis of social justice and care for the land.

Kathe Koja's *Straydog* (2002) is more typical of the traditional story about the bond between a young person and an animal. The protagonist, Rachel, a volunteer at an animal shelter, tells the sad story of a beautiful but feral dog. Rachel's strengths are her empathetic imagining of the dog's understanding of the world and her writing ability, and these come together in an essay that her English teacher has pressured her to write for a creative writing contest. Rachel is unable to rescue the dog she identifies with, feeling the dog's fear and anger: it would take time to calm and tame the dog she calls Grrl, and there simply are not enough resources and time for even the most sympathetic shelter personnel to save every animal, especially after Grrl bites two of the workers. Despite her grief when the dog is euthanized, Rachel's commitment to the injured collie fuels her effort to memorialize her and convince others to care in the essay that is, unfortunately, finally judged too "raw" to earn her acceptance to a summer writing workshop. In the process, however, Rachel confronts her own fear of trusting others and begins to open up to a new classmate, Griffin, also a talented writer.

Rachel is essentially a loner, and her intense emotions sometimes lead her into conflicts. An outsider at school, she is taunted by classmates who, once they hear her evolving essay on the dog, begin calling her a dog and barking at her. This situation escalates until she ends up in the principal's office, along with Griffin. In another violent incident sparked by her enormous grief and pain, she trashes the shelter director's computer after Grrl's death, an action that angers her father, who sees it primarily as a matter of financial irresponsibility, and that results in her dismissal as a volunteer. Her conflict with her father, however, is nothing new; she does not respect him and says she disagrees with everything he says. Her mother, in contrast, understands the intensity of Rachel's feelings and, after Grrl's death, expresses her wish that Rachel had shared her fear and distress before the crisis. This is something that Rachel finds too difficult to do, though.

Rachel makes an exception of Griffin, however, with whom her insightful English teacher has paired her for creative writing peer response. The tentative bond established when they share their writing quickly flowers into tentative friendship—tentative because each is a cautious loner. They also share empathy with animals, and as they pursue the goal of taming Grrl, they grow closer—close enough that he can offer her comfort after Grrl's death and become a real friend. As a shelter employee notes, those who have been hurt are those who understand how to be kind.

As sad as Grrl's story is, Rachel's story is a hopeful one. Her compassion enables her to love another animal, and Griffin, less invested in saving Grrl and only Grrl, welcomes having another dog, whom they share. Rachel releases some of her grief through writing, and she finishes her essay with a view of dog heaven, free of pain and hunger and fear of humans, where all the "straydogs" are "gooddogs."

ADDITIONAL READING RECOMMENDATIONS

Bristle Face by Zachary Ball, 1962
When the Legends Die by Hal Borland, 1963
Sounder by William Armstrong, 1969
M. C. Higgins, the Great by Virginia Hamilton, 1974
Taming the Star Runner by S. E. Hinton, 1979
Every Living Thing [stories] by Cynthia Rylant, 1985
The Island by Gary Paulsen, 1988
It Happened at Cecilia's by Erika Tamar, 1989 (discussed in Jobs: Assuming Adult
    Responsibility)
Mariposa Blues by Ron Koertge, 1991
Yaxley's Cat by Robert Westall, 1992
Lockie Leonard, Scumbuster by Tim Winton, 1993
California Blue by David Klass, 1994
Out of Nowhere by Ouida Sebestyen, 1994
Pictures in the Dark by Gillian Cross, 1996
The Exchange Student by Kate Gilmore, 1999 (discussed in Imagined Futures)
Hoot by Carl Hiaasen, 2002
Saving the Planet & Stuff by Gail Gauthier, 2003 (discussed in Older People's Impact on
    Our Lives)
My Contract with Henry by Robin Vaupel, 2003

Beauty's Meaning

Izzy, Willy-Nilly by Cynthia Voigt (1986)
One Fat Summer by Robert Lipsyte (1977)
Staying Fat for Sarah Byrnes by Chris Crutcher (1993)

The relationship between appearance and reality is a prevalent theme in literature. Mistaken identity, solid character under an unpleasing facade or beautiful appearance covering moral deficiency, exploitation of appearance for comedic effect—all have been explored throughout the history of Western literature. In popular culture, we still repeat adages such as "handsome is as handsome does" or "beauty is only skin deep." Nonetheless physical appearance is very important in our image-conscious culture, ranging from facial features and skin health to weight and muscle tone to fashion. Looks are assumed, to a large extent, to reveal who a person is. Beauty can dominate the thoughts of young people, who are consciously identifying themselves as individuals and developing as sexual beings. As a result, many teens concentrate more on physical features, weight, and skin than on personal growth and development in the areas of intellect and character.

Is preoccupation with physical appearance unhealthy or superficial? This is clearly a matter of degree. Focusing on the surface without regard for character will lead one astray, but a growing body of evidence suggests that success in many areas of life comes more easily to those deemed attractive, indeed may come as a direct outgrowth of pleasing physical appearance. Much of literature reinforces the message that beauty brings success, through its role in winning successful romantic relationships or power, as well as the converse message that lack of beauty brings unhappiness, through its role in obscuring qualities of manhood and womanhood that may prove more enduring over a lifetime. Additionally, many instances of discrimination and prejudice are based solely on physical appearance. So making the effort to present as pleasing an appearance as possible is clearly a realistic goal. Indeed, coping with obesity or disfigurement often contributes to a refocusing of a young person's energy that results in growth in character. Literature that addresses the significance and meaning of beauty, then, can help young adult readers assess its importance in their own lives.

Izzy, Willy-Nilly (1986), by Cynthia Voigt, is a novel about adjustment to disfigurement after a car accident takes fifteen-year-old Izzy's leg. She is pretty, popular, active, a cheerleader, with the right friends and attention from the right boys, but in the hospital she realizes she has become a pariah, and her return to school challenges all the students for whom she makes real the thought that something like this could happen to them—anybody could become a "cripple." There is a lot for Izzy to handle: her own depression, her damaged sense of herself, her discovery of who her friends really are, her sensitivity to each parent's way of attempting to make things right for her, one brother's urge to kill the boy responsible for the accident, her younger sister's jealousy of her new, "privileged" status in the family, which is accompanied by pity so deep that she cannot confront it and hence acts out her anger and fear. Izzy comes from a "nice" family, and handling her own anger and pain is more challenging than it needs to be because of her "nice" background. The one true friend she has is a surprise to her—the odd, self-conscious, undiplomatic, and exceptionally bright Rosamunde, who is the oldest of a large brood of kids, with an offbeat craftswoman for a mother and a city policeman for a father. Izzy's conventional, comfortably middle-class mother is overwhelmed by a sense of Rosamunde's inappropriateness as a friend, a factor that complicates Izzy's real gratitude for Rosamunde's deep empathy. Izzy's growth is painful but impressive as she learns to meet the physical challenges of getting around as well as the emotional challenges of facing friends' and acquaintances' changed attitudes toward her, of seeing another girl take her place on the cheerleading squad, of being seen as handicapped in public places, and of understanding the different ways that her family adjusts to her changed self.

Clearly, beauty is an issue for a young woman who has lost a part of a limb. Izzy grieves over her loss, anticipating a complete end to romance in her life now that she no longer draws appreciative looks from males young and old. Izzy and her friends have thought a lot about looks, clothes, makeup, and hair. As a matter of fact, it is Rosamunde's looks that are against her with Izzy's former friends and family—her wild hair, lumpish clothes, and aversion to makeup. In cheerful moments, Izzy longs to see her friend's eyes made up and her hair cut becomingly. Yet just as she is—intellectual, empathetic, individualistic—Rosamunde attracts the interest of one of Izzy's older brothers. Rosamunde focuses Izzy's recognition of her former friends' changed attitudes toward her; their comments on Rosamunde point up the superficiality of their assessment of others' worth. One friend, indeed, a beautiful young woman who aspires to be a model, is so distressed that she cannot visit Izzy in the hospital, talk to her on the phone, or be anywhere near her in school after the accident; her fear of confronting Izzy's loss of beauty is palpable. On several levels, the accident has forced Izzy to define herself and her beauty in terms other than bodily wholeness. For instance, ·she pays attention to other kinds of beauty, with Rosamunde's help, abandoning the prepackaged needlepoint kit her mother has bought for her to design her own needlepoint picture of a memorable tree whose autumn foliage glows golden against a cloudy sky. She learns empathy for the black therapist who works with her, coming to understand that racism is an inability to see beyond surface difference. Becoming more thoughtful, more empathetic, and more assertive, Izzy becomes more interesting. The handsome senior she has admired does not ask her out, but he provides the occasion for demonstration of Izzy's true triumph over adversity when he dashes off after his girlfriend without remembering to hand her crutch to her—the signal to Izzy that he sees her as a friend, a girl, not as a cripple. Izzy, now ready to be Isobel, has grown as a person, whether she will or not ("willy-nilly").

Throughout her period of adjustment and growth, Izzy has envisioned her true self as a homuncular "little Izzy," who has done back flips before realizing she is handicapped, has limped, has looked deep into other people's fears, has turned beet-red in embarrassment and had hysterics while the outer Izzy has presented a stoic front to the world. Ultimately, little Izzy, dressed in a black velvet skirt and shimmering blouse, takes her first tentative steps toward dancing as Izzy embodies what she has learned about adjusting to accidents, about true friendship, and about class prejudices, as well as about beauty.

In contrast, Robert Lipsyte's *One Fat Summer* (1977) is about being a hero, about work, about class difference (with brief reference to anti-Semitism), and about a father-son relationship and family relationships in general—but all of these themes are subsumed in the role that appearance plays in teens' lives. Bob Marks at age fourteen weighs more than two hundred pounds and is unlikely to stop gaining weight, given his tendency to secretive binge eating and antipathy to activity. In a family of slender, active, sociable people, Bob has become a liar about his habits and is adept at avoiding his father's schemes for transforming him into a son he can understand. To avoid his father's scheme to ship him off to day camp as a junior counselor, Bob conspires with his best friend Joanie first to work on a school project and then to find his own job. Joanie, a smart, funny girl with whom he has had a companionable relationship since they were both toddlers, is shy with others because of her appearance—her nose is long and crooked—but she is funny and supportive of Bob, and it is she who pushes him into answering an ad for lawn-mowing before disappearing back to the city for her own mysterious purposes. Whether he really wants it or not, Bob finds himself with a grueling, poorly paying summer job for a perfectionist, who is a professor—and (like Bob) a Jew, which means both are viewed with antipathy by the local, Gentile year-round residents, some of whom have profited from the summer people's influx, some of whom have lost land and status. By taking this job, Bob has especially antagonized a young veteran, an ex-military bully who feels entitled to it. He and his cronies harass Bob every time they catch him, and the situation nears real danger on more than one occasion. Bob finds a surprising ally in the local diving champion–sex god, who is fascinated by Bob's beautiful older sister.

Bob is as secretive about his job as he is about his eating binges, though he has to negotiate a trade of secrets with his sister to keep it from their father. Their mother is working on her own problems with their father: studying to be a teacher, she is trying to talk him into countenancing her working, and their relationship is tense. When she leaves Bob and Michelle on their own to spend time in the city with her husband, she gives Michelle's romance the perfect condition for flourishing, but when she later learns about it, she puts an end to it for reasons that are not entirely clear. In the course of these machinations, we see a family with serious communication problems. Indeed, Bob's father seems to have little real voice in the household. As Bob begins to lose weight, an inevitable consequence of the hard work he is doing, his mother tries to get him to eat more, and she buys him pants that are too large, assuming his weight will spiral upward again, while his father's protests go unheeded. She seems to be unable to see the real changes occurring in her son.

Bob's changes go much deeper than weight loss. Despite humiliation and threats— and being marooned overnight on an island by his enemies—he refuses to be bullied out of his job and even stands up to his employer, who has tried to underpay him. Bob is sustained by a rich inner life—he envisions himself as a superhero, Big Bob Marks, or as a military man, Commander Marks or Captain Marks, whose heroic perseverance will save the day. These heroic fantasies keep him going in a grueling job and help him envision how he will handle the next attack by the rural bullies. He also sees himself as a writer, and his wry sense of humor is expressed in his vision of the book he could write about his summer, which he would call *The Secret Summer*, as he learns of secrets between members of the group that bullies him at the same time as he helps his sister keep her secrets.

The biggest secret is Joanie's nose job—she eventually reappears on the scene with a red and swollen but healing nose. Their relationship is significantly changed, after close friendship since toddlerhood. She is focused on appearance now; she is not as funny as she was; she enjoys leafing through fashion and beauty magazines; and ultimately she is not very interested in Bob anymore. She does not even notice his weight loss, merely mentioning in puzzlement that he looks "different," so that he has to point out his loss of twenty-five pounds, and then she suggests that this weight loss may be weakening him.

The biggest change is in Bob, as he demonstrates in his final confrontation with the bully, which Pete and Joanie witness. After Bob has succeeded in physically over-coming his enemy, Pete takes advantage of the situation and grabs a gun to humil-iate the defeated man. Puffed up with class pride, clearly scorning the poorer man, he defends his action as proving that "they" should not be able to push "us"—him and Bob—around. He calls Bob a hero, but this does not make Bob any prouder of their success at turning the tables. Bob sees that though Pete looks gorgeous, he has not yet figured out what makes a man a man.

Another close friendship between a young woman and a young man whose appearances set them apart from their peers is depicted in Chris Crutcher's *Staying Fat for Sarah Byrnes* (1993). The novel revolves around the relationship between appearance and reality, variously depicted in physical beauty, emotional health, dat-ing relationships and friendships, parent-child relationships, toughness and vulner-ability, and the depth of professed religious commitment. The novel also explores the need for courage within these various situations.

"Staying fat" has been Eric Calhoune's goal. His huge girth has earned him the nickname Moby since he joined the swim team, but he accepts it from teammates, fans, and the coach, who is his favorite teacher, Ms. Lemry. She also teaches a contro-versial course in contemporary American thought for a select group of second-semester seniors, including several members of the swim team. Classroom discussions focus on important issues that the novel explores, including whether the world is essentially a good or a bad place and whether abortion is justifiable.

The novel uses flashback to explore the central relationship, between Eric and his longtime friend, Sarah Byrnes. Sarah Byrnes goes by given name and surname all the time to forestall some of the jokes about her appearance: her face and hands were heavily scarred when she was three, with reconstructive surgery forbidden by her frighteningly cold and mean father. An outsider most of her life, Sarah Byrnes is tough. Eric has stayed fat for her by binge eating, so that his growing acceptance by others (and the weight loss his grueling swimming workouts bring) will not break the bond they developed through sharing outsider status. Eric is thinking back through their friendship because, at first, Sarah Byrnes is confined to the psychiatric ward of the local hospital, apparently catatonic, and later because he is desperately seeking information about her past that will help her get away from her father, who not only prevented her from having plastic surgery but actually burned her, the reader learns, by pressing her face to a wood stove in a horrifyingly sadistic act that drove Sarah Byrnes's mother away.

Some of the courage and wit with which the friends have faced danger in the past—in the form of bullying by an older, larger boy and school authorities' disapproval of their subversive attitude toward school—is shown in the underground paper they started in middle school, *Crispy Pork Rinds*, which refers to burns ("crispy"), weight ("pork"), and the discarded remnants ("rinds") of news outside the official channels. As Eric learns that Sarah Byrnes is not really catatonic but is figuring out how to escape from her father, who is becoming crazier again, he draws her father's attention and becomes the victim of stalking and assault with a knife, and it takes wit and courage for both teens to survive this deadly situation.

Upon Sarah Byrnes's return to school, she makes a compelling personal contribution to Ms. Lemry's class's intense argument over abortion—that it is better for a fetus to be aborted than for a child to endure what she has at her father's hands. The argument also brings out the ugly reality underlying the romance between a conservative Christian couple in the class: Mark, the vocal spokesman for a narrowly defined, legalistic God, insisted on his girlfriend's having an abortion when he got her pregnant, but he left her to face it alone. Confronted with public knowledge of his hypocrisy, Mark attempts suicide, but as he recovers, he begins to grope his way toward a more tolerant Christianity, represented by the pastor father of Steve Ellerby, another swim team member and Eric's good friend. Although he is a PK (preacher's kid), Steve appears to challenge much of what organized religion stands for—or perhaps just any hypocrisy he sees in the practice of organized religion, a theme that appears in other works by Crutcher—but the course of events, as well as class discussion, shows him to be a serious reflective thinker about the relations between human beings and their responsibility to one another. It takes courage for Sarah Byrnes to face her life, and it takes courage for Mark to face his, for very different reasons, and Steve comes to honor his peers' courage.

Finally, though all the bad guys in this novel are adults and teen villains prove themselves otherwise, adult help is needed to resolve the dangers and emotional landmines of the novel. Ms. Lemry acts as more than teacher and mentor, taking an active role in resolving Sarah Byrnes's threatening family situation and then adopting her, filling the void left by her mother's desertion and the destruction of her fantasies of being rescued by her mother's return. Eric's mother's boyfriend takes the law into his own hands and makes sure that Sarah Byrnes's father will not continue to harm the people who love Sarah Byrnes (the people whom this man is coming to love), revealing himself as a quiet hero. Thus he earns a solid place in Eric's affections that promises to fill the void left by his father's absence since before he was born. Everyone, adult and teen alike, learns to look deeper to see what people are really made of in this chronicle of survival, friendship, and, ultimately, beauty.

ADDITIONAL READING RECOMMENDATIONS

High Cheekbones by Erika Tamar, 1990
Twenty Pageants Later by Caroline B. Cooney, 1991
Life in the Fat Lane by Cherie Bennett, 1998
I Was a Teenage Fairy by Francesca Lia Block, 1998 (discussed in Abuse, Sexual Violence, and Healing)
The Skin I'm In by Sharon G. Flake, 1998
Box Girl by Sarah Withrow, 2001
Stand Tall by Joan Bauer, 2002

Breaking Silence, Speaking Out

Dance on My Grave by Aidan Chambers (1982)
Speak by Laurie Halse Anderson (1999)
The Facts Speak for Themselves by Brock Cole (1997)
The Other Side of Silence by Margaret Mahy (1995)
The Book of the Banshee by Anne Fine (1992)

Many of the most serious problems children and young adults face are exacerbated by silence. Abuse, family dysfunction and family secrets, rape—all may fester in silence, continuing the most horrible conditions in young people's lives. Speaking out is the first step toward coping, but it is a very big step, which may seem to involve more danger than relief is worth. Naming and facing the most serious challenges to one's own survival as an individual are important steps in maturing, as well. In most of the novels discussed here, a character who has chosen silence, in some cases for years, takes that step toward healing.

Aidan Chambers's 1982 novel, *Dance on My Grave*, is a less-than-strictly-linear narrative constructed in bits by sixteen-year-old Hal, after his arrest for desecrating the grave of his friend—and lover—eighteen-year-old Barry. Hal refuses to speak in his own defense, to explain to authorities that he has promised Barry he will "dance on [his] grave," but this narrative is eventually drawn from him by the teacher who has encouraged Hal to study literature and prepare for college. A lengthy descriptive subtitle appears on the cover page: *A Life and a Death in Four Parts One Hundred and Seventeen Bits, Six Running Reports, and Two Press Clippings with a Few Jokes, a Puzzle or Three, Some Footnotes, and a Fiasco Now and Then to Help the Story Along.*

Such play with genre and the black humor of linguistic antics with regard to so serious a theme are typical of Chambers's writing. One of the greatest pleasures of reading this novel is being entertained by the wordplay, which can be further illustrated by one brief example, Hal's list of fifteen words beginning with *re* to describe what a hot bath would represent to him after his near-drowning.

The first newspaper clipping appears on the page before the title page, reporting the arrest of a teen for performing "strange antics" on the grave; the second clipping is the last page of the novel, reporting the resolution of the legal matter, following Hal's sharing his narrative with the court. Running reports chronicle the authorities' interactions with a silent Hal. Hal's narrative bits range from a few lines to a few pages in length, numbered consecutively from 1 in each of the four parts.

Each part of the novel is headlined with an epigraph. The quotation from Kurt Vonnegut, Hal's favorite writer, that opens part one focuses on appearance and reality, cautioning that we must be careful in pretending to an identity. This section focuses on Hal and Barry's meeting when Hal nearly drowned. Hal recounts his earlier experiences with friendship and homosexual attraction, his longing for a "bosom friend," a relationship like that of the biblical David and Jonathan. There is little effort at pretense about the flirtation that underlies the budding friendship. Hal's interest in death is noted in this section as well, since it is his essay about death that has sparked his teacher's encouragement of his further study.

Part two begins with an epigraph from John Donne's "The Perfume," focusing on the "escape" into illicit passionate love, and Hal's fondness for a passage from Vonnegut's *Slapstick* identifies the most meaningful sexual experiences as characterized by "common decency" rather than love. In this section, Hal is caught up in romance and Barry's wild escapades. The real seriousness of his love for Barry is recognized by no one until after his death, when the girl who briefly came between them sympathetically acknowledges it, as she agrees to help him view Barry's body, in order to move toward closure.

The brief, numerically oriented part three prepares the reader for Barry's imminent death, beginning with Hal's summing up of the length of his time with Barry—only seven weeks—and the number of times or length of time they did various things together. The epigraph identifies death as a "kick."

Part four, headed with a sketch of Laurel and Hardy and the quotation "Another fine mess you've gotten us into," chronicles the emotional explosion that led to Barry's death, Hal's learning of it through a radio news broadcast, and his subsequent grief, including his fulfillment of his promise to Barry, the dancing that has seemed so inexplicable to authorities and so offensive to Barry's mother.

Finally, as Hal nears the end of his narrative, he reflects that his writing of the story has changed him more profoundly than his living the events he relates, as he uses the raw material of his experience to create himself as a character. He has moved into artistry, and to recapture the real, raw emotion of his grief, he must include extracts from his diary in the days immediately following Barry's death, a diary he plans to destroy, which he refers to as "effluent" and "excrement." His visits to Barry's grave, and the frenzies they produce, are most fully explained by this effusion of grief onto the typed page, which he calls the "diary of a madman." Writing his experience has released him from the worst of his emotional pain, and he acknowledges that life must continue.

The price of silence after a rape is a painful wound that will not heal, and this is what the ninth-grade protagonist of Laurie Halse Anderson's *Speak* (1999) suffers from. Melinda begins high school as an outcast: no one knows why she called 911 at a late-summer party, but everyone is angry with her. She has lost her friends and is not close enough to her parents to confide in them—she is not even sure where they were that night, but neither one came in until long after she had taken a long shower and crawled into her bed, the place where she would like to stay every day. Her silence about the rape creeps into other areas of her life, until she refuses to speak in uncomfortable situations—being called on in class, dealing with her parents' disapproval of her sliding academic performance, and coping with authorities who misunderstand her, interpreting her depression as sullenness, resistance, a bad attitude. Ironically, Melinda's internal voice, the voice of the first-person narrative, is witty and sarcastic. Her wry observations of high school life continually entertain the reader, who only gradually becomes aware of the intensity of her pain.

Her chewed lips, perpetually scabby, attest to her turmoil; she feels as though she might almost be able to consume herself and disappear some days, while other days she just tries desperately to hold in the screams that build inside her. Another symptom an adult might notice is her lack of attention to her appearance. Her grades decline: starting out mediocre—even the ones she gives herself for playing nicely, attitude, social life, lunch, and clothing—they move to Fs as she neglects homework and cuts class. All the clues are there that something is wrong, but no one figures them out.

Melinda works at maintaining invisibility, especially around the senior who raped her, whom she cannot even name to herself for some months, referring to him as "IT" or "the Beast." She puts away or covers mirrors. She hides in her bedroom closet, the only place where she ever indulges the need to scream—many months later, her mouth stuffed with cloth. She freezes like a rabbit, like the stuffed rabbits in her bedroom (last redecorated in fifth grade), when stalked by the rapist. Surprisingly, she finds a refuge that no one else seems to know of, a disused housekeeping closet, which she slips into when she skips class and later even naps in after school, feeling safer there than she does at home. The poster in her closet-refuge features Maya Angelou, author of *I Know Why the Caged Bird Sings*, the autobiographical work in which Angelou narrates her own rape as a young teen. Melinda hears Angelou encouraging her to speak out as her former best friend Rachel is drawn into a relationship with Andy (the Beast), and Angelou covers the mirror that Melinda ultimately uses to fend him off when he attempts a second rape.

The rapist is good-looking, rich, and popular, and girls seek his approval and company, despite a few rumors. Melinda's immobility may come, in part, from her sense that she was somehow responsible for the rape: she forced herself to drink beer and thus impaired her ability to take care of herself. Andy continues to take advantage of her fear and anger, accusing her in the climactic scene of having wanted intercourse as much as he did. She is sickened by his smell, which brings back blocked memories, partial at first, then increasingly detailed, in a technique that allows the reader gradually to discover just what happened to her.

Melinda's salvation comes through art. Mr. Freeman, a free-spirited artist, promotes artistic expression as a survival skill. He is also the only teacher who encourages Melinda to talk to him, though she does not do so until finding her voice in her confrontation with Andy. Mr. Freeman reads the pain and darkness in her work, especially in the turkey carcass sculpture she creates after Thanksgiving, to which she attaches a Barbie doll head with, significantly, tape over its mouth. In assigning the subject of trees, Mr. Freeman furnishes a metaphor for her life. Melinda at first produces very dark work; for a long time she produces stiff, unnatural trees. It is Mr. Freeman who tells her that trees are not perfect, as she observes herself when the tree in her yard has to be cut back to eliminate dead wood, enabling it to devote energy to new growth. She eventually succeeds in creating images of trees that satisfy her, bringing to bear a developing knowledge from biology class and the insights she has gained from cleaning up her yard in her own burst of springtime energy.

Working in the yard creates a climate for family communication. Her parents are generally preoccupied with their jobs, do not get along very well with each other, and only pay attention to Melinda when she gets bad grades or they are called into the school for a conference, where they express the belief that her behavior is motivated by an immature desire for attention. She is lonely and disappointed at holidays, missing the rituals of her childhood, easily touched by a Christmas gift of drawing materials that indicates they have noticed her interest in art. Instead of responding to her depression, however, they endorse suppression of feelings as being grown up. When Melinda begins to clear the old leaves out of the yard, which no one has paid much attention to, her attention calls forth her father's, and together they begin fostering new growth. Even her mother can see, without prompting, that Melinda is doing hard work. Though the companionship this inspires does not result in her confiding in them, it does initiate a much more pleasant family atmosphere.

Despite Melinda's pain, the predominant tone of the book is very funny. She identifies a long string of cliques and shows the difficulty of a new person's fitting in, as "Heather from Ohio," Melinda's only acquaintance for much of the school year, attempts to do. Heather is the person Melinda could have been had the party not changed her: she is eager and enthusiastic and innocent, generally likable until she bows to peer pressure and dumps Melinda. As an outsider, Melinda comments sarcastically on the school hierarchy. Her depiction of the teachers and their classroom behaviors plays on humorous stereotypes—the conservative, bullying Mr. Neck in social studies, the no-nonsense Ms. Keen in biology, the frantically gesticulating Spanish teacher, the English teacher Hair Woman. Another foil for Melinda is free-speech advocate David Petrakis, an outspoken opponent of Mr. Neck's blatant suppression of student opinion. David gives Melinda a model for speaking out, though it has limited usefulness for her because her silence is a result of rape rather than timidity under normal classroom bullying.

Melinda's former friends take small steps toward reestablishing a connection, and this support helps her take her own small steps toward speaking out, by adding to the restroom graffiti a "guys to stay away from list," which she heads with Andy's name. When he attacks her in the closet and she defends herself with a shard of mirror glass, it is Nicole's lacrosse team that comes to her rescue and subsequently spreads the word that brings her much-needed support throughout the school. The secret that has been eating Melinda's courage and confidence can now come out, and she acknowledges to herself that the rape—now the "IT" she refers to—will not destroy her.

Brock Cole's *The Facts Speak for Themselves* (1997) is a more disturbing story of thirteen-year-old Linda's history of sexualized relationships with the series of men in her dysfunctional mother's life and of responsibility for her half brothers and an elderly man, one of her mother's "husbands." Neglected and abused, she has developed strong survival skills and a matter-of-fact bluntness when she chooses to break her silence about her personal history, through the support of a social worker and a compassionate nun. The reader meets Linda when she is numbed by the murder and suicide of two of the men in her life: her most recent stepfather has shot her lover (who is also her mother's boss, with a daughter Linda's age). The present-time narrative chronicles her interactions with authorities, the police, and the nuns who run a shelter for children who have been removed from their homes. As Linda begins to interact with others, she begins coping with her history, a history that she wants to tell herself, after she reads her social worker's account, which she believes makes her sound like a fool.

Linda's introduction to the facts of sex is crude, as they are explained to her first by her father, drunk and distraught due to her mother's affair. She finds that most of the men and boys she meets subsequently are more than willing to satisfy her early-aroused curiosity about bodies. Linda's mother is usually either depressed and unable to care for her children or pursuing a new man and unavailable to care for her children. She marries the elderly man who takes her and the children to Florida, hoping for comfort and a man's care, but when he disappoints her by having a stroke, she turns responsibility for him over to Linda. There is no one else to lean on. Linda's mother's parents have racist objections to Linda, whose father was Native American, and they disapprove of the elderly Jewish husband. Linda's mother leaves her behind, and Linda's subsequent silence about her home life and a period of sexual activity with boys from school are her defenses against the abandonment by her mother and abuse by her stepfather. In the last phase of Linda's life with her mother, Linda becomes involved with the two men whose lives end with the murder-suicide that finally lands her in a shelter, where she finds adult care.

In the firm but loving care of the nuns, Linda begins learning how to form relationships with girls her own age, though their grave problems are barriers to friendship. She also learns constructive alternatives to destructive anger, discovering that cleaning is very therapeutic. Finally, she meets women whose lives are not governed by continual efforts to manipulate men sexually so that they will take care of women—women whose lives offer an alternative model to her mother's. With their support, Linda takes control of her own life as she tells her own story, presenting the facts as she sees them.

A more complete and literal silence locks in the protagonist of *The Other Side of Silence* (1995), by Margaret Mahy. The novel is the first-person narrative of twelve-year-old Hero, composed at age fifteen as she reflects on her three years of voluntary mutism and the consequences of being drawn into a dangerous relationship with a solitary older woman. This relationship attracts her because it feels like one of the fairy tales she loves to read. Hero's "real life" has a soap-opera quality to it, given her family's fame and media attention. All are "word people," articulate and assertive, and the only way that Hero, always quiet, could gain power was to stop speaking. Ginevra, the oldest sibling, after years of loud arguments with her mother, has left their New Zealand home to do who-knows-what until she returns bruised and pregnant, accompanied by the biracial thirteen-year-old son of her most recent boyfriend. With Ginevra's return, many of the old family arguments resume. Their brother, Athol, the only person to whom Hero speaks, is supposedly working on a graduate degree but secretly writes soap-opera scripts based on real family dialogue. The youngest child asserts her right to attention by using highly unusual words culled from a reference book—and then calls attention to the words by defining them, whether or not anyone asks their meaning. Hero deliberately persists in not speaking, secretly deriding the psychologists' and special educationists' misdiagnosis of her choice as a speech phobia generated by family arguments. Hero knows that she has her own kind of power, almost magic, in mutism within her flamboyant family.

Hero quickly relinquishes mutism, however, when faced with the crisis of imprisonment in a locked room with a young woman who truly cannot speak because she has been deprived of the opportunity to learn human language. Hero speaks to this young woman and to her jailer, then to Ginevra's charge—who follows her, concerned about her absence—and thereafter she speaks. Moreover, she writes the narrative that forms most of the novel—only to revert to silence about the episode by deleting the file from the computer and consigning the only hard copy to the flames. This is her final claim to ownership of her own words: she denies them to others.

Hero slips through her mad family life, living the stories in her head that she calls her "true life." She is mesmerized by stories and practiced bibliomancy till age eleven, opening a book of fairy tales and placing her finger randomly on the page to discover her fate in the selected passage. Her given name seems almost to have predestined her to a love for tales. The dangerous story she chooses to enter is woven by the true madness of Miss Credence, the postmistress, daughter of a brilliant, now-deceased university professor, who lives apparently alone in a turreted old house immured within a shabby, wild, walled garden. Hero gains entry by climbing trees, at first believing herself invisible, but that illusion is dispelled when she takes a spill and makes Miss Credence's acquaintance. The woman offers her a gardening job, assuming Hero to be truly mute and therefore incapable of betraying her private life to outsiders. Lured by the money and intrigued by the story this adventure promises, Hero allows herself to be drawn into the story of a sophisticated manipulator of reality, a brilliant but unbalanced woman who has spent years weaving stories about herself and who proves to have several personalities.

From the outset, Hero sees Miss Credence (whose name seems to suggest an ability to create a reliable identity for herself) as sharing Hero's own division of life into "real life" and "true life"; thus she believes she is seeing true life when Miss Credence strides through the garden, cloaked and hatted in black, smoking, and feeding the birds. Miss Credence calls her "Jorinda, Queen of the Birds," and makes up stories about her that feature an evil bird-catcher named Nocturno. Hero discovers the Grimms' tale of Jorinda and Joringel: an evil witch turns the beautiful maiden Jorinda into a nightingale and cages her to keep with seven thousand other caged nightingales; her fiancé, Joringel, finds a magical flower that releases the spell. Hero will become the "hero" who releases Miss Credence's daughter, Rinda, from her cage.

The first hint of the dangerous extent of Miss Credence's eccentricity comes when she asks Hero to photograph her posed as a big-game hunter with the corpse of the tame neighborhood cat that she has shot dead, protecting the birds. Hero discovers the woman has other lives and personalities. Inside the house Miss Credence is a chatty, nervous woman whose life and talents were subordinated to her father's need for a housekeeper after her mother's death. Hero also learns, to her surprise, that Miss Credence had a daughter named Rinda who apparently left her.

Drawn to the locked door that she realizes must lead to the tower, and the mystery behind it, Hero invades the house, and Miss Credence's privacy, when her employer is supposed to be at work, feeling like one of Bluebeard's brides. She has no sooner discovered Jorinda Credence chained to a bed in a chamber bolted from the outside, her only window barred, than Miss Credence arrives home and bolts Hero in with her, playing out her merged role of Bluebeard and Jorinda's jailer. The other girl has been denied human language and all stimulation in the barren room, and Hero is truly frightened once she knows that the witchlike Miss Credence really has been hiding a melodramatic secret. Miss Credence's story comes out as she paces around her house, telling the story the way she has told it to herself, convincing herself she has done the right thing and prevented any stain from besmirching her brilliant father's reputation. Jorinda has grown up as a classic "closet child," kept from human contact and consequently denied the opportunity to develop language. One can see how Hero's mutism appealed to Miss Credence, allowing her to let down her guard.

Miss Credence finally silences herself through suicide, rather than face others' versions of her story that might expose her as mad or wicked. Jorinda is rescued, to be studied by university psychologists—among whom Hero's mother figures prominently—who will tell new stories about her. Hero's curiosity and imagination have drawn her into a family history more dramatic than her own. The soap opera elements of the family's interactions are noted throughout the novel, not only by Hero but by the workmen remodeling the house, who almost openly eavesdrop. The children have emulated the workmen, using the scaffolding outside the house to eavesdrop on conversations they have been excluded from. Even the neighbors express concern for their privacy, voicing their resentment of the scaffolding, from which their family life may be viewed. There are many secrets in people's ordinary lives, the reader realizes, and people pretend in many ways.

Hero prefers that all stories be anonymous and that authors get no more fame than other people, so that people do not end up being manipulated in other people's stories. This reaction is very natural, given the media exposure her family has lived with and the way Miss Credence's life story was written by her famous father. But stories also give us good advice, as *Old Fairy Tales* gave Hero when she sought random words of wisdom, and they help us shape our own lives. There is powerful magic in words as well as in silence, and Hero has elected to make her choice between the two on a daily basis in her life that is both "real" and "true."

Anne Fine's more light-hearted *Book of the Banshee* (1992) employs mock epic to demonstrate the destructive impact of adolescent emotional turmoil on family relationships. Inspired by a World War I soldier's account of his war experience, the gently named Will Flowers decides to chronicle the war initiated by his younger sister Estelle. Estelle's anger and constant pushing of her parents' reasonable rules occupy their attention, and Will feels that he is being ignored because he is a "good lad." Four-year-old Muffy responds to the turmoil by refusing to speak most of the time and sucking her thumb. The family seems locked into codependency and dysfunction, but their story is humorously told in Will's narrative, as he describes his parents' preparations for battle, the ammunition used and shots fired in each battle—over whether Estelle will go to school, what parties she may attend, what she may wear. Even the professionals who cope with adolescents—the headmaster and teachers—seem to revel in grim acceptance that warfare will be the order of the day.

Will has reread William Scott Saffery's *The Longest Summer* several times, feeling kinship with the author, with whom he shares a first name, because he was Will's age when he joined the army, lying about his age, and he draws on Saffery's account for analogies in his home life. Though he treats his theme humorously, Will comes to an important realization: despite the stupidity and pointlessness of much that Saffery witnessed, he and other soldiers never protested or took a stand, but rather chose to bear witness as participants in the senseless carnage. Will comes to see Estelle's rebellion, her absolute refusal to engage in appeasement, as the kind of conscientious protest that may sometimes save the majority from flinging themselves over a precipice in their herd mentality. And indeed, Estelle does speak up for Will when his parents express annoyance at his clumsiness, a clumsiness attributable largely to his simply growing rapidly. Having discovered the importance of holding firm when the issue is important, Will refuses to read to Muffy unless she uses words to let him know what she wants him to read.

The story that Muffy has demanded over and over again is *Rumpelstiltskin*, a story in which correct naming is essential to preserving a young family intact. Even Will finally speaks out, protesting his parents' arranging his time for babysitting without discussing their plans with him, and demanding lunch money (to which one would think any child was entitled) after months of rummaging around for spare change—his requests for money fell on deaf ears while his parents geared up for daily battle with Estelle.

Throughout the narrative, the reader is told that this is Will's book. Why is it, then, "the book of the banshee"? The banshee is associated with the surprise attack, appearing suddenly and threatening doom. As Will's friend Chopper explains, adolescence is the emergence of a new self, and the old self must die for the new self to emerge. Only at the end of the novel does Will tell the reader that the title is an ana-gram of the name on the old ledger (the Beshoohoefte Bank) that he found, where he writes this story. Like the writer Alicia Whitley, who writes as Alec Whitsun and has inspired Will's writing venture, Will chooses a pen name for himself before send-ing his manuscript out to a publisher, and he arrives at the name Anne Fine. So the book ends cleverly, as it is written throughout, using word play and humor but con-veying the serious point that people must speak up and speak out to make sure peo-ple around them pay attention to what is important. Also, *The Book of the Banshee* makes it clear that the growth and change of one family member impacts the whole family and that growth sometimes, if not always, entails a sense of loss.

ADDITIONAL READING RECOMMENDATIONS

Staying Fat for Sarah Byrnes by Chris Crutcher, 1993 (discussed in Beauty's Meaning)
Freak the Mighty by Rodman Philbrick, 1993 (discussed in Friends Forever?)
When She Hollers by Cynthia Voigt, 1994
Don't You Dare Read This, Mrs. Dunphrey by Margaret Peterson Haddix, 1996
Silent to the Bone by E. L. Konigsberg, 2000
Box Girl by Sarah Withrow, 2001

Crime, Suicide, and Their Aftermath

After the First Death by Robert Cormier (1979)
Breaking the Fall by Michael Cadnum (1992)
The Buffalo Tree by Adam Rapp (1997)
Many Stones by Carolyn Coman (2000)
24 Hours by Margaret Mahy (2000)

Teens in contemporary American society have a lot of freedom. Old enough to participate in adult behaviors, often highly mobile when they have a car or know others with cars, many of them living in households with little parental supervision in the long hours between the end of the school day and the night's rest, they may encounter opportunities to stray into criminal behavior themselves or to be victimized by others' criminal behavior. Perhaps more disturbing is that suicide is the third leading cause of death for fifteen- to twenty-four-year-olds, after accidents and homicides. Given their prevalence in young people's lives, these instances of violence become the subject matter of novels written for them. Acts of violence take a tremendous emotional toll on survivors; acts of violence demand restitution from perpetrators. The subjects discussed here range from failed suicide to actual suicide, from robbery to terrorist killings. Additional texts focusing on crime are discussed in Chapter 14: Guilty or Innocent?

Robert Cormier's gritty novels often illustrate the loss of innocence, and *After the First Death* (1979) explores this grim theme in a quiet New England town, in the context of a hostage situation precipitated by terrorists from an unnamed land. Their hijacking of a busload of small children is related through two alternating narratives. First-person reflections on the event several months later apparently reveal the aftereffects of the violent drama on both the military mastermind who negotiated with the terrorists and his fourteen-year-old son Ben, who acted as go-between. But the reader eventually learns that these narratives are not what they seem to be. Between the first-person segments that are presented as though being written on the typewriter as they are thought, a straightforward chronological third-person narrative of the incident gives insight into several of the actors' thoughts and feelings. The central characters in the narrative of the hostage drama are the youngest terrorist, sixteen-year-old Miro, and the teenage bus driver, Kate. Each of these teens, along with Ben, must play an adult role, whether it involves taking innocent lives in a quasi-military action, trying to escape from trained and armed terrorists while simultaneously protecting small children, or walking unarmed into the hands of violent men to face possible torture and death. Afterward, Ben's father must reconcile himself to the consequences of the actions he has taken in the name of his patriotic duty.

The hostage situation gets out of control, failing to go as planned by either the perpetrators or the military unit responding to the crisis. More questions are raised than answered as all the actors in the drama must follow through on the course they have committed to, with or without hope. All must face fierce testing of their personal courage and make choices that reflect their differing senses of responsibility to others. Unresolved issues for Ben's father are the meaning of patriotism and the degree to which one has freedom to act once involved in a military unit, issues raised in his use of Ben. Kate acts out of a sense of personal responsibility both in her relations with the children in her care and her desire to be brave and do her best, which she assesses by imagining her parents' approval of her actions. Guilt over having perhaps made the wrong choice must be assumed by survivors, but few questions arise for Miro, who has long since accepted the ideology of his military training as a terrorist in the refugee camps where he and his brother spent their childhood.

Kate concludes that Miro is a monster, from her observations throughout the long hours, when she desperately attempts to understand him in her effort to survive the situation. In his freedom from moral responsibility for the pain that he has inflicted and will inflict on innocent victims, she sees that he is innocent, and his innocence is evil rather than good. He simply lacks what she thinks of as normal human feelings, including sympathy for the small children. Miro is surprised to discover feelings in himself at times during the long hours of waiting, despite his rejection of feeling, and it may be argued that his final action is a response to intense emotion rather than dedication to his original assignment. Kate and Miro each have a motive for understanding the other, though their profound cultural differences make such understanding impossible to achieve in the short, intense period that brings them into terrible intimacy, the intimacy of the killer and his designated target. Miro has been told by his leader, Artkin, to win Kate's trust, and Kate sees the potential in her treating Miro as an individual, even as a desirable young man, for dulling the edge of his alertness. Each has tremendous physical awareness—Kate of the ways her body betrays as well as aids her, secreting sweat and urine in crisis, Miro of the ways her body attracts him. Their final minutes together are spent in perverted embrace, as Miro holds her body close as a shield, his gun jammed against her ribcage.

Unhealthy intimacy pervades the novel, not only the forced intimacy of the hostage situation but also intimacy manipulated in the use that each military commander makes of his son. Ben's father's detailed psychological knowledge of his son enables him to use Ben as a pawn in the negotiations, exposing him to the shame of betraying under torture his knowledge of the planned military assault. Artkin's knowledge of Miro, whether the knowledge of a biological father or a father-figure, enables him to command Miro's absolute loyalty. All three teens are motivated by their desire to prove themselves courageous in their parents' eyes.

Ultimately, the reader has a fuller picture of the situation and the characters than any of the characters can have, through the combined narrative methods. Ben's father has suffered a breakdown after the crisis of choosing between conflicting loyalties to his family and his country. The reader is privy to some of the history that has shaped the monstrous innocence of the surviving terrorist, Miro, who melts into American life unknown to authorities and, undoubtedly, is committed to future acts of heartless violence. Miro has scorned the immaturity, vulnerability, and weakness of young Americans; contrasting his history as an orphan scrambling for inadequate scraps of spoiled food in refugee camps with the life of the youthful Americans he encounters, the reader understands, at least in part, Miro's motives.

The novel's epigraph is the last line of Dylan Thomas's "A Refusal to Mourn the Death, by Fire, of a Child in London," a poem that is an "elegy of innocence of youth" and alludes negatively to the possibility of Christian afterlife: "After the first death, there is no other." There are several "first" deaths in the novel: what has been promised to Miro on this mission, his first opportunity to kill an enemy; the death of the first child on the bus, which reshapes the terrorists' strategy in dealing with the American military; the death of the first terrorist that results in another child's death; the impact on Miro of his brother's death, which marked a significant emotional change, the end of family love. In the final analysis, it seems to refer most fully to the death Ben's father deals with, Ben's shooting, after which he reappears in the general's own psyche, despite the father's efforts to bury Ben deep in his memory as well as in the earth.

In *Breaking the Fall* (1992), Michael Cadnum relates a more ordinary story, showing how a teen who faces challenges on several fronts can begin slipping into crime. Stanley feels "dead" much of the time until his classmate Jared offers him the taste of adrenalin that comes with playing "the game": breaking into a home while its inhabitants are sleeping to take some small personal item from the bedroom. This is not the only dangerous game that Jared plays—he also crosses the interstate by walking on top of the mesh-enclosed pedestrian bridge. Jared's sheer nerve pressures Stanley to prove himself, but he is ambivalent about playing the game. When he participates, Stanley enjoys feeling fully aware and alert, as engaged as predatory animals are when they are hunting. Yet he is capable of begging off, of recognizing that he is doing wrong.

Stanley has been drawn into this foolhardy behavior by several circumstances that have caused his feeling of deadness: he is no longer on the baseball team, having had difficulty coming back from an injury; his workaholic parents barely speak to each other and speak with him in short, cryptic bursts; he feels he is holding his parents' marriage together by sheer willpower; he walks through school alert enough to function but not truly involved. The only counterbalancing force to Jared's temptation is his attraction to Sky Tagaloa, until Jared ends their budding romance by telling Sky about the game. After that, he no longer sees Sky, but her brother Tu's friendship outlasts the romance.

Stanley is dealing with loss of innocence, some of it imposed by the circumstances of his growing up as his parents grow apart, some of it self-chosen when he allows Jared to tempt him into illegal behavior. He suffers several literal falls in the course of his escapades, and Jared himself falls to his death. Stanley is drawn to danger, even though ultimately he rejects it, so that Jared is alone at the final moment. Jared must fall, having reached a point at which only the closest brushes with death can give him a thrill.

Adam Rapp's controversial novel *The Buffalo Tree* (1997) portrays life in a brutal juvenile correctional facility in which thirteen-year-old Sura must work at surviving, as well as coming to terms with the consequences of his crime, stealing hood ornaments. His redemption is impelled more by the sad example of his roommate, Coly Jo, whose despair ends in suicide, than by the punishments imposed by administrators (chief among them Dean Petty, whose name indicates the significance of actions taken by authorities) or the by-the-book sessions conducted by the minimally engaged psychologist. Throughout his imprisonment, Sura is aware of the slow measuring out of time, made audible by the guards' nightstick rapping during their rounds, a measurement that governs all the inmates' actions, whether institutionally regulated or negotiated by mutual consent of the "juvies" (as keeping watch through the night by turns, to prevent having their belongings stolen, is timed). The "buffalo tree" is always visible, casting a shadow like a hand over the window at night; the facility's bullies force others to climb the tree and sit, visible to everyone, in humiliation, and it is here that Coly Jo ends his life.

The slang that Rapp creates for the world of the juvies is probably the novel's most distinctive feature. The crimes he and Coly Jo have committed are fairly minor: while Sura stole, he did not hurt people; Coly Jo broke into people's homes to watch them sleeping. But the rules they must play by in the correctional facility seem designed to harden rather than rehabilitate them. The moments of happiness, identified with the pleasure of drinking chocolate milk, are rare; the moments of fear and pain are frequent. Rules are imposed both by the authorities, who punish by, for example, running all the inmates up and down the stairs to the point of exhaustion and beyond, and by the most powerful inmates. The brutality of the center's administration is most cruelly demonstrated when Sura is severely paddled for staring at a photograph of Dean Petty's daughter. The most powerful juvies, however, are responsible for despicable offenses—pouring human waste all over Coly Jo in his bunk and stabbing another juvie with a sharpened pencil in the shower because his frequent sustained erections suggest to them that he is gay. Sura has his own reputation in the facility: he is a fast runner who keeps winning footraces. He stays safe mostly by avoiding trouble, as demonstrated by his unwillingness to fight for his bunk and his possessions when Coly Jo's successor, Long Neck, becomes his new cellmate, whereas Coly Jo, for all his vulnerability, has brought down the bullies' wrath by trying to get back the hat they stole. The older, most powerful inmates have developed a way of life that satisfies them; one of them, given the opportunity for release when it is discovered that one of his friends, rather than he, blinded an old woman, begs to stay in the facility rather than go home to his family, a circumstance that suggests he has been thoroughly brutalized at home.

Sura, in contrast, has a close relationship with his mother, who was only fifteen when he was born. She visits him, and they exchange letters; he hides hers in his textbooks to pore over during study periods. Her disappointment in him is one of the primary factors in his rehabilitation. They have long lived in temporary rooms—he refers to the YWCA, specifically—but since his incarceration, she has set up housekeeping with an older man who promises to take Sura in after his release. The picture of the shabby house they have moved into, with the letter promising him a pair of skates and telling him of the track at the nearby school, sustains him, even though he seriously considers escape, having received information about an escape route from his friend and mentor, Slider, who on his sixteenth birthday was transferred to a facility for older prisoners.

Coly Jo is the other factor in Sura's redemption, a real friend until his spirit is destroyed. Coly Jo is vulnerable, crying in his bunk at night, and Sura comforts and befriends him. Coly Jo's spirit is broken after he wakes to find himself covered with urine and excrement, and he avoids the showers altogether until he is forcibly cleaned publicly with a fire extinguisher by one of the guards. A desperate act of resistance to another punishment results in his being isolated in the "stink hole" for a period of weeks (the longest anyone else has been sentenced to it is a few days), after which he is supposed to be sent to a stricter facility, a situation that drives him to despair and suicide.

Sura is a thoughtful prisoner, observing the hard lives of fellow juvies inside and outside the facility. His sympathy extends even to Long Neck. After Coly Jo's death and his punishment during the investigation of Long Neck's escape, he withdraws from efforts to establish and maintain his place within the juvies' social order, no longer caring to run races. His sessions with the psychologist give the reader, though not the psychologist, insight into the memories that scar him and the fears he lives with day to day. Over the course of his imprisonment, he gives up the plan for the future that he entered with: to dig up the bag of stolen hood ornaments he buried before incarceration, sell them, and take off on his own. Instead, he returns them, taping them to the cars he took them from, in a self-imposed act of restitution, before going to join his mother and her boyfriend in their new home, where he envisions Coly Jo's spirit now free, flying like a bird, and dreams of running track at his new school.

In contrast to the novels that focus on perpetrators of crimes, *Many Stones* (2000), by Carolyn Coman, explores the difficult aftermath of the random murder of a family member. Berry's adored older sister, Laura, was in South Africa, working at a Catholic school, when she was robbed and beaten to death with a stone. Now Berry collects small stones that she keeps in her bedroom, sometimes placing them on her chest to weigh her down as she lies in bed. She lives with fear herself, needing a light at times, while at other times she simply refuses to go home to an empty house after school. She escapes feeling and thinking by swimming, and it is because of the swimathon her father organized that she visits South Africa with him for a ceremony at which she will present the money raised by the event to the school where Laura taught, and a memorial will be dedicated to Laura's memory.

Berry's trip with her father, who left her mother years ago and who always seemed closer to Laura, is fraught with tension. Berry is angry because he tries to manage things, to do things, apparently escaping his grief through organizing the swimathon and memorial service. In her pain and loss, Berry is unable to open up even a little to her father, her anger at his having left them mixed with her sorrow for her sister, as she experiences the aloneness created by the destruction of her sense of family, the loss of those whose support she could trust in. Her trip to South Africa, however, shows her the power of reconciliation in a land where racism still taints relationships and everyone has lost someone precious, yet they go on, making a future and commemorating a painful past in tours of Soweto and Nelson Mandela's prison. As Berry tours these sites with her father, sees the beauty of landscape and animal life as well as persistent inequality, and meets the people whom her sister loved, she moves toward lifting the weight of many stones from her chest and, finally, is able to articulate what her sister's loss has meant to her and others, along with the hope that Laura's idealism and love brought to those with whom she shared a brief life.

In *24 Hours* (2000), New Zealand author Margaret Mahy shows how a seventeen-year-old comes to terms with a friend's suicide and prevents another teen's suicide in a twenty-four-hour period of crazy adventures involving three sisters whose lives have been significantly altered by their father's having shot their mother and brothers. When Ellis meets up with the brash, disreputable-looking Jackie Cattle, whom he knew in grade school, Jackie attaches himself to Ellis in order to get to a party he intends to crash, at the home of Ellis's parents' friends, the well-to-do Kilmers, who are celebrating their separation in grand style. Jackie intends to disrupt his friend Ursa's connection with their son, Christo, whom Ellis has loathed since he tried to drown Ellis years ago. When Ursa angrily gathers up her sister Leo (Leona) and leaves the party, she draws Ellis into a world of odd people and threatening events and sets off Christo's dangerous temper. The chain of events indirectly helps Ellis discover the knowledge that he needed two months earlier in order to dissuade his friend Simon from suicide: that death is really final. This insight, coupled with his growing skill as an actor, allows him to prevent Christo's suicide and the murder of the sisters' one-year-old foster child, Shelley, whom Christo has kidnapped.

A lot happens in a short time in this novel, but the fantastic events are believable largely because of Ellis, who heads into this situation with the desire to let go and have some new experiences during his holiday. It is clear that he is troubled by Simon's death because he thinks of him frequently though fleetingly. The experiences include crashing the Kilmers' party, drinking to the point of passing out among the odd party-goers at the seedy motel where Ursa, Leo, and their twelve-year-old sister, Fox, live with their foster father, having his head shaved and getting a skull tattoo, chasing street kids though the cemetery, driving wildly in a car chase after the child's biological mother and her boyfriend, convincing himself he is in love with Leo, and finally maneuvering his way into Christo's family's city apartment and following him up onto the roof, where he talks Christo out of dropping the child and jumping to his death. In the course of these adventures, Ellis learns significant information about Leo after his first glimpse of her convinces him she is the woman for whom he has been waiting his whole life: she tells him how she prepares the dead for burial at a funeral home. The tattooist Phipps relays the family history in exchange for Ellis's getting a tattoo, telling how the girls' father killed their mother, then woke his children and took them into the cemetery, where he shot the boys before shooting himself; and Ursa, after retelling this story with more detail, explains that her sister needs a job where death is merely normal and a man for whom it is normal and ordinary.

By the time Ellis receives this last, matter-of-fact explanation of Leo's life, he has used some of the details she has shared with him—that the dead pass gas, for instance—with Christo as part of his argument against Christo's suicide, convincing him that he will not have some privileged vantage point from which to enjoy observing the regret of those who mourn him once he has died. Simon was just stupid, Ellis tells Christo, when he worked himself up to the act, imagining how sorry others would be, because he overlooked the fact that in death he would not be able to enjoy the drama of his suicide. The lines from *Measure for Measure* that have haunted Ellis throughout the novel clearly express the dread of death that binds the living to even the meanest life, in preference to the body's dissolution, and he quotes them as he talks Christo out of suicide, puzzling through them with new insight. Ellis tests his acting talent as he plays to this audience, whose reaction really counts.

The sisters' strange history gives another insight into the impact of suicide on families. They are casually unconventional and independent. The youngest sister, Fox, is precocious and apparently psychic, using her crystal ball to foretell that Ellis will eventually marry her; Leo deals with death routinely and enjoys her job; Ursa is assertive and outspoken, critical of Jackie till someone else criticizes him, when she defends him. The sisters are protective of each other and of their guardian, who has at some point become sexually involved with one of his foster children when she was fifteen—it is not clear whether this was Ursa, Leo, or another unnamed foster child. Ursa attests to Leo's physical protection of Fox the night of their father's rampage, and Ellis at first thinks Shelley is Leo's child, seeing her care for the baby. Despite this protectiveness, Jackie warns Ellis away from Leo, saying that they are all "damaged," and it is difficult to imagine that they are not, but these three survivors have gained an appealing interdependency shown in their care for each other.

This twenty-four-hour period chronicles Ellis's intense self-discovery—he tells Ursa that he has done everything he had planned for himself for the next two years—but the title also serves to underscore how one day can completely transform people's lives when traumatic events reshape their futures.

ADDITIONAL READING RECOMMENDATIONS

Dreamland Lake by Richard Peck, 1973
Tiger Eyes by Judy Blume, 1981
Remembering the Good Times by Richard Peck, 1985 (discussed in Friends Forever?)
Girl in a Box by Ouida Sebestyen, 1988
We All Fall Down, 1991, and *Tenderness*, 1997, by Robert Cormier
Letters from the Inside by John Marsden, 1994 (discussed in Friends Forever?)
Soulfire by Lorri Hewett, 1996
Remembering Mog by Colby Rodowsky, 1996
Edge by Michael Cadnum, 1997
Bad by Jean Ferris, 1998
Tightrope, 1999, and *Phoning a Dead Man*, 2002, by Gillian Cross
The Other Side of Truth by Beverley Naidoo, 2000
Black Mirror by Nancy Werlin, 2001
When Dad Killed Mom by Julius Lester, 2001
Martyn Pig by Kevin Brooks, 2002
The Long Night of Leo and Bree by Ellen Wittlinger, 2002

Dating's Challenges

Dinky Hocker Shoots Smack! by M. E. Kerr (1972)
Good Moon Rising by Nancy Garden (1996)
A White Romance by Virginia Hamilton (1987)
Lombardo's Law by Ellen Wittlinger (1993)
Hard Love by Ellen Wittlinger (1999)

Developing special relationships with peers is a major feature of teens' lives, and it plays an important role in fiction for young adults, as it does in literature for mature readers. Discovering the thrill of romance is an intensely personal experience, which no doubt many would like to keep private. Reading the signals from potential dating partners, understanding one's own feelings, deciding what actions to take and when to take them—all can be challenging to lovers at any age. Young people's earliest, tentative moves toward love inevitably occur within complex social networks involving family members, friends, and community members. This can make scary emotional experiences even scarier, but the pull of attraction generally wins over fear of embarrassment, making for poignant or humorous or serious treatment in fiction.

M. E. Kerr's 1972 novel, *Dinky Hocker Shoots Smack!* is a portrait of 1960s political attitudes and perhaps oversimplifies parent-child relationships, but it is timely and true to life in its depiction of one of dating's greatest challenges: overcoming parental objections. Tucker becomes interested in Natalia, the cousin of Dinky Hocker, whom he met when he had to find a home for his calico kitten. Tucker's desire to take Natalia to a dance results in his approaching a classmate, P. John, and setting him up with Dinky for the evening. Thus the two romances begin. Tucker and Natalia are both quiet and bookish; their problem is generally to get started talking. Both Dinky and P. John are large, opinionated people, who get along well from the outset. However, Dinky's parents, who are Natalia's guardians, raise objections to both dating relationships, in the name of protecting their daughter and niece. Nonetheless, Mrs. Hocker draws Tucker into her community projects, helping rehabilitated drug users and creating an opportunity for underprivileged children to complete art projects at the church, giving him the opportunity to continue his friendship with both girls.

The initial phase of Dinky and P. John's relationship develops out of their mutual concern with losing weight. P. John gives Dinky (whom P. John calls only by her given name, Susan) a motive to join WeightWatchers, and he is willing to support her willpower, in contrast to her mother, who urges Dinky to eat chocolate cake because politeness requires it and who dismisses Dinky's obesity as "baby fat." The conflict results in P. John's dismissal, since his outspoken conservative political views have already contributed to the Hockers' dislike. P. John recognizes Dinky's unhappiness and anger since he lives in a similar situation, angry with his political activist father, who is willing to give away whatever he can to liberal causes but cannot give his son what he needs. Similarly, Dinky's mother is callous about Dinky's feelings, while she has apparently bottomless sympathy for the poor and the addicts. After P. John is sent off to his aunt's experimental school, Dinky reverts to constant overeating, preoccupation with the bizarre, and withdrawal—convinced by her mother that P. John is a budding fascist who only wanted to exert control and did not really care for her.

At his aunt's school, P. John is required to do hard physical labor, and he undergoes a political conversion, so that when he returns to Brooklyn Heights and visits Dinky, he is transformed into someone both attractive and acceptable to her parents. Sadly, her mother chooses to surprise Dinky with P. John's visit, oblivious as usual of her daughter's feelings, and Dinky emerges from her bedroom sloppily clad as well as fatter than when they parted. In her pain and humiliation, she finally wins her parents' attention by spray-painting "Dinky Hocker shoots smack" all over the neighborhood during the dinner at which her mother receives a community service award.

The course of true love does not run smooth. P. John tried to keep in touch with Dinky via Tucker, encouraging her to respect herself and take charge of her own life. But her mother's need to control her daughter—amounting to emotional abuse—has resulted in her twisting all of P. John's messages and misrepresenting his Christmas gift of a WeightWatchers' cookbook so that Dinky distrusts her own judgment regarding P. John. Mrs. Hocker is equally controlling of her niece's relationship with Tucker, going so far as to enlist his mother's aid in keeping them apart, using the strongest weapon at her disposal, her knowledge of Natalia's fragile emotional state after her mother's mental illness and her father's suicide. Natalia's stress manifested itself linguistically: at first she did not speak. When she did begin speaking, she spoke in rhyme, and she still reverts to rhyming when nervous, a behavior Dinky unkindly identifies as a way of calling attention to herself—though it seems that in the final analysis, Dinky finds a much more dramatic way to call attention to herself, helped to better self-understanding by Tucker's statement that people who do not use illegal drugs may also have problems.

Mrs. Hocker's objection to Tucker's interest in Natalia arises from her misreadings of their behavior together. When tensions in the household set Natalia to nervous rhyming again, her aunt attributes Natalia's discomfort to Tucker rather than the submerged anger in the household (a situation that also inspires bad behavior in the cat). Mrs. Hocker also reads more sexuality into Tucker and Natalia's relationship than is there because they spend time quietly in the bedroom, where they are drawing and writing messages to each other in a game that breaks the ice when conversation is difficult for them. The basic message that they manage to share, under the adults' radar, is that of Antoine de Saint-Exupéry in *The Little Prince*, "If you tame me, then we shall need each other," the message that Tucker originally associated with the cat. Their mutual attraction is expressed subtly as it grows, despite the efforts of adults to distort it into something unhealthy.

Tucker and Natalia get their chance when the Hockers start paying attention to Dinky/Susan. It is clear that Natalia has begun to cope with the challenges her parents' lives have created when she speaks to Tucker of her father's suicide. Tucker's parents become more understanding as their personal and financial difficulties are resolved—his father gets a new job (and when he does so, his allergy to the cat disappears, enabling Tucker to take her back and restore her to a healthy weight and calm behavior); his mother begins law school; and Tucker himself gains a more equitable role in the household as he begins cooking and doing housework, something he is more willing to do as he recognizes his mother's need to be more than just his mom. Tucker and Natalia's relationship, like the abortive one between Dinky and P. John, has grown out of mutual sympathy, understanding, and respect, qualities that promise to help them develop into mature adults, starting with the summer jobs that separate them at the novel's end, jobs that involve helping other people. Since they have helped Dinky, by respecting her and taking her feelings seriously, seeing her as an individual, it is likely they will do well.

Dating becomes much more challenging for the teen who suspects or knows that he or she is gay. In such situations, the line between friendship and dating may be blurrier than it is for straight teens: a girl attending a movie with her friend questions whether the relationship is really what she hopes it is, afraid of making a misstep, and she must decide whether to come out to family and friends as well. When one is still uncertain about one's own sexuality, it may be premature to come out, especially when challenged by homophobia at school or a family's disapproval. Nancy Garden deals with such sensitive issues in *Annie on My Mind* (1982) and *Good Moon Rising* (1996); in each novel, girls move from friendship to dating each other, and the couple relationship is complicated by differing degrees of willingness to acknowledge the nature of the friendship. The more recent novel is discussed here.

In *Good Moon Rising*, written in the 1990s when gay teens might count on more acceptance than in the early 1980s, Jan and Kerry move by small degrees from friendship into love in the small circle of their high school's theater community, which is staging Arthur Miller's *The Crucible*. While this small-town school's artistic community is probably more liberal than the rest of the students, actors' egos—added to the typical cliquishness of the high school community—complicate reactions to Jan and Kerry's obvious closeness. In addition to the "crucible" of discovering her love for Kerry in the high-pressure context of putting up an emotionally charged show, with the drama teacher whom she respects visibly succumbing to cancer, Jan must diplomatically resolve the issue of sexual attraction with her longtime buddy Ted, who wants desperately to date her until he finds another girlfriend and then realizes Jan's unwillingness comes from her sexuality. Jan fears she will not have her family's support if she comes out to them, but she does have a confidant whom she met in summer stock, a gay man who came out in high school himself. Kerry is less sure about identifying herself as a lesbian in the face of her homophobic costar's ugly campaign to expose her, with her parents traveling abroad, and with her elderly aunt urging her to spend more time with boys.

Jan and Kerry's romance evolves out of a friendship that begins with a "good moon rising." Kerry is new to the school, and Jan's first response to her acting ability is jealousy, when her mentor, Mrs. Nicholson, gives the coveted role of Elizabeth Proctor to the inexperienced but talented Kerry. Jan's important role as stage manager–assistant director seems at first a poor consolation prize before she realizes how important her help is to Mrs. Nicholson and how good she is at it. Jan generously acknowledges Kerry's talent, but it is probably her attraction that makes her so willing to coach the new girl. It does not take either of them long to find out how much they enjoy each other's company, identifying themselves as "weird" but grateful that they can share their weirdness in friendship. They have so much fun together that it seems natural to pass up a big dance so they can attend a one-time showing of the 1948 film version of *Hamlet* starring the great Olivier. Both are nervous as they figure out whether this evening together constitutes a date; both seem equally attracted and involved, though Jan, herself certain of her feelings, is too ready to back off, fearing that Kerry is just experimenting in order to gain more of the life experiences she hungers for. Once past this barrier, they explore what it means to be in a lesbian romance together, with almost no reliable information. In a judgment-free self-description, Jan frames her gender identity from an early age as being just "a different kind of girl." Her certainty about her sexual preference later enables her, in the confrontation at the cast party, to come out to her theater friends, bolstered by Kerry's own willingness to acknowledge their romance and the support of her gay friend Raphael.

The heady intensity of first love is counterbalanced by other intense emotions. Jan must take an increasingly responsible role as assistant director, a position that stretches her in invigorating new ways and requires the utmost diplomacy in coping with the conflict that erupts around her relationship with Kerry. Maintaining a professional stance, furthermore, requires her to set aside her grief when Mrs. Nicholson dies. In any other circumstances, she would probably derive greater emotional satisfaction from becoming an aunt on the eve of the show's performances, but she just does not have time to fully appreciate her sister's new baby, especially amid her ambivalence about telling her family about her newfound happiness with Kerry, given her sister's obvious ignorance of homosexuality.

Some of the novel's power comes from its allusions to plays—Jan's familiarity with *Medea*, Kerry's with *Faust*, their use of scene references from *Hamlet* to communicate through a third party. The third party is Ted, who shows his friendship by supporting Jan's authority in the theater and taking her acknowledgment of her sexual identity in stride. Kerry's costar, Kent, is responsible for most of the ugliness of the homophobic accusations: his ego is fragile, and he protects it with an aggressive offensive against Jan's taking over for Mrs. Nicholson, bucking her authority by refusing to shave a scruffy beard that he also uses to hurt Kerry's face in their scenes that call for physical closeness. Most of the novel's action revolves around the mechanics of putting together a production, an interesting context for relationship dynamics. In the final analysis, though, its power comes from Jan and Kerry's sensitivity and joy.

In *A White Romance* (1987), Virginia Hamilton depicts the difference between true caring and the mesmerism of a merely sexual attraction through the contrasting dating relationships of Talley and David ("Hollywood") and Didi and Roady, in a high school environment made volatile by the busing of white students into an urban black neighborhood. The "white romance" is Didi and Roady's, and it fascinates Talley, who first names it and teases Didi about it. Not yet dating at the outset of her friendship with Didi, Talley is comfortable with her identity as a good student and athlete; she has friends in her neighborhood, notably the good-looking school leader and athlete Victor, whose interest in her is apparent to nearly everyone else before she recognizes it. But she is curious about Didi's nearly all-consuming sexual involvement and love and tries to get from Didi as much information as she can about what sex and love are really like, information that she cannot get from her straitlaced father.

Talley's home life is bounded entirely by her Poppy, who does not approve of her friendship with whites and certainly expects his "young lady" to grow up sexually pure. Since he threw her mother out, Talley has not been close to any woman other than Didi and Didi's mother, an interracial friendship her father would not approve of. However, he works multiple night jobs, and they see very little of each other. He would be even more upset if he knew she regularly meets Didi at Roady's apartment, but when she begins a sexual relationship with David, she knows she is really flouting his values. However, when she learns that he has an unacknowledged sexual romance of his own, Talley feels more comfortable about making her own choices about sex.

It is Roady's drug use, and therefore the company that he and Didi keep, that pulls Talley into a relationship with the handsome, charismatic David. David makes his desire for her plain, pursues it relentlessly, and then treats her as *his* until he tires of her. Talley, in her innocence, is slow to acknowledge that David is a dealer, but from the start of their relationship, she is as often hurt as not by his bewildering behavior. Yet Talley is caught up in the demands that her own body makes on her, and at first their time together is mostly good, though spent almost entirely between the sheets. At school, neither reveals that they are dating, though rumors of their biracial involvement quickly spread.

As significant as his whiteness is to others, what really shapes their relationship is David's habit of exercising control over other people. Talley soon finds she is less happy than she thought she would be, missing out on romance. The heavy metal concert they attend brings matters to a head: noise, drugs, and crowding make Talley violently ill because she is coming down with the flu. After the concert, David offers something to ease her nausea, the first clear evidence of his drug dealing. The other evidence comes with her discovery the same evening of just how much money he has, shown in his real estate investments. Thus, the evening's events force her to confront the truth, a truth she refused to accept when her friend Victor whispered it to her in the halls. Her illness enforces a few days' separation, allowing her to see that a distance has begun to grow between them, and the gulf rapidly widens when he tells Talley that he would not like to share her with a "black dude."

Victor, whose friendship Talley has taken for granted and who has seemed so dull and safe, really cares for Talley, and Talley begins to see the difference as the mesmerism of David's charm starts to fade and she moves toward a healthier, perhaps even truly romantic, relationship with Victor. She has learned the hard way that she does not want to be touched unless she has granted permission.

The racial dynamics involved in integrating the new magnet school take a back seat in this novel, on the whole, to the personal dimension of discovering what love and sexuality mean. Yet race is an ever-present element in these teens' lives as they learn to interact with each other in classrooms and halls, and on the sports fields. Talley observes that the adults have a much harder time coping with integration of the school than the students have. The teens must live in this environment every day, and student leaders have been well prepared to defuse potential confrontations. Victor's leadership is clearly a more constructive way of life than David's drug dealing. When Talley cheers for "the good guys" before going home from Roady's with Victor, race has little to do with her definition of goodness.

Ellen Wittlinger brings wit, an intellectual atmosphere, and emotional verisimilitude to her touching portrayals of young people sorting their way through the challenges of dating. The protagonist of *Lombardo's Law* (1993), Justine, is a solitary, intellectual fifteen-year-old, who is—most of the time—content with solitude. She spends her school lunch period reading a book at a table with two girls named Jennifer, who also read through lunch; she goes to classic and foreign films with her father, even on Saturday nights, when no teen would be caught dead at the movies with a parent. Her mother, however, has great hopes for Justine, remembering the best friend she herself had as a teen, and when the Lombardos move in across the street, she promotes a relationship. Alas, the cute, stylish Heather Lombardo soon finds her own popular crowd and dates the handsomest, coolest guy in school (who makes Justine stammer, even though she recognizes that he sees himself as God's gift to women). Justine finds Heather superficial, like most girls her age, but Heather's brother, Mike, two years younger than the girls, proves to be smart, funny, and as interested in film as Justine is. They begin attending movies together, having a great time without the pressure of dating, and then decide to make a short movie together, spoofing ditzy girls and *2001: A Space Odyssey* through the story of a computer named HALICE and her teen owner.

Justine's problem is her increasing awareness of Mike as a male, accompanied by her lack of real interest in the boys her age who ask her out. Mike is cute but clearly younger than Justine—several inches shorter—and she finds herself defending and explaining their relationship to one person after another. When she double-dates with Heather, she ends up evading a gorilla who thought she would be interested in necking with any male who asked her on her first date. The evening ends in disaster when Heather's gorgeous steady wrecks the car and they all go to the hospital. After this fiasco, Justine goes on several dates with smart, reserved Jeffrey, though neither of them is very interested in the other; their dating is more for the sake of fitting in, meeting others' expectations, than the result of any real attraction. All they have in common is that they are both smart.

Fortunately, Justine figures out that Mike, though younger, not only is smart and shares her interests, but also is good-looking. When he kisses her in celebration of the showing of their film, his action creates a brief period of awkwardness before she takes her courage in both hands and acknowledges the attraction, a feeling that by this point is obviously mutual, although Mike is nearly as cautious as Justine is about confronting it, both of them bound by social expectations. The title grows from Mike's proclivity for naming his observations and opinions as "Lombardo's Law." The first one is that anyone he likes is incapable of liking his sister, the last one that someone who takes a fall from a balcony—as Mike has just done—has earned a kiss. These two "laws" nicely frame the development of their relationship.

The novel is about friendship as well as dating. Justine's mother finds the friend she needs in Mrs. Lombardo, and Justine's friendship with one of the Jennifers develops through quirky bits of dialogue that betray some of the challenges of being both intellectual and a teenager expected to engage in social posturing. Above all, the story makes a strong argument for romance based on friendship and companionship.

Wittlinger's *Hard Love* (1999) raises more complex issues. It is set in the world of the zine—the small, quirky, self-published magazines that writers photocopy and distribute free or for minimal cost. Putting a zine out for public consumption is an act of self-assertion and an act of faith that somewhere there exist unknown readers who are receptive to what the author has to say. John Galardi, using the penname Giovanii, writes *Bananafish* and begins distributing it in a Boston record store, where he lurks to meet the writer of *Escape Velocity*, a self-proclaimed adopted Latina lesbian named Marisol (which means "bitter sun," an identity she embraces).

John/Gio's detached emotional state adds an admirable irony to his writing, but unfortunately it is rooted in his pain over his parents' divorce several years earlier. The divorce has essentially destroyed his relationship with each parent: he lives in a small Massachusetts town with his depressed mother, who sits alone in the dark, naps after work, and scrupulously avoids any physical contact with her son; he spends each weekend at his father's place in Boston, where they silently consume

Friday's dinner in a restaurant, after which his father feels free for the rest of the weekend to date and bring his dates home to bed. John is cynical about relationships and distrustful of intimacy. His lack of interest in girls his age has even led him to speculate that he may be gay, though that possibility is quickly dismissed by Marisol's gay friend Birdie. John/Gio becomes friends with Marisol because both are truly passionate about writing, and it seems that none of the tensions of physical attraction will interfere with their companionship.

Marisol is cautious about involvement. She has been hurt in her first romance, with a young woman who decided she was not a lesbian after all, and she is working through her sense of abandonment by her birth mother. Her adoptive mother is on the surface sanguine about Marisol's sexuality while apparently covertly "encouraging" any indicator that Marisol may ultimately discover she is heterosexual. Marisol's initial feeling of safety with John/Gio is short-lived. Though she repeatedly reminds him that she really is what she says she is, John does not really hear, choosing not to notice his growing love for her. He enjoys correcting his father's misconception about their relationship, clearly dissociating himself from his father's playboy behavior, but when Marisol agrees to attend the junior prom with him—he is under pressure from his friend Brian to double-date—he never gets around to telling his mother and friends that Marisol, too, is just a friend. When he allows himself to express his desire, he ruins their evening and opens a rift between them. Poor John/Gio has been leading a split life, lying to himself—he never even told Marisol his real name before the prom—so how could he be expected to recognize the nature and depth of his own feelings?

In a second, equally painful venture into others' company, they attend a zine convention in Provincetown, where Marisol immediately takes up with a group of lesbians, leaving John more confused and vulnerable than ever in his still-raw postprom emotional state. Though Marisol has made it clear she will be moving on with her life, leaving him when she goes to college on the other side of the country, it is at the conference that she decides she has reached "escape velocity," enabling her to head to New York with her new friends so she can work out who she is in an environment where neither her parents nor John can interfere, no matter how loving their intentions toward her. This is indeed a case of "hard love"—difficult love that, as the song says, is constantly a struggle but nonetheless worth the effort.

The most valuable lesson John learns from loving Marisol is how to reach out to another person. Even while deluding himself, John has been writing to another zine writer, whom he will no doubt find more responsive as a romantic partner. He recognizes that Brian, whom he has routinely patronized, really is his best friend, someone to be counted on in a crisis. Listening to Marisol talk about the letters she writes to her birth mother but will never mail, John writes a letter to each of his parents. Unlike Marisol, he makes sure his parents receive them, in the emotional turbulence of the week following the prom, at a time when he is out of reach. While his action is hurtful, it succeeds in breaking down his mother's emotional barrier and leads to the possibility for healing.

During the period John has known Marisol, his mother has accepted a proposal and has begun planning a wedding, adding to John's hurt every time he sees his mother allow her fiancé's touch, while she still shrinks from his. They have arrived at an impasse over his mother's decision to move into Al's house and her insistence that he live there too, a decision that John has resisted because he does not want to be uprooted for his senior year. As their communication barrier begins to crumble, John is able to encourage his mother to risk loving again when she has a moment of fear that Al too will leave her, but perhaps more importantly, when they speak on the phone after she has read his hurtful letter, John is able to hear how nice, how calm Al is and begins to envision getting to know him, especially once the couple have decided to live in her house until his graduation. The fallout from "hard love" can be significant—it can take a long time to heal, and it can affect much more of a person's life than he or she realizes, but it is important to keep on opening oneself to love.

The novel has an appealing visual format that introduces the reader to the zine world, weaving in the texts that the characters have written for publication, as well as poems Marisol and John write to each other and the letters to their parents. The characters are articulate, intelligent, and artistic; the adults are educated professionals. John's friend Brian and his girlfriend have parts in the school musical. John's mother is a teacher, his father is in publishing, and Marisol's adoptive mother is a social worker who comes from a monied family. Early in their acquaintance, John swears on a copy of J. D. Salinger's *Nine Stories* he will tell Marisol nothing but the truth, and Marisol recommends he read John Berryman's *77 Dream Songs*. These allusions help to characterize the young people and their relationships.

ADDITIONAL READING RECOMMENDATIONS

Night Kites by M. E. Kerr, 1986
The Amazing and Death-Defying Diary of Eugene Dingman by Paul Zindel, 1987
Rats Saw God by Rob Thomas, 1996
Shots on Goal by Rich Wallace, 1997
Lucky Me by Lisa Fiedler, 1998
Lives of Our Own by Lorri Hewett, 1998
If It Doesn't Kill You by Margaret Bechard, 1999
The Lullaby by Sarah Dessen, 2000
Angus, Thongs, and Full-Frontal Snoggin by Louise Rennison, 2000, and sequels
What's in a Name?, 2000, and *Razzle*, 2001, by Ellen Wittlinger
Fifteen Love by Robert Corbet, 2003

Disease and Disability

The Bumblebee Flies Anyway by Robert Cormier (1983)
A Time for Dancing by Davida Wills Hurwin (1995)
Stuck in Neutral by Terry Trueman (2000)
Cruise Control by Terry Trueman (2004)
Stoner & Spaz by Ron Koertge (2001)
Of Sound Mind by Jean Ferris (2001)

With accident, homicide, and suicide the leading causes of death for young people, we may not associate disease or disability with youth. Yet some diseases and disabilities make no allowance for age. Such challenges can be formidable obstacles to normal social life, as well as conditions requiring strength and courage on the part of those who suffer from them. Some of the same coping issues confront teens whose parents or siblings live with disease or disability. A range of such situations are discussed in this chapter.

In *Illness as Metaphor*, Susan Sontag writes, "The most truthful way of regarding illness—and the healthiest way of being ill—is one most purified of, most resistant to, metaphoric thinking." In these novels, illness is real: it imprisons its youthful victims or the suffering adults related to protagonists, and the sick, their friends, and their families must confront mortality. Thus, these are primarily novels of friendship and of family relationships. In each, however, one or more characters find freedom—in a variety of ways.

The Bumblebee Flies Anyway (1983), by Robert Cormier, introduces the reader to a small group of terminally ill outsiders and misfits hospitalized in the Complex. First-person narrator Barney Snow does not know why he is in this special wing where teens undergo experimental treatments, and the truth of his situation is obscured by the euphemistic jargon in which he persistently cloaks the reality of their suffering and the drastic measures taken to counteract it. He refers to the drugs as "merchandise" supplied by "the Handyman," their physician, and administered with "doodads" in an Isolation Room, new treatments announced in advance in the Hit Room, a consultation room. Barney himself has more mobility than most of his peers, a circumstance that enables him to construct the car that they refer to as the Bumblebee, which brings a kind of control over their own fate to the desperate patients.

Rhythm is important to Barney, giving him the illusion of control over his circumstances. He believes that if he and others can just establish the right rhythm for performing tasks, including breathing, they will be successful. His sidekick, usually wheelchair-bound, is known as "Billy the Kidney," a sobriquet that identifies his malady, unusual because the Handyman encourages them not to become involved with each other; they are to keep to themselves because they are all "in transit"—in reality, close to death. Barney's behavior flies in the face of this dictum.

Barney's erstwhile antagonist, Mazzo, has wealth, a telephone, and a beautiful twin sister (as well as his own beauty, though ravaged by illness), but he lacks mobility and is bitter, an understandable feeling for a former athlete. Mazzo attempts to strengthen his control over circumstances by flaunting his telephone, enjoying Billy's obvious neediness. Billy's life has always been spent in transit—in a succession of foster homes. Now he longs to use the telephone to make random contact with people in the outside world. Ironically, in negotiation for Billy's use of the phone, Barney begins to form a friendship with Mazzo, and ultimately he finds himself emotionally engaged.

The Handyman seems detached in conversations with Barney that chill Barney's blood. He, too, deals in euphemism, applying the word "discomfort" to the pain "residents," or patients, experience and the terms "demonstrations" or "proceedings" to "treatments" or "experiments." He explains that Barney's treatments will obliterate memory, under controlled circumstances. Barney's last name, Snow, suggests a pure white field, typifying his forgetfulness of his terminal condition—a blank slate or clean slate every time he receives treatment. It also suggests the manipulation of his consciousness: he is the victim of "a snow job." When Barney undergoes treatment, he has difficulty regaining a sense of himself, but after treatment, he feels rested. His artificially induced sense of well-being distinguishes him from the other patients, who have greater awareness of their futures than he has of his own. Mazzo's sister Cassie manipulates Barney (as does the Handyman) because she wants information, and Mazzo refuses family visits. Her need for information is driven by desperation: she experiences her twin's pain vicariously.

Barney's vision of power, accompanied by the thrill of a frightening vision as well, is sparked by his glimpse of a red sports car in the junkyard bordering hospital grounds. From his first sight of it, he imagines hurtling downhill in it, a girl stepping off the curb into its path, in a waking dream that echoes his nightmares. Billy, too, dreams of cars, having stolen—or "borrowed," he explains—twenty-four cars for hour-long joyrides. Barney discovers the MG is a vo-tech class's project, built of plywood. When he learns that Mazzo misses driving more than anything else, he uses this knowledge to open up communication, promising Mazzo one last car ride. Thus the plan for the Bumblebee is born, and its execution is accelerated when Mazzo, his condition deteriorating, pleads with Barney to disconnect him from his life-support equipment life. Barney reconstructs the dismantled plywood car within the Complex, planning to launch it from the roof, an improbable flier like the insect for which he names it.

Barney acquires self-knowledge but loses confidence in his future when he realizes that his nightmare is a screen, a powerfully frightening emotional image to shield him from the knowledge that he, like the others, suffers from terminal illness, recently in remission, a condition that he has not come to terms with. As the doctor honestly answers his questions about his past, he learns that even his most comforting memory of his mother is largely induced by treatment; his parents died when he was seven, and he, like Billy, has lived in a series of foster homes. More terrible, even the thoughts he thinks of as his, including his preoccupation with rhythm, are inspired from without. Faced with removal from the Complex, the only world he knows, he fights panic. Any of the patients, now his friends, are good candidates for the Bumblebee's flight from the roof, but rather than commit suicide himself, Barney chooses to send Mazzo out in style in an act of self-sacrifice that he, however humble, can recognize as a noble gesture. Barney's grim story is one of resistance to an unkind fate, finding freedom even in the most restrictive circumstances, and finally taking charge of one's own fate.

A Time for Dancing (1995), by Davida Wills Hurwin, is the poignant, realistic story of a sixteen-year-old dancer's losing battle with cancer, told in first-person chapters presenting her and her best friend's narratives of the yearlong ordeal. It is a story of terrible isolation. Juliana copes with pain, intensive treatments, exhaustion, and her fear and anger, while Samantha copes with loneliness, stress, and her own fear and anger. Both teens' stories are compelling.

Julie and Sam have been dancing together since they were nine, and their individual identities, as well as their friendship, are bound up in dancing. They are used to pushing their obedient bodies in performance. As Julie goes through the progressive pain and exhaustion caused by lymphoma and its treatment, willing herself to dance in a last concert and pushing past exhaustion to rehearse for it, she steadily loses control over the body that once did whatever she and her teachers demanded of it. Her love of dancing makes it difficult for her—and Sam—to let go and accept that her body simply will not do everything she expects it to, even just wake up and get out of bed on a lot of days. Julie is a fighter, at the end clinging to life longer than anyone expects her to.

The cancer is well advanced when it is diagnosed, and the oncologist who makes the diagnosis recommends an aggressive course of treatment. Despite the grueling chemotherapy, X-rays continue to show the disease has advanced. For a long time, no one voices what this means. It is only late in Julie's illness that she learns she is "terminal," when she eavesdrops on the specialist's conversation with her parents, a conversation from which Julie herself has been excluded. From the point when Julie realizes she must face death, she is conscious of a split between her outer self, which accepts what she is told about treatment and complies while appearing calm, and her inner self, which is terrified and silently screaming. The struggle she consciously undergoes at this point reflects a disconnect from her facade, which everyone accepts in order not to face the imminence of Julie's death.

By eavesdropping, Julie learns that her parents will not allow the doctor to be honest with her. They themselves refuse to confront the possibility the disease is not yielding to treatment, though they cope with the challenge in very different emotional ways—her mother through infinite patience and encouragement, her father through impatient anger and withdrawal. Julie's own emotional ups and downs, along with her exhaustion, make it difficult for her to communicate with her healthy friends who, consequently, fail to address the reality of her condition, pretending that she is normal when she occasionally attends a social event and eventually returns to school and dance lessons.

Sam, Julie's best friend, like Julie's mother, treats her as though she is still Julie rather than a victim. When Julie refuses to answer the phone, Sam goes to her house; she helps Julie put on her wig and takes her out. But, refusing to see that Julie will not recover, Sam allows a distance to grow between them for a time, in a period of partial estrangement that is as much Julie's responsibility as Sam's. Julie's world is bound by disease and treatment; she becomes angry when people ask her how she is or treat her with a cheerful patience that betrays how little they know of her struggles; she resents her five-year-old sister's self-centeredness and occasional boisterousness, and she allows herself to feel self-pityingly that her parents are paying more attention to Rosie than to her. Julie often is too tired to talk on the phone or lacks the stamina to explain what she is going through.

Sam meantime has other challenges in her life: her divorced parents are pursuing their own lives without much real communication with her; she falls in love and dates; she faces the demands of dance class and practice as well as of school; and she maintains an active social life with the other dancers that enables her to spend some time laughing and having a good time without thinking of Julie. Additionally, she bears a burden of pain and sorrow, intensely missing Julie's friendship. Some of their interactions are not very rewarding: when Julie accuses her of not calling, Sam points out that Julie does not call either; Julie is rude to Sam's boyfriend when she finally meets him, and the boyfriend callously advises Sam to walk away from the friendship.

A surprising source of peace and a kind of happiness come to Julie in a mental state that she experiences after chemotherapy, a state she calls the "Between Place." It is a dreamy place where she sees images, often a somewhat frightening old man, and it is an escape from her outer being, the body that suffers. The old man helps her reconcile herself to death's imminence, acting as a sort of spirit guide, bringing her some sense that she is less alone in facing death than she usually feels.

When Julie and Sam were younger, they visited a psychic who foretold many of the circumstances of Sam's parents' breakup but said of Julie that she would take a long journey alone. Julie is very much alone on each step of her journey, even with so courageous and staunch a mother and best friend. Fortunately, she is able, finally, to share a close, wordless grieving with her mother that helps both come to terms with her impending death. Her differences with Sam, too, are reconciled before the final weeks. Although it is painful for Sam, especially unsupported by her own family, she manages to be with Julie and Julie's family in the final hours.

Julie and Sam have a couple of significant conversations about what happens after death, both before her illness is diagnosed and later, near the end, both times at the ocean. Julie does not believe in God, but she does believe in a surviving spirit, not tied to the body. On the day of their second conversation, they observe gulls whirling in a "dance" in the air. This memory comforts Sam after Julie's funeral, when she imagines her friend's spirit free as the gulls to dance over the ocean.

Terry Trueman's brief and thought-provoking *Stuck in Neutral* (2000) imagines the interior world of severely handicapped fourteen-year-old Shawn, who suffers from cerebral palsy. Shawn has no muscle control, which means he cannot communicate and cannot control any bodily functions—he swallows food when his swallow reflex kicks in, not through deliberate choice, and he cannot so much as choose what he wants to look at, nor does he have any control over vocalizing or laughing. He experiences several grand mal seizures a day, which created significant pain for him when he was younger but, now that they are confined to brain activity, no longer seize his muscles. The premise of Trueman's book is that a normal, even high, intelligence might dwell within a body that cannot communicate its insights to others; thus, the novel is a first-person narrative that relates what Shawn's life is like, including his growing suspicion that his father is planning to euthanize him, imagining that Shawn's life contains nothing but pain.

Shawn lives with his mother, a woman of infinite patience who has largely devoted her life to his care, and his older siblings Cindy and Paul. His father apparently could not bear the emotional drain of seeing Shawn's "pain" from an early age. A prize-winning writer, he has gained fame with a poem about his sorrow that has brought him a career of television appearances as, essentially, a professional victim. The circumstance that most rouses Shawn's suspicions of his father's intentions is his new writing project: a biography of a man who killed his brain-damaged two-year-old son in an act of "mercy killing." The suspense is high, and is still unresolved at the novel's end.

In a sequel, *Cruise Control* (2004), Trueman chronicles the emotional challenges faced by Shawn's brother, Paul, a seventeen-year-old athlete who performs well in academics as well as several sports. It is as though, Paul reflects, he has everything that Shawn does not. Paul struggles with fierce anger—at his father, who left the family; at thoughtless or cruel people who threaten Shawn; at anyone who crosses him. He feels trapped by circumstances: since his father has left them, though he supports them financially, Paul believes he must stay close to home instead of attending Georgetown University, his dream college, across the country. Feeling responsible and protective, Paul is deeply ashamed of his occasional embarrassment over Shawn's condition, most deeply ashamed of a time of crisis when he allowed himself to imagine life free of Shawn. Because he is so angry with his father for leaving them with this burden, his own desire for freedom disgusts him, as he recognizes his father's supposed feelings in himself. However, his mother clarifies the circumstances of his father's leaving and, in their different ways, both his parents help Paul let himself off the hook, convincing him he is *not* responsible for his brother and it is okay to pursue his own dreams.

Freed from his exaggerated sense of responsibility and his disproportionate anger at his father, Paul finds his internal rage dissipating, to the extent that he can play his final basketball game without overreacting to the other team's insults and an aggressive deliberate foul, a situation that in the past would have ensured his getting into a fight. This freedom also simplifies Paul's love for his brother, a love that he finally is able to express to Shawn, and he dedicates his last game of high school basketball to his brother in a public acknowledgment that he has never felt able to make before.

Paul has particularly important assistance with coping from his friend Tim, who has patience with Paul's sudden anger as well as enormous compassion. Tim's ability to see and treat Shawn as a person comes, no doubt, from the compassion he also shows his mother, whose marriage to Tim's abusive stepfather gives him a similar feeling of entrapment in family responsibility. When the stepfather's violence finally pushes Tim into fighting back, Tim is literally imprisoned, and his snap startles Paul into realizing how close his own predilection for violence has brought him to ruining his life.

Covering the same time period as *Stuck in Neutral*, *Cruise Control* similarly fails to resolve the suspense as to what Shawn and Paul's father may do, alone with Shawn while the rest of the family is at the basketball finals. Both novels deal realistically, from the author's personal knowledge, with the day-to-day challenges of coping with a profoundly disabled family member, one whom the rest of the family love but who cannot express any response, if indeed he feels any. Both novels raise the question of the meaning of life—whether a life that is not normal in any way should be considered by healthy humans to be less than life. Memory, Shawn reflects, is all that is left of a lived life, and Shawn remembers, even though no one he loves will ever know that he does. Trueman postulates Shawn's finding control of his body in the hallucinatory experiences of his seizures as well as his enjoying a rich inner life the rest of the time. As one character observes, a brain scan shows no differences between Shawn's brain and others' brains. Shawn is "stuck in neutral," subject to whatever forces move him forward or back, unable to engage in gear to govern his own movement. Paul is on "cruise control," barreling down the highway at high speed. Neither has a choice in the body or the family circumstances he has been placed in.

A milder case of cerebral palsy characterizes the protagonist of *Stoner & Spaz* (2001), in which Ron Koertge chronicles a brief, transformative relationship between sixteen-year-old Ben (Spaz) and the sexy drug user Colleen (Stoner). Their meeting is improbable: when her macho, drug-dealing, motorcycle-riding boyfriend is pursuing another girl, Colleen hooks up with Ben in the movie theater where he spends a lot of his time watching classic films and gives him her phone number so that he can help her write a paper on *The Great Gatsby*, thus beginning a friendship that turns into an unlikely romance.

Ben is a loner, self-isolated by his disability and unwilling to take chances on rejection from his peers. Both his parents are gone, and he lives with his grandmother; his mother's departure has made him cautious about trusting others. Ben's grandmother dresses him expensively but conservatively, further isolating him from his peers. When Colleen staggers into his life, reeling, sick (she vomits out the window of his grandmother's car), in need of his help with schoolwork, ready to take him dancing but equally ready to abandon him when her boyfriend shows up, she shakes things up! Colleen is charming and likable, despite her unreliability; she is frank and curious. Ben has lived primarily through the movies, and he knows a wealth of movie lore, which he uses to envision his possibilities for action, calling to mind famous scenes for appropriate dialogue—though he is smart and funny in his own right. Their relationship attracts notice at school, bringing more interaction with others, starting him on a path to gradual integration into the community of his peers.

After Ben pushes Colleen into a rehabilitation program, their friendship blossoms into romance. But it is moviemaking that propels him into real interaction with others, into seeking better understanding of his peers, bringing him out of preoccupation with himself when he undertakes a documentary on high school life. His new neighbor Marcie introduces him to video editing on her computer and loans him her video camera, and when she invites him to work on his movie at her place while she is out of town, his two new interests—moviemaking and Colleen—absorb him. In the course of filming interviews, Ben opens up himself, finding that other students have as many questions for him as he has for them. Marcie pushes Ben to get beyond superficial, stereotypical portrayals of various groups from teen moms to jocks to stoners, and she encourages him to submit the resulting documentary to a gallery. The exhibit introduces him to other teen filmmakers, and he begins thinking about his college plans. Ben grows significantly through this experience, and it is timed well because Colleen cannot stay drug-free. If he pinned all his hopes for a normal social life on his relationship with her, his prospects would be limited, but instead she proves to be only one of two catalysts that propel him into connecting with others his age.

Of Sound Mind (2001) by Jean Ferris takes the reader into the world of the deaf as seen by high school senior Theo, the only hearing member in his family and, thus, their liaison with the hearing world. Bilingual in English and American Sign Language (ASL), Theo has led a life of interpreting and making phone calls for his parents, especially for his mother, Palma, a well-known sculptor whose gallery exhibits must be negotiated and coordinated. Because the most noticeable thing about Theo's family is their deafness, he tends not to question or analyze their characteristics as a family. He resents the demands his famous prima donna mother makes on him: she has no patience with hired interpreters or the TTY phone and expects him to drop whatever he is doing every time she needs him. Interpreting is tiring, demanding work, and sometimes conceptually beyond him, as when he inter-preted at the closing on their house at age eleven. His father, Thomas, a furniture maker, bends over backward to avoid making demands on Theo, and Theo worries about Thomas's health because he is not sure that Thomas's communication with his physician through writing has fully convinced Thomas of the gravity of his medical problems. Theo's own vocational orientation is to mathematics—he helps his younger brother, Jeremy, with homework every day—and he dreams of going to MIT, but Palma expects him to stay close to home in Philadelphia.

Theo's life changes dramatically when he meets an interesting, attractive girl who is also fluent in sign and interprets for her deaf father, who otherwise, however, is self-sufficient and temperamentally rather solitary. Ivy's parents are divorced, and she never sees her mother. Ivy's passion is cooking, and though new to the area, she is soon cooking regularly for several elderly neighbors, building a small catering business. Theo begins helping her deliver food; soon Jeremy begins hanging out with Ivy's father, whose hobby is building model airplanes. (Theo notes that many deaf people adopt hobbies or practice trades that require skilled hands). Before long Thomas is joining their model-building and flying sessions. Since Palma spends most of her time alone in her studio, this arrangement works out just fine, and Theo and Ivy's romance blossoms—until Thomas suffers a stroke.

Suddenly the demands on Theo are overwhelming. Thomas has provided the steady, responsible anchor in the household—he is a warm and loving father and the solid center in Palma's dramatic emotional life. Already difficult and self-centered, Palma is insecure and hysterical as Theo pushes aside his own fear and pain to cope with the hospital—where medical personnel have struggled even to diagnose the nature and extent of Thomas's malady, not knowing he is deaf—and then to pick up Thomas's household responsibilities (Palma does not cook or keep house or do laun-dry) and care for Thomas when he comes home from the hospital. Palma is convinced Theo should leave school to be her live-in caretaker, housekeeper, and interpreter. Fortunately, two of Ivy's elderly customers, Harry and Hazel, a widowed sister and brother, step in, in a solution that works to everyone's benefit.

As a result, Theo suddenly has to struggle with a perverse sense of rejection, even though it is clear that Harry and Hazel are good for Thomas, and for Jeremy, and they in turn enjoy being needed. He lashes out at Ivy when she identifies the source of his malaise, pointing out that her need to feed other people is a thinly disguised effort to mother others, when Ivy herself needs mothering. The stress both have been under temporarily ruptures their relationship, but Thomas's second, fatal stroke just before Christmas brings them back together. Palma, Jeremy, and Theo all need the warm support that Ivy's cooking and Harry and Hazel's knowledge of loss can give them. For once, Theo can just grieve, but at the same time, in the midst of his grief, he takes the MIT application out of his desk drawer again and fills it out.

A final, brief chapter shows the family in August: Theo is packing for MIT, and Ivy will attend culinary school in Boston. Hazel is excited to be helping Palma arrange her next exhibit, and Harry is about to take Jeremy back-to-school shopping. While grief is still fresh, life goes on. The unimaginable has happened, and everyone has grown, though even the reader has to feel the loss of sweet, gentle Thomas. Any reader who is unfamiliar with the challenges of living with deafness will learn a great deal from this novel, but it is also a compelling narrative of finding a balance between family demands and personal goals. Ferris has represented ASL as though it were syntactically equivalent to English, a strategy that keeps it from sounding like a pidgin or imitation of English and that keeps the narrative moving. Theo comments on personal expression in various characters' signing, and he describes Palma's sculptures of hands in the act of communicating. Theo can admire his mother's art even if he resents her assumptions about his availability to serve her needs.

ADDITIONAL READING RECOMMENDATIONS

A Summer to Die by Lois Lowry, 1977
Night Kites by M. E. Kerr, 1986
After the Rain by Norma Fox Mazer, 1987
The Chemo Kid by Robert Lipsyte, 1992
Freak the Mighty by Rodman Philbrick, 1993 (discussed in Friends Forever?)
The Eagle Kite by Paula Fox, 1995
Saying It Out Loud by Joan Abelove, 1999
Both Sides Now by Ruth Pennebaker, 2002

Emotional Problems Confronted

The Language of Goldfish by Zibby Oneal (1980)
Humming Whispers by Angela Johnson (1996)
Damage by A. M. Jenkins (2001)
America by E. R. Frank (2002)

When teens are their own worst enemies, what saves them from self-destructive behavior? All too often, it is a suicide attempt that brings help. Suicidal feelings are often not reported, due to the stigmatization of emotional problems by peers or lack of attention on the part of adults in their lives. In some cases, adults in the family do not take behavioral changes or mood swings as seriously as they should, believing them to be normal in adolescence. Furthermore, many teens experience stresses and traumas that trigger depression. It is not surprising, therefore, that emotional disturbance is a major theme of many young adult novels. In the novels discussed here, teens confronting depression and other emotional problems find their way back to emotional balance, or begin their journey back, through the support of close friends or mentors who recognize the nature of the problem and help the suffering teens face the challenge.

The Language of Goldfish (1980), by Zibby Oneal, chronicles a teen's growing sense that she is "going crazy," her family's denial, a suicide attempt, and her long journey back to emotional balance. Carrie's eighth-grade year is shaped by her resistance to change: she clings to memories of a childhood and best friend she lost when the family moved, as she clings to the games and magical beliefs of childhood. She does not want to begin acting like a teen socially, seeming perfectly content in her quiet isolation in school. She loves drawing and math. Her art teacher, who gives her private lessons on Saturdays and encourages her to submit work in competitions, is her only friend. When episodes of dizziness and forgetfulness begin, Carrie tries to enlist her busy parents' and older sister's help, but it takes a suicide attempt to bring the help she needs, and even then, her family hides the truth from themselves as well as others. However, Carrie is capable of healing, with the support of daily visits to her psychiatrist and her drawing and painting, and eventually, early in ninth grade, she comes to her own understanding of her fear of maturation.

The goldfish pond in the backyard becomes an important symbol of childhood for Carrie. With her older sister, Moira, she has fed the goldfish, calling them with whistles, and the sisters imagined they could ride the fishes' backs to the small rocky island in the middle of the pool. The island symbolizes a destination of some sort, envisioned in her waking moments when she slips out of touch with everyday life around her, and then, after her suicide attempt, becomes the subject of a series of paintings that she eventually sees, with her art teacher's help, as an emergent vision.

Carrie's unease with growing up teases the edge of her vision in her discomfort at an exhibit of Aubrey Beardsley's exuberantly sensual drawings and her embarrassment at her art teacher's identification of the ever-present sexuality in their lines, as well as in embarrassment during an English class discussion of Keats's "Eve of St. Agnes," with its focus on sexual initiation. She actively resists her mother's and sister's efforts to spark her interest in what they consider age-appropriate activities, specifically school dances. Even after hospitalization and months of daily sessions with her psychiatrist, Carrie seeks the company of younger children in her summer job. Her relationship with an eight-year-old enables her, finally, to leave childhood behind by bequeathing the magic of the goldfish pond to the younger girl.

Often misunderstood within her family, Carrie feels like a piece from a jigsaw puzzle that is different from the one that makes up their lives. Her parents have an active social life, entertaining regularly, going out; her sister listens to rock music and is popular in school and interested in boys. Carrie's physician father responds to her dizziness by drawing blood for an anemia test; her mother simply refuses to listen to anything Carrie says about her mental state both before and after she overdoses on medication. In the aftermath of her suicide attempt, Carrie finds the hospital, where her actions are recognized and acknowledged for what they are, a much safer place than home.

Carrie's family loves her, even if it takes her art teacher's assertion to make this clear to Carrie. Both her mother and sister have expectations of what Carrie should be doing and thinking about, and she feels judged by them, longing for the simpler relationships of the past when her mother wore an apron and cooked for her and her sister played with her. She is most comfortable with her younger brother, Duncan. The shabby Christmas ornaments of her childhood remain as beautiful to her as they were in former years because of the memories they carry, and when she places her chipped Christmas angel on the mantle in its fresh, elegant display, her mother relents and allows it to remain. Carrie's embarrassment about discussing her body's changes with her mother leads her to ask her sister to purchase a bra for her, something Moira readily consents to, showing Carrie that she does not have to face change alone. She also finds support from Moira when she finally decides to attend a dance, just to prove to herself that she can do it.

Carrie's progress is signaled in the subjects of her artwork. Before and immediately after her breakdown, she draws abstractly. Her series of island pictures helps her emerge from the isolation that follows the episode. As she begins to reconnect to other people, she shifts to drawing people and animals.

The friendship with her art teacher, such an important part of her life, undergoes a significant change when Mrs. Ramsay announces she will be moving to Milwaukee with her children during the summer, leaving her husband, and Carrie learns through gossip that she is leaving him for another man. This revelation hints at an undercurrent that has run through their relationship: it gives a pattern to several exchanges between them that individually suggested no deeper meaning. By the time that Carrie learns that the sexuality Mrs. Ramsay identified in art is also reshaping her life, she is strong enough to face it, and to face change in general.

In *Humming Whispers* (1996), Angela Johnson presents fourteen-year-old Sophy's troubled love of her schizophrenic sister, Nicole, along with Sophie's fear that she too will hear the "humming whispers" that lead Nicole away from home. Sophy is especially concerned for herself at this point because Nicole's disease became apparent at age fourteen. Lately, Sophy has seen her face change in mirrors, and she is not sure whether she is experiencing delusions. She looks like her sister, and when she was small, she wanted to be just like her sister. Now she fears sleeping in the same room as her sister, troubled by the dreams and shadows of her own life, while she continues to love Nicole and struggles to find a way to live with both her fears and her love.

This family has learned to live with sad and harsh realities. The girls' parents were killed in an automobile accident, forever changing their young aunt's life as she took over their care. Sophy still remembers being left alone while Aunt Shirley tried to find Nicole the first time that the whispers led her away. At the time of the novel, the family lives daily with the possibility of Nikki's following the whispers again when her medication is not just right or when she fails to take it on schedule—and she does follow "Them" the day after her birthday.

Nikki's boyfriend, Reuben, is a gentle artist, sweet and considerate, faithful in love despite Nicole's vagaries. He joins the girls and their aunt in their unusual birthday celebration: they take a picnic to the cemetery to spend hours "with" their parents. He also watches out for an elderly woman, Miss Onyx, the friend of his now-deceased grandmother. Miss Onyx is an important part of Sophy's life, sharing stories of her life as a dancer and displaying in the faded tattooed numbers on her wrist just what humans can survive, the extreme privations of concentration camps.

Sophy, too, is a dancer who attends a high school for the arts. Nicole is usually a "secret dancer," but when her illness is pulling her into her private world of compulsions, she begins dancing around the apartment more openly. In contrast to this behavior, Miss Onyx reassures Sophy that she can "find herself" in dance, that it is a matter of control, a kind of control that Nikki lacks. Sophy's response is to wonder why she must find herself because she does not feel "lost."

Sophy, however, "finds" *things*—she steals. When Nicole returns after a stay in the hospital, which follows being picked up by police on a runway at the airport, she discovers the box of oddly assorted jewelry, candy bars, CDs, and household items under Sophy's bed, but Sophy tells her the collection is for a school project in her first-ever lie to Nicole. Her other reaction to her sister's illness is a sleep disturbance—she falls asleep when any disturbing things are going on, and thus she tends to sleep through her sister's departures and odd behaviors. In a gesture that indicates she will have more control over her life than her sister has over her own, Sophy finally lets go of her box of stolen goods, distributing them among prostitutes in the neighborhood after a store clerk gently confronts her about stealing from his store.

Each of the women in this family is concerned about each of the others, and they all watch each other and worry about each other. Miss Onyx functions as an elderly relative in their lives, and in her presence, Sophy, at least, finds comfort and peace. Sophy has worried about her sister from an early age: she fears that Nicole, deep in a medicated sleep, will not wake during a dangerous storm and will be hurt. Nicole, ten years older than Sophy, feels responsible for alleviating Sophy's fears, especially her fear of airplanes, which Nicole claims she herself inspired by telling Sophy a scary story about a plane during what was apparently an earlier delusional episode, when Nicole took Sophy with her and they wandered homeless and hungry for days. Now, in compensation, Nicole takes Sophy to a spot near the airport where they can lie on the ground, holding hands, and be swallowed up in the noise of planes swooping close overhead. One brief passage, near the end of the novel, presents Nicole's sense of what is going on, her understanding of Sophy's fear and the pain that she hides away by stashing stolen goods under the bed. Nicole's evident love and clear insights are mixed with delusional suggestions as well.

Both sisters make lists. Sophy's lists show her ability to empathize with Nicole and Miss Onyx. But after Miss Onyx's stroke, Sophy writes a list that demonstrates the lessons she has learned from the elderly woman, verbalizing her ability to claim dancing as a healthy activity, her right to a life without fear, and her commitment to living. Her list also announces her intention to find a summer job, something she earlier thought she could not do because she feared mental illness. By the end of the novel, Sophy has come to terms with mirrors, and she faces her fear of storms by dancing in the rain with her sister. She is not guaranteed a life free of emotional disturbance, but she is no longer paralyzed by her dread of mental illness.

Damage (2001), by A. M. Jenkins, depicts Austin Reid's slide into depression, bringing him almost to suicide before he finds salvation in friendship. The novel is one of those rare ones written in the second person, a technique that draws the reader in, inviting empathy with the protagonist. Austin is all too aware of the irony that he is not enjoying life as he used to. He expected his senior year to be the best year, given his easy way with girls and his football-star status, not to mention his sheer enjoyment in playing the game. He goes through the motions of flirting with girls, defusing tension between his friends, and teasing and joking with the people he knows, but that is all he is doing—going through the motions. The Baptist church's signboard enjoins him to "Be joyful always," but his joy has fled, seemingly perma-nently, drawing him inexorably toward a dramatic escape from pain.

Austin's lifelong friendship with his buddy, teammate, and next-door neighbor Curtis gives him the lifeline he needs only because the timing is right. The astute Curtis has asked several times whether Austin is okay, but Austin has refused to acknowledge how depressed he is until the day he arrives home ready to slit his wrists, no longer able to imagine any other way to end the deadness that has consumed him for months. But Curtis is on his porch, and as Austin talks with him, he recog-nizes that even if he is no longer hanging onto the cliff's edge by his fingernails, there is an alternative to falling. The novel ends with the acknowledgment that a future, whatever it may be, awaits him.

Curtis's ability to anchor Austin grows from the crises they have survived together, especially the loss of a father. Austin's father died of cancer when Austin was three, and his earliest memories turn out to be memories of Curtis's father, whom he more or less shared. Austin also shared Curtis's pain when his father left his mother for a pretty, much younger woman five years earlier. He has been sup-portive as Curtis has worked through the more recent pain of a failed romance, to which Curtis committed himself wholeheartedly once sex became part of the rela-tionship. Curtis is steadfast, immovable, honest, and loyal, and he has integrity. Loyalty to his mother precludes his forgiving his father, whom he has steadily refused to visit. As much as Curtis loves football, when it is tarnished by their new coach's "drill" designed to punish any player who makes a mistake, he turns his back on the team, and Austin knows that once he has done so, he will never change his mind. Opening up to Curtis is safe, and the first step to getting professional treat-ment, because Curtis will not allow him to pretend again.

The precipitating factor in Austin's decline into near-suicidal depression occurs when his girlfriend, Heather, dismisses Austin as abnormal. He has welcomed the way his relationship with her consumes his hours, keeping him from being alone with desperate depression. From time to time he has sought more emotional intimacy with Heather, but she is in tight control of her emotions, unwilling to let go even during sex and angry when Austin puts her pleasure ahead of his. Heather's father committed suicide, and eventually she reveals that it was she who found him, but instead of drawing Austin closer with this admission, she uses it to express her anger at him as well as her father. Heather is not ready to confront her emotions and to heal, as Austin ultimately is due to Curtis's friendship.

America (2002) is the compelling story of a teen who has been abandoned, abused, and numbed with alcohol, who has sought love, rebelled, sunk into depression, and tried to commit suicide, but who ultimately works his way through trauma, rage, and despair with a patient therapist. Author E. R. Frank creates the fictional Dr. B and the troubled youth America as composites of therapists and teens she has known as a clinical social worker. America's name may suggest that he embodies the stories of many troubled teens today, though in the novel his name seems to reflect his crack-addicted mother's unsureness of what racial mixture he will exhibit. America is silent and withdrawn in the wake of his suicide attempt, but over the course of a couple of years in a stable counseling relationship, he confronts his past as a child who "fell through the cracks" in the system of social agencies that should have prevented his abandonment and abuse. The other set of "cracks" that America confronts are cracks in the wall he has constructed against his enormous emotional pain. He tries to avoid thinking about the past, but Dr. B's questions trigger memories, and gradually the reader acquires a full picture of his life. It is the small things that matter, his foster mother used to tell him, and the details of his experience force small wedges into festering memories, lancing them to ultimately release their poison. Dr. B sparks America's imagination by asking him what he thinks is in his own file. Dr. B's success in drawing America out of the prison he has built around his feelings derives from the foundation deep in America's past, the one solid, loving relationship he remembers.

America is reluctant to expect continuity in any relationship because of a number of temporary, unsatisfactory relationships with counselors in institutions, as well as because of the separation from his loving foster mother, Mrs. Harper, on two traumatic occasions. His earliest memories of Mrs. Harper are joyful ones of being hugged and tickled and of helping her paint angels for sale. The fun of hide-and-seek is in being found, but when he is lost in the city, no one can find him. Mrs. Harper and her friend tried to prevent this by teaching him telephone numbers and how to make a collect call, but America cannot find an operating telephone once he is in his mother's apartment. He obsessively scribbles the memorized phone numbers over every surface he can write on, even after he has forgotten their meaning.

The sense of needing to be found is buried deep in him, even during periods of extreme withdrawal. An early crisis in his sessions with Dr. B is the outcome of B's taking a two-week vacation. America is always certain that he will be abandoned again, sure he is unworthy of being found. This conviction is reinforced when his half brother, Brooklyn, refuses to acknowledge their family relationship when he shows up in the same institution for treatment for drug dependency. However, when others demonstrate that they care about him, his conviction is shaken. America's recovery is aided by his elementary school friend Liza's finding him—caring enough to find him. Though his second separation from Mrs. Harper lasts a long time, and he is slow to seek out the aged woman in her nursing home, once he sees her room, he cannot help but believe in her enduring love for him: her room is filled with little angels painted to resemble America at five, the time of his first separation from her.

The blues, oranges, and yellows that she used in painting inspired America's early obsession with flames. The gift of a lighter marks the beginning of his difficult relationship with the abusive Browning, Mrs. Harper's caregiver, who lives with them after her health has begun to fail. At first, America lights Browning's cigarettes in the room they share. Later, he burns a paper of his mother's that he finds among Mrs. Harper's possessions, as though trying to end his connection with her. It is hardly surprising that he sets Browning's blanket alight after being raped by him. From then on, his guilt over Browning's death, which is chalked up to smoking in bed by the authorities, leads him to play obsessively with lighters.

America's obsession with shoelaces begins when he runs away after starting the fire, when his shoelace frays as he leaves the only home he has known. He feels that he must replace the lace, like the happy family life he knew in his earliest days, and thus begins years of stealing or buying as many pairs of shoelaces as he can. He later develops a wide variety of fancy lacing techniques that become his trademark, and, at the first residential facility he is sent to, he is even called "Shoelace" by the other children. His braided shoelaces make a rope strong enough to hang him, when he attempts suicide. At the end of the novel, after successfully confronting his past with Dr. B and graduating to life in a group home, when he is finally willing to part with a collection of shoelaces, America ceremonially burns them as he prepares to face life (after which he throws away the lighter as well), possibly marking the end of his obsessive-compulsive disorder.

America is also drawn into endless games of War with Dr. B, the card game America learned from Brooklyn. As they play, he comes to trust Dr. B and gradually to reveal bits of his past. Not until after his breakthrough, though, does he discover the world of miniatures on Dr. B's shelves. In early sessions, all he saw was the tiny soldiers lined up to take aim at him. Later he finds other figures—sports teams, circus performers and animals, and finally, a whole "army" of angels. This last discovery marks the connection between his early relationship of love and normal childhood dependency on Mrs. Harper with his healing relationship with Dr. B. It also marks the ascendancy of the good in his nature, the victory of the angels over his conviction that he is bad and unworthy of love.

A school trip to an IMAX movie on mountain climbing and Mount Everest has given America an image for withdrawing from abuse. Like other victims, he has had the sensation of floating up above his body. The purity of the unmarked snow and the sensation of being high above everything that he experienced in the theater have continued to take over America's thoughts when he feels threatened. Gradually, he learns not to withdraw in his therapy sessions but to confront and dispel the negative images of the past.

Cooking and gardening help him emerge from withdrawal and also provide him with ways to think about his past. Having learned to cook well at a young age, America is a real artist in the institution's kitchen, though he destroys all the carrots that come his way, remembering the threat that Browning reinforced with the image of peeling a carrot. When America learns to take out negative feelings on the carrots, his healing progresses, and later, his love for cooking leads naturally to planting a garden at the group home. He learns that "soil" is not "dirt" and that manure fertilizes new growth in a metaphor that helps him think about building a strong new sense of self on the frightening and humiliating experiences of his past.

Psychotherapy itself is often best understood through metaphors for how the mind works, and patients find it useful to understand their experiences and to reconceive their ways of handling challenge through appropriate metaphor. Thus the reader's understanding of America's struggle becomes clearer as the character's understanding of his own past increases through reinterpretation of recurring metaphors and symbols.

The first-person narrative is America's story. At first, it is told in episodic sections, with scraps of his past and gaps in the novel's present time. Later, the narrative is more sustained, alternating between the past and the present. His history is a heart-wrenching tale, but the terrible circumstances he endures make his victory all the more inspiring. His progress assures readers that the most broken of individuals can indeed recover, though the road back from such trauma and despair is anything but easy.

ADDITIONAL READING RECOMMENDATIONS

I Am the Cheese by Robert Cormier, 1977
Remembering the Good Times by Richard Peck, 1985 (discussed in Friends Forever?)
Gruel and Unusual Punishment by Jim Arter, 1991
Round the Bend by Mitzi Dale, 1991
Strange Objects by Gary Crew, 1993
The Hanged Man by Francesca Lia Block, 1994
Iceman, 1994, and *Freewill*, 2001, by Chris Lynch
I Am an Artichoke by Lucy Frank, 1995
Taking It by Michael Cadnum, 1995
The Toll Bridge by Aidan Chambers, 1995
Ironman by Chris Crutcher, 1995
Dancing on the Edge by Han Nolan, 1997 (discussed in Families, Traditional
    and Redefined)
Stephen Fair by Tim Wynne-Jones, 1998
Dive by Adele Griffin, 1999
Tribes by Arthur Slade, 2002
Warrior Angel by Robert Lipsyte, 2003

Families, Traditional and Redefined

Jacob Have I Loved by Katherine Paterson (1980)
The Glory Field by Walter Dean Myers (1994)
Like Sisters on the Homefront by Rita Williams-Garcia (1995)
Dancing on the Edge by Han Nolan (1997)
The Spring Tone by Kazumi Yumoto (1995; translated by
   Cathy Hirano, 1999)
Homeless Bird by Gloria Whelan (2000)

Families play a major role in shaping individuals, and they come in a wide array of types. Some people live in multigenerational households, some in single-parent households, some as only children, some with step-siblings. Family history and traditions shape the daily lives of some individuals, while others live in relatively isolated nuclear families. Families are shaped by cultural expectations, and those expectations shape the possibilities for individuals as well. Gender roles, socioeconomic status, educational opportunities—all reflect the families in which people grow to adulthood. A variety of family patterns shape young protagonists' lives in the following novels.

In *Jacob Have I Loved* (1980), Katherine Paterson chronicles protagonist Sarah-Louise's often-painful growing up during World War II on isolated Rass Island in the Chesapeake Bay. Louise ("Wheeze") is a tomboy who at thirteen would like nothing better than to follow her father into a life of crabbing, a life considered inappropriate for a woman. The bane of her existence is her twin sister, Caroline, the beautiful, gifted, fragile darling of the family and the community, in whose shadow Louise struggles to establish her identity and to claim her share of others' love. Her dilemma is that of the twin who is, or believes herself to be, unloved regardless of merit or birthright while the less deserving twin finds love and fortune. Her grandmother spitefully quotes Romans 9:13 to her: ". . . Jacob have I loved, but Esau have I hated," only confirming Louise's conviction that she cannot earn as much love as Caroline. Like Esau, Louise forfeits her right to others' love until she takes responsibility for her own success and happiness, breaking out of the jealousy and anger that has confined her to a narrow range of choices during her teen years.

In those years, 1941 to 1945, Louise is repeatedly wounded as Caroline gains the lion's share of the family's resources for music lessons, earns in a few hours the approval of those Louise has spent weeks helping, and finally wins the love of Louise's best friend, Call, just as Louise is recognizing the depth of her own caring for him. These situations seem to confirm that she is entitled to less from birth, a difference established by the purely physiological fact that Caroline was tiny and required medical attention off the island, a situation that also removed her mother's care during Louise's first weeks of life. Caroline has extraordinary musical talent as well, a talent that brings pleasure to the entire community and that her parents and Louise nurture through routine sacrifice for her lessons, a situation eventually relieved when their neighbor, Captain Wallace, makes a generous gift to support her training on the mainland and she is subsequently admitted to Juilliard. Caroline's confidence constantly irritates Louise, but she has received applause all her life, so it is natural for her to expect she will one day be famous.

Louise, in contrast, limits her choices in the anger and resentment she bears her twin. She fails even to inform her family of her own dreams—of seeing the mountains, getting an education off the island, studying medicine. Two external circumstances help her rationalize this reticence: the war and a hurricane, both of which negatively affect family finances. The war, however, takes men and boys away from the island, a circumstance that brings her the opportunity to work with her father, when she discovers that he sings to the oysters. It is clear to the reader, if not always to Louise, that her parents love and appreciate her. She works hard, and she shows surprising patience with her paternal grandmother, increasingly irascible as she ages, who makes the girls' mother miserable by calling her a harlot and accusing her of stealing her husband. Louise is increasingly soured by her jealousy, which diminishes her joy in the carefree years of her early teens; the ensuing period is marked by competition for the friendship of the Captain; and Louise is finally eclipsed when Caroline's musical education is supported and Call falls in love with her. Throughout these years, Louise reflects on the Bible and her Protestant upbringing, trying to understand her place in the world. She identifies with Joseph when he dreamed of his brothers' bowing to him; she reasons that David, God's "pet," was forgiven for much greater sins than she herself has committed; and she searches the Bible to find some way out of the damnation she fears God will visit upon her. The war that rages in the world outside the island and the bay—as remote from her immediate experience as *Silas Marner*, which they read in school—seems to epitomize the deep divisions between human beings for which only God can be considered responsible.

As Louise begins to be attracted to boys and men, she has a limited number of men to respond to. She is chagrined by an intense physical attraction to Captain Wallace, that she first feels in a neighborly hug. Reminding herself that he is older than her grandmother, she nonetheless continues to find particular beauty in his hands. Indeed, it is only her grandmother who notes her wakening sexual response to the Captain, but her grasp on reality is weak enough that no one takes seriously her insight into Louise's love. After Call enters military service, Louise realizes her feelings for her long-time buddy have matured into love. Again, her grandmother accurately identifies Louise's feelings, asking her, when Call returns, where she thinks she is going with "that man."

Louise allows the island environment to confine her when she fails to pursue her own dreams with the tenacity that Caroline exhibits. She notes that women on the island generally resent the water, treating it like a mistress that pulls their men away from them. Louise, in contrast, has always found peace on the water, a peace she shares with her father during the time she works with him, a period she later recognizes as the happiest part of her early life. Later, she finds a fulfilling life similarly islanded in the mountains, where she practices as a nurse-midwife and marries a widower. It is in her capacity as a midwife that she finally comes to terms with her twin status and the difference in the family's treatment of her and Caroline. When she delivers twins, she neglects the larger, healthier infant and exerts every effort to bring its tiny sister alive through her first hours. Discovering how fully the tiny infant has absorbed her attention, she understands her family's anxiety for Caroline's well-being.

The words with which her story closes are from the Appalachian-inspired "I Wonder as I Wander," sung to the plaintive, haunting melody recorded and adapted by John Jacob Niles in the 1930s. This is the solo that Caroline sang in the 1941 Christmas concert following the attack on Pearl Harbor. The song affirms the loneliness of life in this world and claims God's attention to every soul, no matter how lowly. Louise has finally found love, a sense of worth, and acceptance of her family's treatment.

Walter Dean Myers's *The Glory Field* (1994) spans several generations in an African American family's life, beginning with the enslavement of Muhammad Bilal in West Africa in 1753 and ending with a 1994 picnic on the family homestead on the South Carolina coast. The Lewis family has taken their white owners' surname after the Civil War, along with an eight-acre farm bordering the plantation. "The glory field" acquired its name when the first head of the household to own the land, Moses Lewis, gathered his free family around him there, and all he could say was "Glory!" It is the site of whippings by whites and the burial in unmarked graves of recaptured runaway slaves. The field bears witness to the family's achievements, even when bought with pain and death, and hence is precious in the same way that the family heirloom, the patriarch's shackles, is.

A series of stories in 1753, 1864, 1900, 1930, 1964, and 1994 traces the continuity of the family traits of strength and endurance and illustrate the family's ongoing challenge to define themselves individually within a white-dominated society while retaining a strong connection to the traditions that bind them to the land. In defining themselves individually—as men and women, not as slaves, boys, or second-class citizens—they also uphold an obligation to the family and to black people in general. As they harvest the last crop of sweet potatoes together at a family reunion in 1994, the crop becomes emblematic of the opportunities they have earned through that persistence and strength, shown over the centuries most especially in the labor they have performed for themselves and their loved ones.

The chains that Muhammad Bilal wore to North America as a youth are handed down from generation to generation. Many of the circumstances his descendants face are equally confining. Indeed, in the last story, young Sheppard Lewis makes a journey that echoes his ancestor's, chained in the throes of withdrawal, confined in a dark, stifling trailer when he and his cousin Malcolm accept a trucker's offer of a ride. As Shep screams his agony out, Malcolm reflects on what it means to be black. A thoughtful young musician, who works in his great-aunt's cosmetics business, Malcolm has been forced to enter a world he has little contact with ordinarily, a world that troubles him. He has entered it because of his sense of responsibility for and to his cousin. At the family reunion, the hard labor of keeping up with his farmer relatives as they pick sweet potatoes bonds Malcolm to the rest of the family, and he feels their strength. Both his journey with Shep and his refusal to give up fit Malcolm to become the next custodian of the ancestral shackles. The elderly kinsman who bequeaths them to him knows that Malcolm will do his best to understand not only the bitter elements of their heritage but the family's pride and worth.

Rita Williams-Garcia's *Like Sisters on the Homefront* (1995) similarly chronicles the reknitting of a family that has gone in two directions—the urban North and the rural South, where the male head of the family continues a family commitment to the ministry and retains the family land, while his mother retains the family's oral history dating to the beginning of their enslavement. The heedless fourteen-year-old Gayle's second pregnancy, ending in an abortion that her mother insists on, results in her exile from New York City to her strict uncle's household in Georgia, where she must take responsibility for her baby son, help with household chores, and attend church, consigned to an apparently joyless existence.

Gayle is brash and hard to intimidate, but on arrival she notes the family's ownership of things—of land, a pillared antebellum house, antiques including the crib where little José will sleep, and patchwork quilts. They own things like her Uncle Luther owns God, she thinks. The atmosphere oppresses her, along with the strict discipline, but gradually it is lightened by her closest relationships—with her cousin Cookie and her great-grandmother. The Georgia folks may be holier than thou, but Gayle discovers her true family resemblance to Miss Great, who remembers what it was like to be young and who coaxes her into making peach brandy according to the family recipe and tells her family stories. Gayle, treating her cousin like a "sister," teaches Cookie how to buy jeans that fit and how to overcome the shyness of the reserved, proper young man who is on the verge of falling in love with her, but she tempts Cookie into pride and disobedience, causing a family fracas that turns the sweet Cookie rude and rebellious.

Gayle's commitment to the family and the land is cemented by her great-grandmother, who prophesies that little José will follow in the family footsteps and become a preacher and then, in her last act of life, chants the family's oral history, entrusting it to Gayle, in the act known as the Telling. Gayle sees the angel of death come for her great-grandmother and knows she is joyous in heaven. To her astonishment, she finds her appreciation and understanding of her family's personalities illuminated, along with the history that she now treasures. Gayle even sympathizes with Uncle Luther, seeing his grief, discovers that she has earned her aunt's faith in her as a young woman with "good sense," and in a surprising role reversal, she prevents Cookie from running off by reminding Cookie that she is saved in a final emotional confrontation that helps each girl realize that she can save the other through their sisterhood.

Han Nolan's novels explore the meanings of love and of physical and emotional wellness in often odd family situations. *Dancing on the Edge* (1997) demonstrates that a family's silences can be as powerful as words in shaping a child's world. Miracle loves to dance, but she dances toward the "edge" of her sanity as her changing living arrangements with different family members challenge her ability to make sense of her world. Increasingly, she questions whether she even exists, until she dances into the flames of a circle of candles, and the flames' impact on her body assures her of her own existence.

Miracle's apparent suicide attempt results in counseling that enables her to confront her doubts about reality, doubts fostered by her psychic grandmother Gigi's stories and charms. Gigi's impact on Miracle's development limits her ability to distinguish between the true and the false. Magic numbers, clothes in colors chosen to enhance one's aura, séances, spiritual healing practices, stories of the past, restrictions on Miracle's activities and contact with her grandfather, expectations of Miracle's future as a "prodigy" like her father Dane's youthful writing of novels—all combine to give Miracle a rather vague sense of how to exert some control over her own life. This heritage of magical thinking combines with a proclivity for withdrawing into an imagined fairy world when the emotional stresses of her life grow too difficult to confront.

Mysteries and magical explanations abound. Her birth coincided with her mother's death, and her name reflects her grandmother's claim that her birth was a miracle. Her father, Dane, vanished from the home he shared with Miracle and her grandmother when Gigi's efforts to nurture his talent became so restrictive that he just left all his possessions behind one night—a disappearance that the family explains as Dane's having melted. Already concerned about her mother's death, Miracle believes she is responsible for her father's disappearance—and a bit unsure as to how and where he has gone, given her grandmother's claim that he melted. This story is largely responsible for her dancing into the flames several years later: she is trying to duplicate her father's feat. After weeks of treatment for the severe burns and weeks in a psychiatric ward, she finally confronts her grandmother with the knowledge that human beings do not melt—they burn.

Miracle's troubled state of mind should be glaringly evident to any of the adults entrusted with her care. She wears Dane's old bathrobe for years, retaining the sash when she is persuaded to take off the robe for dancing lessons and bike-riding, and finally clinging to a piece of it. She asks her mother's sister, Aunt Casey, to cut her hair like her father's. In each home where she lives, she attempts to re-create Dane's "cave"—the basement room full of books and candles where she enjoyed his early companionship. Her wild expressive dances lead her to bump into furniture all over the room, in early efforts to establish her reality, and she is covered with bruises. Yet none of the adults pays enough attention to notice what is going on in her thinking, and over the years, Miracle builds a worldview compounded of the decidedly eccentric adults' influences and her own fantastic interpretations of what she hears. When she learns of black holes from Grandaddy Opal, Miracle develops an elaborate theory that her father has gone back in time through a black hole to adjust events so that he can circumvent her mother's death and return, with her mother, to Miracle in a tornado. When the tornado results in destruction of the house but not her parents' reappearance, Miracle blames herself. Her Aunt Casey, taking psychology courses at the local university, is the person best qualified to detect the extent of Miracle's disconnect with reality, but Miracle and Gigi have moved away, Casey has problems of her own, and she shuts out awareness of her niece's problems.

Miracle's dance lessons are a secret she shares with Grandaddy Opal because her grandmother is opposed to her dancing. It is his decision to get her a bicycle and teach her to ride. He represents some degree of normality in her life, coaxing her into giving up Dane's bathrobe so that she can bicycle, and offers her love, but the heart attack he suffers after the tornado, along with the literal homelessness it brings, prevents Miracle's continuing to live with him. The family is divided—Gigi with a new husband with whom she opens a psychic cure center; Grandaddy Opal with his friend Miss Emmaline Wilson, to whom Aunt Casey's husband, Toole, objects because she is black; Aunt Casey and Uncle Toole, with whom Miracle ends up after the tornado, finally separating. Each of the households Miracle has lived in has been oddly cluttered—Dane rings himself with candles in bottles; Opal stacks *National Geographics* in precarious pillars; and Toole, a household mover, fills his home with customers' damaged castoff furniture. Similarly, the evasions and revised stories of the past have accumulated to almost completely hide Miracle's real being.

After Miracle dances into the flames, her injuries bring her the professional help she needs. Working with her aunt Casey and with Dr. DeAngelis, in the guise of an angel of deliverance, Miracle realizes a significant truth: her mother committed suicide. She was unable to cope with her loss of freedom and the knowledge that she would never achieve her dream of being a dancer. Casey realizes that no one has truly *loved* this child, and she offers Miracle the love that will help her survive and come back from "the edge." The insights of Casey and Dr. DeAngelis come just in time for Miracle to escape Gigi's attempt to kidnap her and set her up for a "miracle cure" to advertise her new business venture. Miracle knows, finally, that she is real, that love is real, and that she can count on her grandfather and her aunt to support her as she grows into a healthy adult.

Family structures in other cultures reflect their context as much as Miracle's family reflects its small-town Southern environment. Kazumi Yumoto portrays a Japanese teenager's coming to terms with family change and changes in herself in *The Spring Tone* (1995; translated by Cathy Hirano, 1999). Tomomi feels as if a monster is emerging from within her, turning her into a monster, as she faces adulthood: adults quarrel with one another; adults sicken and die. Since she has even wished for her grandmother's death during the last phase of painful terminal illness, Tomomi now believes herself to be monstrous.

At home, Tomomi faces changes wrought by her grandmother's recent death and her father's apparent separation from her mother, and her mother easily becomes angry. Living with her grandfather, Tomomi observes changes in his behavior as well as his stubborn refusal to stop smoking and seek medical attention for his persistent cough. Along with changes in her home life Tomomi struggles to accept the changes in her body that prompt the phys ed instructor, the male hairdresser, and a stranger she passes on the street to stare at her or touch her. She has begun getting headaches in response to the pressures of school and impending adulthood. She envies her brother Tetsu his child's privilege of self-centeredness until she realizes that he also feels the pressure of responsibility—for her, for the feral cats he cares for at the dump, for his attempts to defend the family by leaving dead cats in the hated next-door neighbor's yard.

The "spring tone" is the feeling the season brings to Tomomi. She is aware of the passage of time as she has never been before, fearing the disintegration of her family, with her father living in his studio, her mother working, her grandfather disappearing into the storage area, Tetsu roaming. Withdrawing from former friends and activities, she spends her spring vacation accompanying Tetsu on his quest for dead cats, a quest that acquaints her with a woman who twice daily lugs great pots of fish scraps and vegetables to several spots where she feeds strays. With Tetsu, she explores a dump near their home, even camping out in a derelict bus, accompanied by their grandfather after he brings them a warm blanket.

Her grandfather releases Tomomi from her fear that she is a monster when he tells her about a time in his youth when his own actions were monstrous. He explains that the incident taught him that one should never fight over material things, a lesson that helps Tomomi understand why he himself does not fight with their neighbor over the wall that encroaches on their property. He teaches Tomomi another lesson as well, pointing out that her wish for the end of her grandmother's pain was a product of empathy and she could not have experienced such empathy had she been younger, so it is a positive result of growing up. Released from guilt, Tomomi recognizes that the passage of time will bring change, no matter what she does (and one of the changes will be her grandfather's death).

The spring ends with health crises that all human parties survive: the woman who feeds the cats becomes ill, and Tetsu and Tomomi take over her cat-feeding job till she recovers; the next-door neighbor collapses in a passion of anger at Tetsu when he misinterprets Tetsu's carrying home a sick cat as another effort to deposit a dead cat in his yard, but he recovers after treatment; Tomomi falls ill and is hospitalized. She feels her grandmother's protective spiritual presence during her illness, brought on the scent of her grandmother's fan. The spring brings the beginnings of reconciliation between her parents. Most importantly for Tomomi, the spring's events have helped her come to terms with becoming an adult: she is ready to face life's ills as well as its pleasures. When Tetsu shares his discovery of three lizard's eggs just hatching, she is able to see her adult self as a hatchling rather than a monster.

The life of a village girl in contemporary India is the subject of *Homeless Bird* (2000) by Gloria Whelan. In this society, a young woman's marriage is arranged by parents; she leaves her family permanently when she marries; the quality of her life is determined by her mother-in-law's and husband's temperaments; and she may be cast aside as a worthless burden on the family when widowed. Bound by traditions that limit young females' education to housekeeping, a girl has no control over her own life, dependent on her husband and his family for every grain of rice that nourishes her. The novel's protagonist is a "homeless bird" with no place to call her own, her life prospects grim until she puts her artistic skills to use to earn her own living, defying the tradition that would keep her dependent and impoverished for life.

Because her family is too poor to feed her, Koly is married off at age thirteen to a boy who is dying of tuberculosis. His parents have lied to her parents about his age and health so that they can get her dowry to take him to the holy city of Varanasi on the Ganges River in a desperate search for healing. It is a hopeless venture; Hari dies almost upon arrival in the holy city. Without having experienced real marriage, Koly loses the little status she held. She lives with her mean mother-in-law, unable ever to satisfy her, working like the lowliest servant, often hungry, her widow's pension appropriated by her in-laws.

Yet for a few years she finds compensations. Her kind father-in-law, a teacher who is delighted by Koly's thirst for learning, teaches her to read, and she finds a sister in Hari's sister Chandra—until Chandra's marriage takes her away, an event followed a year later by her father-in-law's death. Ever an optimist, Koly eases her loneliness by feeding a mangy stray dog until her mother-in-law discovers it, and then taming the bandicoot that lives under the house. She has a loving nature and, throughout most of her three years under her mother-in-law's domination, tries to please her. Koly is a skilled artist who brings her own fresh perspective to the scenes of village life that she embroiders on her wedding quilt, on a quilt for her mother-in-law memorializing Hari, and on a wedding quilt for Chandra. However, she loses the pleasures of both reading and embroidering after her father-in-law's death: her mother-in-law believes women should not read, so she keeps Koly too busy for reading, and she refuses to supply the materials for any more quilts.

Given her mother-in-law's unkindness, why does Koly not return home to her own family? Nothing but shame and disgrace would attend her return home, and she cannot visit such humiliation upon her family, who, she is sure, would be hard-pressed to feed her even if they were willing to take her in again. Koly hopes for eventual escape, but her prospects are slim after she gives up her silver wedding earrings in exchange for her father-in-law's cherished collection of Tagore's poems. Her mother-in-law's meanness, however, leads her to abandon Koly in Vrindavan, a city where thousands of unwanted widows live on charity, and ultimately this proves more blessing than curse. A rare chain of events leads Koly to protection, delivering her from the need to live literally on the streets or to chant prayers all day in a temple in return for food. A benefactress helps her find work embroidering saris at a decent, though meager, wage that brings her independence.

Independence has its price, though. When her friend, a young rickshaw driver turned farmer, proposes marriage, Koly is reluctant to choose love if it means giving up her freedom again, along with her income, although she appreciates his offer, knowing that many people consider it bad luck to marry a widow. She misses him when he returns to his land, and when he builds a room in his modest house for her embroidery, his action convinces her to follow her heart and marry him. The home-less bird finally finds a home where she will be loved and honored.

ADDITIONAL READING RECOMMENDATIONS

Home before Dark, 1976, and *All Together Now*, 1979, by Sue Ellen Bridgers
Sweet Whispers, Brother Rush by Virginia Hamilton, 1982
Night Kites by M. E. Kerr, 1986
White Peak Farm by Berlie Doherty, 1990
The Book of the Banshee by Anne Fine, 1992 (discussed in Breaking Silence, Speaking Out)
Shadow of the Dragon by Sherry Garland, 1993
Adam and Eve and Pinch-Me by Julie Johnson, 1994
Zero at the Bone by Michael Cadnum, 1996
Flyers by Daniel Hayes, 1996
Dangerous Angels: The Weetzie Bat Books by Francesca Lia Block, 1998
One Thing That's True by Cheryl Foggo, 1998
Backwater by Joan Bauer, 1999 (discussed in Survival)
Ties That Break, Ties That Bind by Lensey Namioka, 1999
A Face in Every Window by Han Nolan, 1999
A Step from Heaven by An Na, 2001
Counting Stars by David Almond, 2002
I Am Not Esther by Fleur Beale, 2002
Holly Starcross by Berlie Doherty, 2002
Son of the Mob by Gordon Korman, 2002
Our Time on the River by Don Brown, 2003

Friends Forever?

Remembering the Good Times by Richard Peck (1985)
Freak the Mighty by Rodman Philbrick (1993)
Letters from the Inside by John Marsden (1994)
The Sisterhood of the Traveling Pants by Ann Brashares (2001)
The Second Summer of the Sisterhood by Ann Brashares
   (2003)
Catalyst by Laurie Halse Anderson (2002)

In adolescence, peers replace family members as the primary confidants and shapers of behavior, and it sometimes seems as if the relationships formed then will last forever. Yet this is also a period of immense growth and change, factors that challenge friendships. Young adults' increasing independence, resulting in jobs, after-school activities, competitions, and dating, bring them into new, stimulating, and challenging situations. A desire for stability vies with a desire for new experiences. Some friendships will survive in the resulting balancing act, and some will not. Friendship is an important element of many novels discussed in other chapters, especially Chapter 31: Teammates, but it is the primary focus of novels discussed here.

Richard Peck establishes an elegiac tone throughout *Remembering the Good Times* (1985), stressing the theme of loss—lost family wholeness, lost rural peace, lost friends, lost innocence. The tone evokes an elderly person's nostalgia for a past that seems the more idyllic for being irrevocable, and indeed Polly Prior, the most important adult in the book, is old. Great-grandmother of the narrator Buck's friend Kate, Polly Prior remembers McKinley's presidency, graduated from high school in a class of three, and lost her older brother in World War I. The changes in the period the novel covers, however, are far more rapid-paced. Buck chronicles the problems caused by suburban life's incursions into the rural community where, after a period of summer visits, he moves into his father's mobile home when his mother moves across the country. Except for a short epilogue, the novel ends after the death of Buck and Kate's close friend Trav at the beginning of their sophomore year when the pear orchard they all cherish is sold to finance Kate's college education and the developers have begun carving the land into residential lots.

Despite this setting in a period of change, the novel has spaces and moments that seem impervious to change. Until Polly Prior sells off the orchard, Kate's special place—a clearing that was her great-grandmother's special place too, before she was confined to a wheelchair—exists timelessly except for the changing of the seasons. Polly Prior's bedroom, in contrast, is crowded with time, a museum to her life's history. When she pulls Halloween/Homecoming outfits for Kate, Trav, and Buck out of drawers and boxes, the four of them move to the clearing for a twilight photograph—Kate in an early twentieth-century dress, Trav in World War I uniform, Buck in a raccoon coat—and Buck feels as though they have been pulled into a "time warp" or another world. The novel's action is confined to a small area, the high school, the orchard, Kate's and Travis's homes. Trav and Buck spend months away from the area, but the narrative skips over these times. It is only the magical space that counts, in which their friendship flowers and they experience loss and separation from parents and each other.

The magic of the orchard is destroyed as much by Trav's suicide in the clearing as by the earth-moving equipment, its timelessness giving way to permanent change, just as the community has undergone permanent change—the importing of impersonal violence along with the suburban houses. Trying to change with the times, Scotty and Irene, friends of Buck's father, transform their Sunoco garage into a twenty-four-hour convenience store, where Scotty loses his life in a late-night robbery that nets the thief eighty-five dollars. Trav's inability to change, to meet his own perfectionist demands of himself in his parents' upwardly mobile life, results first in breakdown, then in suicide.

Trav's suicide is foreshadowed in his clinging to his own past, preserved in neatly arranged collections of Matchbox cars, marbles, and baseball cards, collections that he unabashedly exposes to Buck and Kate's view when they attend an upscale Christmas party in his home. His self-imposed doom is more significantly foreshadowed in his poem about remembering the pear blossoms in threatening early winter weather. Just before taking his life, he bestows gifts of his possessions—his prized pocket calculator for Buck, his old Paddington Bear for Kate—but they miss the significance of this act because he has just returned from a summer of outdoor work on his cousin's farm in Iowa, and he gives Polly Prior a newly purchased gift at the same time.

The nostalgic mood is underscored with Kate's discovery of her acting talent in Tennessee Williams' "memory play" *The Glass Menagerie*. Like this novel's central characters, the play revolves around an older woman, a young woman, and two young men and shows fragile people under pressure.

The elegiac tone is also reinforced by the relative absence of their parents' generation in the novel. Buck refers to his father's good qualities at several important moments, but Kate's mother is flashy and flighty, and it is Kate who takes care of Polly Prior, while Trav's parents are reserved, subdued, always correct. Buck sees his father's grief when his friend Scotty dies, and he realizes that his father is not always calm, collected, and wise, though the reader suspects he has already lost faith in his parents when they divorce and his mother moves away. Polly Prior is as outspoken and full of life at the end of the novel as at the beginning, and it is she who can utter the words that bring healing to the community, helping them confront their grief at Trav's suicide by moving them from assigning blame or offering glib explanations. It is Polly Prior, too, who gives utterance to the novel's title, declaring that she may not always remember everything correctly because she only "[remembers] the good times."

Of course, the young people change and grow out of the prepubescent innocence in which their friendship was established. Such innocence cannot last, and the characters' physical maturing is marked by emotional tensions—especially Buck's jealousy of the special closeness he suspects between Kate and Trav. Violence impinges on their idyll, initiated by the school bully, who beats up Buck and threatens a pretty young teacher until Kate takes uncharacteristic action to wreak shockingly violent revenge. These tensions, the pressures that drive Trav, and the violence that accompanies change all contribute to their exile from Edenic bliss as they reach the brink of adulthood. In this novel, change is sudden and fast-paced, bringing an increase in violence. Hence it is no surprise that the effects are violent too.

In *Freak the Mighty* (1993; reprinted as *The Mighty*), Rodman Philbrick shows the inspirational power of heroic tales as he tells a poignant story of the friendship between Max, a huge young teen who is isolated by his apparent learning disability and the emotional effects of his having witnessed his father's murder of his mother, and Kevin, his tiny, highly intelligent and imaginative neighbor whom disease has crippled. Their unlikely friendship is permeated with the romance of chivalry, as Kevin's imagination transforms everything they do together into a bigger-than-life story. With Max's strength and Kevin's wit, they unite—Kevin literally riding on Max's shoulders—as an unbeatable hero, Freak the Mighty, in an act of naming that redefines Kevin's nickname, "Freak." Basking in Kevin's friendship and his faith in Max's intelligence, which has been hidden by Max's silence in school, he is briefly released from loneliness and revealed as a sweet, gentle soul deeply hurt by his mother's death rather than the monster that his size and incommunicability suggest to others. Kevin convinces Max that his visits to the hospital are fitting him for a bionic body, and not until after Kevin's death does Max realizes that these tales were mere fantasy, a way of coping with his terminal disease. Though Max mourns his friend's death, their time together frees Max from a prison of self-doubt and enables his grandparents to begin to appreciate him.

Max's withdrawal is symbolized by his life in the Down Under, his basement bedroom where he has nothing better to do than read comic books until Kevin moves in next door. Max likes his isolation from his grandparents, with whom he lives, because he recognizes their fear of what he might become now that he is at the "dangerous age" of early puberty. He looks more and more like his father as he grows taller and his shoe size reaches fourteen, and he fears discovering even more resemblances in himself. Strangers, even Kevin's mother, Gwen, blanch when they first see him, but Gwen is quick to see beyond his likeness to her friend's killer. She appreciates the value of Max's friendship with her son, who is isolated too—by disease, his pedantic language, and his unself-conscious dramatization of ordinary events.

Max's narrative is very funny, largely due to the quirky Kevin, who imagines Max equal to any physical assault, even though Max himself eschews violence. His huge polysyllabic vocabulary, coupled with his predilection for glamorizing every event, lends his language a humorous formality. The Arthurian veil he casts over their little adventures is suggested from the beginning by his calling his mother the Fair Gwen or the Fair Guinevere. The particular appeal that the Knights of the Round Table hold is their robotic or bionic element, he explains to Max: their armor is a forerunner of the cyborg-populated future he wants to pioneer. Kevin's wit and logophilia are encapsulated in "Freak's Dictionary," appended to the narrative, a brief dictionary of terms humorously defined by Kevin, his gift to Max at the end of his life.

Kevin's biting sarcasm nearly leads Max into confrontation with the neighborhood's knife-carrying bullies. In the aftermath, Max's grandparents reveal their innocence and their treatment of him, as Gram encourages Max to "run away" from the "hoodlum boy" and Grim (whose taciturnity makes this sobriquet appropriate) endorses this recommendation as "taking evasive action." The reader, privy to Max's thoughts, recognizes the degree to which Max protects his grandparents, who underestimate the real danger he is in. This danger, however, is nothing compared to that threatened by his father, "Killer Kane," who escapes from prison and kidnaps Max, until the combination of Max's strength and Kevin's intelligence frees Max and delivers his father into the hands of the police.

Kevin's ability to see Max for who he is helps others view him more clearly and accurately. In school, Kevin encourages Max to speak out, revealing his freedom from learning disability. Max's deep empathy is an important support to his friend, and his friend's mother, in the last months of Kevin's life, though Max allows himself to believe in Kevin's fantasies about survival in a bionic body. It is their friendship that empowers each boy, and, while Kevin readily shares stories of heroes, what this narrative finally reveals is the power of collaboration to create a hero.

Australian writer John Marsden's epistolary novel *Letters from the Inside* (1994) leaves the reader with the mystery of an unresolved ending. The letters chronicle a friendship between an inmate in a juvenile correctional center and a teen who leads a largely normal suburban life. The correspondence extends over nearly a year, beginning when Tracey places a personal ad in a teen magazine and Mandy responds, not knowing her new pen pal is in jail for a serious crime. When she learns the truth about Tracey, Mandy continues to write to her, hearing in those "letters from the inside" a genuine, vulnerable voice that she wants to believe represents the "real" Tracey. Keeping up the correspondence represents a growth in Mandy's understanding of others, rather than a truly equal friendship. Tracey never wants to hear about genuinely dark moments in Mandy's life, and when Mandy confides her fears of her older brother Steve's potentially sociopathic violence, Tracey simply ignores them. As their mutual understanding and friendship grow, Tracey explores some of her discomfort over the crime that led to her incarceration, a crime that is never identified though hints emerge, and she sheds some of the tough exterior she maintains for self-preservation in cellblock A. About the time that the reader hopes for real transformation of Tracey's character and her ultimate rehabilitation, Mandy simply disappears. Now dependent on Mandy's friendship, Tracey becomes depressed and increasingly desperate when several letters are returned. The reader is left speculating that the constant threat of violence that has shadowed Tracey's every action on the inside has been realized in some way—most likely in the fashion of the violence at Columbine High School—in Mandy's apparently safer life.

At first, the fifteen-year-olds' friendship develops within a veil of lies that expose some of the most superficial elements of "typical" teen girls' friendships. Tracey describes a fantasy life—with a loving family, plenty of money, a horse and dogs, a dream of a boyfriend, designer-label clothes, expensive vacations—but Mandy ferrets out the truth when she attempts to have a letter hand-delivered to Tracey via a foreign exchange student at the school Tracey claimed to attend. Tracey finally reveals her incarceration, explaining that she really wants to hear about normal teen life. Indeed, she seems to hunger for the life she might have had and will miss, having been sentenced to move directly from the juvenile facility to a women's prison when she turns eighteen. Confronted with the gravity of Tracey's problems of simply surviving in Garrett, Mandy reevaluates the ups and downs of her own life. When she brings herself to confide in her parents that her pen pal is incarcerated, she is surprised by the outcome: her father admits to a short stint in a correctional facility as a teen and tells her how important letters can be to an inmate, and her mother slips a little chocolate into the Christmas gift Mandy mails to Tracey.

Tracey's revelations of the truth about her life come slowly—through her sharing of the prize-winning essay she has written about her grandmother's slow slipping toward death, in a letter about her father's violence and murder of her mother.

Mandy, less threatened on a day-to-day basis, nonetheless fears her brother but tells Tracey she's been unable to convince her parents of the gravity of the threat he poses. In the last of her letters, she reports his outcast status as he graduates, his lack of prospects for the future, his preoccupation with the guns his grandfather has bequeathed to him. The plot unfolds entirely through the letters, so the indeterminate ending appears through several unanswered letters from Tracey to Mandy, ending with clear indications of her depression and withdrawal due to her fears for Mandy and the loss of her friendship. Tracey's inability to receive news and her lack of family make it unlikely she will learn what has become of Mandy for years to come.

Mandy's importance to Tracey is clear when she begins calling her "manna" in her letters, in reference to the "bread from heaven" that sustained the Israelites as they wandered for forty years in the wilderness under Moses' guidance, caught between enslavement in Egypt and the promised land. The Hebrew root of *manna*, like its Arabic cognate, means "to show favor" or "to be kind," meanings that aptly describe Mandy's letters to Tracey.

A more lighthearted mood prevails in *The Sisterhood of the Traveling Pants* (2001) and its sequel, *The Second Summer of the Sisterhood* (2003), by Ann Brashares. Four teens' friendship is symbolized in the "traveling pants," the magical blue jeans that fit, flatter, and therefore empower each member of the "sisterhood." The girls' friendship predates their birth within seventeen days of each other: their mothers became friends in an aerobics class for pregnant women, where they were known as the "Septembers" for their babies' due dates. The girls are a diverse group to be so close, representing a range of family structures, ethnicities, talents, and even schools. Their summers together have cemented their friendship as their experiences grew in different directions. In the first novel, they spend their first summer apart, and the pants become their symbol of continuing love and support, passed from one friend to the next to be worn in situations that require confidence. This novel brings out the importance of appearance, showing how it affects young women's self-esteem and confidence. The second novel, with a special focus on romantic love, involves less geographical separation and actually shows friendship in action more fully, as well as characterizing their mothers more fully as the surviving Septembers move toward reunion.

The four friends' separate stories are interwoven through their communications, which generally accompany the pants in the mail, with brief email exchanges, phone calls, and face-to-face conversations fleshing out interactions in the sequel. In *The Sisterhood*, Tibby faces the challenge of being left behind to start her first job and evade playing mother's helper to two much younger siblings in diapers, while the rest of the sisters venture out of their suburban world. Tibby meets new people and reevaluates the way she judges others. Lena steps outside the wall that her beauty, along with her intense need for personal privacy, forms around her and connects to her Greek heritage. The passionate Carmen copes with the stepfamily that her father springs on her at the outset of her first summer visit with him—a stepfamily, moreover, whose restrained Anglo ways contrast dramatically with her ethnicity and emotional openness. The athletic Bee is challenged to keep a lid on her volatile emotions at a high-powered soccer camp in Baja California.

These girls are smart, talented, and, much of the time, confident. Lena paints and, because of her beauty, is cautious but secure; in Greece, she discovers her temperamental likeness to her grandfather. Carmen's confidence in her mathematical skills is not balanced by confidence in her father's love; she is afraid of being angry at her father, afraid of losing him. Bee is a high-powered competitor and able to wield considerable sexual power with her spectacular blond hair, though both traits, combined with sometimes reckless impulsiveness, can get her in trouble. Her mother, from the Netherlands, suffered from unspecified emotional problems, and as Bee's story unfolds, the reader begins to suspect she is bipolar. Tibby's talent is in filmmaking, and she acquires, against her will, a twelve-year-old assistant in her summer documentary project, an assistant who Tibby learns has leukemia. Only because her friends are gone does Tibby find herself growing close to this odd and endearing younger girl, an experience that proves quite meaningful for both of them. All the girls need courage to get through their special challenges, and the pants help them find their courage.

In *The Second Summer*, their friendship is more clearly in evidence, through phone calls, emails, and time spent together. Family relationships play a bigger role on the whole: both Lena and Bee seek more information about their mothers. Carmen and Tibby repeat their mistakes of the previous summer. The magic of the pants seems to work more for Carmen's pretty, youthful mother than for the sisters, until late in the summer when the heartbroken Lena needs their magic to regain confidence in her own beauty and lovability.

Despite the many serious issues addressed and the emotional veracity of these novels, a light, often comic, tone is maintained most of the time, reinforced by the elevation of the pants to the status of magical object through ritual and rules governing their use. Collectively, the four friends face a wide range of challenges in the two novels: recognizing love; readiness for sex, especially when they look more confident than they are; the ability to distinguish the genuine from the false in others; understanding of family dynamics in the form of younger siblings, death of a parent or grandparent, alienation or distance from parents or grandparents, and single parents' search for new love; death of a contemporary with leukemia; handling weight gain and depression. The mothers are more diverse than their daughters and their lives have taken significantly different courses, but they reforge the friendship that lapsed with Bee's mother's death at the end of the second summer, bearing witness to the elasticity and enduring nature of friendship. The celebration of love with which the second novel ends acknowledges the many manifestations of love they have encountered.

In *Catalyst* (2002), Laurie Halse Anderson revisits the high school community of *Speak* (discussed in Chapter 7: Breaking Silence, Speaking Out) to focus on science geek Kate Malone, who is awaiting MIT's admission decision. Kate's life is methodical and structured. She takes care of her minister father and fourteen-year-old brother, runs cross-country, earns top grades, and attends church social functions as well as services. Lately, though, she has suffered from insomnia and gone for late-night runs; at these times the reader sees beneath her calm surface into her bifurcation into "good Kate" and "bad Kate," which enables her to sardonically voice her negative feelings. Chaos and change erupt into Kate's life when her neighbors' house fire brings the hostile and aggressive social outcast Teri Litch to share her bedroom, especially when Teri's two-year-old brother, Mikey, insists on sleeping in her room as well. Kate's concerns—relationships with friends and anxiety over her college future—are swallowed up in the Litch family's tragedy, and an unlikely friendship takes fragile root, giving Kate's life a new direction.

As in *Speak*, Anderson interweaves a number of themes and symbols. Content of sections, chapters, and subchapters is signaled with chemistry terminology. Each of the three parts of the novel begins with a quotation from a high school chemistry textbook, pointing up parallels between chemical reactions and human relations. Kate describes her family structure as an atom, with herself and her brother as proton and neutron and her father as loosely bonded electrons. Sections of chapters are numbered like sections of a scientific report (e.g., 1.1.1, 1.1.2), except for the climactic event of the novel, which is numbered 0.0.0 and titled "Quantum Shift."

Also, each chapter begins with a safety rule for a chem lab, but lab procedures ensure no safety in life. Kate's dominant concern has been her failure to apply to "safety" colleges, having staked her whole future on MIT, her dead mother's alma mater. Kate defines herself through science because it operates through regular laws, unlike her pastor father's religion. She further defines herself in opposition to the humanities and professes her surprise at having a boyfriend who plans to major in history and become a college professor. She drifts through a mythology class, certain that it has nothing of value for her education, caricaturing the student teacher who, she notes, is three years older than she is. Despite her dismissal of art and the art students, it is the artist Melinda (protagonist of *Speak*) who offers comfort immediately after Kate's rejection by MIT.

Yet Kate the scientist has no more control over her fate than do the tragic Greek figures she studies. Despite her concern with safety, following procedures and observing rules to obtain predictable results, she cannot ensure consistent results in life situations. Under pressure, Kate threatens to explode, and early signals of the stress she's experiencing are her insomnia and her running, the latter looking more like obsession than disciplined cross-country training, especially when the reader learns that Kate began running in fourth grade by literally running away from her mother's funeral.

As emotional pressure mounts, bifurcated "good Kate/bad Kate" begins to shatter into fragments, losing her ability to cope and keep things in order. At the same time, her new contact lenses give her clearer vision, enabling her to see her relationships more clearly, and this helps her see the narrowness of her friends' and her concerns over grades, class rank, and college acceptance.

Kate's family suffers from chronic health problems: migraines, asthma, allergies. Part of the job Kate has taken on at home is to remind her family to take their medications, and she works in a pharmacy. Her mother died of pneumonia, quite suddenly, so health has become a preoccupation. Throughout the novel's crisis period, Kate keeps questioning whether she may have the flu, and she suffers from a sore pectoral muscle throughout the novel. Thus, stress takes a toll on the family, though they do not talk about it. Every time Kate's father takes a normal fatherly interest in her college plans, she avoids his questions. Much of the stress she is under, therefore, is the result of her refusal to be open about her doubts and fears. Whatever it is, Kate thinks, she can handle it.

One of the novel's major themes, then, is the conflicting explanations of life given by religion and science. Another, related one is safety: are there rules we can follow to protect us from accident, illness, death? Volatile individuals and emotions cannot be controlled, and life circumstances cannot be controlled through observing the rules.

Friendship is central to the novel. Circumstances unite Teri and Kate in unforeseeable ways, forging an unlikely bond. Teri's family has suffered dramatic effects from abuse, a circumstance that offers an explanation for her larger-than-life, vindictive anger, which at first repels calm, controlled Kate—"good Kate," at any rate; she allows her "bad" alter ego to snipe at her controlled behavior and demeanor. Kate's own loss is reawakened by new tragedy and her brother Toby's questions about the funeral he cannot remember.

The house that Teri first attempts to rebuild, then attempts to destroy, and finally reverts to rebuilding, serves as another metaphorical frame for family relationships, echoed in Kate's fondness for cleanliness, order, and perfectly ironed clothes and her boyfriend Mitch's dramatic cleaning of his room and change of career goal from history prof to economist, from the impractical to the practical. Just as Kate learns that practicality cannot protect us from all of life's misfortunes, Mitch embraces it.

As a budding scientist, Kate has avoided essay writing, and ironically it is her writing skills that play a large part in MIT's admissions decision. She is, however, an inveterate maker of lists—listing supplies for house construction one day and strategies for circumventing MIT's rejection another. Bored and frustrated by the apparent irrelevance of Greek mythology, Kate suddenly sees Teri as a figure out of Greek tragedy, her sorrow and loss of Mikey undeserved and benumbing in their immensity. In her preoccupation with what is "practical," Kate has overlooked the relevance of Athena and Artemis to understanding herself: Athena's birth as a father's daughter, from the head rather than the loins, dispassionate and intelligent; Artemis' fleetness of foot and association with the moon. Yet Kate's practicality pales in comparison to Teri's know-how: Teri's ability to hot-wire a car or drive a nail with elegant precision demonstrates to Kate the limits of her own abilities, revealing that Kate is largely imprisoned in abstract intellectualism. Ultimately, though, none of the characters has the skill to build a safe haven from accident and grief.

The central metaphor is the catalyst, the substance that facilitates a reaction. Small Mikey is the catalyst, bonding those who love him. Kate's vision clears at last, as she abandons her obsession with colleges, test scores, and grades to form a real, supportive relationship with another young woman, who—surprisingly like Kate herself—has had to assume adult responsibilities for others at an early age.

Like Melinda's voice in *Speak*, Kate's voice is smart, caustic, and funny. Anderson's most impressive feat in both novels is to reveal a character fully while putting off until the end the reader's crucial insight into what has made her what she is, in order to maintain narrative suspense. Both deal with painful subjects in satisfyingly complex ways.

ADDITIONAL READING RECOMMENDATIONS

The Planet of Junior Brown by Virginia Hamilton, 1971
That Was Then, This Is Now by S. E. Hinton, 1971
Trying Hard to Hear You by Sandra Scoppettone, 1974
The Trouble with Lemons, 1991, *Eye of the Beholder*, 1992, and *No Effect*, 1993, by Daniel Hayes
The Boy in the Moon by Ron Koertge, 1991 (discussed in Sexual Identity, Sexual Desire)
Life Belts by Jane Hosie-Bounar, 1993
A Time for Dancing by Davida Wills Hurwin, 1994 (discussed in Disease and Disability)
I Am an Artichoke by Lucy Frank, 1995
Far North by Will Hobbs, 1996 (discussed in Survival)
The Schernoff Discoveries by Gary Paulsen, 1997
Violet and Claire by Francesca Lia Block, 1999
Safe at Second by Scott Johnson, 1999
Amandine by Adele Griffin, 2001
Damage by A. M. Jenkins, 2001 (discussed in Emotional Problems Confronted)
God of Beer by Garret Keizer, 2002 (discussed in Accidents and Adjustments)
Big Mouth and Ugly Girl by Joyce Carol Oates, 2002 (discussed in School Days)
Buddha Boy by Kathe Koja, 2003 (discussed in Religion and Spiritual Life)

Guilty or Innocent?

If Beale Street Could Talk by James Baldwin (1974)
Monster by Walter Dean Myers (1999)
The Killer's Cousin by Nancy Werlin (1998)
The Body of Christopher Creed by Carol Plum-Ucci (2003)

Many readers love the mystery genre, enjoying the suspense created when a crime has been committed and investigation into the identity of the criminal motivates the plot. A satisfying mystery leaves the reader with a clear resolution, but such resolutions may be rare in real life. In reality, guilt may be partial or shared; heroes and villains are not so sharply divided as genre fiction would have us believe; society may play a more significant role than individuals. Acceptance of moral ambiguity and qualified culpability is a mark of adulthood, and several interesting novels avoid simplistic explanations of responsibility for crimes, or in one case disappearance.

James Baldwin's powerful novels address complexity in relationships and actions; *If Beale Street Could Talk* (1974) revolves around twenty-two-year-old Fonny, who has been arrested for rape in this story narrated by Tish, his fiancée. Tish is pregnant, and her family and Fonny's father are determined to save Fonny, for the baby's, Tish's, and Fonny's own sake. Each family member contributes in some way to purchase him a good defense, doing research and legwork themselves, and Tish visits Fonny daily to keep prison life from destroying him before he comes to trial. As she adjusts to pregnancy and develops her ability to endure emotional strain, she reviews the events that led to Fonny's present situation, in the process giving the reader a detailed picture of Black life in 1960s–1970s Harlem.

Is Fonny guilty? Tish's mother, Sharon, cannot imagine it. Yet Fonny has alluded to visiting prostitutes and suggests he has sought more than run-of-the-mill sex. The rape victim is a prostitute, who identified Fonny in a lineup—a lineup in which he was the only black man—and then went home to Puerto Rico. Sharon pleads with her to reconsider her identification, but the victim adamantly refuses, then suffers a breakdown that leads to institutionalization. Fonny's best friend, Daniel, is at first willing to give Fonny an alibi, but Daniel has recently been released after two years in prison, an experience that broke him, and the defense attorney fears that the prosecution will pressure him to change his testimony.

At the heart of the accusation is the brutality of a racist society. Fonny has made an enemy of a white police officer, an officer who has pressured Tish for sexual favors and who earlier tried to arrest Fonny for assault on a white drug user who harassed Tish at a fruit stand. Both Tish and Fonny fear they have made a dangerous enemy, and the power that white authority and institutions hold over young black men is evident at every turn.

Just as insidious are the anger and the effect of racism within Fonny's family. His mother, a light-skinned beauty from Atlanta who has built her life around her evangelical religion, believes her son and husband are lost. With her daughters, she is willing to testify that Fonny has run wild and is capable of any criminal act. Fonny's father, already troubled by alcoholism, turns to stealing from his employer to raise money for Fonny's defense, though for many years he led a respectable, if not evangelical Christian, life.

Passions drive this novel. Black rage underpins the tenderness of sexual and family love, and this rage takes the form of profanity in the novel. Anger brought Tish and Fonny together as children. Fonny describes overhearing the sounds of his parents' Sunday night sexual routine, combining his mother's conviction of his father's damnation with his father's deliberate blasphemy. Fonny's first sculpture embodies the black man's fierce struggle against being caged in American society. Indeed, the physicality of the novel is forceful. Tish's first sexual experience with Fonny is described in enough detail to convey the combination of pain and joy that she feels. While the description of Daniel's prison life is not graphic, Tish realizes that he has been beaten and raped, and he is only a shell of his former self. Anger rages between Tish's and Fonny's families over Tish's pregnancy and Fonny's prospects for life as a responsible father.

Characterization is complex, avoiding any easy black/white good/bad victim/oppressor dichotomies. In this novel, black characters are powerful but profoundly challenged people.

Twenty-five years later, in *Monster* (1999), Walter Dean Myers invites the reader to join a jury in assessing felony murder defendant Steve Harmon's innocence, through a felicitous union of structure, graphic presentation, and content. Is Steve a "monster," as the prosecutor portrays him? Or is he a good person who has been drawn into complicity in a crime he did not actually commit? The story unfolds through brief passages from a journal Steve is keeping during the days of his trial, presented as hand-printed words on gray pages, and highlights of the trial, presented as a screenplay that Steve is writing during his trial, using it to make sense of the trial, which seems to him like a black-and-white movie, a drama in which he does not have a role. The novel also has a few illustrations, grainy gray photographs of Steve.

As the reader pieces together the evidence presented—in the courtroom, in Steve's journals, in pictures, and in the screenplay—the story that unfolds shows a young Harlem man from a strong, religious family, a bit of a loner, sharing his neighbors' consensus that it is increasingly difficult to get along financially. When Steve's screenplay takes the reader out of the courtroom to view interactions in the neighborhood, he is shown in a passive role, listening and indicating brief agreement as neighbors discuss the best prospects for robbery. Apparently, the other defendant in the case, twenty-three-year-old James King, turned the store owner's gun against him in a struggle, killing. The fourteen-year-old gang member who has previously taunted Steve as a "lame," as shown in a flashback, claims to have been coerced into acting as lookout for the crime. The third man involved, in his twenties, has worked out a plea bargain in return for his testimony. He claims that Steve's role was to check out the pharmacy before the two men entered to rob the proprietor.

Is Steve a reliable narrator? The reader witnesses the trial only through Steve's screenplay, titled "Monster." In his journal, Steve writes that his attorney has warned him not to record anything in it that he wouldn't want the prosecuting attorney to read. Consequently, the journal portrays Steve's feelings—his hatred of jail, his constant fear, his uncertainty about how the trial is going, his worry over whether he is indeed the "monster" he is being portrayed as, but it is ultimately no more reliable than his movie. Steve is concerned that the prosecutor intends the jury to see him as the same kind of person as the unsavory witnesses on the stand. In addition to the others implicated in the crime, who freely admit their roles in the crime while accusing James King of having actually murdered the pharmacy's owner, the witnesses include two inmates who learned of the crime through purchasing stolen cigarettes. Their own characters, and truthfulness, are at least suspect.

In the company of these young black men whose history includes breaking and entering, dealing drugs, and committing gang-initiation-related violence, Steve protests his essential goodness. But clearly his hold on his concept of himself as a good person is tenuous, especially when he is confronted again and again with the facts of the murder, along with skepticism about his innocence from detectives, prison guards, and his own attorney. Even his difficult brief interactions with his bewildered parents fail to convince him that he is still good. In one brief, poignant scene, we see Steve in happier days watching TV with his younger brother, talking about what it would be like to be a superhero who saves people. This scene follows upon a silhouetted depiction of two prisoners' beating of another prisoner that culminates in a sexual assault. Clearly, Steve has not lived up to the heroic image he imagined for himself and, to his lasting pain, the big-brother image he presented to his brother, Jerry.

The degree of Steve's responsibility for the crime is not resolved. His sense of himself is shaken as a result of his experience, and at the end of the novel he continues to question whether he is a monster; the reader may question it too.

Nancy Werlin's *The Killer's Cousin* (1998) is a psychological drama with ghostly elements. This narrative, too, is a first-person account by a teen who has been tried for murder. Eighteen-year-old David lost much of his senior year of high school in the murder trial after his girlfriend's death, so he is finishing high school at a private school in another city, living in an attic apartment in his uncle and aunt's home. David was acquitted and Emily's death was ruled accidental, but his relationship with his parents, especially his father, has been seriously damaged. Moreover, David is famous, and although he's in a different city, people recognize his name, even his face. Despite his acquittal, many people still believe he murdered Emily, but no one articulates the suspicion like his younger cousin Lily.

The family situation that David moves into in Boston is more strained than his own. Soon after his arrival, David discovers that Vic and Julia communicate through twelve-year-old Lily, even at the dinner table. The apartment he is using was previously inhabited by Lily's older sister, Kathy, a victim of apparent suicide. Lily is, not surprisingly, an odd child. She watches him, expressing hostility, invades his space because she believes it should have been hers, spies on David when he kisses a girl, then reports made-up stories about their sexual activities to her parents, and trashes his computer and CDs.

Upon David's arrival, she asks him if he felt powerful when his girlfriend died. Eventually, David learns that Lily was present when Kathy died—drinking household chemicals and drowning in the bathtub—and this confirms his belief that she is in serious need of psychological help, even before he realizes that Lily murdered her sister by bringing her the glass of water laced with chemicals when she had a cold and could not detect the poison. After confessing to David, Lily sets the house on fire and locks herself into his apartment. David is quicker than anyone else to realize what she has done, and he heroically rescues her from the fire, telling her that the two of them face the punishment of living on after causing the deaths of those they loved and that she is not to punish herself by dying in this fire.

David's understanding of Lily—her jealousy of her sister, her guilt, her need for being a go-between with her parents—has been partly inspired by apparent communications from his cousin Kathy's ghost. He has seen the outline of a young woman in his apartment from time to time, accompanied by a humming noise. Surprised that it is Kathy rather than Emily who seems to haunt him, David gets distinct messages in the form of insistent impulsions to "help Lily." As tension mounts between him and Lily, he has vivid dreams of Lily's troubled state and Kathy's promptings. Fearing that he is hallucinating, having tried to convince Lily's parents of her problem and been accused himself of being "crazy," David researches symptoms of mental disorders, unsure whose mental balance is threatened, who is stable and truthful. The ambiguity of the title reinforces the ambiguity of the situation: throughout much of the novel, the reader is uncertain whether David did indeed murder Emily, making Lily "the killer's cousin," but as Lily reveals herself, the reader finds that David is the cousin of a murderer.

The Body of Christopher Creed (2003), by Carol Plum-Ucci, is the tale of a scapegoat: as in Old Testament ritual, a goat—or a person—is sent into the wilderness bearing the sins of the people away. Christ is the quintessential scapegoat, dying to expiate all the world's sins. In the Towne of Steepleton, New Jersey—historic, conventional, its name suggesting commitment to religion—when a young person disappears, the ensuing accusations and blame expose the falsity of the town's appearance of morality. As competing versions of reality come into conflict, exposing hidden sins and hidden virtues, the crisis caused by Christopher Creed's disappearance ultimately cleanses the community. Well-heeled suburbanite existence has afforded no insulation against misery for Chris. His disappearance, after an ambiguous email to the principal, reenacts an earlier, equally mysterious disappearance during his parents' teen years, and it is this reenactment that suggests the community's need for a recurring ritual of expiation.

The suspenseful mystery is related by Torey Adams, who more than a year later rereads a narrative of his search for Chris that he wrote after a nervous breakdown. Torey's search for the truth was motivated by a sense of responsibility—everyone, at some time or another, hurt Chris—and his observation that his peers' and neighbors' reactions betray competing versions of the reality of life in Steepleton. His search drew the suspicion of those who believe Chris was murdered (no body has been found), and some of his former friends still maintain that he collaborated in the murder with one of the town's poorer teens, Bo, who has a long police record. A year and a half later, Torey is continuing his search for Chris via the Internet in an ongoing quest for understanding that is motivated by compassion, though his search is now less urgent.

Torey initially becomes involved in searching because in the ambiguous email announcing Chris's imminent disappearance Torey is mentioned as one of the people whose life Chris would rather lead. Torey's friends frequently describe his life as perfect, a label that makes Torey uncomfortable.

Because nobody liked Chris Creed, immediately after his disappearance, most of the conversations Torey hears include tasteless jokes. Torey is a sensitive person: his memory of hitting Chris brings him a sense of shame and responsibility as part of a community that ostracized the boy from an early age, and he has serious questions about religion, as well as about the obligation to be humane. He is troubled by his peers' hypocrisy, superficiality, and glib judgments of others and disgusted when his friends, including his churchgoing girlfriend, suggest that one of the "boons"—low-income people from the area known as the boondocks—has done Chris in, a judgment based on the boons' bad skin, shabby clothes, and supposed bad smell. Torey is a musician and songwriter who is a better listener than many of his peers. He is also sensitive to the suggestion of the supernatural, a quality that leads to his frequently feeling as though Chris's body or ghost is nearby. This sensitivity also makes him accept a psychic's prediction that he will find a body and thus leads him out to the Lenape burial ground—where he sees an Indian ghost, for the second time in his life, and does indeed find a body, that of a much earlier suicide.

The route to his discovery brings him a new perspective on the lives of his peers and the town's adults. He reestablishes friendship with his long-time friend Ali, known to his current friends as the school's "turbo-slut," and discovers some of the awful challenges she faces on a daily basis: her mother uses drugs and has sex with a series of boyfriends, some of whom are decidedly weird. Ali's new boyfriend Bo is the leader of the high school boons, and although he is guilty of several episodes of breaking and entering, he is basically a good guy, protective of Ali, her younger brother, and his own younger siblings, whom he looks after because his mother's life is much like that of Ali's mother's. Bo's run-ins with the police, who at Mrs. Creed's urging, are determined to charge him with Chris's murder, are shown in a new light when the police chief urges Torey and Ali to allow Bo to take the blame for something he did not do. Later the chief assaults Bo while he is in custody because Bo has revealed his affair with Ali's mother to the chief's daughter.

By this point, Torey has discovered most of the weirdness in Mrs. Creed's treatment of her son. He was skeptical of their motives from the point when the Creeds sought their church's aid, affirming that their son was happy and normal—skeptical because the annoying Chris was seen as anything but normal by his peers. Almost every kid has hit Chris at some point, and Torey remembers how Chris would respond to his physical pain with utter despair but almost immediately rebound, refusing to be shaken off and appearing happy. When Torey resumes his friendship with Ali, at the price of his current romance, he learns from her that Chris had no privacy, his ex-military mother raised him and his younger brothers with a military approach to rules, and Chris kept a diary well-hidden in his bedroom. The surface of respectable adult behavior is undermined by lies—lies that are ultimately exposed by the testimony of Chris's younger brother and the principal, as well as by Torey's lawyer mother in her negotiations on Bo's behalf.

Nearly everyone in the community seems intent on blaming someone else, and no one takes responsibility for his or her own actions. Mrs. Creed's vendetta against Bo is explained by her own Freudian slip: after describing the abuse she suffered during her childhood as a boon, being suspended out a window by her father, she affirms her determination to "see Bo hang" too.

When Torey's mother is drawn into the mystery, Torey finds out about the town's major skeleton in the closet. Something similar happened in her youth: Digger Haines vanished without a trace, and a similar phase of gossip and blame followed. Ultimately, Digger's father could not handle the accusation that he had driven his son to run away or, worse, commit suicide, and he also disappeared. Digger survived—Torey's mother met him years later. She is incorrect in assuming, though, that his father also left town. It is the elder Haines's body that Torey finds when he searches for Chris's body, hoping to prove Bo's innocence with evidence that Chris committed suicide.

Chris's diary has prompted this phase of the search. Ali, Bo, and Torey discover his story of a summer romance, but they discover that it is a pathetic fiction. Meeting the girl's aunt, the psychic who told Chris she saw "death in the woods," sets Torey on the course that results in his falling into the Lenape burial chamber, where Mr. Haines shot himself. The bodies' exposure to oxygen causes instant, dramatic deterioration, so that Torey—who is also suffering the pain of a broken leg—reports that he has seen hell, and he subsequently suffers a nervous breakdown.

This mystery ends without full resolution. Torey concludes the narrative by quoting some of the email responses he has received in his Internet search for Chris. This is a mystery in which texts are important: the email that may be a farewell or a suicide note and may have been written by Chris himself or by his abductor or murderer; Chris's treasure map, that may have marked the spot where he hid the money that facilitated his running away; Chris's diary, that misleads but nonetheless sets Torey on the right track for figuring out what has happened to Chris; and the Web site Torey creates to continue his search, along with the narrative he has written that he emails to the individuals whose names match or approximate those listed in Chris's email. Torey's song lyrics also play a part in the story. And he refers to a poem he wrote in elementary school, titled "Inhumane," after a visit to a wax museum depicting a chamber of horrors, in a prefiguring of his visit to the burial chamber. Understanding the mystery requires reading between the lines, noting the clues that Torey has overlooked in his quest, and paying attention to Chris's pompous style of speaking. The reader's acceptance of Torey's story depends on how one interprets his seeing ghosts, the psychic's predictions, and his reliability after treatment for severe emotional trauma.

Torey insists throughout his narrative that the town's inhabitants maintain contradictory versions of reality; he notes that everyone has a skeleton in the closet. By the time he finds the hidden body, he is so tired of lies and selfishness that he asserts he is more afraid of the living than of the dead.

The Body of Christopher Creed contains important elements of religious symbolism. The name "Christopher Creed" is suggestive: "Christopher" means "Christ bearer," and "Creed" signifies belief. Saint Christopher, formerly the patron saint of travelers in the Roman Catholic faith, gained this reputation by bearing a crushingly heavy child across a stream, whose identity was then revealed as the Christ, his weight attributable to his bearing the world's sins. Torey's given name is "Victor" and his surname is "Adams," suggesting a victory, possibly over Adam, the first sinner. "Victor Adams" is the name signed to the email with which the novel ends, a response to Torey's Internet search that appears to come from Chris in his new identity.

Torey's questions about hypocrisy begin in church, where he questions why Christ is always depicted wearing a loincloth when historical testimony asserts he was crucified naked. Much of the novel is concerned with seeing—seeing truth, accepting the unseen as real. When Torey has become convinced that Chris is still alive, he recognizes that his disappearance enabled him to truly live. Torey is concerned with the balance of good fortune and ill fortune in the grand scheme of things: his early "perfect life" is bound to be balanced out with some bad times later. He attributes this view to Christian teachings, and it is reinforced in a reference to the biblical parable of the rich man (sometimes known as Dives) who, in hell, seeing the beggar Lazarus in Abraham's bosom, asked that he might return to earthly life to warn his brothers of the retribution to come if they did not become more charitable. He was told that they would not believe him if he returned as a ghost. Recalling this story, Torey recognizes that even an otherworldly visitation could not convince some of his neighbors to be charitable—and indeed, he is the only person to see and listen to ghosts. In his search for Chris, Torey falls into an underground sepulcher, only to find that Chris, like the resurrected Christ, is not there. Torey feels he has seen hell, and in the weeks following his nightmarish discovery of the bodies, he is unable to eat because he is haunted by the smell of burning. The hell he has visited proves to be figurative, but like the rich man of the parable, Torey returns to tell his story and advise others about the need for charity. While many of the elements of his story can be explained in rational terms, the lesson that Torey himself seems to draw from his experience is that one must practice charity—as he does with Leo, the weird kid who is the butt of practical jokes and the object of suspicion in his new school. If no one else hears what Torey has to say, at least he has experienced rebirth, as has Christopher.

ADDITIONAL READING RECOMMENDATIONS

Killing Mr. Griffin by Lois Duncan, 1978
The Accident by Todd Strasser, 1988
His Dark Materials trilogy by Philip Pullman, 1995–2000 (discussed in
     Imagined Places)
Heat by Michael Cadnum, 1998
Counterfeit Son by Elaine Marie Alphin, 2000
Big Mouth and Ugly Girl by Joyce Carol Oates, 2002 (discussed in School Days)

Heroism: What Does It Mean to Be a Hero?
Mary Tasillo

Westmark by Lloyd Alexander (1981)
The Kestrel by Lloyd Alexander (1982)
The Blue Sword by Robin McKinley (1982)
A Hero Ain't Nothin' but a Sandwich by Alice Childress
  (1973)
The Adventures of Blue Avenger by Norma Howe (1999)

Young adult literature of the past thirty years departs from the classic hero, who is unfailingly admired, a member of the dominant culture, male, and a brave battler against whatever forces threaten his domination—corrupt humans, devils, or the natural world. Readers encounter him in classics such as *Treasure Island* and *The Call of the Wild*, movies, and accounts of the founding fathers of the United States. However, contemporary readers are much less likely to identify with this hero in an increasingly multicultural and global society, and a postmodern hero with weaknesses, an antihero, or an unlikely hero may well be more satisfying than the classic hero.

Young adult works that come closest to the classics in their depiction of the hero, such as Lloyd Alexander's *Westmark* trilogy and Robin McKinley's books about the kingdom of Damar, occur in the realm of fantasy. These books, while featuring unlikely heroes, follow a relatively traditional notion of the hero who reaches success by physically subduing evil forces in battle, fighting dragons, or using scientific reasoning. The reader can identify with the hero's self-doubt and position as an outsider but can also accept these figures as reliably heroic because they exist in a time and place outside the reader's own—that is, they exist in the imagination.

Other works self-consciously address what it means to be a hero. They may contain the word "hero" in the title—*A Hero Ain't Nothin' but a Sandwich*, for instance; even *All-American Girl* is evocative of the heroic in its appeal to American patriotism. These books are set in the present or recent past in familiar places, and their heroes are people the reader knows. Often the reader finishes the book with a decidedly cynical viewpoint: these tales debunk the national hero through exposing him or her as cowardly and immoral at heart, opening a window into a hero's self-doubt, or showing the irrelevance of the traditional hero to everyday lives. They do not revision the hero; the hero no longer exists.

Yet other works treat notions of the hero with humor. Meg Cabot's *All-American Girl* and Norma Howe's *Blue Avenger* books, for instance, take a farcical approach, simultaneously parodying the heroic and providing witty commentary on the challenges of making it through the teenage years in contemporary culture. The acts portrayed as truly heroic in these books are admitting one's romantic interest to another person, remaining true to a unique personality in the face of peer pressure, and challenging societal injustices perpetrated largely by adults. The heroes of these books are portrayed comically with all of the embarrassing awkwardness of youth, yet in the end triumph over their challenges if not over adolescence, gaining something for the good of society as well as getting the girl—or boy.

The unlikely hero is ubiquitous in young adult literature because it is classically a literature of the outsider. Teenagers generally feel alone and misunderstood, often powerless even to make decisions about their own life. The most positive outcome of the new heroic literature is its potential for providing hope and realistic notions of the hero at the same time that it deconstructs this staple figure of our culture.

In Lloyd Alexander's *Westmark* series (*Westmark*, 1981; *The Kestrel*, 1982; *The Beggar Queen*, 1984), the protagonist Theo is a morally torn vagabond hero, the apprentice in a printer's shop who is sent on his journey when armed guards destroy the shop and kill his employer. Theo, a classic good boy—an orphan who does excellent work—is forced into an evil action by circumstance: he beats one of the guards over the head with something heavy and runs for his life. Though his moral sense dictates that he return and confess, a local police officer convinces him to leave the city, and thus Theo takes to the road. His actions involve him in a moral dilemma: he realizes that he wanted to kill the guard, and this does not fit into his moral code. Interestingly, Alexander uses the term "printer's *devil*" rather than "apprentice" to describe Theo's employment, and Theo begins to wonder if he is not a devil in more than one sense.

Theo falls in with a couple of men who make their living by swindling and trickery, and, feeling compelled by circumstances to stay with them, soon finds himself not only participating in their swindles to save his skin and earn his keep but also even suggesting a fantastic trick that brings them the most success they have had. Apparently he is cut out for the vagabond's life, but he simultaneously works hard at denouncing this lifestyle. Yet the reader is won over to the vagabond's side and sees a world where the outlaws in the end are more moral than upright law-abiding citizens. The vagabond is morally superior in several significant aspects. Westmark's monarchy is corrupt. Power is actually wielded by Carrabus, the power-hungry adviser to the sickly king. He closes universities and has printing presses destroyed throughout the kingdom, thus destroying knowledge. Censorship becomes another important issue. Theo and the group of former students he falls in with challenge the monarchy's injustices; they are heroic in morals and in deed as they fight against injustice by rebuilding a press to distribute information as well as preparing for physical battle to destroy the corrupt government. Their ringleader Florian questions whether it is a corrupt leader or the system of the monarchy itself that causes these problems. For Theo, the evidence is inconclusive, and, as his friend Mickle turns out to be the princess of Westmark, one sees that he will have to straddle these two worlds. For Florian, the end of this government justifies the violent means that may be necessary. Theo is torn—violence helped to save his friends and yet he regrets the bloodshed. This is what defines Theo as the hero in *Westmark*—that he can see both sides of the argument; thus it appears that he will find a way to bridge the gap for both himself and the kingdom. He is not the traditional heroic savior but a mediator.

However, in *The Kestrel*, Theo gives himself over to the violent fighting, resisting the notion that he would be of better use as mediator and adviser. When Theo is attacked, he rejoins Florian's people, and the neighboring kingdom of Regia invades the country. Theo asserts his masculinity in battle: he does not want to go back to the castle, even to his dear friend and romantic interest Mickle, when everyone else is going off to fight. Gone are his innocent morals that led him to question his ability to do battle and kill; instead, he seeks to prove that he has the courage of his convictions regarding the government and can ensure the kingdom's safety. Theo's travels have led him to question the system further, and he is now more inclined to agree with Florian. Though he does well in Justin's army, he still stands outside, questioning the ruthlessness of Justin's wrath as general—a wrath that is frightening in its cool calculatedness. However, when Theo finds his friend Stock's mutilated body, he too gives himself over to wrath, to that part of him that enjoyed killing the officer at the beginning of his adventures. Now Theo hardly seems to know himself except as an army-commanding machine, and indeed, his friends barely recognize him. In place of moral questioning, Theo has only anger, calculation, and the battle as he commands troops as Kestrel, a bloodthirsty colonel. The reader must question how it is that men get to this point, for are they not born peaceably inclined as Theo once was?

Even when Mickle and Theo are reunited, Theo initially is too far gone to figure out whether he still loves Mickle because he cannot feel anything. Mickle, on the other hand, has kept her head and become a hero in her own right, after sneaking out of the palace to track down the missing Theo and finding herself instead commanding her own armies near the invader's border. Mickle's leadership plays counterpoint to that of other (male) generals: her first priority is saving her people's lives, and she will retreat to achieve that end. Nonetheless, Mickle devises cunning and unexpected plans; she sneaks across the Regian border in disguise to meet with the young Regian king and orchestrate a truce. The two young monarchs, having just witnessed battle, are anxious to avoid further battles because they, refreshingly, care about their subjects. Not only is peace made, but Mickle seeks to give up her sovereign power to a three-person governing body. Clearly, she is a hero as she steps forward courageously, despite her youth and lack of experience, to maintain Westmark's boundary and save villages from the Regians' plundering. A creative thinker, Mickle disguises herself to meet with the Regian king herself rather than negotiate through the traditional means.

Thus, while Theo's narrative seems to be the dominant one, it is Mickle who emerges as the true hero over the course of *The Kestrel*. Feminine creative thinking triumphs over masculine weaponry and military planning, thus inverting traditional notions of heroism.

Robin McKinley's *The Blue Sword* (1982) is the story of Harry and an ancient sword carried by a legendary dragon-slayer (whose story is recounted in the prequel *The Hero and the Crown*, 1984). Harry's name cues the reader immediately to her oddity—that she is immune to traditional feminine interests and graces. Orphaned as a young woman, she is brought from the Homeland by her brother, Richard, to his station near the Hills, where the odd Hillfolk live, near the border with the mysterious and ominous North. Harry's adventure begins when she encounters the Hillfolk.

Upon a rare visit to the outpost, Corlath, king of the Hillfolk, notices Harry because her presence preoccupies his *kelar*, a sort of magic power in the Hillfolk that is especially strong in their king. He decides to kidnap her, an action that quickly makes it apparent that she herself possesses some very strong *kelar*, which manifests itself in her ability to see visions as well as in physical prowess and an immense capacity for learning. She sees visions of battles and of the dragon-slayer Aerin, who becomes a guiding figure for her. Horsemanship and swordsmanship come to her naturally with her strong *kelar*; clearly Harry was cut out for this role, and she fears that her proclivity is like a disease in her blood.

Questioning why she has been chosen, particularly as a Homelander, an outsider, Harry suggests the preconception that one's lineage plays a part in the hero role. The Hillfolk wonder why they are bothering to kidnap this despised foreigner. The idea that destiny is tied to lineage is confirmed when Harry later discovers that in fact she has Hill, or Damarian, blood, and she shares status as blood-outsider with Aerin, also an outcast in her youth due to her Northern blood. Harry's role is additionally confirmed by the way animals take to her—both the horses and the wild cats that sometimes accompany the Hillfolk. The cat Narknon takes to Harry as he takes to no one else, following her to her training and providing comfort and food. Harry is able to use his reactions as a judge of character as well, for Narknon takes to Harry's nearest and dearest.

After five weeks of intense training, she returns to the king for the Hillfolks' laprun trials, in which, despite the brevity of Harry's training and her lack of preparation for the format of the trials (she is only just learning Hillspeech), she wins the trials, becoming the first *damalur-sol*, or lady-hero, in generations. She is rewarded with the sword Gonturan and is made one of the king's riders. Everywhere Harry goes, she awkwardly must confront the respect, adulation, and curiosity shown her by the people.

However, the festivities of this laprun trial are cut short due to the impending threat of the North. The Hill forces are small, the Northern large and demonic. The Hillfolk must face them in the hopes of saving some enclaves where they can hide and preserve their existence. Their small forces have been strengthened, however, by the presence of the *damalur-sol*, which inspires more women to join the army than in recent memory. Yet Harry abandons this army, urged by her *kelar*, to attempt to block an unprotected pass farther south. She is followed by her companions Senay and Terim, and she seeks the assistance of her friend Captain Jack Dedham at the Homelander outpost, who essentially abandons his career, disobeying orders with a small band of men to assist her in defending the pass against the Northerners. Along the way, they acquire more fighters from Senay's village and from the *kentare*, women archers of the forests who all but disappeared to the eyes of the Hillfolk many years ago and who return to offer their service to the bearer of Gonturan. Thus Harry, as a woman and carrying a woman's sword, is able to gather a stronger army.

The group reaches the pass the night before the battle, a cold and evil wind chills them and carries word of their numbers back to the Northerners, and Harry can hardly sleep for dreaming. The next day Harry and her band fight valiantly, holding their ground, but they are vastly outnumbered. The first battle culminates, before they retreat to regroup, in a pitched battle between Harry and the head of the Northerners. Harry feels she can hardly function; in the vicinity of his strong evil power, everything seems hazy, her arm seems to have a mind of its own, and she is fortunate that her horse is superior to that of her foe's. Her companion Hill cat, Narknon, deals the final blow in knocking down the Northern standard, before both sides retreat to regroup. Thus affiliation with supportive friends plays an important role in Harry's success as a hero.

Alone before they head back to face the regathered Northerners, Harry calls on both Corlath and Lady Aerin to aid in whatever way they can. She finds her arm lifting; blue fire pools and travels the mountains and skies; she speaks in the Old Tongue; and the mountains crumble underneath, covering and crushing the Northern army. When Harry's army regains its composure, the mountains have rearranged themselves and forests have taken the place of the scraggly trees the *kentare* hid in earlier. Harry wakes weak and with no idea what has just happened or for how long she has slept.

Harry becomes even less sure of herself as it comes time to return to Corlath's army. She has seen that his army is winning; this brings great hope and joy to her weary troop. Harry tries to disband her followers, as she is quite unsure of her reception upon return to Corlath, but they refuse, recognizing in Harry the hero she fails to recognize in herself. Her reception is more than warm: Corlath asks Harry to marry him, and she accepts. In the years to follow, they live happily. Harry learns the many stories of Aerin from Corlath, and teaches new ones to him, for Aerin appears often to Harry, a slyly grinning elder sister. *Hariman-sol*, as the Hillfolk call her, seems to come to peace with her role and the promise that she can, in a sense, retire from it with the major battle won.

In the contemporary realm of the 1970s ghetto, Alice Childress's *A Hero Ain't Nothin' but a Sandwich* (1973) is the story of Benjie, a thirteen-year-old black heroin addict, and the people close to him who might conceivably function as role models. The story is told from the first-person viewpoint of quite a number of characters—starting off with Benjie and including his mother, Rose; his grandmother; his near-stepfather, Butler; two of his teachers; the school principal; the neighborhood pusher; and a couple of Benjie's friends. The point of the title is underlined for the reader throughout the book by a sheer absence of heroes. Every voice seems to have a defeated tone; everyone is just trying to get by—and being tried by general life experience. The first-person narratives are occasionally interrupted by items from the local newspaper or church bulletin, bringing a perspective on the broader community. They report that crime is increasing and that old women (including Benjie's grandmother) are being mugged when leaving the church during the week. The announcement of a local fashion show serves as a springboard for discussion of the relatively elite moneyed and intelligentsia in the community, and the ad of Madam Snowson, a fortune teller, draws Benjie's grandmother and mother, who know it will do no good but are willing to try anything to get Benjie and their family on the mend.

The question raised, though often obliquely, throughout the course of the book is whether a selection of heroes to choose among is a sufficient condition to save young people from drugs and a life of crime in the inner city. Nigeria Greene, one of the teachers at Benjie's school and the one ultimately responsible for turning him in to the authorities for being on the nod, replaced the classroom photos of white founding fathers, including illustrious slave-holders such as George Washington, with black heroes for his classroom of students of color, heroes such as Marcus Garvey and Harriet Tubman. The teacher Bernard Cohen, one of the only white people in the community who is not a social worker, also hangs pictures of black heroes for the students, even the militant Malcolm X. However, these heroes on the walls seem not to be doing the students much good, particularly if Benjie is any example. Benjie reveals himself to be a smart kid through his sharp-eyed perceptions of the world around him—recognizing who is and who is not dishing out lies—and Nigeria Greene's faith in him attests to his abilities as well.

Nigeria's own authority is established by his educational attainments and by the credibility given him with students' respect. But Benjie sees school as stupid, boring, and pointless, and when he is not skipping school, he spends his time there drugged, staring out the window, and trying his hardest to ignore his teachers' talk. The principal addresses the difficulties of trying to provide appropriate role models and assemblies and holiday observances for all his varied students. When he occasionally schedules an assembly to address drug use, he fears the ex-addict is being presented as a hero: drug use is okay as long as the user cleans him- or herself up at some point. This attitude is reflected in Benjie's own justification of his behavior as he declares that he is not an addict, claiming he can give up drugs when he wants to.

This notion of choice is belied when Benjie starts stealing from his family to support his habit—first money that he "borrows" from his grandmother's purse and later the suit that he steals from Butler's closet when he first comes home from detoxification. It is this stealing that wreaks havoc with family dynamics. Taking the suit precipitates Butler's move to another apartment.

Benjie has already been giving Butler a hard time for trying to step in as a strong father figure and tells him he need not try to prove anything because they live in a time when "a hero ain't nothin' but a sandwich," thus refuting the potential for or relevance of heroes in contemporary urban America. However, the need for a hero or role model of some kind is affirmed later, when Benjie declares that he just needs someone to believe in him. Indeed, Butler seems quite heroic on one level when he chases down Benjie on the building roof and saves him from jumping to his death. Benjie pleads with him to let him go, to let him die, but Butler refuses to do so and with much straining pulls Benjie back up to safety.

After this proof of Butler's care, Benjie decides to allow Butler to be a father to him. Butler simultaneously makes the commitment to treat Benjie as his flesh and blood instead of running away from him when the going gets bad. Thus Butler is the humble real-life hero who steers Benjie back on course. When an adviser at the rehab center recommends to Butler that he provide Benjie with some male hero figure from the pages of black history, the movie screen, or the baseball field, Butler retorts that some of these celebrities have the same problem as Benjie. In contrast, he points out, he is supporting a family on a limited salary and cannot even claim them as tax exemptions, so perhaps he deserves the medal for heroism. And as the book closes, Butler is outside the center in the cold waiting for Benjie to show up to his appointment, trusting that Benjie is running late and has gotten distracted by the shop windows en route. Is a hero a celebrity or an upright man who is holding it together? Will either save anyone from a life of drugs, crime, or poverty?

Norma Howe takes a humorous approach to the concept of the hero in *The Adventures of Blue Avenger* (1999). On his sixteenth birthday, David Schumacher decides to officially change his name to Blue Avenger, the comic book superhero he has been drawing for the past three years as an outlet for his frustration about his father's untimely death and other injustices in the world. A comic book superhero is a fanciful character, fighting the largest injustices unaided. Blue Avenger parodies this superhero.

As soon as David becomes Blue Avenger, the world changes for him. He addresses previously unthinkable tasks with ease, telling his classmate Omaha Nebraska Brown suavely that he loves her, saving the school principal from a swarm of killer bees (by carrying her off and dumping her in a swimming pool), and discovering the winning recipe for a "weepless" lemon meringue pie. All this and more he accomplishes with ease. Blue is admired and respected for such embarrassingly awkward acts as dumping his school principal in the swimming pool, and his heroic acts are dutifully covered in the local newspaper.

However, a comic book superhero lives for the public only in media coverage and in his rare appearances while fighting crime. Blue Avenger differs in leading his life as Blue Avenger twenty-four hours a day, seven days a week. What portion of this personality is Blue Avenger, hero? What portion is David Schumacher? In her parody, Howe occasionally describes Blue's stony face when addressing a new task—pure fancy because, while Blue can accomplish amazing things, the reader still sees him as a weird, smart, carrot-topped sixteen-year-old whose superhero costume consists of his father's old blue fishing vest and a blue towel turban. Ultimately, the Blue Avenger conceit is a talisman that frees David from some of the doubts and insecurities that threaten to overwhelm teenagers.

The humor of this book depends on its application of heroic efforts to the daily problems encountered by socially conscious teenagers, instead of the more adult problems addressed in the typical hero or superhero tale. Blue is heroic because suddenly he walks through his adolescent life with unbelievable ease, unlike the blundering that everyone else does throughout their teen years. He is not without doubt, which renders him believable as a teenage protagonist. He is also, like many young people, preoccupied with the ageless philosophical question of whether people are in control of their own actions. His sincerity in seeking an answer to this question, his conviction that an answer can be found, keeps him firmly in the realm of naive young person. The reader knows that his question is unanswerable. But this question is actually fundamental to the question of heroism. Would the heroic soldier have thrown himself on the grenade, thereby saving his fellows, regardless of his wish to die? Do people choose to become heroes or can they not help themselves? And is heroism a result of being thrown into the right circumstances or of how the individual is genetically wired to react, or is it a result of one's choices, character traits, and morals?

Howe's offhand style and the political consciousness of Blue and Omaha lead one to expect heroes with somewhat radical mores. However, Blue Avenger is a hero who takes an admirable and just but relatively conservative stance. David does not swear, and though this does provide occasion for a comic book–inspired use of various punctuation sequences, it is conservative behavior for the contemporary teenager. Blue's and Omaha's antigun sentiments and their weird high school quirkiness come across as progressive. However, Blue's role as hero is really the more moderate role of the peacekeeper. As a babysitter, he charms children into entertaining themselves; he charms the student newspaper kids into pulling graphic depictions of proper condom use so they will keep the newspaper's funding; and he charms the city of Oakland into a best-of-both-worlds compromise on gun laws, whereby citizens can still carry their guns but can use only a special nonlethal stun-bullet. His job as hero is to win people over with his newfound charm and to encourage compromise—to know how to make friends and influence people.

ADDITIONAL READING RECOMMENDATIONS

The Lord of the Rings by J. R. R. Tolkien, 1954
The Prydain Chronicles by Lloyd Alexander, 1964–68
The Outsiders by S. E. Hinton, 1967 (discussed in Insiders and Outsiders)

Freak the Mighty, 1993 (discussed in Friends Forever?), and *Max the Mighty*, 1998, by
     Rodman Philbrick
The Watcher by James Howe, 1997 (discussed in Abuse, Sexual Violence, and Healing)
Harry Potter series by J. K. Rowling, 1997–
Blue Avenger Cracks the Code, 2000, and *Blue Avenger and the Theory of Everything*, 2002,
     by Norma Howe
The Arthur trilogy by Kevin Crossley-Holland, 2001–3 (discussed in Old Tales Retold: Fairy
     Tales, Legends, Myths)
Troy by Adele Geras, 2001
All-American Girl by Meg Cabot, 2002

History Is about Young Adults, Too

The Midwife's Apprentice by Karen Cushman (1995)
Catherine, Called Birdy by Karen Cushman (1994)
High Seas trilogy by Iain Lawrence (1998–2001)
Lyddie by Katherine Paterson (1991)
Jip: His Story by Katherine Paterson (1998)
The Borning Room by Paul Fleishmann (1991)

The best historical fiction for young people not only is factually accurate but also gives the reader interesting and believable characters to care about and identify with. This latter characteristic sometimes gets lost when youthful characters seem to exist only for the purpose of reporting on the actions and thoughts of prominent historical personages. Another challenge to authors is to create characters the contemporary reader can sympathize with while remaining true to the cultural values that shaped individuals' actions during the period when the story is set.

The novels discussed in this chapter by no means cover the whole range of historical periods in which good young adult fiction is set, but each one revolves around an adolescent fictional protagonist. Thus the focus is on a young person's confrontation with the issues of other young adult literature—family matters, romance, illness and death, vocation—within a particular time and place. (Novels focusing on war are discussed in Chapter 32: War's Impact.) Quite foreign to a contemporary reader is medieval Europe, whose beliefs are so remote from our own, and Karen Cushman is skilled at conveying this belief system while creating interest in the fates of her young women characters. The romance of the high seas has a magic that Iain Lawrence effectively creates in a series of adventures in the tradition of *Treasure Island*, combining suspense with the ever-relevant theme of a son's relationship with his father. The values of nineteenth-century American life—hard work, independence, freedom, and literacy—shape the lives of youthful characters in memorable novels of New England by Katherine Paterson and rural Ohio by Paul Fleischmann.

Medieval Europe

The Midwife's Apprentice (1995), by Karen Cushman, is a cheerful tale of the transformation of a solitary waif who steals or works for bare subsistence and burrows into a dung heap for warmth at night into a clean, pretty, literate apprentice to a knowledgeable midwife in fourteenth-century England. Jane, the midwife, is a hard taskmaster who jealously guards her knowledge of birthing babies, but from the time she takes in the girl, known as Dung Beetle, the child is assured of regular food and a place to sleep. Because Beetle is told she is stupid and is tormented by the village boys, she fails to recognize just how much herb lore she is acquiring while she does her mistress's bidding, and she accepts her lot in life until circumstances give her a greater sense of self-worth that enables her to choose the direction of her life and pursue her real vocation for midwifery.

Three circumstances transform her: she is given a comb by a kindly merchant; she helps a villager deliver twin calves and later helps a small boy find a secure place to work and live; and she learns to read. The first episode, which gives her some pride in her appearance, leads her to choose the name Alyce for herself, marking the beginning of self-respect. Her ability to help others suggests to her that she might be useful to the community, though her knowledge is limited because of lack of training and experience. When she fails to help a village woman struggling to give birth, Alyce flees to a nearby inn to work, where her shy eavesdropping allows her to learn reading and writing and then helps her understand her mistress's real evaluation of her worth, when the midwife visits the inn. From this conversation, Alyce learns that Mistress Jane can and will teach her what she needs to know to deliver babies but she must be persistent, because no matter what the limitations on the midwife's knowledge, babies will come, and the midwife can never give up.

As Alyce's natural intelligence and good-heartedness appear not only to the reader but to the villagers, she is increasingly accepted by the community. For a time, her only friend is an orange cat, but her ability to use the villagers' superstition enables her to right some wrongs, and, after saving a boy from drowning and helping deliver the calves, as well as threatening the other boys with curses, to gain a little respect. She inspires real affection in the boy whom she feeds and sends off to the manor house in search of employment. When she proves herself capable of helping a woman in labor at the inn, she redeems herself in her own eyes. Suddenly Alyce finds herself respected and able to choose between different ways of life, so that midwifery becomes her choice, not a matter of happenstance. The humorous tone and Alyce's delightful personality make this novel a real pleasure to read as well as a good introduction to medieval life.

Cushman's *Catherine, Called Birdy* (1994) uses the diary genre to record the restricted life led by members of feudal society, especially women. Birdy, so called because her love of birds is manifested in the aviary she has created in her bedroom, spends the year between her thirteenth and fourteenth birthday vigorously resisting her father's attempts to marry her off, seeing in them the same kind of negotiations he would make in the sale of livestock. Her gentle mother admonishes her not to fight so hard against the cage in which she lives, and other, older women give her similar advice, suggesting that she may learn how to be herself and enjoy what freedom she may find within the limits of her station in life. Birdy's mischief is often childish, but in everything she does she exhibits a loving heart and a desperate desire for more freedom to run and jump outdoors and indulge her boundless curiosity about animals, people, and life's deeper meaning. Her journal is the gift of her favorite brother Edward, a monk, intended to school her to more mature behavior, a goal she attains in spite of herself throughout the year that she keeps it.

Birdy is passionate in her emotional responses to people, whether they are servants, family members, villagers, or prospective suitors. She has a great distaste for the boisterous, sometimes cruel, loutish behavior that many of the men exhibit, especially her betrothed, a much older man who exhibits disgusting table manners and nearly kills one of her beloved dogs. She loves all animals, not just birds, and finally gives her consent to marrying the man she despises by accepting his gifts of silver so that she may rescue a bear from the torments of bear-baiting. Her tender heart is wounded by ordinary events in thirteenth-century English life like the hanging of thieves and the death of a young man mortally wounded in a brawl in the manor hall.

The villagers' lives seem infinitely preferable to hers. The young people may marry whom they choose, in contrast to her friend Aelis, her uncle George, and her brother Robert, whose marital arrangements are practical economic matters. The villagers spend their lives in the open, doing chores that have far more appeal to her than her own: embroidery, spinning, making smelly batches of soap, and brewing home remedies for injuries and ailments. Furthermore, she fears childbearing, a dangerous business for the medieval woman, and all too often resulting in sorrow over a child's death.

Birdy imagines a number of alternative fates to the one chosen for her. She thinks of going crusading, only to learn that the Crusades are over and that, moreover, the killing of pagans is a harrowing business. She thinks of posing as a boy and entering a monastery to make pictures in manuscripts, but her brother Edward, the monk, observes that her breasts are too fully developed to fool the monks. For a year she plots and brainstorms, avoiding the recognition she must finally grow into: that she has a well-established and limited role in the society she was born into, and her only chance of happiness is to face her life with courage and make the best of it—exactly what all the adults have tried to tell her. She sees this acceptance in action in her uncle's marriage, even though his loss of the woman he loves has changed his personality.

It is a relief to the reader's feelings, as well as to Birdy's, that once she has reached this acceptance, she learns that she will marry the polite and literate, not to mention much younger, son of her betrothed because her fiancé has died in a tavern brawl. She has gained more insight into human nature during this year of journal-keeping, reevaluating her father when she observes his fierce battle for her mother's life after childbirth and grudgingly appreciating her brother Robert when he makes arrangements for rescuing the bear (though she is still surprised at her friend Aelis' pleasure in being betrothed to him).

The omnipresence of medieval Christianity, with its strong element of superstition, is felt throughout the novel. The cycle of the year is marked with religious festivals and traditions originating in pagan fertility rites. Each day is a saint's day, and many of the tidbits of information Birdy records about the saints are bizarre. The story of the relics brought from Rome will not convince any modern reader of their efficacy. Equally important is the feudal system, the strict hierarchy that structures social life and economics. The belief system that governs Birdy's life, along with the details of village and manor life, is fully integrated into the entertaining narrative of her coming to terms with the marriage that will take her away from everything that is dear to her, indeed all that she has ever known.

Sea Stories

Iain Lawrence's High Seas trilogy (*The Wreckers*, 1998; *The Smugglers*, 1999; *The Buccaneers*, 2001) traces protagonist John Spencer's fortunes at sea from age fourteen to seventeen at the turn of the nineteenth century. Steeped in their author's sailing experience and knowledge of boats and the sea, the novels convey a strong

sense of life at sea through accurate historical detail and the use of nautical terminology. As John matures, through the successive adventures, he becomes a better
judge of character in a series of spine-tingling episodes that reinforce the reader's
sense that a few men working together to navigate and sail a relatively small vessel
far from land are mutually dependent on one another, and their survival often
depends on accurately sizing up another person's strengths and weaknesses.

In *The Wreckers*, John's desire to go to sea is tested by his merchant father, who
takes him on a voyage that ends with the loss of the ship. It is there that the adventure begins, with John and his father the only survivors on the Cornwall coast where
the villagers who lured their ship to the rocks want only their death. Befriended by the
sunny, sweet Mary and under her uncle's protection, John must discover where his father
has been imprisoned and rescue him from a horrifying death. To do so, he must sort out
truth from appearance and then muster great courage to face numerous threats. The
truths of several villagers' pasts are shrouded in ghost stories and sightings generated by the losses they have suffered and witnessed and the guilt some of them bear.

In *The Smugglers*, John has the task of bringing the *Dragon*, the ship his father
has just purchased, safely to London, subordinate only to the captain, a madman who
seesaws between affability and rage. A number of hidden elements in the seamen's
pasts and present allegiances come to light as events unfold, even as the ship's hidden compartments and stowaway are revealed. John ultimately proves more astute
than his father, though at first he too is taken in by likable exteriors of the captain
and most colorful crew member. Having discovered their involvement in the smuggling trade with France, however, he finally delivers them into the hands of the king's
revenue officers.

In *The Buccaneers*, John takes on more authority as his father's representative on
the *Dragon* during a trading voyage to the Caribbean, under the captaincy of a long-
time family friend. On this trip, he must make a number of decisions and, on several
occasions, must stand on principle, most notably when he refuses to take slaves as
cargo. Determining which men are truthful and which are false is crucial on the
many occasions when his life is at risk, whether from storms and damage to the ship
or from former naval officers turned pirate. John's judgment improves, showing
itself much better than his father's, and he shows himself capable of taking charge of
a ship, with a little guidance from more experienced mariners. Coming near to
wrecking a second time on the rocky Cornwall coast, John reencounters Mary, now
old enough to entice him to stay on land, but his life-course is set: he will remain a
seafaring man, though he promises to return. It is clear at the conclusion of this trilogy that John's love of the sea is stronger than any other love.

While the thrill of exciting plots, realized through dramatic scenes and dialogue, is
what a reader is most likely to take away from reading the trilogy, John's relationships with a series of mentors enable him to come of age and act on his own, testing
his own judgment against his father's in a maturing father-son relationship that
could occur in any period.

Nineteenth-Century America

In *Lyddie* (1991) and *Jip: His Story* (1998), Katherine Paterson depicts the emergence from two kinds of slavery—the constrictions of poverty and preemancipation
enslavement of blacks—in midcentury New England. In the first novel, Lyddie leaves
her family's debt-ridden Vermont farm as the family is separated so that she may
earn a meager pittance working at a tavern, but when she is fired for going back to

visit the farm in her mistress's absence, she takes advantage of her release to find work in the textile mills of Lowell, Massachusetts, where her new independence as a wage-earner overcomes any sense of her enslavement to factory life. In the later novel, the foundling Jip works as hard on the poor farm near Lyddie's home as Lyddie worked. Always longing to know about the parents who abandoned him on the road, he eventually learns that his birthright is an even harsher confinement than the poverty and farm work that cage him. Both novels bring the protagonists self-knowledge, friendship with people of integrity, and a profound thirst for education when they discover the joys of literacy.

Lyddie comes of age through a series of challenges that she likens to facing bears, after literally facing a hungry black bear in the family's cabin at the outset of the novel. At thirteen in 1843, Lyddie is virtually the head of the household in her father's absence, helped with farm chores by ten-year-old Charlie. Her mother's fear and susceptibility to predictions of Armageddon's imminence make her undependable in a crisis, and Lyddie's two sisters are too young to help. After the bear's invasion of their home—which he leaves in a hurry with his head stuck in a pot of hot oatmeal—her mother and the girls depart to live with Lyddie's aunt, in an arrangement that ends in the mother's eventual commitment to an insane asylum. After Charlie and Lyddie have scraped through one winter on the homestead alone, they are forced to go to work, Charlie as a miller's apprentice, Lyddie as a kitchen girl in a tavern, with their small income sent directly to their mother. However, Lyddie has salvaged their earnings from the sale to their kindly Quaker neighbor of the calf she and Charlie bred, using the neighbor's bull. The trip home that culminates in her dismissal from the tavern is for the purpose of hiding the money to pay off debts.

At home, Lyddie is confronted with a moral decision, one that her warm heart comes to quickly, when she encounters a fugitive slave hiding in her family's cabin. She has heard rumors of escaped slaves in the area, and she well knows the monetary reward that reporting him would bring her, but when she gets to know Ezekiel, she not only keeps his secret but turns over the profits from the calf's sale to help him journey to Canada in an act of spontaneous generosity that has a long-range effect on her life, and later on Jip's.

Lyddie's heart has been touched by the plight of the escaped slave, but it begins to harden during her employment as a mill girl in Lowell, where she is driven by the desperate desire to pay off her father's debts and redeem the farm for herself and Charlie. Though helped generously by a skilled older worker, Diana, Lyddie avoids becoming too close when she learns that Diana is organizing workers to seek better conditions and is, hence, a dangerous person to associate with. Lyddie's drive to earn money makes her unwilling to risk any displeasure on the part of her supervisors. As she becomes skilled, she resents having to help a new Irish girl, as Diana once helped her, because it slows her down and limits her earnings, until she rediscovers the kindness that was once a part of her nature.

While Lyddie does not easily make friends with other young women who live in the boarding house, she is entranced when her roommate Betsy begins reading aloud to her from *Oliver Twist*. After they have finished the book together, Lyddie parts with two of her precious hard-earned dollars to purchase her own copy, and reading it over and over significantly improves her rudimentary literacy to the point where she is no longer ashamed of her letter-writing skills. Betsy's dream of saving enough for a college education in Ohio is thwarted when health problems make it impossible for her to continue working in the mill, but it is a dream that eventually inspires Lyddie herself.

Still, it is only the stress of circumstances that sets Lyddie on this course. Her mother's incarceration and death leave her surviving sister, Rachel, on her hands, and in the brief period when she stays with Lyddie and works in the mill, Lyddie rediscovers the sweetness of family love. However, it is better for Rachel to live with Charlie and the miller's family, who have treated him as their own, and Lyddie must acknowledge that her two siblings have a much better life there than she could possibly provide for them. She discovers that there are limitations on her own great strength when she falls ill. Betsy has left, and Diana has become pregnant and left for Boston, leaving Lyddie to form a new attachment to the young Irish girl, Brigid, whom she teaches to read. It is Brigid's plight that ultimately ends Lyddie's employment at the mill. Having successfully eluded sexual harassment by her supervisor herself, Lyddie rescues the younger girl from his predations, overturning a water bucket on his head in an act of defense that sends her into gales of laughter as she recalls the bear. She is dismissed the following day on charges of "moral turpitude." While Lyddie would not have chosen freedom from being a wage slave in the mill at this juncture, perpetually asked to manage more looms at an ever faster pace with a diminishing piece rate, it is a release that enables her to reconsider and reshape her life.

With her mother's death, her uncle has sold to their Quaker neighbor the family farm that she wished so desperately to save, so there is no returning there. However, Lyddie's prospects for the future are more promising than she could have dreamed when she left home. Luke Stevens, the son of her Quaker neighbor, has proposed to her; and the fugitive slave, Ezekiel (who has selected the surname Freeman for himself upon reaching Canada), has repaid her loan fivefold. Lyddie is surprised to learn of Luke's interest but unwilling to live on the farm that was formerly her family's as his wife, feeling that it would be charity, an act on Luke's part much like his aid to the fugitive slave. Instead, Lyddie chooses to go to college.

The many challenges that Lyddie has overcome have seemed like so many bears to her—so many threats from the outside. She comes to see, however, that the real bear that must be stared down is whatever lack of generosity she finds in herself. When she comes to this realization, she also acknowledges her need to become something more than she is before binding her fate to another person's.

The sadly misspelled letter from her mother that Lyddie and Charlie received their last winter on the family farm has furnished them with a running joke that Lyddie quotes from time to time to Charlie. After announcing her disappointment that the end of the world has not come when expected, Mrs. Worthen commented, "But we can stil hop." Each time Lyddie repeats this sentiment, she affirms the strength of her own spirit and life-force as well as the optimism for the future that her mother misnamed. Lyddie applies the statement, uttering it only in her thoughts, to her new sympathy with Luke at the end of the novel that tells her story. In the later novel, *Jip: His Story*, Lyddie's budding warmth of spirit is realized in her teaching, and she and Luke finally come together in an effort to save Jip from enslavement under the Fugitive Slave Act.

Jip's story unfolds in the mid-1850s. His name recalls "gypsy," an identity that his coloring suggests, and he has lived on the poor farm since he was found along the road in rural Vermont. The elderly, weak-minded, and infirm inhabitants of the poor farm are unable to do much work, but the young Jip does the work of a man, alongside his friend Sheldon, a strong young man with the mind of a child, until Sheldon is sent to work at the dangerous quarry, where he quickly gets himself killed. Jip regularly acquires extra chores through his empathy for living creatures—both farm animals and infirm humans are called his "pets" by the manager and his wife as an excuse for assigning Jip the sole responsibility for their care. Indeed, the odd humans who stir little sympathy in townsfolk and governing officials become Jip's friends, and this is the case with the lunatic Put, an intelligent, cultured man whose periods of insanity result in his consignment to a cage at the poor farm—cheaper than the asylum. Jip's first opportunity for friendship with someone his own age comes when a family is remanded to the poor farm, and this friendship leads in turn to Jip's opportunity for schooling, an important step that links him with adult friends Lyddie (known to Jip as Teacher) and Luke Stevens.

Jip has been deprived of education to this point because it is in the manager's interest to have his able-bodied help on the farm. Hence the manager and his wife argue that he is deficient in understanding. When his new friend Lucy refuses to attend school without Jip, he has a brief opportunity—interrupted when the manager insists on keeping him home to help with farmwork—to learn, and his real intelligence is recognized by Lyddie. She reads daily to the class from the novel that mesmerized her, *Oliver Twist*, an especially meaningful story for Jip, who like Oliver does not know his parents' identity. Jip's father does prove to be rich, like Oliver's, but unfortunately his mother is a slave, and therefore his father wants him back only as property, in a twist on the Dickens story. Lyddie's recent gift of books to Jip includes *Uncle Tom's Cabin*, a text that gives him more insight than *Oliver Twist* into the direction his life is headed if found by his father, so Jip flees to Luke, the man whom Lyddie has told him he can trust if he finds himself in any kind of trouble.

Jip's exciting escape, capture, and second escape are the means by which Lyddie and Luke's romance finally ends in marriage. Jip believes his freedom would be meaningless to him without his friend Put's freedom, and the old man's sacrifice of his life for Jip is the clinching argument for his final run to Canada, where he heads for the care of Ezekiel Freeman, becoming a son to him. Jip's later resolution to return to the United States to become a soldier in the Civil War attests to the value of freedom and a responsibility to one's fellow beings that connects the two novels.

In *The Borning Room* (1991), Paul Fleishmann narrates an Ohio family's experience from the point of view of Georgina Caroline Lott, who was born in 1851 and is recounting her childhood to a visitor shortly before her death in 1918. Her grandfather Lott left New Hampshire thirty years before her birth and cleared the family's land out of forest. His new home included the "borning room," a room where the women of the household give birth and the dying await their final hour, a room that bears witness to the struggles, pain, and peace of the events recorded merely as names and dates in the family Bible. Georgina's memories give substance to that list of names and dates.

Much of the narrative focuses on the years surrounding the Civil War, Georgina's life from age eight to eighteen. The first episode in the borning room that she remembers brings together two instances of delivery, or deliverance: the birth of her brother Zeb and the help exchanged with a runaway slave. Shortly after Georgina discovers and hides the slave, Cora, she and her sister are alone in the house with her mother as labor begins. The older Lucilla is dispatched on foot to fetch the midwife, ten miles away. Knowing that Cora has borne several children, Georgina brings her out of hiding to help her mother. In return, the men of the family, supporters of the Underground Railroad, help Cora on her way, and Cora leaves behind a cornhusk doll for Georgina. In a more lasting act of gratitude, Georgina's mother asks her to hang a lantern in the garret as a signal of help for future runaways.

The death of Georgina's grandfather has an equal impact on her and helps to shape her subsequent values. She is twelve when he suffers a stroke on a Sunday when Georgina is worshipping at home with him. A freethinker, her grandfather communes with nature and discusses his reflections with whichever child is with him, an observance he substitutes for the local Protestant service. Georgina respects and understands her grandfather's nature-oriented philosophy of life. She reveres his oft-repeated story of having shaken Benjamin Franklin's hand and his wide knowledge, gleaned through reading; he often quotes Franklin in conversation. After the stroke, neighbors who sit at his bedside work desperately to convert him, luridly depicting the torments of hell. Georgina, in contrast, brings a vase of violets to comfort him, and she is pleased to learn that he dies staunch in his beliefs, pointing to the violets in refutation of the arguments he has been forced to listen to. She is further comforted when her father plants a fruit tree at his grave, a family tradition already established at her grandmother's death, one that will memorialize her own parents later.

Her mother's death is one of the most difficult trials Georgina faces. Impressed by the credentials of the community's new doctor, her father arranges for his attendance, rather than the midwife's, at her mother's next confinement, unaware that the man has delivered only two babies. The inexperienced doctor not only loses his patient and the infant he delivers but also fails to notice the second tiny twin, who survives with the patient nurturing and good sense of an embittered aunt who has recently moved into the house after the death of her husband and children. Georgina never feels as close to this youngest brother as to Zeb, because he always reminds her of her mother's death, and the house becomes a yet colder place for her when Lucilla marries, leaving Georgina and her two little brothers in her critical aunt's stern care. Before the youngest is two, both boys contract diphtheria, and Zeb nearly dies before Mr. Bock, the new schoolmaster who rooms with the family, breaks the membrane that obstructs his breathing, an action that endears him to Georgina. The outcome is their courtship and marriage in 1869.

These momentous births, illnesses, and deaths, occurring in the same room, the same bed, bring Georgina an understanding of the continuity of life, an understanding that is reinforced by the tree-planting custom and the custom of making death portraits of the dying and dead. As Georgina nears death herself, she recalls how she placed her first daughter in a cedar cradle made by her father, wrapping her in a blanket woven by her mother, and set Cora's cornhusk doll beside her. The infant was christened with her mother's given name and the name of the apple variety that her grandfather brought from New Hampshire to plant in Ohio. When her tiny daughter grasped her finger, Georgina felt she was bequeathing her grandfather's legacy: the child touched a hand that had touched a hand that had touched Benjamin Franklin's hand.

Franklin's values are seen in life on this Ohio farmstead. The education available through local schooling is extended considerably through the family's wide reading, their musical evenings, drawing, and discussions of religion and politics. Against the family's firm rationality and solid humanistic knowledge are set the more outmoded beliefs of the era: Georgina's maternal grandmother's superstitions about childbirth and the often contradictory home remedies for illnesses. This is a memorable family, whose participation in the transformation of Ohio from a frontier to part of a technologically advancing twentieth-century nation is chronicled in the memory of one strong woman, who learns to accept change even as she cherishes tradition.

ADDITIONAL READING RECOMMENDATIONS

The Eagle of the Ninth, 1954; *The Silver Branch*, 1957; *The Lantern Bearers*, 1959; and
     Sword at Sunset, 1963, by Rosemary Sutcliff
The King's Fifth, 1966, and *My Name Is Not Angelica*, 1989, by Scott O'Dell
Smith, 1967; *Black Jack*, 1969; *The Strange Affair of Adelaide Harris*, 1971; *John Diamond*
     [*Footsteps*], 1980; and *The December Rose*, 1987, by Leon Garfield
Roll of Thunder, Hear My Cry, 1977; *Let the Circle Be Unbroken*, 1981; *The Road to*
     Memphis, 1990; and *The Land*, 2001, by Mildred D. Taylor
Jacob Have I Loved by Katherine Paterson, 1980 (discussed in Families, Traditional and
     Redefined)
Beyond the Divide, 1983; *Beyond the Burning Time*, 1994; and *True North: A Novel of the*
     Underground Railroad, 1996, by Kathryn Lasky
Cat, Herself by Mollie Hunter, 1986
The Winter Room, 1989, and *The Rifle*, 1995, by Gary Paulsen
The Star Fisher, 1991, and *Dragon's Gate*, 1993, by Laurence Yep
A Break with Charity: A Story about the Salem Witch Trials by Ann Rinaldi, 1992
Dove and Sword: A Novel of Joan of Arc by Nancy Garden, 1995
The Pirate's Son by Geraldine McCaughrean, 1998
Anna of Byzantium by Tracy Barrett, 1999
Fever 1793 by Laurie Halse Anderson, 2000
The Book of the Lion by Michael Cadnum, 2000
The Playmaker by J. B. Cheaney, 2000
Girl with a Pearl Earring by Tracy Chevalier, 2000
Queen's Own Fool: A Novel of Mary Queen of Scots by Jane Yolen and Robert Harris, 2000
Post Cards from No Man's Land by Aidan Chambers, 2002
The Arthur trilogy by Kevin Crossley-Holland, 2001–3 (discussed in Old Tales Retold: Fairy
     Tales, Legends, Myths)

Imagined Futures

Eva by Peter Dickinson (1989)
The Giver by Lois Lowry (1993)
Phoenix Rising by Karen Hesse (1994)
The Exchange Student by Kate Gilmore (1999)

The genre of science fiction has long functioned as a vehicle for social criticism. Social trends that we see around us, such as increased conformity, and the development of technology, such as "weapons of mass destruction" and genetic alteration, as well as the dangers inherent in disregard for the environment, suggest frightening futures. Thus most tales depicting the future are cautionary tales, meant to alert readers to the potential negative outcomes of current actions. Such tales are often frightening, but the ones discussed here offer optimism in their shared theme of humans' capacity to learn.

The topic of xenotransplantation—the replacement of diseased organs in humans with animal organs, typically from baboons or pigs—is no longer just the stuff of science fiction. However, far more extensive merging of human with animal is represented in Peter Dickinson's *Eva* (1989). When Eva's body suffers irremediable damage in a car accident and her neural memory is transplanted into the body of a young chimpanzee, Kelly, a spectrum of ethical issues is raised, along with the question, what does it mean to be human? The first issue has to do with the decision made by Eva's parents. Eva herself wakes into consciousness eight months after the accident, and eight months after the decision has been made. She wakes to a world controlled by the scientists who have created her new identity and only gradually comes to recognize the ramifications of being Eva inside Kelly's body. As she comes to terms with it and learns to inhabit her body anew, becoming a new creature consciously as well as physically, Eva becomes a spokesperson for the chimpanzees' right to ethical treatment as well.

Expected by scientists to be only the first of many new humans reborn into animal bodies, Eva settles into her gap-bridging role because of her early life among chimps. Her father works with the pool of chimpanzees available for human research purposes, created for a world in which the expanding human population and incursions into the environment have eliminated most of the large animal species. As an infant and toddler, Eva developed an extraordinary depth of understanding of the chimpanzees through daily contact. Thus she does not resist merging her identity with the ghostlike echo of Kelly that remains in the body she now inhabits, unlike the humans later merged into chimp bodies in disastrous attempts to replicate Eva's success story. Eva never forgets Kelly but welcomes her memory and her ability to function in the world, an ability that includes her need for a social group of other chimpanzees. While the adult humans seem to have expected to have a human Eva in a chimp's body—thinking, feeling, and acting much as she did before the accident—and strangers meeting her sometimes see her as an extraordinary chimp, Eva herself is the only creature fully capable of understanding the implications of the synthesis.

She finds, however, that she can communicate well with the young environmental activist Grog, who accepts her as she is but nonetheless, like every adult Eva has contact with after her new identity is forged, has an agenda for her. An animal rights activist, Grog sees in Eva the potential leader of a band of chimpanzees able to return to the wild, if sufficient appropriate land can be found for them, something chimps in captivity cannot do without a guide. It is ironic that Grog, who ultimately succeeds in engineering the project that results in Eva's living largely as a wild chimpanzee for the rest of her life, comes to know her through his mother's direction of the commercials for the company that funded the experiment with Eva and Kelly, commercials that feature chimpanzees in human clothing. For their money, the company expects to get some lucrative programming, raising from the outset the question of who actually owns Eva herself and who can legally speak for her. Before she has even awoken from her coma, she is committed to commercials by her parents' and the Chimpanzee Pool's acceptance of corporate funding.

In accepting the physical and social aspects of her chimpanzee identity, Eva loses her relationship with her mother, who never stops missing the beautiful little human girl she bore and is made uncomfortable by Eva's grooming her. She becomes nearly frantic at the thought of Eva's being among the chimpanzees as she goes into estrus. Eva's father sees her as a wonderful research opportunity, a covert agent among the chimpanzees. Eva herself brings all the knowledge she has acquired to her development of relationships with the Pool chimps, which subsequently helps them make the transition to living in the wild. She wants to avoid taking over as leader in an unnatural way, and therefore she must forge a close alliance with a bright male chimp who can become the leader of her group as they escape from the fenced area on Madagascar to repopulate the jungle. It is ironic that Eva loses her bond with her mother through her transformation because the mother-daughter bond is the strongest bond in her chimpanzee life, and the last creature to give her comfort on her deathbed is her own daughter.

Eva succeeds by accepting her life as an animal, though she teaches her family and kinship group how to tie knots and plant vegetation, passing useful (human) skills to them. Thus she achieves a fulfilling life by being a chimp, and she serves both chimpanzees and humans by establishing the apes' right to a life in the wild independent of humans, bringing hope for a future world in which balance between civilization's good and nature's basic claim on all animal life may be achieved.

Lois Lowry's powerful, thought-provoking novel *The Giver* (1993) has rapidly acquired the status of a modern classic. An antiutopian novel, it underscores the dangers of creating a peaceful and egalitarian society at the price of rigid conformity that stigmatizes not only intense emotion and spontaneity but also privacy and creativity. Jonas, citizen of a peaceful conformist society in an unidentified place and time, is apprenticed to the community's only Receiver, the sole repository of memories of human experiences from a past predating climate control, the elimination of war, and the substitution of socially engineered families for biological ones. This is a society where sexuality is suppressed via voluntary daily medication; large animals such as elephants and hippos are considered mythical; and daily life in the community involves no high-powered vehicles, presumably in an effort to maximize citizen safety. Chances of the citizens' suffering pain are minimized, but at the expense of minimizing their pleasures as well.

The first few chapters introduce the reader to the structure of community life. Individuality is suppressed through the regulation of the stages of life: at a yearly ceremony, each cohort of children receives the same symbols of growth (for example, clothing with buttons or bicycles); the youngest children are assigned to adult couples, whose marriages have been arranged and who do not engage in sex, so that all may experience an approximation of family life; the oldest children are given their adult job assignments. When the children are grown, parents live with other childless adults; they spend their last years living with other elderly people. Children do not know who their birth parents or grandparents are. The concept of love is foreign, deemed too abstract.

Nurturing babies is one of the community jobs, the job that Jonas's father performs. His position becomes important in Jonas's growing disaffection with community values. Because nurturers must ensure that infants are ready to be integrated into family life, they decide if a child is too fussy, too wakeful, or otherwise unable to meet expectations. Such infants are euthanized. This is a portion of the job that Jonas has no knowledge of until he watches his father kill one of a pair of twins, to keep the community from having to deal with the confusion rearing twins would entail. The practice of ridding the community of unsatisfactory members, both young and old, is kept from the people. Individuals who have been eliminated are described as having been "released."

Like infants who cry too much, the elderly residents are released from the community when they are deemed more trouble than they are worth. Release is the normal way of death, but most community members do not witness it; instead, they attend a celebration for the individual about to be released in which his life is recalled, its worth noted, and when the individual departs into another room, none of the celebrants is aware that this person is being executed. It is a chilling practice. Release is also practiced on criminals. Only once in the community's memory has it been voluntarily sought, and Jonas learns that this suicide was chosen by his predecessor, the most recent Receiver's apprentice, who has subsequently been labeled a failure.

This is only one of the ways in which language use is distorted and regulated in this society. In daily dinner-table discussions, all members of a family are expected to share their day's experiences, identifying their emotions so that the emotional experience may be dispelled. Only when Jonas begins to understand how narrow a range of human experience is available to the community does he realize they have misapplied the words to pale copies of the emotions they represent: his sister, for example, has identified her "anger" when, Jonas later realizes, she has experienced only annoyance. Lies are forbidden, and apologies for minor deviations from routine behavior, such as any apparent curiosity about an individual, are habitual. Precision of language use is instilled in children from an early age, but "precision" means that observable concrete experience is privileged and imaginative thought dismissed as "imprecise." Children learn appropriate language use through instruction, as well as through public humiliation and even punishment. Jonas's friend Asher actually stopped talking altogether for a time when he regularly confused the words "snack" and "smack" at age three, a speech error that led to his receiving an increasing number of stinging blows with a discipline wand each time he repeated his mistake. Such severe punishment of a small child and such unyielding expectations of conformity make it clear that freedom and individualism are vices in this society.

Both privacy and change have been ruled out as well. Public announcements are made via an audio system that places an invasive speaker in every dwelling, and communication is two-way; only the Receiver has the capacity to turn off the one in his room. Any suggestion for a better way of doing things is referred to a committee, and community members share a standing joke about consigning any matter to a committee—it is the same thing as saying that nothing will change. Communal child production and child-rearing, standardized occupations, daily family routines, and the composition of families are all regulated by a council of elders, a group committed to preserving things just as they are. Even names are carefully regulated: when an elderly person is released, his or her name becomes available and will be assigned to a "newchild" at the annual ceremony when the infants are placed in homes and the children move up a year in age and privileges. More fundamental changes have been implemented as well: no one sees color, except the Receiver and those rare children who show some aptitude for following in his footsteps, like Jonas, who begins to see red just before his assignment; the climate is controlled and the terrain has been leveled to maximize food production.

This society remains stable, leading a bland but secure existence, because so many elements of human experience have been regulated out of existence. Memories of the whole spectrum of experience are held only by the Receiver, who takes on the role of the Giver as soon as Jonas begins learning from him. As memories are transmitted to Jonas in full experiential detail, the Giver loses them, lightening the burden he carries. It is his job to be the community's sage, but he can share his wisdom only when the elders request it. For most of his extraordinarily lonely existence, he lives with the most mundane as well as the most profound experiences of the past, as well as their intense emotional component, unable to share his richer, deeper knowledge with anyone. This is the burden he begins passing to Jonas, and this is the burden that led to his last apprentice's request for release, a failure of strength for the immensity of the burden that is made more poignant by the fact that she was the Giver's daughter. The distress caused by this child's release was felt throughout the community when the unsettling memories she had already received were dispelled at the moment of death and picked up by every member: memories of loneliness, hunger, and terror.

It is the convergence of Jonas's understanding of release with the news of the impending release of the newchild his family has been fostering, whom Jonas has begun to love, that makes him decide to flee the community. He knows that his escape will set all his memories free among his neighbors, an outcome he believes is preferable to their remaining ignorant of what life really means. His motivation is personal—he seeks freedom from his society's constraints; he wants to save the foster brother he loves; and he wants to find a part of the world where love rather than regulations binds people in relationship. Babies represent hope for the future, and though Jonas's escape brings him fear and suffering, the end of his journey suggests the beginning of a new and more fulfilling kind of life.

The ambiguity of the ending can lead to a more pessimistic sense of the novel's meaning: the reader may interpret Jonas's closing thoughts as a dream state brought on by starvation and exposure, only to be terminated by death. This reading is reinforced by the fact that Jonas is seeing and feeling experiences that were previously transmitted to him by the Giver. However, Lowry has suggested a more positive reading: Jonas is headed toward a new life, and whether the reader interprets this as an afterlife or simply survival in a different part of the world, it will undeniably be better than the life he has been living—with freedom, music, color, and love.

Karen Hesse's poetic books establish a strong sense of place in support of the themes they develop, and *Phoenix Rising* (1994), the story of the aftereffects on rural New England of a nuclear power plant accident, is no exception. Nye lives with her grandmother on a Vermont sheep farm that stays largely radiation free, but the impact of the disaster is brought home to them when they take in sick Boston evacuees, the wife and son of the manager of the plant. The environmental effects of the spread of radiation are widespread, and the long-term outlook for the health of the region's inhabitants is gloomy. Nye's relatives living nearer the site must destroy their large dairy herd and lose their livelihood. They also suffer severe illness, an illness that threatens the life of Nye's youngest cousin, Bethany. These health and environmental effects are magnified by the ignorance and prejudice that surround the event. Nye's grandmother keeps their visitors' presence quiet as long as she can, and Nye does not tell even her close friend Muncie about them because Muncie's family shares the local fear of contamination through contact with evacuees from the plant's vicinity. Muncie nastily dismisses all the evacuees as "mutants," and their neighbor Ripley later transfers his grief over his dog's death in the contaminated area to rage at the evacuees.

Having a bedridden fifteen-year-old suffering from radiation sickness in the back bedroom of her home adds work to Nye's daily round of chores, and she resents her grandmother's extending hospitality without consulting her. The situation exacerbates her anger in reaction to the power plant accident—science, which once was a subject studied in a textbook, has now become unpleasantly real to her. She also resents the intrusion of Ezra and his mother and resists becoming emotionally involved with them because the last two people who inhabited the back bedroom—her mother and her grandfather—died. Thus, they abandoned her as surely as Nye's father did when he deserted the family after her mother contracted cancer, and she does not want to make any kind of emotional connection with anyone else who is going to die. When she first begins sitting with Ezra for brief periods to give his mother some respite, he does not talk or acknowledge her presence at all, but she reads aloud to him and talks about her life. By the time he regains enough will to live that he is ready to interact, they are more connected than Nye has realized, since Ezra has been listening to her and getting to know her all along.

Ezra must overcome agonizing fear as he regains strength. Having refused to leave his dying father, who in his turn had stayed in the highly radioactive plant as long as he could to help his employees, Ezra has become violently ill through exposure, and he fears contamination of the air, the soil, all his surroundings. Still, during the time he has been bedridden, he has conceived a longing for the sheep-farming life Nye and her grandmother lead, admiring their apparent self-sufficiency, and Nye is able gradually to coax him out onto the farm, though she takes issue with his belief that they can be truly independent. Her position is underscored by her grandmother's concern about the economic aftereffects of the accident: with Boston deserted, she wonders who will buy their cheese.

Ezra recovers enough to attend school briefly, but the ugly bullying of Nye's neighbor escalates into a brutal beating, and Ezra's medical emergency reveals that he is suffering from leukemia. Against her will, Nye has again become emotionally involved with someone who is dying. Facing this death is painful, and she is also forced to deal with the earlier deaths that have bereaved her, this time with more maturity and understanding. What the nuclear accident has demonstrated to Nye and others most clearly is that all are connected—all humans, all their natural supports of oxygen, water, and food supply. This means, of course, that what injures one geographic area, one group of people, harms everyone. It also means that all must take responsibility for their link to others, a responsibility that Nye has accepted. After Ezra's death, she is resolved to take further action, to claim the citizen's right to inform her congressmen of what she has seen and learned.

Her fear of trusting others nearly costs Nye her only friendship when Muncie learns what Nye has concealed from her. When Ezra is attacked, however, Muncie joins in the fight, and her friendship with Nye is cemented anew as they clean up afterward while Nye's grandmother and Ezra's mother take Ezra to the hospital. Muncie sees Nye more clearly, in some ways, than Nye sees herself, pointing out that she is just like her grandmother, doing things her own way without regard for other people. Though Nye comes to know Ezra only to lose him, and with him her first romantic attraction to a boy, she gains self-knowledge from him too, when he writes her a letter that thanks her for inspiring him to live. Ezra admires Nye's nonjudgmental acceptance of him as an obligation she must shoulder—because someone must. In the final analysis, this memorable novel is about responsibility and interdependence.

A future after ecological near-disaster is imagined in the year 2094 in Kate Gilmore's novel, *The Exchange Student* (1999). After contact with intelligent beings on another planet is established, nine young alien "exchange students" move into widely scattered homes on earth. The Chelans maintain a facade of normal curiosity about every aspect of life on this planet, though from the start they manifest an intense reverence for animals. Secretly, they hold conversations with each other that gradually reveal their concealed mission to steal animals for their home planet. With a high degree of intelligence and extraordinary technological development, they hope to re-create their own ecosystem to include a full range of animal life. When it becomes obvious that they cannot steal the animals they covet, they plot to raid the DNA stores of an organization dedicated to preserving earth's endangered species, all the while manipulating and deceiving their hosts. The drama of the Chelan plot highlights humans' own eco-collapse in 2025, history from which the earths' inhabitants have learned to value and protect the ecosystem by 2094.

Fen, the Chelan who masterminds the plot (though he must be pushed into it by the leader of their group), is fortunate enough to be placed with a host sister who is a budding zoologist. Daria maintains a menagerie and participates in a breeding program coordinated by the experienced director of the Ark, the organization that Fen eventually plans to raid. All of Daria's family are talented individuals committed to their special interests: the mother, Gloria, is a writer of fiction; the father, Roger, is a landscape architect and city planner; Daria's brother, Tim, is a musician; and her sister, Lily, designs clothing. Daria's experience in caring for and studying almost fifty animals on the premises makes her an ideal observer of her visitor's physiology, and their shared love of animals leads to their spending a lot of time together. Daria early discovers that Fen becomes uncomfortable and deflects nearly all questions about animals on Chela, a behavior that is somewhat surprising given his obvious fascination with earth fauna: his discomfort is readily apparent in the Chelan chameleon-like chromatic changes in response to intense emotion or stress. Fen's empathy and nonhumanness enable him to get quite near any animal without disturbing it, a quality that makes him quite useful to her in dealing with frightened animals. Despite her ability as an observer, however, Daria has no inkling of Fen's secret mission, even after he steals one of her new fennec fox kits from its mother. Their shared love of animals, however, leads to successful resolution of both Chelans' and humans' dilemma in a cooperative venture using Chelan technological expertise and earth's DNA storehouse.

This novel requires the reader to consider what it would be like to live in a world without any large animals. Gilmore is convincing in envisioning an ecological disaster that might accelerate rapidly from small beginnings, while she comfortingly depicts a world in which humans have learned the hard lesson of respect for the fragile ecosystem. The challenge in creating believable aliens is always to find sufficient common ground for mutual sympathy between humans and others while making them sufficiently different to reflect the biology of an imagined different world. The device of color change works well in this regard as a feature humans share to a certain degree and one that allows for a learning process in communicating across unimaginably different cultures. The label "exchange student" is turned on its head, since Fen has no intention of attending a high school in the Hudson Valley, and given his training and his culture's sophistication, the idea of his being able to acquire academic knowledge is ludicrous. Yet ultimately the leading zoologists of both planets, with their disciples, study each other's knowledge in a balanced exchange that gives the title added meaning.

ADDITIONAL READING RECOMMENDATIONS

House of Stairs by William Sleator, 1974
Z for Zachariah by Robert C. O'Brien, 1975
The Hitchhiker's Guide to the Universe, 1980, and sequels by Douglas Adams
The Ear, the Eye, and the Arm: A Novel, 1994, and *The House of the Scorpion*, 2002, by
    Nancy Farmer
Galax-Arena: A Novel by Gillian Rubinstein, 1995
Feed by M. T. Anderson, 2002

Imagined Places

Harper Hall trilogy by Anne McCaffrey (1976–79)
His Dark Materials trilogy by Philip Pullman (1995–2000)
Howl's Moving Castle by Diana Wynne Jones (1986)

Fantasy, legend, and science fiction can take a variety of forms. Some texts are set in an imagined past or future; some focus on magical powers, magical people, or magical creatures; some focus on special places that may or may not be accessible from our world. J. R. R. Tolkien created so complete and compelling a world that fans learn to write in Elvish, study the extensive body of legends that Tolkien wrote in support of the *Lord of the Rings*, and gather to celebrate Bilbo and Frodo's birthday. J. K. Rowling's enormously successful series is set in imaginary spaces located within contemporary Britain: Hogwarts School of Witchcraft and Wizardry reached via the express that departs from Platform 9¾, Diagon Alley, Sirius Black's house, and others. Philip Pullman draws on physics' many-worlds explanation of reality when he places an Oxford of another world just a window away from his own Oxford. Imagined worlds hold magic for the reader, whatever creatures or devices embody that magic for the characters who dwell in them.

Anne McCaffrey's long-running series is set in Pern, where humans ride dragons, and an intense empathic bond between the dragon and his or her rider enables them to cooperate for the common good. In this very different world from ours, deadly Threadfall from a sister planet can slice a person to ribbons, and the dragons defend the human population from the menace; social structures are governed by the need for defense and protection; and communities are structured around safe places. Communication, history, and education are facilitated by harpers, members of a guild trained centrally at Harper Hall. In this imaginary setting, McCaffrey tells very human stories. In her Harper Hall trilogy (1976–79), she focuses on gifted young people's separation from families, negotiation of school culture, and vocational choice, while they cope with the challenges of burgeoning relationships and with other changes, their interactions complicated by strong bonds with fire lizards, small cousins of the dragons. The trilogy focuses on two characters: Menolly, a girl (fourteen at the outset) who cannot stop music from pouring out of her despite all her parents' efforts to keep her from conduct deemed unseemly in a woman, and her younger friend Piemur, a smart scapegrace whose talent is his clear soprano voice until it changes, when he must find a new vocational path. The first volume, *Dragonsong*, focuses on Menolly's escape from her father's stern conservative rule to live in a cave with nine fire lizards, beasts believed mythical by the hard-nosed practical seamen of her home community. Here she proves her ability not only to survive but also to recognize the power of her musical gift, whose expression in her home has brought her beatings. The middle volume, *Dragonsinger*, is a satisfying school story that develops Menolly and Piemur's bond in the context of school rivalries, intimidating masters' requirements, and a position on the fringes of changes in the greater world in which young people may play an important role in promoting needed cultural change. In this context, which values originality in musical expression and fosters social change, Menolly is taught to stop apologizing for who and what she is and to develop her gift. The third volume, *Dragondrums*, shows an opposite course of development for her younger friend Piemur, whose musical talent is appreciated and rewarded until the loss of his boy's soprano sends him off to learn new skills. Like Menolly, Piemur too must live in the wild alone for a time, using his wits and his love of the graceful, coveted fire lizards to survive and, ultimately, discover his vocation.

The ability of communities to change in response to changing circumstances is an important theme. Humans on Pern have a social structure that has served them well, and their love of tradition is manifested in their fondness for the time-honored ballads that all the harpers learn. Each community has its harper, who teaches the children through song. The importance of song in everyone's life makes it potentially a powerful vehicle for changing attitudes and values. Menolly, whose musical gifts are extraordinary, is prohibited by her dour traditionalist father from performing the songs of her own making, but her ability to compose lilting, appealing tunes is the very talent most valued by the master harpers. Her plight is a comment not only on patriarchal society's waste of girls' abilities but also on the plight of the gifted artist whose originality goes unappreciated in communities too rigidly schooled to conformity and tradition.

Both Menolly and Piemur undergo unplanned initiatory experiences. Menolly helps a female fire lizard move her eggs to the safety of a cave, where she herself makes a home and is reborn as an esteemed individual, emerging from the womblike enclosure bonded to nine newly hatched dragons-in-miniature, whose bond with the humans they imprint on is almost mystical. Her experience with only these small creatures for company gives her another kind of expertise, in addition to her musical genius, that wins her immediate acceptance in the larger world, once she has been rescued from her father's domain. Piemur, after stealing a fire dragon egg on a spying mission, hides in a wagon and wakes outside of any geographical area he knows, without means of communicating with the harper community and with the very pressing need to find food for himself, avoid Threadfall, feed and protect his fire lizard hatchling, and then care for a crippled young runner beast before he can find his way back to civilization and reestablish contact with his friends and mentors of the guild. In the course of his wilderness adventure, he becomes a man.

Both young people are severely challenged by their peers' envy of their abilities and the dullness of less talented or soured elders who cannot appreciate their originality, even in the elite Harper Hall community. Menolly, though, has suffered her cruelest injury in her healer mother's failure to properly treat a deep gash in her hand, in the hope of keeping Menolly from playing music. After being abused for her ability, the minor persecutions of fellow apprentices simply rouse her ire.

Both she and Piemur suffer hazing and undeserved punishment and learn discretion. Both are intelligent and good-natured, curious about the world, and likable, but it is clear that there will always be people who underestimate them or undermine their successes, something each must come to terms with. It is equally clear that their sense of vocation and the respect of those they themselves respect will sustain them.

The empathic communication between humans and their fire lizards and dragons is one of the most appealing features of this world. The intensity of the bond is almost embarrassing to witness, its loss leading to utter desolation. When a hatchling imprints on a human, the joy felt by each is much like a mother and child's joy in each other. Similarly, when Menolly's and Sebell's fire lizards mate, they consummate their own love, its intensity increased by the lizards' union. The communicative dimension of their emotional bond makes it more intense than human-pet bonds in our world.

An animal is envisioned as the visible soul of each human in Philip Pullman's His Dark Materials trilogy (1995–2000), one of the most unusual features of the world parallel to our own where the protagonist Lyra lives. This ambitious saga replays the battle against the Kingdom of Heaven by rebel angels, this time led by a human and joined by other creatures in revolt against the Authority, or "Ancient of Days," who has withdrawn from the worlds, and in whose name a destructive, joyless power is exerted by the Church, whose doctrine prevents people from accepting and living fully in their bodies. Amid these momentous events, a second Eve, Lyra, whose importance has been prophesied in the world of her birth, grows through the last days of childhood toward temptation to knowledge of her body's needs and desires in a second "fall," a fall that brings out human potential rather than undermining the divine and paves the way for humans to build the Republic of Heaven.

This rambunctious Eve is an imaginative liar, appropriately named "Lyra," who, ironically, possesses preternatural ability in reading the alethiometer, a truth-reading instrument, also known as "the golden compass." Lyra's friend and protector, the armored bear, names her "Silvertongue" for her persuasive abilities, her storytelling, and her prevaricating. Joined with Will, the unwavering wielder of "the subtle knife"—a tool that cuts windows between the many worlds that have diverged at crucial decision points—Lyra brings an end to death as it has been ordained, a perpetual dreary limbo, and frees the deceased bodies to mingle freely, and happily, with the elements, restoring their affinity with the natural world in the kind of "immortality" that arises from decomposition and atomic recombination into new lives.

Several important motifs develop this ambitious tale. Each book is titled with the name of a tool, a tool that enables its wielder to weigh truth, see consciousness, or enter parallel worlds, and the person in whose charge that tool resides plays a leading role in that volume of the story. (The first volume was titled *Northern Lights* in Great Britain; its retitling as *The Golden Compass* in the first American edition more effectively balances the titles of the second and third volumes, *The Subtle Knife* and *The Amber Spyglass*.) The relationship between body and soul is explored through the visible form of "daemons" in Lyra's world. Particles of consciousness permeate each world, more or less visible to inhabitants, known as "Dust" in Lyra's world, "dark matter" in ours, and indicating a relationship between body and mind that is seen as sinful in Lyra's world and prompts excesses on the part of the Church reminiscent of the Spanish Inquisition.

The titles point to connections between religion and science, each of which is concerned with ultimate reality. Lyra's alethiometer is more useful than a library of human knowledge; it is a tool for discovering truth, difficult to read and requiring years of study—except by the imaginative Lyra, who intuitively reads its ambiguous answers until her fall into adult knowledge of love destroys this ability. While it tells truth, it does not predict the future, suggesting that the future is not fixed. Will's subtle knife cuts anything, including the fabric of the material world, opening windows from one world into another. It is manipulated by concentration of the will rather than the heart, and it shatters when the bearer, distracted by love, fails to direct it. The knife even takes Will and Lyra to the land where the dead reside, enabling them to lead the poor shadows out into another world where they can finally find dissolution. Every time it is wielded, however, it creates a specter that feeds on adult human souls, leaving them as hollow shells, and hence his last task as bearer of the knife is to seal all the windows, leaving humans to work out their own destinies within the context of the world they were born into. Dr. Mary Malone, a nun turned scientist, makes the amber spyglass in the world of the gentle mulefa, so that she can detect the conscious Dust particles, and with it she discovers that they are rapidly flowing out of the mulefas' world. Her research in our world has been directed to understanding dark matter, and her brief meeting with Lyra brings insight into its conscious nature, prompting computer communication with it that impels her escape into the world in which she can play her vital role in the second Fall. Each of these mechanical instruments connects spirit or mind with the physical.

The concrete form of the spirit, or soul, is manifested as a daemon in animal form in Lyra's world. The daemon is a constant companion of the individual, inseparable from him or her till death, who talks with the person and, often, expresses an emotional state that the person masks. It is appropriately changeable in form up to puberty, expressing the malleability of the child's personality. Generally of the opposite gender from the human it is affiliated with, it takes a fixed animal shape appropriate to the human's personality. Thus Lyra's father, the powerful Lord Asriel, has a fierce snow leopard as daemon, and her mother, Mrs. Coulter, has a quick-witted, heartless but beautiful monkey as hers. Will, coming from our world, does not know he has a daemon, though Lyra readily recognizes that his is inside him, until he enters the isle of the dead and, like Lyra, must leave his daemon behind. Both Lyra and Will suffer enormous pain at this separation, and later their daemons hide from them and tease them, no longer trusting them, demonstrating that the daemon may keep secrets from its person if it wants to. At the human's death, the daemon vanishes in instant dissolution. When Lyra leads the dead out of confinement, they anticipate reunion with their daemons in a similar dissolution, no longer confined to a joyless limbo, cheated of the heaven that religion promised them.

Lyra may be afraid when she gets to the land of the dead, and on its shores she meets her own death, but she acts with courage. This liberation brings an end to a shadow life following ordinary physical life in the body, paving the way for future generations to find salvation and joy in living rather than postponing it to an imagined afterlife. Her courage is strengthened by her sense of responsibility to those she has betrayed—her friend Roger, whose daemon was severed from him by her father in order to open a path between worlds, and her very own daemon Pantalaimon.

Lyra is a very stout-hearted heroine, on the whole, though as Will gains stature, her dependency on him grows. Nonetheless, they form a balanced partnership: Lyra is always loving, calling the bear king "my dear" and trying to love her parents, inspiring strong loyalties in the adults who know her as herself, regardless of whether they are aware of the prophecies surrounding her; and Will never becomes so caught up in the adventure that he does not care deeply for Lyra nor does he lose sight of his tender concern for his mother. The crises through which they pass together bring them closer, preparing the way for the all-enveloping love that will be the outcome of Lyra's temptation by the "serpent," Mary.

Mary's temptation comes in the form of a narrative of her decision to leave the church, a narrative that emphasizes joy in one's body and awakens in Lyra a sense of opening within. Her daemon and Will's, now visible, are close, sharing secrets, and as the human pair seeks the daemon pair, the occasion, the "garden," and the temptation conjoin. This is what Lyra's parents have, finally, enabled. Lord Asriel, fierce and proud, has opened the way between the worlds and built a citadel to lead an assault on "the Authority," on God, joining the dissatisfied angels who similarly rebelled with Lucifer. Lyra's mother, who has long sought worldly power for herself through the church, follows a devious path only to finally join Asriel in overcoming the powerful angel Megatron. The destruction of the fragile, aged Authority—who has not been seen in the worlds for thousands of years—is a mere by-product of the massive conflict that involves bears, witches, specters, and the dead. What their victory brings is an end to human lives lived without joy; their happiness in the physical postponed to the promise of surpassing heavenly reward. The name of Lyra's daemon, "Pantalaimon," suggests "pantheism," finding god in nature.

Lyra and Will make a very difficult decision at the end, severing the connection between their worlds so that both will live full lives in their respective worlds, taking their knowledge, their joy, their love, and their conviction into their own societies. Pullman's subject matter is the epic matter of Milton's *Paradise Lost*, and if opinion is divided as to his artistic success in discussing so fundamental a theme, he nonetheless furnishes plenty of matter for thought. Many fantasies, however, are far more lighthearted, without loss of quality as literary works.

Diana Wynne Jones combines humor with fantasy in entertaining novels in which, often, young people learning about themselves discover that they have magical powers, and, often, must cope with their powers, the forces of evil, and growing up simultaneously. In *Howl's Moving Castle* (1986), Sophie Hatter must overcome her ideas about the preordained role of the oldest of three sisters, as well as gain control over her magic, protect herself from the wizard who eats young girls' hearts, and cope with the aches and pains of a body that has been charmed into an old woman's body. This novel does away with the classic fairy tale's sequence of three siblings off to seek their fortune or to overcome danger. The first always botches the matter, Sophie knows, and the second child is equally unsuccessful. Hence, she and Lettie have always encouraged the youngest sister, Martha, to prepare for the role of successful adventurer. Their fortunes seem fixed after their father's death, when Sophie and Lettie's stepmother—young, loving, but impoverished—sets all three girls to apprentice so they can learn respectable trades. She sends beautiful Lettie to the bakery, where she hopes the girl will get offers of marriage; she sends clever Martha to a witch; and she puts Sophie to work in her own hat shop, which she plans to bequeath to the girl one day.

Sophie seems ready to settle into exploited drudgery without a murmur, increasingly isolating herself from other people, talking only to the hats she trims—until she crosses the Witch of the Waste and is bewitched. Unable to explain that she is really young Sophie under a spell, she hobbles off to find her fortune and, no longer afraid of lecherous Wizard Howl in her transformed body, she seeks a night's lodging in his peripatetic castle when she is benighted.

What Sophie is slow to recognize, as she finds a home with the wizard, his apprentice, and a fire demon, is that her transformation has liberated her. As an elderly woman, she can be bossy and crotchety, and she need not fear the attentions of the opposite sex. Although there is much about wizard and castle that she does not know, she asserts her right to a place with them and earns their respect through her magical power, a power that, however, she often uses without thinking through the ramifications of her actions.

Instead of being the family's failure—the dull-witted firstborn bound to mess up the heroic task—Sophie discovers she is skilled and lovable as herself, even before her beauty is restored. Moreover, pretty Lettie is interested in learning magic from the witch to whom Martha has been apprenticed and clever Martha wants ten children, so they change places within a couple of weeks of taking up their apprenticeships. All three young women thus confound the rigid expectations of conventional tale structure. All three nonetheless find true love as well as demonstrate their quick-wittedness.

A story about magic inevitably addresses the relationship between appearance and reality. Dogs and scarecrows are bewitched men; the Wizard's reputed heartlessness is repeatedly contradicted by his kind acts; the obtuseness Sophie sees in him belies his insights; and the Witch of the Waste's fire demon masquerades as a schoolteacher in Wales, the only "real world" locale that Howl's castle door opens into. Much of the novel's action occurs within the castle, in part because Sophie is unable to move from there when the castle appears in other locales.

John Donne's "Song" beginning, "Go and catch a falling star," is the spell cast on Wizard Howl by the Witch of the Waste. It is completed when Howl is honest with Sophie in the midst of a wind he has whipped up, and he very nearly loses his life to the Witch's demon but is rescued by Sophie, who has the power of talking life into things. Howl's appealing fire demon decides to stay on voluntarily, once the contract that binds them to each other is broken. Once Howl has fully destroyed both the Witch and her demon, he is free to suggest a "happily ever after" resolution to Sophie, who acknowledges that "happily ever after" will be eventful with him.

ADDITIONAL READING RECOMMENDATIONS

The Lord of the Rings by J. R. R. Tolkien, 1954
The Time Quartet by Madeleine L'Engle, 1962–91
The Prydain Chronicles by Lloyd Alexander, 1964–68
The Earthsea Cycle by Ursula K. LeGuin, 1968–90
Red Shift by Alan Garner, 1973
The Dalemark Quartet, 1975–94, and The Chronicles of Chrestomanci, 1977–2005, by Diana
     Wynne Jones
Riddle-Master trilogy by Patricia McKillip, 1976–79
Dragon of the Lost Sea, 1982, *Dragon Steel*, 1985, *Dragon Cauldron*, 1991, and *Dragon War*,
     1992, by Laurence Yep
Pit Dragon trilogy by Jane Yolen, 1982–87
Kingdom series by Cynthia Voigt, 1985–2001
The Chronicles of the Enchanted Forest by Patricia C. Wrede, 1985–94
Eight Days of Luke by Diana Wynne Jones, 1988
Dream Spinner by Joanne Hoppe, 1992
The Abhorsen Trilogy by Garth Nix, 1995–2002
The Thief, 1996, and *The Queen of Attolia*, 2000, by Megan Whalen Turner
Harry Potter series by J. K. Rowling, 1997–
The Wee Free Men, 2003, and *A Hatful of Sky*, 2004, by Terry Pratchett

Insiders and Outsiders

The Outsiders by S. E. Hinton (1967)
Necessary Roughness by Marie G. Lee (1996)
One of the Boys by Scott Johnson (1992)
The Harmony Arms by Ron Koertge (1992)

The Outsiders dramatizes a major theme for adolescents in every generation: the need for insider status, for belonging. A teen herself when she wrote this now-classic novel, S. E. Hinton expresses the desire that every young person has: to be an accepted and important part of a family and of a valued social group. Hinton expressed it more poignantly than many more experienced writers have. The centrality of this theme in literature of the past forty years marks a significant departure from most of the literature written for teens before its publication, and many historians of the genre date the contemporary phase of YA literature to this 1967 novel. In much of the YA literature that has followed it, protagonists are alienated from the mainstream in some way—by race or ethnicity, social class, sexual identity, degree of intelligence or talent, or personal problems—and may or may not be integrated into society in order to resolve the immediate conflicts facing them.

The essence of gang membership is belonging, and Hinton's gangs are relatively innocent. Their violence is largely limited to fighting, or rumbling, sometimes with fists but, when threatened, with blades or broken bottles. Only the hoods, the real JDs (juvenile delinquents), possess guns or commit crimes more serious than minor shoplifting. What runs through Ponyboy Curtis's narrative is the need to be valued and to establish connection on the basis of what he sees—beautiful sunsets—and thinks about: Frost's poem "Nothing Gold Can Stay," with its Edenic longings for perpetual innocence, and Mitchell's *Gone with the Wind*, with its gallantry and courage in the face of defeat.

The nature of heroism is explored through several characters' actions. Abused, gentle, and timid Johnny Cade becomes a fugitive when he kills a Soc—a rich boy looking for opportunities to punish his social inferiors—to prevent Ponyboy's death by drowning, and then becomes a hero when he and Ponyboy save several children from a burning church. Even the toughest member of the gang, the dashing criminal Dallas (Dally) Winston, faces fire to try to rescue Johnny in turn. After Johnny's death, he commits a crime and faces police officers with an empty gun, willing his death at their hands. His gallantry may be considered suicidal rather than heroic, unless we take into consideration Ponyboy and Johnny's fondness for *Gone with the Wind*. Like the young Confederate heirs to plantations riding off to war, Ponyboy and Johnny undertake the rescue of the children boldly but unreflectively; Dallas, in contrast, faces physical danger when all hope is lost and without any expectation of winning glory after Johnny's death, throwing his life away much as Rhett Butler seems likely to do when Atlanta is burning. This kind of heroism wins admiration, and the surviving hero, Ponyboy, finds more acceptance in his community as a result of his actions.

Another kind of heroism is represented by Ponyboy's brothers. Daryl (Darry) illustrates an everyday kind of heroism in his steady self-discipline and hard work to keep his younger brothers together in the wake of their parents' death, and Soda drops out of school to help support their household. It takes the drama of Ponyboy's near drowning, his escape with Johnny, his heroism, and finally his fear for Johnny to bring him to the realization that Darry's daily sacrifices constitute a mature heroism. Darry's abilities would allow him to bridge social groups, but his family responsibilities prevent his being an insider in the world he would like to belong to.

Unlike the Curtis boys, Dallas and Johnny are doomed heroes. Johnny's physically brave actions are undertaken on the behalf of others, with total disregard for his personal safety. Sacrificing himself for others, finding peace and freedom only when apart from society in the quiet of a deserted church, leaving a message of encouragement to Ponyboy urging him to "stay gold," or innocent, Johnny may be considered a Christ-figure. It is by his own choice that he is crucified, and his death expiates sins that have not originated with him. Always outside, Johnny also achieves wisdom, which he passes along to Ponyboy.

Ponyboy, in contrast, survives the classic stages of formal initiation into adulthood—separated from friends and family, facing physical and emotional challenges, suffering loss, and coming through his ordeal with newfound wisdom, to be restored to his friends and family a changed individual. His account of the events is the vehicle by which he will be fully reintegrated into the community.

The Edenic world the main characters inhabit at the outset is largely a nonsexual one in which parentless boys eat what and when they like and roughhouse in sheer animal joy. Ponyboy's conversations with the popular and pretty Soc Cherry are genuine human-to-human contact, innocent of sexual desire. Part of the knowledge that Ponyboy acquires occurs when Soda's girlfriend betrays their love. The most important lesson, though, is that the young people are united by their common humanity, whatever social forces seem to divide them. When the Soc Randy later forswears violence and hatred, sickened by what has happened, it is Ponyboy who is able to express the wisdom that other characters lack, as he explains that his former enemy is "just a guy." He symbolizes what they share in terms of watching the sunset, which not only represents the beauty that Ponyboy appreciates but also subtly reminds the reader that like all dawns succeeded by day (in Frost's poem, "So dawn goes down to day"), all humans must face death, and thus all share what may be their most important experience.

Human relationships dominate this novel, and people are classified as "insiders" or "outsiders" purely on the basis of the classifer's perspective. The relations between Greasers and Socs, the relationships of Greasers to each other, and the relationship of the three brothers who share a parentless home and a common grief are the dominant elements of the novel. How people interact with each other, care for each other, hurt each other, destroy each other, and save each other are matters of import today as surely as they were to Hinton when she was a teenager.

Necessary Roughness (1996), by Marie G. Lee, portrays the uphill battle for tolerance that Korean American twins Chan Jung Kim and Young-Boon Kim face when they move from Los Angeles to a Minnesota mining town of fewer than eight thousand inhabitants. Although very close to each other, their battles are as different as their personalities and activities. Chan, from whose point of view the narrative unfolds, also faces a constant battle with his father, whose expectations are high. Chan's father, known as Abogee (Father) throughout the novel, was a chemist in Korea, though he is constrained to support the family in America by owning or managing small shops, and he has no respect for Chan's athletic ability and better-than-average but not stellar grades. Young, in contrast to her twin, is a stereotypically successful and obedient Korean American teen; she is an outstanding student, excelling especially in mathematics, and a musician, as well as a compliant daughter who earns her father's praise by succeeding in L.A.'s competitive Korean American community. Chan, on the other hand, has found his happiness on a county soccer team, most of whose members are Latino. Chan's soccer experience, along with his tae kwon do training, furnish his route to acceptance in their new high school, where he learns to play football after the team's kicker sustains serious injuries in an automobile accident. However, despite gaining entry, Chan continues to face the unpleasant challenges of racial discrimination, which sometimes takes the form of "necessary roughness," a term used by the assistant coach to describe the physically aggressive side of football.

The family has encountered racism from the moment they arrived in Iron River, where Mr. Kim is taking over his ne'er-do-well brother's franchised convenience store. Their position in this all-white town is not helped by Uncle Bong's preceding them. When they attempt to rent an apartment, they are not only turned away but physically ejected from the building where Bong lived, just after paying his last two months' rent in cash. The store has been trashed, but it is not until several months later that Chan learns this is because Bong was dealing drugs (as well as selling pornography, something Abogee learns the first time the magazine distributor delivers the store's standard order). Mr. and Mrs. Kim's hard work in the store, as well as their friendship with their elderly landlady Mrs. Knutsen, begins to replace the bad image that Bong created.

In this small town, the twins stand out in the mostly blond student body, but a few other students suffer discrimination as well: Jimmi Beargrease, a football player from the reservation an hour's drive from the high school, and Rainey Scarponi, called "the sausage queen" by students who look down on Italian Americans (her father has a successful sausage business). Beargrease is, however, accepted on the football team because of his friendship with the cocaptain Chan refers to as "Monster," a coarse bully who insults and eventually assaults Chan in the locker room and whose antagonism to Asian Americans, the reader eventually learns, has been fostered by his physician father, who lost a brother in Vietnam. Monster and Beargrease part company, though not in public, over administering "necessary roughness" to Chan: when several team members jump Chan from behind and cover his face with a towel so that he is not positive who roughs him up. It is reassuring that Monster's star status is not enough to protect him from dismissal from the team, because the head coach is a fair and kind man.

Young's experience is less challenging, or appears to be so because her story is not as central as Chan's and comes to an earlier end. She finds a good friend, Donna, and a boyfriend, Chan's friend Mikko. Neither of the twins is allowed to date until college, so the moments they can steal with potential dates (Chan with Rainey, Young with

Mikko) occur in school or after-school activities or are represented to their parents as time spent with same-sex friends. But Young's untimely death in an automobile accident puts questions of acceptance by peers, and even by the community, into a different perspective.

Following her death, Chan finds acceptance in school and on the team. Her funeral both emphasizes and diminishes the family's cultural differences from the rest of the town, as Mrs. Knutsen's women's club and the team gather round Chan and his parents, while their closest Korean American friends and Uncle Bong arrive on the scene. Instead of being embarrassed by the wailing of the Kim, Lee, and Park women in the Lutheran Church, Chan's parents appear to find it comforting, and the foods brought by their friends from California restore familiar smells and tastes to the gathering. The most dramatic moment comes when Abogee throws himself onto his daughter's casket at the cemetery. Chan's status at school seems to have changed significantly; he notes, somewhat ironically, that he is now known as someone whose sister died instead of as an Asian. His friendship with Mikko is cemented in their shared grief. Furthermore, it is the football coach's concern about Chan's emotional state that leads to a long heart-to-heart conversation in which Chan finally talks about his teammates' locker room assault.

Football ultimately unites Chan and his parents with the community, as the team goes to the finals, buoyed by community support (and Chan's parents finally attend a game). The tragic events also lead to reconciliation between Chan and his father, in a shared moment of grief when Chan finds him burning incense to the Buddha. (He earlier asked why the statue, a relic of their Korean past, had to be brought to Minnesota, since the family had long since became Christian.) As the two share their grief, Abogee explains his concern that Young's spirit should safely journey to its next place, and Chan relieves his mind by telling him that he placed Young's flute in her coffin. As justification for his adherence to Korean traditions, Abogee states his faith that all religions support each other. From this healing moment, a new mutual understanding grows. A final moment of healing closes the novel, as Chan visits Young's grave to place his football trophy on it, only to discover that Mikko's jersey and a souvenir teddy bear from Minneapolis, where the finals were held, already adorn the grave. This peaceful though deeply sad moment seems to add emphasis to the title: the "necessary roughness" of life demands that humans pull together to meet its challenges.

Many young adult novels take the perspective of the outsider, but Scott Johnson's *One of the Boys* (1992) presents the insider's dilemma: Eric is "one of the Boys" but, increasingly often, is not sure he wants to be. The leader of the Boys, Marty, whom Eric thinks of as a friend before he better understands Marty's capacity for manipulating others, is good at thinking up "mischief" for his gang to execute. Eric finds these pranks funny, and he has an established identity in school society within this small group. A rift begins to develop, though, when Eric is pushed by his hard-working parents to get a job to earn money for college, a commitment that leaves him less time for acting on Marty's orders and makes him the butt of Marty's jokes. Unlike Marty, Eric is not really mean, nor does he want to become involved in crime, so he ultimately pulls back from being one of the Boys when he sees what life is like for someone who has made the wrong choices and, additionally, discovers Marty's actual crimes, a string of thefts that he tries to pin on Eric. By taking a stand for decency and responsibility, Eric steps back from the brink of a life of dishonesty, and he learns the meaning of manhood.

At first, Marty's gang confine themselves to leaving around condoms filled with white glue and water, jamming the girls' bathroom door shut to trap girls inside, and playing similar pranks. But Marty's ingenuity takes on a harsher edge with "the Christmas Concert Caper." Although Marty's pranks lack the complexities or ritual of the underground Vigils in Cormier's *The Chocolate War*, Marty may nevertheless remind a reader of Cormier's Archie. Marty engineers his Boys' pranks but does not always take an active role in pulling them off. The Christmas Concert episode involves breaking into the band room to hide all the instruments an hour before the concert, and it is the first plot that affects and implicates Eric in ways that worry him. Eric is in the band, though he often fakes playing his trumpet, and his lack of skill has led to a mutual dislike between him and the band director. Eric has given Marty the band room security alarm code, which he knows because his father installed the system. Thus, the prank endangers Eric, but he finds the episode funny—until he realizes some of the instruments have been damaged. Then instruments begin to go missing. Over time, Eric is forced to recognize that Marty is stealing and pawning them, in a lucrative little business he has not told his boys about, and when Eric confronts him, Marty convinces him to steal something himself—an old, beat-up trumpet—in the last raid on the band room. Eric plays along, hoping to give the instrument to a homeless alcoholic who used to play jazz. This turns out to be the last raid because Marty is finally apprehended and defends himself by accusing Eric of his own role as mastermind. Eric is saved from serious trouble by several circumstances, the most important of which is his decision to return the trumpet he took to the principal, making it an occasion to tell him all that he knows or suspects about Marty.

Eric decides to confess when he looks around the rundown area of town where his homeless buddy Ole hangs out. He wonders what life has in store for him. A life like the alcoholic Ole's? Ole, who flatteringly calls Eric "Jazzman," makes it clear that getting his education is Eric's first responsibility; he attributes his own life on the streets to choices he has made, and he has to work hard to convince Eric that it is really too late for him to do things differently—in contrast to Eric himself, who still has options. In his attempts to convince Ole that life can change, Eric fully persuades himself, paving the way for his confession to the principal. But for change to occur, he must first face the fact that he has done wrong, not just make excuses or simply try to forget the past.

Eric has a clear-cut moment of decision between confessing or taking the apparently easy way out when he must decide whether to return the stolen trumpet to the school or pawn it to get rid of the evidence. After Eric gives back the trumpet, he is relieved by his return to honor and accepts, perhaps even welcomes, his punishments—suspension, community service, grounding. His own conscience makes him feel worse than other people's reactions to his guilt. Paradoxically, he finds, his parents are proud of his shame—because it demonstrates that his values really are intact. The epigraph is from *To Kill a Mockingbird*: "The one thing that doesn't abide by majority rule is a person's conscience."

In *The Harmony Arms* (1992), Ron Koertge tells the story of a summer romance that redeems what promises to be an awful month for Gabriel McKay, alone with his eccentric father, Sumner, in Los Angeles. Staying in the Harmony Arms, Gabriel and Sumner find harmony and balance through their interaction with a group of eccentrics. Gabriel is at first reluctant to leave his friends and summer baseball in Bradleyville, Missouri, to accompany Sumner to California, where he is under contract to work on a movie based on his children's book about an otter named Timmy. Gabriel's mother, however, is off on an extended bicycle tour with her boyfriend, and Gabriel has no choice. Gabriel is constantly embarrassed by Sumner in their small hometown because Sumner always carries his Timmy the Otter hand puppet and speaks through him. The elementary school children that Sumner teaches may find Timmy entertaining, but Gabriel objects to conversing with a squeaky-voiced puppet or giving Timmy a hug when asked. At the Harmony Arms, a long way from Bradleyville physically and psychically, Sumner's behavior doesn't seem as odd. They share the condominium complex with an aged alcoholic psychic named Cassandra, who Rollerblades for exercise and wears huge muumuus that she makes herself from bargain print fabrics, and an even older nudist, Mr. Palmer, whose main occupation is swimming laps in the pool but who also demonstrates for animal rights. The complex is managed by Mona, a dancer whose only current work is in commercials and whose tofu-and-vegetable diet reminds Gabriel and Sumner how different California culture is from their own. Mona is under pressure to settle for work that brings in a paycheck, even if it demeans her, and she takes jobs as a dancing aspirin and an ant. The pressure to commercialize and undermine Timmy the Otter's integrity ends Sumner's dreams of fame and fortune in the movies.

Despite the eccentricity of the group at the Harmony Arms, they quickly form surprisingly close bonds, encouraging and supporting each other. It is Mona's daughter, Tess, though, who dramatically changes Gabriel's summer for the better. Tess carries a video camera everywhere, shooting footage for *Mondo Tess*, which she is planning to complete at age eighteen when she enters film school. Tess tends to patronize Gabriel at first, but he soon comes to enjoy her quirkiness and respect her knowledge of film and her street smarts. She can find her way any place in L.A. via public transportation, and she has an instinct and repertoire of strategies for handling drunks and potentially violent confrontations. Tess's sophistication and toughness do not extend to her dealings with her father, however. When he shows up on the doorstep during a Harmony Arms gathering, she runs off in fury and begins pitching patio furniture into the pool. It does not take long for Gabriel to discover Tess's appeal as well as her passion, and from the moment when he kisses her foot at the pool's edge, the two spend most of their time coping with hormones. Both teens have to negotiate their time together with parents who fear they will be swept up in desire when they are alone, and it is a fear Gabriel and Tess must confront as well.

Left under Cassandra's watchful eye the day after a group beach outing—when Mr. Palmer was noticeably distressed by his loneliness, changes on his favorite clothes-optional beach, and the deterioration of his own body—they find themselves swept up in a somewhat harebrained adventure rather than in passion. Mr. Palmer has died by his own hand, peacefully, in Cassandra's company, and his last wish was that his body be left to weather in the high desert, so the three remove his body to Cassandra's ancient Nash, intending to sneak it away. But Cassandra's driving skills are even less reliable than her clairvoyance, and she crashes into a bus stop bench. There is a happy ending, however, when the conspirators have to settle for a conventional cremation and ceremonial scattering of Mr. P.'s ashes in the desert.

Cassandra's prophetic abilities are often distorted: the child in a red raincoat that she "sees" being struck by a car turns out to be a red fire hydrant. While everyone around her takes her predictions with several grains of salt, she ultimately articulates a profoundly liberating truth for Gabriel, that his personality is the perfect balance between his mother's fierce energy and his father's dreamy, eccentric creativity. Sumner has changed too, and father and son have grown closer during their month in L.A. Sumner has begun swimming and dressing more stylishly, and he acknowledges that his humor, expressed through Timmy, is often inappropriate and a way of covering his discomfort in serious situations. Gabriel has stood up for his father at the beach when Sumner was threatened by several tough guys who object to the "fruity voice" he uses for Timmy (and both of them have been rescued from a violent outcome by Tess's diplomatic intervention). Most importantly, Gabriel has grown more accepting of behavior outside the norm, and he says good-bye to Cassandra—easily the most eccentric character of the novel—with real regret, though she promises astral visits to Missouri. Harmony prevails, as their L.A. adventure comes to an end, ending Gabriel's summer romance on an upbeat, friendly note.

ADDITIONAL READING RECOMMENDATIONS

When the Legends Die by Hal Borland, 1963

The Soul Brothers and Sister Lou by Kristin Hunter, 1968

Tell Me That You Love Me, Junie Moon by Marjorie Kellogg, 1968

One Fat Summer, 1977 (discussed in Beauty's Meaning), and *The Summer Boy*, 1982 (discussed in Jobs: Assuming Adult Responsibility), by Robert Lipsyte

The Goats by Brock Cole, 1987

Scorpions by Walter Dean Myers, 1990

How the Garcia Girls Lost Their Accent by Julia Alvarez, 1991

The Brave, 1991, and *The Chief*, 1993, by Robert Lipsyte

The Proving Ground by Elaine Marie Alphin, 1992

American Dragons: Twenty-Five Asian American Voices (stories) edited by Laurence Yep, 1993

Deliver Us from Evie by M. E. Kerr, 1994

Confess-O-Rama by Ron Koertge, 1996

Gideon's People by Carolyn Meyer, 1996

An Island Like You: Stories of the Barrio (stories) by Judith Ortiz Cofer, 1996

Shark Bait, 1997, and *Jungle Dogs, 1998,* by Graham Salisbury

The Perks of Being a Wallflower by Stephen Chbosky, 1999

Tightrope by Gillian Cross, 1999

Breaking Rank by Kristen D. Randle, 1999

145th Street: Short Stories by Walter Dean Myers, 2000

Locked Inside by Nancy Werlin, 2000

Whale Talk by Chris Crutcher, 2001 (discussed in Accepting Difference)

Heaven Eyes by David Almond, 2001

Lord of the Deep by Graham Salisbury, 2001

Behind the Mountains by Edwidge Danticat, 2002

Buddha Boy by Kathe Koja, 2003 (discussed in Religion and Spiritual Life)

Jobs: Assuming Adult Responsibility

The Summer Boy by Robert Lipsyte (1982)
It Happened at Cecilia's by Erika Tamar (1989)
Rules of the Road by Joan Bauer (1998)
Hope Was Here by Joan Bauer (2000)
Lucy the Giant by Sherri L. Smith (2002)

Adolescence is said to be an American concept, a category of human life that does not exist in less developed societies where children pass quickly from childhood pursuits into adult responsibilities. Adolescence is an in-between stage, and the jobs that many teens hold down are similarly in-between: work rather than child's play, but less work, perhaps, with less pay and less responsibility than jobs that most adults hold. Yet economic necessity, along with an American belief in the value of work experience in developing teens' sense of responsibility and, hence, character, makes having a job an important part of many teens' lives. The teen who grows up on a farm or with responsibilities in a family business, of course, has little choice in the matter but is a full-fledged member of a working culture.

Yet work does not play a central role in much of the fiction for young adults. In the novels discussed here, nonetheless, the job is essential to plotting and characterization. The characters are concerned about work issues—fairness, ethics, division of responsibility, initiative for change in working conditions or production, the impact of work commitments on education, social life, and family relationships. These protagonists gain maturity and self-esteem, at the very least, through their job experience.

In *The Summer Boy* (1982), Robert Lipsyte continues the chronicle of Bob Marks's career begun in *One Fat Summer* (discussed in Chapter 6: Beauty's Meaning), set in the 1950s, when unionization appears not to have reached the Poconos. A despised "summer boy," between his freshman and sophomore college years, Bob lands a job at the local laundry, where he soon discovers the dangers of working conditions both inside the facility and outside in the poorly maintained delivery trucks. It looks as if the owner Roger Sinclair is trying to run the business into the ground. Sinclair is also an outsider to the community, an exile from a Ph.D. program in English who has married into laundry ownership. Bored, literate, disdainful, and full of himself, he embodies the worst qualities of the summer visitors to this year-round community, flashing his wealth conspicuously in expensive tweeds and a foreign sports car while refusing to spring for tires with tread, truck brakes, and valves on the hot water lines inside the laundry; the company restroom is a pigsty. Clear gender inequality reigns: the women do the backbreaking labor of the actual washing, drying, and folding, working longer hours for less pay than the handful of men who pick up dirty sheets and towels and deliver clean ones to the area restaurants and hotels. Supervisors call elderly women "girls" and pat behinds, regardless of age, on their way through the facility. Nearly all the workers support families; all need their jobs, except for Bob.

Hired by Sinclair himself, Bob is suspected of spying for him, and he finds it hard to win the employees' trust. Indeed, during his first week, his coworkers bet on when he will quit. His lasting the summer seems unlikely his second day, when he is demoted from driving to folding, but the same stubbornness he exhibited at age fourteen when mowing Dr. Kahn's lawn keeps him going here until he lays his job on the line by becoming the workers' spokesperson and delivering a petition for some repairs to ensure safety. He wins the concessions in return for his departure and, in a hollow victory, walks out unnoticed as his coworkers celebrate.

As in *One Fat Summer*, the community is full of secrets, and Bob gathers material for a future as a writer. The biggest secret is abortion, illegal in the 1950s. When his best friend Joanie needs one, pregnant by a lover whose identity she keeps secret from Bob, Bob knows where to take her—to their kindly summer neighbors, who run an abortion office in New York City. Hypocritically, the couple express their disapproval when he delivers Joanie to their door, until Joanie clears his reputation with them. Bob has abetted her romance by covering for her with her parents, but when he learns that the man involved is his married boss, he uses the information to win his victory for the laundry workers.

The division between the Jewish summer people and non-Jewish locals runs below the surface. The abortion doctor and his wife are said to have barely escaped Nazi Germany, and thus there is some irony in his performing abortions. The secrecy that surrounds the operation in those pre–*Roe v. Wade* days and the suggestion that the couple are not quite respectable are hinted at but not explicitly discussed. Though Lipsyte portrays community tensions that may sometimes seem dated, the novel evokes social, economic, and political divisions and issues that remain relevant.

In contrast to Bob's outsider status, *It Happened at Cecilia's* (1989), by Erika Tamar, presents an insider's view of a small family restaurant catering to the artistic community of Greenwich Village. Ninth-grader Andy Szabo lives with his widowed father, Lazlo, and his cat Katie in a small apartment upstairs from Cecilia's, the Hungarian-Cajun restaurant that Lazlo co-owns with ex-con Cajun Jack. Andy spends afternoons and evenings in the restaurant, developing relationships with his extended family, which includes the perennially out-of-work actor who tends bar, the neurotic stand-up comic who eats there every evening before nervously performing his routine across the street, the beautiful college student who works as night waitress, and others. Sometimes he buses tables. It may not be an ordinary after-school routine, but it suits Andy just fine.

Andy's mouth sometimes gets him in trouble at school, especially with the school bully, and he finds himself sneaking home by circuitous routes after getting on "Bear" Abbott's bad side. This strategy makes him question whether he is the man that his fiery-tempered Hungarian father is. Andy also admires from afar a Chinese-Irish-American girl named Kim O'Hara, not quite ready to start dating though aware of his father's dating life. Andy puts up with the occasional weekend at his well-to-do maternal grandmother's suburban home even though she dislikes his father and disparages his partnership with Cajun Jack. So life and the issues of maturation are pretty normal for a ninth grader—until a series of dramatic changes disrupt his existence.

His father, who has not seriously dated since Andy's mother, Cecilia, died, hires a waitress and falls in love with her. A restaurant reviewer raves about the food in his column, which overnight brings in far more customers than the restaurant is prepared to handle, and chaos ensues. Amid complaints by new customers, departure of the neighborhood regulars, and general havoc, local mobsters pressure Lazlo and Cajun Jack for a cut of the substantial profits the restaurant's new fame should bring them, torching the restaurant when Lazlo refuses to pay them off.

It takes Andy a while to learn that Cecilia's is being targeted by the mob, though, because his concerns are more personal. Lorraine, aka the Chipmunk, moves into the cramped apartment with Lazlo, and Andy feels that his life has been turned upside down. No one consulted him about the living arrangements, and he fails to share Lazlo's enthusiasm about his impending marriage. Furthermore, when Lazlo protects Andy from the mob's threats by sending him to his grandmother a week before his scheduled Christmas break, he does not tell Andy why he is sending him away, so Andy assumes that he is being gotten out the way because of his father's romance. Then his beloved cat disappears from the apartment and Andy returns to the city to find her. In his confrontation with his father over whether Andy may stay in his own home, Lorraine proves a surprising ally, urging Lazlo to tell Andy about the gangsters' threat and sharing sentry duty with him on the roof, thus acknowledging Andy as part of the network of adults deeply concerned in the restaurant's fate.

The danger to the restaurant, and to their lives, is real until the restaurant reviewer writes a column retracting his positive comments. At that point, business drops to nearly nothing, with the regulars gone and no prospect of a new clientele, giving Lazlo, Lorraine, and Andy some much-needed time for working out the dynamics of a new family. Alas, Katie the cat has not returned, presumably so terrified by the noisy fire trucks' arrival that she has left for good. Andy tries not to envision the fate of a trusting though terrified pet trying to fend for herself on the streets.

But the restaurant's—and Andy's—fortunes change significantly once again with an ironic twist in the fortunes of the nervous stand-up comic. In near-despair, he vows to give up his act, discards his planned routine, and veers into an inspired improvised monologue about the crazy events at Cecilia's, wowing his audience and gaining fame that leads to TV appearances and a movie role—and brings new business to Cecilia's. The restaurant will stay solvent, after all. Then Andy solves his problem with the bully in an unexpected way, using Lorraine's trick for keeping city predators away—acting crazy, talking to herself, waving an umbrella. Best of all, though, Katie finds her way home, half-starved but alive. Finally, Andy's love interest, Kim O'Hara, calls. Much has, indeed, "happened at Cecilia's," remaking Andy's life but extending his sense of family and showing that he is not so unlike his father after all.

Several of Joan Bauer's novels depict strong, courageous female characters, both as protagonists and as role models for the teen protagonists. In two of these novels, *Rules of the Road* (1998) and *Hope Was Here* (2000), the characters' development as mature working women dominates the novels.

Rules of the Road tells the story of sixteen-year-old Jenna Boller's trip from Chicago to Dallas as driver for the elderly widow who owns the chain of shoe stores where Jenna works. Mrs. Gladstone is taking a farewell tour of stores, planning to retire at the stockholders' meeting, reluctantly resolved to turn over the business to her son although he is poised to sell out to a chain of bargain shoe stores. The crusty seventy-three-year-old Madeleine Gladstone sees something in Jenna that reminds her of herself when she was young, and as the story unfolds, the reader sees the resemblance. Jenna loves selling shoes and is a conscientious employee who has absorbed her boss's attitudes toward quality merchandise and customer service, and has an eye for store display and layout. Her expertise, along with her developing assertiveness and her determined optimism, makes her a perfect assistant to Mrs. Gladstone, even though her status as a new driver initially makes her nervous about this job. Jenna's height is an asset when she has to assert her authority with adults. Furthermore, Mrs. Gladstone has observed her handling of her alcoholic father, so she knows Jenna can handle challenges with poise.

Mrs. Gladstone's bad hip makes her more dependent on Jenna than she would like to be, and Jenna is progressively drawn more fully into the intrigues that swirl around the impending vote on the merger. She learns about the politics of management decisions in a series of encounters with the unpleasant son and Mrs. Gladstone's supporters: the influential super-salesman, Harry Bender, and the elderly shoe model, Alice Lovett.

Harry Bender is an alcoholic who has stayed sober for twenty-three years and is active in Alcoholics Anonymous. He is the perfect foil for Jenna's father, who refuses to acknowledge his problem with alcohol. He shows up in town every once in a while and makes drunken calls to his family in the middle of the night, embarrasses them, makes promises he breaks, and generally causes pain and hurt until he disappears again, causing more pain and hurt. On this trip with Mrs. Gladstone, Jenna is able to confront her anger at her father, something she has always been afraid to face, feeling that if she expresses anger she will no longer be the perfect daughter and will lose him entirely. Jenna's admiration for Harry Bender is increased by her understanding of his daily victories over alcohol, and she even wishes that he were her father. It is bitterly ironic that he should lose his life to a drunk driver, but the shock of this event gives Jenna the strength she needs to stop her father's car and request a police officer's help when he tries to drive drunk with her in the car, putting an end to the real danger his behavior poses.

Similarly, Mrs. Gladstone serves as a foil for Jenna's grandmother, who has Alzheimer's and lives in a nursing home. Having had a close relationship with her grandmother, Jenna finds her decline very painful. She shares some of her grandparents' wise sayings with Mrs. Gladstone, to encourage her when things are looking bleak, and she takes her own inspiration from Mrs. Gladstone's continued acumen. The challenges that Jenna faces lead her to reflect on the absence of rules for life like those for driving—"rules of the road"—when she has to face the fact that life is unfair: that she can love a father whom she cannot trust, that she can lose the relative she trusts to disease.

The painful situations Jenna must deal with are eased by several wonderful women in her life. Her mother is strong and loving. Her younger sister, Faith, is sweet and tries hard to fill Jenna's shoes by visiting their grandmother in Jenna's absence. Jenna has a good friend, Opal. Her grandmother has shared her life lessons with Jenna before beginning to slip away. The feisty Mrs. Gladstone and her friend Alice initiate Jenna into business and travel; Alice cuts her hair and takes her shopping, transforming Jenna's appearance and helping her gain self-confidence and poise. Jenna is not alone in her battles with life, and this network strengthens her, supporting her growth. Jenna's own wry wit sustains her as well—the novel is very funny, despite the serious problems that Jenna must confront.

One of the most determinedly optimistic attitudes a reader may ever encounter radiates from Hope Yancey, protagonist and narrator of *Hope Was Here*. Hope's name is not merely a felicitous match of name to personality: she chose her name and had it legally changed from Tulip, the name her mother saddled her with before leaving her to the care of Addie, Hope's aunt. Addie is a cook by trade, and, having hung around diners most of her life, Hope steps quite naturally into waitressing, her mostly absent mother's profession. She models much of her personal behavior on Addie, but she models her waitress work on her mother.

Hope sees the world in terms of food. Addie's special dishes are works of art, and Hope's serving is a form of love: by paying attention to her customers' bodily needs she frees them from care and sends them on their way feeling satisfied and as optimistic as Hope herself. Her optimism has suffered a recent blow, however, when Addie's New York City business partner absconded with nearly all their restaurant's funds. As a result, she and her aunt are forced to start over at the Welcome Stairways in tiny Mulhoney, Wisconsin. After this betrayal, Hope is less willing to open her heart to others.

Yet she continues to carry her hope for a father's love with her as they pack up and move, in the same way they have moved on from disappointment before. Hope's longing for parental love and guidance takes the form of a series of scrapbooks that chronicle her life. Hope daydreams that her unknown father will find her some day, and she wants to be ready to share all the significant moments of her life with him through her scrapbooks. Her trust in others has gotten off to a rocky start, with her mother's abandonment while Hope was a premature infant struggling for life, but Addie is the strong, reliable mother-figure who has raised Hope to be adaptable, hardworking, and kind. Hope's experience enables her to encourage another waitress whose infant is not thriving. Hope takes her mother's brief visits in stride and writes down her mother's waitressing tips. Still, love seems chancy, and Addie and Hope are cautious in seeing in their new employer the husband and father he will become.

G. T. Stoop is nothing but admirable. He has built his restaurant with welcoming double stairways to honor his Quaker forebears' tradition of hospitality and makes Addie and Hope at home instantly. No sooner have they arrived than G. T. enters the mayoral race, despite his leukemia. When asked why townspeople should vote for a terminally ill man, G. T. points out that he will work for the town, not to establish a long-term bastion of personal power. He is motivated by a genuine desire to serve the town—and to end the corruption of the current mayor. G. T. easily gains the support of the town's young people, because they, unlike their elders, need not fear losing jobs with the big dairy that is the town's main employer and also the main supporter of Mayor Millstone, who earns the dairy's support by turning a blind eye to their failure to pay taxes. Hope is drawn into the community when she helps G. T. campaign, and into an optimism about the future that is briefly threatened by his defeat—until Hope's keen interest in her customers and the campaign enables her to uncover the fraud, and when G. T. is finally declared the rightful winner of the election, her faith in the democratic process is cemented.

When G. T. invites Addie to go out for dinner, he initiates a romance that will culminate in marriage. His teenage cook, Braverman, apparently inspired by G. T., asks Hope out, and after an initial graceless response, Hope finds happiness in dating him through her high school years. When G. T. asks Hope if he may adopt her to further cement their new family relationship, she finally recognizes him as the father she has been looking for. Though their happiness is brief, by the time G. T. dies, Hope feels that her willingness to accept love has been worth the pain.

As in a play, much of the novel's action occurs in a restricted locale, in this case, the diner, and the mechanics of food service, as well as its opportunities for human connection, get plenty of attention as Hope explains how to treat the cook, how to

handle rushes, how to relate to other waitresses and busboys. Throughout her transient work life before the Welcome Stairways, Hope has always left a tiny, printed
message, "Hope was here," in each place before she left it. At the end of this novel,
the "Hope" whose presence she claims is faith in people and optimism about the
future, as well as a memorable character.

Sherri L. Smith's *Lucy the Giant* (2002) depicts the dangerous and intensely challenging life on a crabbing boat on the Bering Sea. Fifteen-year-old Lucy towers over
most of her classmates in Sitka, an outcast because of her size and her father's alcoholism. Cautious about relationships, she underestimates the depth of her friend
Sheila's loyalty, and feeling alone when circumstances precipitate a crisis, she runs
away, shrinking from any suggestion of pity. In her town, everyone knows that her
mother abandoned her when she was seven, her father's alcoholism cost him his job,
and he is a mean drunk—verbally abusive—when he is not ignoring her. Their
poverty makes Lucy even more self-conscious and, perhaps worse, physically uncomfortable in her own home: she has few clothes, and her attic bedroom is too small for
her. These circumstances briefly lose some of their power to depress her when a stray
dog adopts her: Lucy is actually happy until disease catches up with the dog, and Lucy
cannot save her.

Her despair results in a somewhat accidental running away: Lucy is mistakenly
rounded up for a flight to Kodiak while she is hanging out in the airport. Her size
leads people to think she is older than she is, a fact that works to her advantage when
she arrives in the strange town. Long observation of her father and his cronies tells
her that a drunk can often sleep in a back room in a bar, so she heads for a bar, planning to feign drunkenness in order to get a place to sleep. Against her will, she ends
up in a drinking contest for the survival suit left behind by a recently drowned crew-
man on a crabbing boat. With the suit, Lucy lands a job because they desperately
need another hand.

The biggest challenge that Lucy faces is figuring out how to act like an adult, so
she keeps quiet and works hard. Her hard work earns the respect of captain and
crew—except for Tracer, whom she outdrank her first night in Kodiak. The work is
grueling—cold, wet, heavy. In a storm, everyone works just to keep the ice from
building up on everything in sight, until they are asleep on their feet. When they are
setting traps and culling crabs, they sleep no more than four hours at a time. She witnesses severe injury to one of the crewmen, a situation that means even more work
for the rest of them. The extreme conditions under which they work bring quick
friendship because of the crew's mutual dependency.

Harley, the captain, is cautious around her, though, despite the fact that her dedication earns his praise. Feeling there is something familiar about Harley, Lucy discovers it is, ironically, alcoholism: she learns from another crew member that he
avoids people and situations that may tempt him to hit the bottle as he did in the
past, and Lucy's ability to drink Tracer under the table makes him distant. As a matter of fact, he nearly lost his license and has not seen his daughter in years, all
because of alcoholism, and now, nearly out of debt and making child support pay-
ments, he expects to rebuild a relationship with his child. He warms to Lucy, though,
but just when she really feels a part of the group, his discovery that she is underage
threatens the ground that Harley has worked so hard to regain. Hiring a minor for
this work is illegal. Lucy is miserable as she learns a lesson of adulthood, that her lie
may harm the people she cares about the most. When she saves the life of her enemy,
Tracer, however, he promises not to expose her. Still, given the choice of staying on
the crab boat or returning home, Lucy chooses home.

The relationship she has begun to develop with Harley, that of a daughter to a father, has given her some insight into what family relationships can be. He has given her the approval she craves. His continuing sobriety has convinced her that people can change. The relationship among the crab boat members has given her a positive model for interdependence, with which she can replace the dysfunctional codependency of her own family life. She accepts her father's point, made many years earlier to a social agency, that he is all the family she has. Having made good money and her own friends, lived comfortably in port for a brief time (with the joy of rooming in a house with a dog), and earned self-esteem, Lucy can voluntarily make a temporary return to her limiting former life, planning to leave for college, where she discovers that she has a real friend, Sheila, in Sitka. Still, her return home seems pretty bleak. One cannot help thinking that teens do not have much freedom or power—not many choices—with dysfunctional parents and must weather the storms until they grow up and leave home.

ADDITIONAL READING RECOMMENDATIONS

The Contender, 1967 (discussed in Addressing Addiction), and *One Fat Summer*, 1977 (discussed in Beauty's Meaning), by Robert Lipsyte
Workin' for Peanuts by Todd Strasser, 1983
The Amazing and Death-Defying Diary of Eugene Dingman by Paul Zindel, 1987
Seventeen against the Dealer by Cynthia Voigt, 1989
Make Lemonade by Virginia Euwer Wolff, 1993 (discussed in Poverty's Challenges)
Striking Out, 1993, *Farm Team*, 1995, and *Hard Ball*, 1998, by Will Weaver
Don't You Dare Read This, Mrs. Dunphries by Margaret Peterson Haddix, 1996
Help Wanted: Short Stories edited by Anita Silvey, 1997
Buried Onions by Gary Soto, 1997 (discussed in Poverty's Challenges)
Gingerbread by Rachel Cohn, 2002

Old Tales Retold: Fairy Tales, Legends, Myths

Beauty by Robin McKinley (1978)
Zel by Donna Jo Napoli (1996)
Quiver by Stephanie Spinner (2002)
Dating Hamlet by Lisa Fiedler (2002)
I Am Mordred by Nancy Springer (1998)
I Am Morgan le Fay by Nancy Springer (2001)
The Arthur trilogy by Kevin Crossley-Holland (2001–3)

Stories from myth and legend persist in our culture because they evoke deep emotional responses from us, shaped as we are by those stories, often from a very young age. Contemporary retellings prove their lasting relevance for readers. The novelist may heighten the psychological realism of the tale by fleshing out its briefly sketched characters, or put the story into a contemporary setting, or reinterpret the theme of the conventional story, or tell the story from the perspective of a character not usually considered the protagonist. Classical myths and fairy tales, the Arthurian cycle, stories of Robin Hood, Shakespeare's plots, and even the Bible have been reinterpreted in creative ways in recent years.

Robin McKinley's *Beauty* (1978) is one of a number of recent novelistic retellings of classic tales from a female perspective. McKinley's "Beauty and the Beast" fills in the outline of the tale's beautiful victim who conquers the beast by learning to love the violent, apparently unlovable creature that would tear her from her grieving father as sacrifice for his unwitting transgression and welcomes her destiny as his extorted prize, only to find a surprisingly happy ending in his transformation into a rich, handsome, and noble human.

Like many a heroine in any genre for contemporary young adult readers—and like McKinley's heroic female protagonist of the fantasies *The Blue Sword* and *The Hero and the Crown*—Beauty is capable, mature, and assertive. She believes her nickname is entirely ironic, failing to notice her own development from awkward early adolescence into true beauty, but she never doubts her ability to live up to her given name of Honor, a name that underscores the character and strength that the tale's heroine must have possessed in order to face and live with terror. Furthermore, she chooses to trust the Beast's honor when he assures her she will come to no harm in his home. McKinley's Beauty, moreover, is intelligent and scholarly as well as courageous. She possesses that definitive characteristic of many romance heroines that may be somewhat inelegantly characterized as "spunk": she tells the truth, daringly at times; she resists conforming to her society's gender roles; and she is an independent thinker, able to engage and maintain a man's interest in conversation.

Another important characteristic of the heroine is her winning way with animals. The strength of her bond with her fine horse enables her to bring him into the Beast's company, and she lures birds and butterflies to the castle walls. McKinley's portrayal thus underscores the important role that empathy plays in this story as Beauty's feeling for animals also helps her bring out the Beast's gentler nature.

At heart, the tale recounts the family story of the daughter sacrificed by her birth family to the "beastly" behavior of sexual conquest by an outsider unknown to the family or clan, and when his beastliness is properly subdued to honorable love, his true nobility is revealed. The magical elements of rose and ring in McKinley's story reinforce this theme. The roses, fragrant emblem of beauty and nubility, bloom profusely on the eve of Beauty's departure, elegantly framing her former life for which she eventually feels nostalgia and longing, as she almost flirts with the Beast, feeding him by hand, and then suddenly senses the intensity of the Beast's passion. She wears the griffin ring, foreshadowing their marriage, to her meeting with him, when she departs from home and family apparently forever. Several elements of her life in the castle are charming: the library of books yet to be written; the breeze that serves her, increasingly outspoken and prompting her intuition of the truth of the Beast's history; the shifting geography of the palace and the grounds. These elements allow Beauty's intelligence and compassion to lead her into clearer perception of the reality underlying the magic. Allusion to the tale of King Cophetua and the beggar maid most clearly underscores the clarity of the Beast's own perceptiveness in choosing Beauty to woo.

The homelier elements of the time-honored romance are the family relationships that have nurtured and sustained Beauty. Her pleasure in home and family seem reasonable, her delayed return to the Beast understandable, but as in the original tale, honor wins out, and the beast is restored to his own beauty.

Donna Jo Napoli has also drawn on fairy tales for a number of absorbing novels. In *Zel* (1996), she fleshes out the story of Rapunzel through the multiple perspectives of the witch-mother, Rapunzel, and her noble-born lover Konrad, setting it in a specific time and place, mid-sixteenth-century Switzerland. Napoli gives the reader a reason to sympathize with the witch by providing her with a history as a barren woman, once married and Christian, who has given up her soul in return for a gift, a special way with plants, which enables her to bargain the rapunzel greens her pregnant neighbor craves for the child she is carrying. For thirteen years, the witch enjoys motherhood, with Zel the center of her isolated mountain life. Just as Zel trembles on the edge of puberty, however, she meets and is attracted to a rich and handsome youth, winning his interest through her love of animals, her unspoiled honesty, and her disregard for wealth. Before her adoptive mother has even suspected the danger, the bond is formed.

In her brief encounter with the youth, Zel has won the gift of a fertilized goose egg. A demented goose's devotion to a nest of rocks has elicited Zel's pity, but when Zel tries to substitute the egg for a rock, the goose suddenly becomes much more important to Mother, who desperately needs to see a happy outcome to this effort, as the goose symbolizes her own adoption of Zel. When the goose rejects the egg, and the tiny creature dies unhatched, Mother interprets it as a judgment on her own robbing of another's nest. The gift also alarms Mother by alerting her to Zel's incipient involvement with a boy.

To preserve Zel's chastity until Zel chooses magical wisdom with a life of celibacy over conventional heterosexual love and child-rearing, continuing their mother-daughter bond, Mother immures her in the tower. To get Zel there, Mother frightens her with stories of an implacable enemy who will take Zel's life, but of course, by depriving Zel of freedom and of choice, Mother becomes the enemy, and in time Zel's sanity is sacrificed as well. When Konrad finally discovers her, she is far more vulnerable than she was at their first meeting, unable at first to distinguish his real presence from her waking dreams in the isolation of the tiny tower room, where she is deprived of her former joy in home, animals, and the freedom to stretch her limbs.

Konrad becomes Mother's enemy without his knowledge, simply by virtue of his search for Zel and the feelings Zel harbors for him. By the time he finds Zel, and their love is consummated, Zel cannot help repudiating her mother as nature takes its course, reasserting its own story of the daughter's betrayal of the mother in Zel's fecundity. The contest between Mother and Konrad is minimal: Mother recognizes that they are united in love of Zel, and she breaks his fall with the thorns that blind him in an act that may proceed from mercy rather than revenge, an act that ends her power. The joyous "happy ending"—for eternity—releases Zel's pent-up emotions in healing tears. All are united—Konrad and Zel with their twin daughters, Mother only a whisper of an animate presence in the place where she raised her daughter.

In *Quiver* (2002), Stephanie Spinner tells the classic heroine Atalanta's story from her participation in the Calydonian hunt to her loss of a foot race to Hippomenes to the couple's transformation into lions after their desecration of Zeus' sanctuary. Her story is told primarily through first-person narration by the protagonist, punctuated by short dialogues between the gods who take an interest in her fate: Artemis, Apollo, Aphrodite, and Eros. Her earlier history as an infant exposed to the elements by her father, King Iasus, and her upbringing as an apprentice of sorts to the bow-maker and fletcher Castor are revealed through her thoughts and dialogue.

Atalanta is a devout young woman who has vowed chastity in Artemis' service, but her fate is largely in the hands of the men who dominate her society and ultimately in the hands of the gods, who take a sporting interest in the affairs of mortals, an interest represented by Artemis' quiver. Artemis loses it in a wager with Apollo over Atalanta's ability to stand up to her domineering and callous father, who reclaims her only because he has no heir. Then Apollo loses the quiver to Eros, when he bets that Atalanta will win yet another footrace, but she allows Aphrodite's apples to distract her. The quiver passes from Eros to Hippomenes when the latter offers thanks for the arrow that struck Atalanta's heart, motivating her to run after the apples. When Hippomenes gives the quiver to Atalanta, she in turn offers it to Artemis. In the final analysis, all has been in the gods' hands, as foretold in the dreams Atalanta receives from Apollo at his shrine after the hunt in Calydon.

Atalanta, nonetheless, has strong feelings and wishes that make her accessible to the modern reader. She enjoys her athletic prowess and friendship; she wants to choose whether to take a husband; she is angry at the father who rejected her and treated her mother cruelly; she feels the lack of a mother—hence, perhaps, her devotion to the goddess; and finally, once she has fallen in love, she enjoys sex and childbearing. She even retains her status as fleet huntress in her final transformation, though it is meant as a punishment.

In *Dating Hamlet* (2002) Lisa Fiedler gives a new perspective on the story of Shakespeare's Hamlet. Ophelia is actively engaged in the story rather than being just an object of the prince's desire and a tool in the hands of their powerful elders. Because Ophelia is resourceful and clever, this version has a happy ending: the characters killed with poison in the play can be revived with the antidote Ophelia brews. The tedious Polonius is still run through with Hamlet's sword as he hides behind the curtains in Queen Gertrude's bedchamber, but no one much cares, because he is not really the father of Ophelia and Laertes. Their birth father turns out to be the much more amusing and caring gravedigger, who aids them in their plot to deceive the world into thinking Ophelia and Laertes are dead.

Fiedler makes all the sleight-of-hand fairly believable—or at least no less believable than Shakespeare—and at the end she sends the surviving lovers off to Verona, to look up a guy by the name of Romeo whom Hamlet has met at school in Wittenberg. Ophelia certainly deserves our sympathy in the original play, but it is difficult to imagine her agency in a situation where her brother opposes her romance, her father is killed by her lover, her lover repudiates her, and she responds with a truer madness than Hamlet's and commits suicide. These circumstances no longer apply in Fiedler's revision. Because Fiedler imagines different relationships among the characters, Ophelia is able to enter into Hamlet's smokescreen of mock-madness and has opportunities for communicating with others—through letters and messages delivered by her friend and servant, Anne. The contemporary reader may find her a more satisfactory character as a spunky girl who dons a boy's britches after faking her own death so she can help Laertes engineer a pretense of Hamlet's demise and run off to enjoy life, leaving Claudius dead and Gertrude in the tender care of the conquering Fortinbras.

Ophelia is a modern girl, who was taught bawdy songs by Laertes and his friend Hamlet when she was just a child, who feels a healthy sexual attraction to the man who plans to marry her and an equally healthy repugnance to the randy Barnardo and the creepy King Claudius who casts a lustful eye her way. Her knowledge of perfumes, poisons, and antidotes comes from her mother. Her biological father, the gravedigger, abandoned a life as a traveling player after falling in love with her mother, and he has stayed at Elsinore to watch his children grow, showing a natural concern and affection for them, unlike the oleaginous Polonius. The friendships and shifting romances that Fiedler imagines among the young people, who have known each other from infancy, seem quite natural, making one wonder why all these young people are so ready to be manipulated by their elders in Shakespeare's play.

Ophelia remains Elizabethan in her ability to see apparitions—her deceased mother as well as Hamlet's father—and to believe what these specters tell her. The progression of events follows Shakespeare, as does some of the dialogue. Nonetheless, Fiedler's Ophelia is thoroughly contemporary, a young woman who claims a role equal to Hamlet's in the momentous events that follow upon the previous king's murder.

Nancy Springer's novels of Camelot, *I Am Mordred* (1998) and *I Am Morgan le Fay* (2001) give understandable motives to the villains of the Arthurian story. Mordred lives out a self-fulfilling prophecy as he first resists but finally embraces his fate as his father's killer. Washed ashore in a coracle full of babies set adrift by Arthur's futile effort to avoid his fate, Mordred, after a few happy years in the care of a fisherman's wife, seeks love the rest of his life, until he gives up his soul so as to live without emotional pain. He gives his heart to Nimue, even though she removes him from his early home, and he adores the white hound she gives him as a link to her, but Nimue leaves him with his mother, Morgause, who turns away from him because he is a reminder of her incestuous liaison with Arthur. Coming painfully, at last, to the knowledge that he is Arthur's bastard, Mordred hopes for some kind of acknowledgment but is disappointed in this hope. He is ostracized, an outcast, his reserve misread, his aversion to brutal violence misinterpreted as cowardice. An act of compassion, the freeing of a caged merlin, results in the death of his beloved

Nimue and his faithful hound. In desperation Mordred seeks to give his soul into his royal father's safekeeping to forestall damnation, but he is tricked and rendered soulless, only united with his father in Avalon in the form of a raven after they have lived out the fate foretold for them both. It is impossible to feel anything other than sympathy for the youth caught in this web woven by others.

Since Morgan le Fay is responsible for Mordred's conception as a doubly cursed infant—both a bastard and the product of incest—it is difficult to imagine how she might be rendered sympathetic, but Morgan similarly seeks parental love unsuccessfully, suffers jealousy of a favored sibling, and tries to hold onto what is good in her life and cheat fate. The fate she tries to escape is twofold: she avoids her own fated nature, foretold as a sly malice-driven middle-aged sorceress and ultimately the black morrigan, vulture of the battlefield; and she tries to deflect the early death in battle foretold for the only man she ever loves. After all her powers as a fay fail to protect him, she succumbs to madness for a time before forswearing the giving life of the fairy people for the selfish earthly power of sorcery, following the hollow-eyed Merlin to Camelot for her hated half brother Arthur's coronation, bent only on wreaking harm. This grim fate is lamentable, given the charm with which Springer imbues her girlhood self and the sadness of her near-orphan status from early childhood—her mother whisked away to wed King Uther and her beloved father dead on the battlefield while the sorcerer's trickery deprived her of the truth of her last memory of him and the child conceived through the sorcerer's agency deprived her of her mother's interest and care. It is a perilous life for women, even fay women, left to fend for themselves, and she learns to make use of all the power she can muster.

One of the most satisfying retellings of the Arthurian stories is Kevin Crossley-Holland's trilogy *The Seeing Stone* (2001), *At the Crossing-Places* (2002), and *King of the Middle March* (2003), which alternates the Arthurian material with the story of young Arthur de Caldicot, later Sir Arthur de Gortanore, beginning in 1199 when he is thirteen and ending with his return from the Fourth Crusade at age seventeen. The intertwining stories show the significance of stories in our lives, and through his growing knowledge of the legendary king's life and defeat, the young Crusader develops the king within himself, entering, with this discovery, into maturity and the possession of his inheritance.

Though it is the second volume of the trilogy that emphasizes the theme of crossing-places, such places play an important role throughout the trilogy. Arthur's home in England lies near the border with Wales, and these years of his dawning self-knowledge and maturation bridge two centuries. Arthur faces several significant turning points in his life, some initiated by others' actions, some by his own decisions. His life intersects in odd ways with the life of King Arthur. As a Crusader, he finds himself at the juncture of very different civilizations from the time of his arrival in Venice. He inhabits liminal spaces throughout this entire period of development.

The agent of his education is Merlin, the Merlin of Camelot, a local wise man who entrusts a magical wedge of polished obsidian to Arthur de Caldicot, in which he sees King Arthur's story unfold. From the outset, Arthur is a bit of a misfit—left-handed, bullied by his older brother Serle, unmindful of his status, a reader and writer who fears for a time that he will end up in the church rather than lead the active life he hopes for. His life is changed dramatically when he learns that the parents he has loved and revered are really his foster parents and he is the bastard son of the much older man he has believed his uncle, Sir William, a brutal, powerful man. Over time Arthur learns that he was taken from his mother, a village woman who was told he was dead, and that his father murdered her husband. He seeks her identity unsuccessfully until his return from the Crusade, after Sir William's death. Arthur's knowledge of his parentage thus echoes King Arthur's discovery of his birth, and he discovers that his bullying older brother is not really his brother.

Like King Arthur, too, he has a strong code of honor and responsibility to those weaker than he. Arthur is truly chivalrous, helping his friend Gatty with farmwork and facing a dangerous bull with her; rescuing his foster sister Sian when she falls through the ice; rescuing a girl whose hem has caught fire and is burning her terrified pony; intervening in a knife fight in France; rescuing a younger, smaller squire from bullies and a shipwright's daughter first from drowning and then from dishonor at the hands of drunken soldiers; and finally facing his biological father, who attacks the gentle Lord Stephen, a second foster father and role model in whose service Arthur left England. On his travels, Arthur sees many acts that disgust him, learning how soldiers' ideals may be betrayed in the contingencies of new situations in strange lands, yet he resists becoming brutalized himself.

His abilities, and especially his personal bravery, earn him knighthood early in his travels, an honor that grants him clear status, regardless of his birth. Arthur learns what he can from his experiences, discovering the common humanity he shares with Muslims when he meets them in France and Italy, learning languages, trying new foods (even if he does this against his will). By the time that he must make the decision to take Lord Stephen home to England to recover from the serious head wound Sir William dealt him, Arthur has become a mature, reliable man before his seventeenth birthday.

One of his biggest worries while he is away from home is whether his fiancée, Winnie, Lord Stephen's niece, will remain true to him, or fall in love with his half brother Tom, although Arthur has loved and trusted Tom all his life, first knowing him as a cousin and then as more than a friend as they negotiate the change in their relationship wrought by the revelation that they share a father. His worries are exacerbated by his observation of Guinevere's divided heart as revealed in his seeing stone. The adjustment that Arthur and Tom have made is more harmonious than Arthur's changing relationship with his half sister Grace, because he and Grace had hoped to marry before discovering Arthur's parentage. Arthur avoids the fate of his famous predecessor, however, because he does not father a child with his half sister. A good outcome of the change in status is the improvement in Serle and Arthur's comradeship, when his foster brother Serle arrives in Venice as Sir William's squire. They are no longer rivals in any sense, and a Serle with battles to fight is a happier youth than he was at home, just as Sir William is a happier man as a soldier and lover, freed from the daily responsibilities of his manor and marriage.

The interweaving of the two stories is masterful, with the core Arthurian narrative, including tales of various knights, true to the major texts but unfolding as dramas to the viewer. The later Arthur must view his seeing stone in secret, and the narrative unfolds over years, its more disturbing mature themes emerging as Arthur de Caldicot reaches a maturity with which he can accept the heroes' flawed natures. The theme of Arthur de Caldicot's own writing complicates the interweaving further, layering Arthur's chronicle of his own life, punctuated by his retelling of King Arthur's story, and weaving in letters, bards' songs, and his own poetry. Arthur's favorite writing places are refuges to which he can retreat from the demands of daily life, places where he reflects—and grows as a person through his reflection. Arthur eventually realizes that the name of the manor his foster father bequeaths to him, Catmole, is an anagram of Camelot, and he recognizes Tumber Hill, where he has walked with Merlin, as King Arthur's resting place. King Arthur's story has become his story as he has grown and is now a part of him, as Merlin points out when he takes back the seeing stone.

ADDITIONAL READING RECOMMENDATIONS

The Once and Future King by T. H. White, 1958

The Weirdstone of Brisingamen, 1960 (rev. 1963), *The Moon of Gomrath*, 1963, and *The Owl Service*, 1967, by Alan Garner

The Merlin trilogy by Mary Stewart, 1970–79

Grendel by John Gardner, 1971

The Light beyond the Forest, 1979, *The Sword and the Circle*, 1981, and *The Road to Camlann*, 1982, by Rosemary Sutcliff

Dragon's Boy by Jane Yolen, 1990

Orfe by Cynthia Voigt, 1992

The Magic Circle, 1993, and *Beast*, 2002, by Donna Jo Napoli

Othello: A Novel by Julius Lester, 1995

Dateline: Troy by Paul Fleischmann, 1996

Ella Enchanted by Gale Carson Levine, 1997

Daughter of the Sea by Berlie Doherty, 1997

Rose Daughter, 1997, and *Spindle's End*, 2000, by Robin McKinley

In a Dark Wood, 1998, and *Forbidden Forest: The Story of Little John and Robin Hood* by Michael Cadnum, 2002

Shadow Spinner by Susan Fletcher, 1998

Just Ella by Margaret Peterson Haddix, 1999

The Rose and the Beast: Fairy Tales Retold by Francesca Lia Block, 2000

Troy by Adele Geras, 2001

Lamb: The Gospel According to Biff, Christ's Childhood Pal by Christopher Moore, 2002

A Time to Love: Stories from the Old Testament by Walter Dean Myers, 2003

Sword of the Rightful King by Jane Yolen, 2003

Older People's Impact on Our Lives

The Pigman by Paul Zindel (1968)
Toning the Sweep by Angela Johnson (1993)
Kit's Wilderness by David Almond (2000)
Saving the Planet & Stuff by Gail Gauthier (2003)

Relationships between the elderly and the young can bring great benefits to both. Grandparent-grandchild relationships, or relationships that imitate them, are often free of the tensions that exist in parent-child relationships. Grandparents, usually free of the day-to-day stress of child-rearing, freely take unqualified pride in their children's children. Often shared family traits or interests that the older generation's own children have rejected are the basis of a bond that skips a generation. Children are sometimes more willing to accept or even seek the guidance of an elderly person than of a parent. Of course, retired elderly people have more time for young people and may be widowed or disabled or otherwise isolated, making them more eager than parents to sustain mentoring companionships.

But relationships between teens and the elderly are shaped in a mainstream American culture that tends to undervalue age, associating debilitation, slowness, and loss of function with advanced years rather than dignity, patience, and wisdom. Furthermore, when parents work, care of the elderly may become difficult to schedule, and teens may find themselves facing unwanted responsibilities for people who can no longer be entirely independent. Also, teens are sometimes reluctant to visit the hospitalized or the terminally ill, feeling uncomfortable in the presence of ill health. They may not want to confront the impairment and mortality of loved older relatives or friends, perhaps avoiding the obvious conclusion that a similar fate awaits them eventually. Such circumstances may spark resentment rather than pleasure in relationships that skip a generation.

Nonetheless, whether it is family responsibility, a job, or happenstance that brings young people together with the elderly, the potential for learning and emotional satisfaction is great. Young people may learn history, especially family history, and specific skills from the old, and, above all, young people learn what it means to age, to confront ill health, to live with the knowledge of mortality. Both age groups may grow in patience, tolerance, and flexibility from cross-generational relationships.

Paul Zindel's *The Pigman* (1968), however, shows how such a relationship can go wrong as well as what young people can learn from it. The novel is presented as a memorial for the elderly man for whose death the narrators admit responsibility. John and Lorraine alternate narrating the chapters that chronicle their involvement with Mr. Pignati, whom they call "the Pigman" because of his wife's collection of pigs, which she accumulated as a joke about their name. Though their friendship with the old man is founded on deception, their real appreciation for him, especially of his interest in them, becomes clear to them; unfortunately, by the time it does, they have hurt and shocked him in an episode that causes his death.

The acquaintance begins with a prank telephone call, followed by a visit to the old man's house under the pretense of collecting for a charity. They enjoy his hospitality and friendliness, skip school the next day to meet him at the zoo, and develop a friendship with him on a series of entertaining outings. Mr. Pignati knows how to have fun, Lorraine observes, and he obviously appreciates their company, unlike her mother and John's parents. It is clear that he is lonely. Though he speaks of his wife in the present tense, they soon discover that she has recently died. Before they take an interest in him, an interest that is at first just a mockery, his only steady companion is the zoo's baboon, so he welcomes companionship and overlooks any false notes in it.

His first heart attack is precipitated by a hectic impromptu chase on roller skates that is innocent fun, though it shows poor judgment. While he is in the hospital, they take advantage of his friendship, playing house in his empty home, and inviting a couple of friends to a party that, almost inevitably, gets out of hand. Mr. Pignati comes home to disaster, finding his wife's belongings desecrated, his trust betrayed. In misery after being taken home by the police, Lorraine wishes she could call him to explain that they were just playing—not intending to harm him. Though he forgives them, he is very ill and simply emptied emotionally. When they coax him once more to the zoo, sincere in their sorrow over their actions, the stress of the baboon's death is enough to precipitate his own death. John and Lorraine must face up to the damage they have done, realizing that they are in grown-up territory now. Unlike the bad behavior of a small child, their part in destroying his home and his life cannot be simply apologized for and forgotten.

John and Lorraine are self-admittedly immature sophomores in high school. John is bored and rebellious, a liar and a prankster. Neither teen has much respect for their elders or their values, though Lorraine claims that both are compassionate, attributing their real emotional involvement with Mr. Pignati to that quality. The narrative often has a flip, pseudosophisticated tone that makes suspect the narrators' assertions about their motives, but this is an attitude that they re-create in telling their story, having outgrown it by the end of the narrative. At last they reflect on their responsibility for their own actions, the primary theme of the narrative, now that they have come up short against the reality—the finality—of death.

Angela Johnson's short novel *Toning the Sweep* (1993) is a more upbeat novel about leave-taking and closure. The narrative covers the week when fourteen-year-old Emmie and her mother help Grandmama Ola pack up her home in the desert to move to Cleveland, where she will spend the final days of her life with family. Grandmama Ola is a formidable, colorful, and eccentric character on whom cancer has so far had little visible effect, and Emmie adores her. Ola's character is revealed in the decision she made when her husband was killed by whites in Alabama in 1964: Ola mourned his sudden, violent death, but she packed up fourteen-year-old Diane (Emmie's mother) with a few cherished possessions and drove her murdered husband's Buick to California, where she made a new life for herself, never looking back at the place where she had experienced her greatest happiness. Now she must once again pack her dearest possessions, give away a lot, and leave a life behind.

Ola's life is full of warmth, beginning with warm friendships. She loves the color yellow, wears flowing scarves and hats, and cultivates plants, even the invasive kudzu vine that she brought from the South. Like her grandmother, Emmie loves the desert, but Diane has rejected her mother's lifestyle in favor of city living in the Midwest. On this last journey to the desert, Diane is more emotionally open with both her mother and daughter, and the three women's differences as well as closeness are brought out in this stressful transitional period. Ola says good-bye to her community in a series of visits, and Emmie videotapes these important last days in the desert, collecting stories from Ola's friends as a gift to her grandmother to ease her transition into her new life in Cleveland. Emmie has been a part of this community every summer of her life, and she participates in the leave-taking visits and final farewell party—a celebration of life, with dancing.

As they pack and say their farewells, all the women reminisce as well as celebrate. Through the conversations and gatherings, Emmie learns a lot about her mother, especially about that fourteenth summer when Emmie's Granddaddy died, and about her Grandmama Ola's cancer. Through this, she begins to understand how pain has strengthened them as well as how her grandmother's life will end in pain. She learns that her grandfather was killed by whites for being "uppity" simply because he bought a big car that he loved, that neither her grandmother nor grandfather anticipated his killing because they were wrapped up in their own cocoon of happiness and were largely oblivious to the impact the Civil Rights Movement was having on the South, that her own mother found her beloved father's body, and that her grandmother drove that Buick right out of the South and kept driving it—driving fast and sometimes carelessly—as a kind of memorial to him.

The Southern custom that gives the novel its name, and that brings closure for Diane, derives from the practice of ringing a dead person's soul to heaven by hammering on a "sweep," or plow. Emmie is reminded of this when she goes through a small box of her grandfather's things. Since she has no plow in the California desert but recognizes the importance of water to this place, Emmie, unexpectedly joined by her mother, takes a hammer to a water tower. On the eve of their departure, together they "tone the sweep" for Emmie's grandfather, letting go of the pain, letting go of the ghosts from the past that haunt the family. This toning foretells another toning ceremony that Emmie and her mother will likely perform as Ola departs life in a future beyond the boundaries of the novel. *Toning the Sweep* ends in life-affirming joy, with the sun breaking through clouds and the underscoring of two of the novel's symbols: the exuberant kudzu whose growth can't be stopped and the big Buick convertible that brings freedom and escape. Community and relationships have broken in the past but re-formed in new surroundings. They will break again, but life continues, and life is full of opportunities for joy.

Kit's Wilderness (2000) shows the origins of the creative process as author David Almond weaves together thirteen-year-old Kit Watson's curiosity about the past and love for his grandfather with the life of his contemporaries in a powerful story of initiation that unfolds in a liminal wilderness where age-old darkness confronts the light. Kit's family has returned to the Welsh mining village where generations of Watsons have lived and worked, alongside Askews and Carrs and McCalls. A memorable early nineteenth-century accident buried more than one hundred young workers, an event memorialized with a marker that lists names still given in present-day families. The first name on the memorial is John Askew; the last, Christopher Watson. They were thirteen when they died. This fact creates a bond between the present-day thirteen-year-old John Askew and Kit, and consequently Kit is drawn into John's after-school game of Death, in which the participants—all from the old families—share a cigarette and sip water drawn from a spring whose source is deep in the old mines, swear oaths, and take turns imagining themselves dead.

In this location, where so many miners' lives indeed were lost, with the days growing shorter as winter comes on, it is easy for the young people to believe in the ghosts whose stories their elders have told, and from the time he is drawn into the game, Kit sees the flickering shapes of the dead children at the edge of his vision. His grandfather shares his own stories and songs with Kit, showing him fossils retrieved from the mines and the entrances to the abandoned mines, and telling of the bright ghost Silky, a mischievous, happy spirit. To Kit's grandfather, descending into the mines is like time travel: he points out that what is mined is the sun's energy, stored eons ago in the plants compressed into coal. His grandfather also attests to the bond between Askew and Watson, telling of the courage and strength of John Askew's grandfather.

The present John Askew, taciturn and loutish but a highly gifted artist, attracts the disapproval of school authorities. Kit's friend Allie dismisses Askew as a "caveman." Kit, however, values Askew's talent, and when his retelling of Little Silky's story earns the English teacher's praise and she suggests it be illustrated, it is John Askew whom Kit recommends as the illustrator. But the same teacher, distressed by Kit's willingness to follow Askew, discovers the game of Death and puts an end to it, with the result that Askew is dismissed from school.

Allie, in contrast to John Askew, is a creature of light. Kit's now-deceased grandmother babysat Allie as a young child, and every time she visits, she brings joy to his grandfather, who sees her as a good-bad girl. Allie's ambition is to act professionally, and she is in her element when she is chosen to play the ice-girl in a midwinter production of *The Snow Queen*. As she rehearses, she learns some simple magic tricks, laying the groundwork for Kit's reflections on the ways that magic, storytelling, cave painting, and religion intertwined in humankind's earliest cultures.

When winter weather descends on the village, Kit's grandfather tells stories of the cold of his childhood; the geography teacher talks of the glaciers' grip on prehistoric people's lives; and the English teacher makes a writing assignment based on the imagined caveman Lak. Kit begins writing, envisioning a story that weaves elements of John Askew's personality and family situation with the magic suggested by the Snow Queen story and his vision of the past that has been stimulated both by school instruction and his grandfather's stories. Present-day events become intertwined in his writing process: his grandfather's lapses from awareness of his circumstances grow more frequent and longer; then John Askew disappears from his home. When his grandfather is ill, Kit dreams of Little Silky, following him into the dark tunnels where he envisions his grandfather wandering until the ghost brings him to the old man, and Kit holds him in his dreams until they are rescued. Each time this occurs, his grandfather returns to alertness and health, though he is growing weaker. Similarly, Kit seeks to bring Askew back from darkness, confronting the other boy's violence and infatuation with darkness and death. Askew's parents are distraught, convinced he has met his death in some kind of accident. Kit begins to conflate Mrs. Askew with the mother of Lak in the story he has been writing, and he envisions himself the magician-priest, able to resurrect, with his stories, those who have gone from sight.

Kit's climactic confrontation with Askew in an abandoned mine shaft reclaims the boy from his dark side, and the reconciliation comes through story. The story that Kit is writing envisions the prehistoric Lak rescuing a baby sister from a bear's grip, then returning to the camp where he left his family only to find they have moved south, presuming both children dead. John Askew, like Lak, has a baby sister who needs protection, protection from their abusive alcoholic father. But the infant that Lak carries also suggests John's lost babyhood, the part of him that cries out to be protected and nourished. By following Askew into the mine, daring to call him friend despite the boy's threats, and then telling Askew the story he has made up as they fall asleep by the fireside, Kit appeals to Askew to come home, to protect his family as Lak has protected his against the bear, suggesting Askew may even be able to save his father from his own self-destructiveness. Kit offers Askew a vision of the light and life that persist outside the darkness of the tunnels and the temptation to death, arguing that life is as real as death, light as real as darkness.

During the time they spend underground, Askew cuts both their thumbs, asking Kit to mingle their blood, affirming their brotherhood in a rite of passage. When Kit dreams of darkness this time, it is his grandfather who comes for him and holds him, until Allie comes in the morning's light to lead them out with a flashlight in a symbolic rebirth. They are reborn into a new year the morning after midwinter's day: born into manhood and responsibility—John accepting his responsibility to his family, Kit having to accept his grandfather's heritage as the old man approaches death within a few weeks of this episode. John Askew prepares illustrations for Kit's story of Lak and returns to school for art classes. Having completed the story in his underground telling of it, Kit is free from the specter of Lak's mother, though he saves the beautiful pebbles he has seen her offering him for his performance of magic in resurrecting her son from his apparent death.

The wilderness and the drift mine lose their mysteriousness for the town's children with the coming of spring. The authorities shore up the drift mine, add gates and electricity, and open it for history lessons. Bringing the past to light, reclaiming the dark history, makes it less magical, safer for the children. The wilderness that Kit has explored both figuratively and literally—the wildness emphasized in Allie's repeated accusation that he drives her wild—has been tamed, brought under control, the dark temptation of death counterbalanced with light and the prospect of new growth, through the artistic process.

Billed on the book jacket as possibly "the first eco-comedy," Gail Gauthier's *Saving the Planet & Stuff* (2003) tells the very funny tale of Michael Racine's summer job at a small environmental magazine founded by a pair of hippies, now in their seventies, friends of his grandparents. On impulse, Michael heads off to Vermont with them, having known them less than twenty-four hours, because his first summer job has fallen through, but almost immediately he finds himself wishing he had learned more about Norah and Walt before leaving home to live in their solar house, eat vegetarian fare, and bicycle to work. From the outset, Michael is drawn to Norah's goodness, but he and the cranky Walt seem destined to get on each other's nerves. Actually, Michael has made a career of setting off his grandfather, so he holds his own fairly well. But learning to turn off lights and find creative ways to recycle old pantyhose and discarded dishes turns out to be nowhere near as challenging as coping with office politics. The staff of *The Earth's Mother* may be small, but it is a hotbed of rivalries and competing visions, not to mention office romance. As Michael works at the magazine and spends time with Norah and Walt, he learns about environmental issues in spite of himself and grows passionate about exposing an insulation manufacturer's cover-up of the fungus growth induced by its product, insisting that his elderly hosts fight for the ideals of their youth. A welcome by-product of the drama is an opportunity for a few casual dates with Amber, a lifeguard and sometime employee at the magazine.

Michael has felt the need of putting something impressive on his college applications, especially when he compares his situation with his friends' summer jobs and travels. He is used to hearing his parents and, especially, his grandparents boast of his smart younger brother's achievements. So he initially jumps at this opportunity to work on the magazine, even if as "office peon," sorting email from readers (some of it pretty absurd), answering the phone when the secretary is at lunch, and picking up take-out meals for the staff. With no interest in or knowledge of environmental issues and little interest in magazine production, at first he tends to react to issues as a normal uninformed twenty-first-century teen, which aligns him with the recently hired managing editor, Todd, at his very first staff meeting. Michael basks in Todd's praise of his creativity, doled out as a reward for his unthinking acceptance of Todd's vision of an updated magazine with a slicker, more upscale appearance with wider audience appeal. As Michael is drawn into the controversy over changing the format from hard news reporting, he does research on magazines on his own as well as the research he is assigned at the office.

An article on fungus in insulation becomes the focal point for the controversy, as Michael takes calls from the building supply store manager who is investigating it. Todd fails to return the reporter's calls, planning to kill the story, as Michael discovers over a couple of weeks, while the threat of exposure subjects the writer to intimidation and, eventually, the loss of his job. When a staff meeting confrontation ends in their meek acceptance of the magazine's going in a new direction, Michael takes action, alerting Norah and Walt to Todd's sneaky tactics and, when Norah admits to feeling too tired to fight, he pushes her to talk to a longtime contact at a major newspaper. Michael has been transformed into an activist by the idealism he sees being lived in his hosts' lives—even though he has caught Walt eating meat on the sly. In addition to catching some of their enthusiasm for an ecofriendly lifestyle—though he looks forward to a return to malls, cable TV, and DVDs—Michael gains insight into his grandfather, whose values are substantially different from Norah and Walt's, and his relationship with him, as well as getting needed perspective on his life by getting away from his family for the summer.

ADDITIONAL READING RECOMMENDATIONS

Gentlehands by M. E. Kerr, 1978

Cold Sassy Tree by Olive Ann Burns, 1984

Dogsong by Gary Paulsen, 1985 (discussed in Animals and the Environment)

Remembering the Good Times by Richard Peck, 1986 (discussed in Friends Forever?)

After the Rain by Norma Fox Mazer, 1987

Bearstone, 1989, and *Beardance*, 1993, by Will Hobbs (both discussed in Animals and the Environment)

Everywhere by Bruce Brooks, 1990

The Sabbath Garden by Patricia Baird Greene, 1993

Tiger, Tiger, Burning Bright by Ron Koertge, 1994

Ice by Phyllis Reynolds Naylor, 1995

Rules of the Road, 1998; *Hope Was Here*, 2000 (both discussed in Jobs: Assuming Adult Responsibility); and *Stand Tall*, 2002, by Joan Bauer

Mind's Eye by Paul Fleischman, 1999

The Spring Tone by Kazumi Yumoto, 1999 (discussed in Families, Traditional and Redefined)

River Boy by Tim Bowler, 2000

Being with Henry by Martha Brooks, 2000

Post Cards from No Man's Land by Aidan Chambers, 2002

Parents' Absence, Parents' Presence

Homecoming by Cynthia Voigt (1981)
Seek by Paul Fleischman (2001)
Walk Two Moons by Sharon Creech (1994)
Shizuko's Daughter by Kyoko Mori (1993)

Parent-child relationships play a significant role in literature for all ages, but the conflicting needs for connection and separation vie most vigorously during the teen years, when children begin making choices—of friends, dating partners, interests, work, school performance, entertainment, purchases, religion, in short all the aspects of life that define a person as an individual. A young person needs to separate from his or her parents in order to forge an adult identity, but a parent's concern and approval form a necessary foundation for the child's sense of identity and self-esteem. Parental rules and supervision often seem too invasive to a teen who consequently struggles to push parents away. If a real break with a parent is going to be made in a person's life, it is likely to happen during the years of young adulthood. Indeed, some young people go so far as to run away.

On the other hand, a young person who feels the absence of a parent may be impelled to seek the parent during this period, whether the absence is due to divorce, adoption, even death, or perhaps due to factors like alcoholism or mental illness that may remove a physically present parent from the child's emotional life. A child who is in some way left behind by a parent is often likely to be aware of an empty place in his or her existence, no matter how well adjusted otherwise.

The novels discussed in this chapter address a range of problems with parents, by no means comprehensive but suggestive of some of the issues raised for young adults trying to come to terms with parents' absence or presence in their lives.

Cynthia Voigt creates strong young adult protagonists in a series of novels focusing on the Tillerman family and their friends. *Homecoming* (1981) establishes Dicey Tillerman's strength, courage, and determination when her mother walks away from her and her younger siblings, James, Maybeth, and Sammy, abandoning them in a mall parking lot with the admonition to "mind Dicey." Reasoning that she may show up at their eventual destination, the home of an elderly second cousin more than two hundred miles from the home they have left, and concerned that any appeal to the police will result in their being separated in foster homes and bringing trouble to their mother, Dicey decides that they will walk to the home of the unknown relative, whose address she has committed to memory. Dicey's resourcefulness is fully tested as she finds food and shelter for the children along the way, taking them fishing and clamming in a park, volunteering to carry grocery bags in a supermarket parking lot for tips, figuring out whom they can trust. She tells the necessary lies to keep them out of sight of any authorities but firmly corrects her younger brothers when they begin to feel that stealing is justified. After their safe arrival in Bridgeport, Connecticut, their relative's personality and home prove to be unsuited for caring for the children, so Dicey sets forth a second time some weeks later, after earning money by washing windows for local businesses, to observe the grandmother she has never met, a solitary eccentric living on a farm on Maryland's Eastern Shore. Dicey's ingenuity and courage are again tested severely, but she wins them a home with the crusty old lady, who is certainly eccentric and fiercely independent but no more so than her grandchildren.

The action occurs over the course of the summer when Dicey is thirteen, and her slimness, short hair, and dress enable her to pass for a boy on several occasions, a strategy that she believes keeps her safe in some of the situations they encounter. Dicey is an active girl who relishes camping and fishing and who, as the cliché runs, is "not afraid of hard work." She is used to taking charge. Her mother, who turns up in an institution in a catatonic state during the time the children are with their second cousin, has relied on Dicey, and in most cases her younger siblings accept her leadership. Her boldness and assertiveness are somewhat atypical for her age, and she knows how to appear more self-assured than she feels. These characteristics help to account for others' mistaking her gender. Dicey does not long to be a boy nor does she always deliberately seek to be seen as a boy, attitudes that suggest strength and resourcefulness are natural in any responsible young person, male or female. Although she exercises authority over her siblings, she also cares for them not only by feeding them but also by encouraging them and loving them, stepping in to fill the missing mother's role. When she meets her grandmother, Abigail Tillerman, she recognizes whom she takes after in her family.

Both Abigail and Dicey carve out places for themselves when left on their own, but neither has actively rebelled against masculine authority, Abigail in the context of her marriage, Dicey in the context of her cousin's dependence upon her parish priest for advice about decisions concerning the children. Dicey does, however, run from the situation that threatens to separate the family and from adult misinterpretation of the younger children's behavior. In protecting her brothers and sister, she shows herself stronger than her grandmother, who allowed her husband's harshness to separate her from her children. As Dicey learns a little more of her family history, she discovers her mother's own stand for her beliefs: she refused to be married and allowed her decision to alienate her from the family. Dicey sees the same stubbornness in six-year-old Sammy, who misses their mother the most. The independence of both Dicey and her grandmother extends to an avoidance of mainstream religion, though both have strong principles, and they seem similarly unconcerned about what other people think of them. In contrast, the middle-aged cousin whose home Dicey flees looks to her church to provide the structure of her daily life as well as to shape her personal decisions. Dicey has a strong sense of justice, and she claims authority over the younger children even in her grandmother's house, countermanding the punishment her grandmother assigns to Sammy when he has disappeared for hours without telling Dicey where he is going. In Abigail's home, Dicey's authority over the children is challenged at times, but the potential for their mutual reinforcement of the same principles for the younger children's behavior seems to be a positive force that counteracts the initial jockeying as they establish a new family structure that takes Dicey's independence into account.

Dicey is too young for the responsibility that has been thrust upon her, but she rises to the occasion and takes charge of her family's fate. It is only at the very end of the novel that Abigail gives in to the temptation to take in her grandchildren and responds to Dicey's direct request. Abigail's ambivalence is shown in her introducing the children as her grandchildren but referring to the younger children as "your family" when speaking to Dicey, rather than as "our family." Dicey needs love, approval, and nurturing herself, but she rarely acknowledges this need during the period in which she is striving to establish a home for the children.

All the Tillermans are unusual in various ways. James is intelligent and thirsty for knowledge. He longs for male role models and thrives in the summer school run by the church in part because he welcomes having male teachers, the priests. Maybeth is so withdrawn that educators keep trying to assign her to special education classes, yet her thoughtful insights, as well as her ability to learn songs rapidly and retain them, keep reassuring Dicey that Maybeth is intelligent. Sammy's governing characteristic is stubbornness. Dicey worries about his unhappiness when she remembers the joy he expressed as a small child, but she appreciates his willingness to fight when fighting is called for, a characteristic that leads to his being identified as a troublemaker. Despite their strong individual personalities, they share a love of music and can find emotional refreshment and closeness when they sing together.

Dicey responds more to the family home, the land, and the bay than she does to her grandmother, choosing the Tillerman homestead as the place she wants them to stay, imagining the life they can live there on the Eastern Shore, rather than choosing her grandmother as an adult on whom to rely. It is a sense of home that Dicey, James, Maybeth, and Sammy are seeking, hoping to replace the feeling of rightness they had in their home on the beach at Provincetown. Their cousin's small home in town, with its tiny back yard, hems them in as much as her attitudes do. On the Eastern Shore, they find flat, open land with a seemingly endless horizon, land with possibilities that they begin to share with their grandmother as they help her see ways to support them all. Dicey briefly allows herself to dream of refurbishing and learning to sail the boat in her grandmother's barn and then, finally, is able to embrace the dream in a decision that will reshape the course of all the Tillermans' lives.

Seek (2001), by Paul Fleischman, describes a high school senior's coming to terms with his need for the father who left before he was born. The novel takes the unusual genre of a radio script written by protagonist Rob Radkovitz in response to the assignment to write an autobiography. He chooses this form because his father was a musician and DJ, and Rob has sought him over the years with ever more powerful radio equipment, hoping to catch an echo of the voice on the taped radio show that is one of Rob's two mementoes of his father. (The other is a recording of Louisiana countryside sounds.) Living with his mother and her family, Rob has experienced a rich family life, and he has a strong male influence in his life in the person of his grandfather, a college history professor. Yet there is always something missing, something elusive.

The pain caused by this missing piece is responsible for Rob's eventually abandoning his search. He has new family challenges to contend with when, in his high school years, his mother begins a serious relationship and marries. Rob's first reaction is total resistance to Andy, but his mother's real love and Andy's kindness and interest reconcile him to sharing his mother. His new stepfather teaches him yoga, and it is in its practice that he realizes he has come to terms with his father's absence, though it requires years of searching, inwardly raging, grieving, trying to ignore, and finally growing through the issue that bring him to this state of calm. He once needed his biological father but now, in the wake of this realization, when his father finally does seek him out, Rob realizes he does not need to develop a relationship with someone who is a stranger to him.

Relying as he does on the airwaves as the medium of his search, Rob finds it natural to chronicle his life as the sounds of voices in dialogue, saying that he is more prone to "listen back" than to "look back" over his past. The radio waves are "an ocean of voices," he discovers as he acquires increasingly sophisticated equipment and seeks stations ever farther afield, hoping to hear the voice he will recognize from the recording he has treasured. He gets into shortwave and rigs a mike to "broadcast" in his household, an activity that reemerges several years later when he and a couple of friends set up a pirate station and begin broadcasting. For a time, having faced supreme disappointment after he has convinced himself his father will show up for his eighth grade graduation ceremony, Rob abandons radio altogether, angry at his father and his own capacity for self-delusion, and in this period he writes, first for the school newspaper, then for an underground paper of his own creation. All these activities attest to his creativity and satirical talent. His creativity always brings his brilliant family's praise. From childhood he has been steeped in the sound of the written word as read aloud and expounded—his grandmother's classic novels and mysteries, his grandfather's labor history, his mother's languages (she teaches Spanish and French and listens to Mexican soap operas on the radio) and poetry—along with broadcasts of operas and baseball games.

Rob composes this polyphonic, dialogic autobiography as testimony to his search. Although it was his father he thought he was seeking for so many years, it is himself he finds. There is reconciliation though no desire for further relationship when his biological father finally does telephone him, in response to Rob's broadcast. After that phone call, Rob forgives his father, realizing how young his father was. Most importantly, though, his autobiography bears testimony to the richness of the family life he has known—a richness that truly compensates for any sense of lack he has known.

In contrast to these tales of abandonment, Sharon Creech's 1994 novel, *Walk Two Moons*, layers several stories to chronicle thirteen-year-old protagonist Salamanca Tree Hiddle's acceptance of her mother's death. The overarching frame of the novel is shaped by Sal and her father's move from a Kentucky farm to Euclid, Ohio, where she contends with the challenges of accepting her father's friendship with the widow Margaret Cadaver, along with entering a new school, supporting her paranoid best friend Phoebe Winterbottom through a short period of being left by her mother, and enjoying a developing interest in the opposite sex represented specifically by the mysterious and likable Ben. The more immediate frame for the unfolding of Sal's stories is the one-week car trip she takes with her grandparents from Ohio to Lewiston, Idaho, a journey timed so they will arrive at the grave of Sal's mother, Sugar, on Sugar's birthday. As Sal relates the story of the momentous trip, she also tells Phoebe's story to her grandparents. In the course of telling Phoebe's story, much of Sal's own life in Ohio is revealed, along with the story of her mother's last year, but Sal never alludes directly to her mother's death, so that an unwary reader may assume that Sugar has simply left her family and may be persuaded to return. Sal's conversations with her charmingly eccentric grandparents (her father's parents) reveal more family history, furnishing insight into Sal's adjustment to the dramatic changes she has had to cope with. In the course of their trip, Sal must rise to the challenge of a new loss as well when her grandmother suffers a fatal stroke.

Most of Sal's stories tell of the loss, whether temporary or permanent, of loved ones, with the loss of her mother occupying center stage. Through the telling, as well as the visit to her mother's grave with which the trip culminates, she reaches acceptance. In the nonchronological telling, the reader begins to see Sugar's restlessness on the Kentucky farm, a restlessness that is at first alleviated when she becomes pregnant but then turns to despair when the infant is stillborn. Sugar left her husband and daughter to allow herself some time to think and to process her emotions alone, but in Idaho her bus plunged over a mountainside, and everyone except Mrs. Cadaver was killed. Sitting next to Sugar on the bus, Mrs. Cadaver has heard a great deal about Sal and her father before the accident, and it is this connection that formed the basis of the friendship that impelled her father to move to Ohio. Because Sal has been so grief stricken that she has not yet admitted her mother is dead and so angry and desolate at being left behind that she shuts her father out, she has not given anyone the opportunity to explain to her that her father is not dating Mrs. Cadaver but that her friendship is helping him deal with his own grief.

While there is much that Sal refuses to admit, her sensitivity to others' feelings and to family dynamics enables her to understand Phoebe's family better than Phoebe can. She has patience with Phoebe, more patience than she has with her own father, and in lending support to her friend, Sal comes to terms with her own mother's having left her. Phoebe's story has significant comic elements as well, provided by Phoebe's paranoia and vivid imagination. Phoebe's mother has led a cautious, conventional, and respectable life as a devoted housewife and mother, so when she leaves, Phoebe is convinced that her mother has been kidnapped, at the very least, and murdered, at the worst. Phoebe has an unfounded theory that the young man who came to their door one day is a lunatic bent on mayhem. Though Phoebe's theory is incorrect, the man is significant: he is the son Mrs. Winterbottom put up for adoption before she met Mr. Winterbottom. Phoebe has been unable to envision her mother as having any life separate from her family; she sees her mother only in relation to her own needs. This is clear to Sal, and because she can see Mrs. Winterbottom's unhappiness when the family cannot, she is able to assure Phoebe that her mother's leaving has nothing to do with her. This recognition, an insight that is cemented by her visit to her mother's grave, helps her let go of her own mother.

Along with loss, the novel deals with love. Sal's grandparents illustrate the love of a couple who have shared a long life together. Sal's father's love for her mother and her is shown in Sal's memories of the past and the motive, once she learns it, for his move to Ohio. The apparently unemotional Mr. Winterbottom provides a touching welcome to his wife when she returns, warmly including her son in the family circle. And Sal herself discovers the joy of kissing and touching Ben, who appears to be her soul mate when both of them draw the same picture in response to a directive to draw their souls. Through the multilayered depiction of couples, Creech shows us that love is a central element of life and that love goes on, even after death.

Shizuko's Daughter (1993), by Kyoko Mori, tells the touching story of a Japanese girl whose mother's suicide leaves her in a loveless world controlled by a harsh father, who has never really felt connected to her, and a bitter stepmother, who resents Yuki as an ever-present reminder of her mother. All that sustains Yuki in the years that follow Shizuko's death is the memory of her mother's love, underscored in a suicide note, and eventually her memories build independence and a strength of character that are interpreted by her stepmother as spoiled selfishness and by her maternal grandparents as lack of respect. Like the persimmons that were sour in the summer when fresh but, dried, provide a sweet remembrance of the summer's happiness, her memories preserve the sweetness of her mother's love during a long winter of lovelessness.

Yuki's loneliness and sadness are seen as character flaws by those who expect her to accept her mother's death and move on, but Shizuko was an extraordinary woman, knowledgeable, an artist, and a loving mother, and Yuki's loyalty to her is intense. Indeed, her father has never truly known Yuki as the happy and talkative child that his wife's family knew, since he himself is uncommunicative. Even with her mother's family, after Shizuko's suicide, she is taciturn. Years after her mother's death, at her aunt's wedding, she dares to voice to her new uncle her distrust of love between men and women, which often leads to unhappiness and imprisonment. Not until she escapes to college from her father's house does she show any interest in a boy. Before that, boys have only drawn away the attention of a potential friend who shares her interest in sports.

Respect is important to Yuki. It becomes increasingly impossible even to pretend to any desire for a relationship with her father and stepmother because they have shown no respect for her mother or for her. She is well aware how trapped her mother was, unable to leave her husband because doing so would separate her from Yuki, unwilling even to entertain a friendship for a kind male friend because he is divorced. The need for preserving face drives her stepmother's and father's actions. Only late in the novel does the reader gain any insight into the father, Hideki, whose thoughts reveal that he felt some pressure to resign from his job after his first wife's suicide. When his second wife, Hanae, threatens to leave him, he goes to any length to placate her because the destruction of a second marriage would force his resignation.

Yuki's stepmother is critical of Shizuko from the start and is ready to find fault with Yuki after Yuki asserts her resistance to the situation by breaking the saki bowl at her father's wedding. Hanae redecorates the house, with less sophisticated taste than Shizuko's, and destroys those possessions that she dares to. Her bitterness over the long wait for Shizuko's husband is compounded by her inability to bear him a child, and she takes out her anger on Yuki. Unrealistically, she expects Yuki to move on with her life, leaving her mother behind, while she heightens the contrast between her and Shizuko with constant criticism and even, on one occasion, physical abuse. Consumed by bitterness herself, she suggests that Yuki is unbalanced, having inherited her mother's insanity.

With Hanae's concern for face, it is difficult to understand why she and Hideki do not attend the school events and athletic competitions in which Yuki consistently excels. Yet she is angry and shamed by Yuki's failure to invite them to her high school graduation ceremony, after years of neglect and abuse. One can imagine Yuki's heart might have been won, suffering as she did from her mother's loss, with kindness. Her mother made her beautiful clothes in many colors, but her stepmother buys her ill-fitting, ugly clothes and then berates her for not wearing them. Consequently, Yuki works to earn the money to buy her own clothes, a strategy that brings the added benefit of keeping her away from her home each evening.

Yuki's memories of her mother are largely dominated by colors and textures, and she follows in Shizuko's footsteps in her love of art. She earns the homemaking teacher's enmity by happily drawing a failed cooking assignment. Sent to gather natural materials for a centerpiece, she substitutes them for the frogs awaiting dissection in her biology class. She loves flowers, as her mother and grandparents do, and likes to watch the stars. But the hours she spends drawing in her room are only another indication to her stepmother that she is mentally unhealthy and selfish. Shizuko's own sketchbook, though, survives through the years when her life and legacy have been shut out of sight, and it finally brings a measure of self-knowledge to Hideki, a sense of responsibility for his first wife's unhappiness along with recognition of her forgiveness. The last word, however, comes from Yuki's grandmother, who has lost people dear to her yet continues to love and to cherish the future represented in the children. Her continuing love provides a counterpoint to the shattering caused by Shizuko's suicide.

ADDITIONAL READING RECOMMENDATIONS

Where the Lilies Bloom by Vera and Bill Cleaver, 1969 (discussed in Poverty's Challenges)

A Hero Ain't Nothin' but a Sandwich by Alice Childress, 1973 (discussed in Heroism: What Does It Mean to Be a Hero?)

Father Figure by Richard Peck, 1978

Rainbow Jordan by Alice Childress, 1980

All Together Now, 1979, and *Notes for Another Life*, 1981, by Sue Ellen Bridgers

A Formal Feeling by Zibby Oneal, 1982

A Solitary Blue by Cynthia Voigt, 1983

Wart, Son of Toad by Alden R. Carter, 1985

Annie John by Jamaica Kincaid, 1985

Midnight Hour Encores by Bruce Brooks, 1986

The Moonlight Man, 1986, and *The Eagle Kite*, 1995, by Paula Fox

The Catalogue of the Universe by Margaret Mahy, 1986

Celine by Brock Cole, 1989

Beyond the Reef by Todd Strasser, 1989

The Heroic Life of Al Capsella by Judith Clarke, 1990, and sequels

Somewhere in the Darkness by Walter Dean Myers, 1990

Mariposa Blues by Ron Koertge, 1991

Ask Me Something Easy by Natalie Honeycutt, 1991

Freak the Mighty, 1993 (discussed in Friends Forever?), and *Max the Mighty*, 1998, by Rodman Philbrick

The Kingdom by the Sea, 1991, and *A Place to Hide*, 1994, by Robert Westall

Two Moons in August, 1992, and *Being with Henry*, 2000, by Martha Brooks

A Bone from a Dry Sea by Peter Dickinson, 1992

Plain City by Virginia Hamilton, 1993

For the Love of Pete: A Novel by Jan Marino, 1993

The Snake-Stone by Berlie Doherty, 1996

Dancing on the Edge by Han Nolan, 1997 (discussed in Families, Traditional and Redefined)

Humming Whispers, 1996 (discussed in Emotional Problems Confronted), and *Heaven*, 1998, by Angela Johnson

Strays Like Us by Richard Peck, 1998

Harley, Like a Person by Cat Bauer, 2000

Miracle's Boys by Jacqueline Woodson, 2000

Holly Starcross by Berlie Doherty, 2002

Sonny's War by Valerie Hobbs, 2002 (discussed in War's Impact)

Tribes by Arthur Slade, 2002

Buddha Boy, 2003 (discussed in Religion and Spiritual Life), and *The Blue Mirror*, 2004, by Kathe Koja, 2004

Poverty's Challenges

Where the Lilies Bloom by Vera and Bill Cleaver (1969)
The House on Mango Street by Sandra Cisneros (1984)
Buried Onions by Gary Soto (1997)
Make Lemonade by Virginia Euwer Wolff (1993)

Poverty is a powerful shaper of young people's lives, marginalizing them in an affluent society, often humiliating and hurting them, and requiring hard work and sacrifices on their part in a struggle for the family's existence. The work to which they commit themselves may demand more of them than they can realistically manage, or they may be taken advantage of in their eagerness to take on adult responsibility. This is the situation that Mary Call Luther faces when she attempts to hold on to her father's home and land and keep her siblings together in *Where the Lilies Bloom*, in a struggle similar to Lyddie's in Katherine Paterson's depiction of the nineteenth-century Lowell mill girl's life (discussed in Chapter 16: History Is about Young Adults, Too).

Urban communities are usually the setting for the theme of poverty. When discrimination is at the heart of the economic conditions that shape a young protagonist's life, he or she may be glad of any job at all in a community where unemployment is rife. The protagonists of novels discussed here keep their eyes focused on their route out of the conditions that imprison them—education. Whatever the context for their struggles, these characters retain their dignity and humanity in the face of their challenges.

Vera and Bill Cleaver's 1969 novel of Appalachian life, *Where the Lilies Bloom* has become a classic. Depicting a poor North Carolina mountain family's life in the aptly named Trial Valley, the novel gives insight into the reasons people might cherish a hard-working, impoverished rural life in a beautiful setting. Above all, this is Mary Call Luther's story. Mary Call is the child that her fiercely independent sharecropper father leans upon after her mother's death, old enough at fourteen to be entrusted with instructions for his burial on the mountainside and his injunction against her older sister's marrying their landlord. Both Mary Call and her father think of eighteen-year-old Devola as mentally challenged enough that she cannot be trusted to make her own decision about marriage, and both are anxious that the children should stay together after his death. On his instructions, they hide his death from prying outsiders and try to make do with the bit of money left behind, their wits, and the proceeds from their wildcrafting—harvesting the wild plants that can be sold to the drug companies for medicinal purposes.

Mary Call is trying so hard to be an adult that she sacrifices her right to her feelings. She may be resourceful and tough, but she needs time to grieve for her father. Unfortunately, her fear of the authorities' splitting up her family drives her, and in turn she drives her family. She can rely on ten-year-old Romey, but he is clearly too young for the burdens she must place on him, and his response is natural—he resists and becomes angry with her. His own struggles to understand the hardness of their lot are touching; at one point, he says that God has forgotten them. The challenges Mary Call encounters in trying to get her siblings to accept her authority just make her that much harder, fighting to succeed in something her father was not very good at—keeping the small mountain farm viable when his first financial obligation is to his landlord and, literally, keeping a roof over their heads and food on the table in a harsh climate with little money. She is strong and quick and fierce enough to kill a fox that attacks their animals. However, she also becomes unpleasantly manipulative at times, maneuvering the landlord Kiser Pease, who wants to marry Devola, into giving them a pig and a cow and a radio and convincing him to leave his car at their home for Devola's entertainment.

Two qualities shine through the hardships, though: the children's love of their wildly beautiful environment and their spirit of fun. With all the challenges they face, they enjoy lighthearted moments, driving the car and laughing at the way Romey scares off the nosy wife of the general store owner by wearing a bearskin. The novel conveys an appreciation of natural riches, the abundant herbs, bark, and leaves that the children can use to eke out an income, and they remember always to reseed the areas they harvest. At the same time, the authors combat the oversimplified stereotype of quaint mountain folk that Mary Call identifies as the "happy pappy" stereotype—the impoverished, ignorant mountaineers grinning on the porches of tumble-down cabins, unaware that their lives could be better.

Though Mary Call's determination is not enough to keep them going, and ultimately she must accept that her father has been wrong in his unyielding opposition to Devola's marriage, her stubborn will keeps them independent of outsiders' and even relatives' charity once she is forced to confront her own limitations and acknowledge that even Kizer Pease has some good points. The nosy, hypocritical Christian woman's husband, owner of the local store, provides practical assistance to help them start making evergreen roping for the holidays. Independence may be an admirable quality, but there are important values in being part of a community as well.

Sandra Cisneros's *The House on Mango Street* (1984), a work often read by young adults because it treats coming-of-age themes, portrays the impact of urban poverty on a young Hispanic girl as well as the hope for the future that her name, Esperanza, implies. The work has been variously called a poetic novel and a book of short stories; the short poetic chapters, each separately titled, are often identified more accurately as "vignettes." Together the brief images provide a portrait of Esperanza's neighborhood. The house, with its appealing street name, is emblematic of the family's disappointment: the parents promise a bigger house, with bedrooms and bathrooms for all, but the shabby tiny house brings shame to Esperanza. However, it is a *house* with a tiny yard, an improvement over the apartments they have lived in. It is temporary, her mother says, but Esperanza fears it will prove permanent.

Esperanza's observations of her neighbors, as well as her interactions with the nuns at school, a store owner, older teens, and relatives, give a varied picture of life in the community. It is primarily a story of women's lives. Women's roles are limited both by their own aspirations and the restrictions imposed by their relatives, spouses, and boyfriends, enforced with violence. Esperanza identifies with the strong women, the wild women like the great-grandmother for whom she was named, who, like her, was born in the Chinese year of the horse. Like her neighbors, Esperanza aspires to something better, but the route she will choose is education and writing. She discovers that with these aspirations she will both belong and not belong.

The neighborhood's connections with Mexico and Puerto Rico are a part of her cultural knowledge. Neighbors maintain contact with families outside the United States, bringing relatives in, planning eventual returns. This separation can cause sorrow when relatives left behind die or when transient individuals, working in the United States away from their families, meet with violent death. New arrivals face the language barrier and must adjust to the climate. The community forms a world apart from the city's white culture: some residents move away because the neighborhood is getting worse, that is, opening to people like Esperanza's family; outsiders who wander into the neighborhood find it threatening.

Girls and boys live different lives, and the girls learn the possibilities for their lives through observation. They model themselves on older teens, learning how to dress and how to attract boys, discussing the development of their bodies. They observe the young woman who must take her mother's place as the family housekeeper after her mother's death, fitting in college studies as best she can because she cannot rebel against her father's authority. They observe the rebellion of young women against strict fathers through sexual activity, and they learn the hard way to avoid sexual assault by not being alone and not taking kindness from older men at face value.

As the text nears conclusion, there are several indicators that Esperanza will leave the neighborhood and this past behind. She wants a house of her own, recalling Virginia Woolf's *A Room of One's Own*, a space and a life in which a woman can write. Her friends' elderly relatives foretell her departure and success but stress her connection, the circularity of her life. She comes back, in the last vignette, to the idea of writing and the repetition of the first couple of sentences of the book, indicating that when grown she will write—or after she has grown she is writing—about her origins.

The street is named after a red, sweet, exotic fruit that cannot tolerate cold temperatures, an Asian import into California. Ironically, the red of the house in which she lives on Mango Street is crumbling brick, not the warm red of organic life. Esperanza has admired and identified with four slender but tenacious trees on her street because their roots reach deep and they reach for light beyond the concrete and bricks.

Gary Soto's poetic novel *Buried Onions* (1997) depicts the grim inner-city life of a poor young Hispanic man, Eddie, who cannot afford college, has difficulty getting and keeping work in the face of white suspicions of his motives and actions, often struggles simply to get enough to eat, and is constantly on guard against the gang violence around him that killed his cousin and nearly kills his friend José, a marine on leave before going overseas. Eddie conceives the fanciful idea that the sadness experienced by many people of color are caused by a huge onion buried under the city. To their perpetual sadness, manifested in tears caused by the giant onion, are added the challenges of poor jobs and ever-present death.

Eddie's father and two uncles are dead of unspecified causes, and his best friend from high school was killed in a factory accident. Eddie struggles, thinking of himself as like an ant, too young for a good job and too old for gang life (a way of life that does not appeal to him), wanting only a solid working-class life built on hard work and a family to work for. He has followed self-destructive paths in the past, but at nineteen, he hopes God will bring him a decent life, though the evidence of life around him does not bode well for that outcome. His tenderheartedness, along with the constraints that poverty makes on it, is illustrated when he visits his godmother, only to find that she is about to take her aged dog to be put down; he helps her, and he grieves for the dog, but his hunger compels him to take half the money she has handed him for the donation expected for the dog's euthanasia. As he moves around the city, he observes that it swallows people up: more people go into the hospital and police station than come out.

Eddie's inability to make a decent living is largely due to the inability of whites to distinguish between the victimizers and the victims in the Hispanic community. He may face police harassment simply by being in a white neighborhood, and when his employer's truck is stolen in the brief time it is parked outside his home, he does not even think of calling the police. When he and José attempt to reclaim it for his employer, José is badly wounded while he is alone on the street with the truck.

Eddie's aunt pesters him daily to avenge his cousin's murder, knowing that the criminal justice system is unlikely to do so, but Eddie resists her pleas. He avoids violence, recognizing that in his neighborhood it takes constant vigilance to avoid offending with a look, and he does not know the true circumstances of his cousin's death. Each time he encounters his cousin's dangerous friend Angel, he feels the simultaneous challenge to fight violence with violence and the fear that perhaps Angel himself was responsible for the cousin's death and will kill Eddie next. When forced by circumstances, however, he fights with a will.

Eddie's sense of the ever-presence of death is symbolized by the mortuary students at the community college where he has been studying the air-conditioning trade until forced by poverty to quit. He is aware of the prospects for steady, well-paying work that the mortuary students have, seeing all the death around him. In some of his bleaker moments, he envisions individuals as corpses laid out for funerals. The hopeless emptiness and hunger he sees around him, often in the person of winos, as well as kids sniffing glue or taking more expensive drugs, are epitomized by the black man who is selling bags of onions out of the car in which his family lives.

Encouraged by Coach, who directs playground activities in his neighborhood, Eddie inquires into the military as a way out of the trap of poverty and racism but does not join up until he is driven into it by the certainty that gang members will be after him. Ironically, even the van that promises to carry him away from inner-city Fresno to boot camp breaks down, enabling him to discover the already-harvested onion fields where black men eke out their living from "leftovers." Despite the intense sorrow that Eddie feels as he realizes the real, physical presence of buried onions, he elects to turn his back on the tears that have plagued his first nineteen years of life, walking away from the violence of brother against brother in the barrio life he has known. Can it be any worse for him to face wars in another country than it has been to live amid war on the streets of his own neighborhood?

In contrast, Virginia Euwer Wolff's optimistically titled *Make Lemonade* (1993) offers hope that education will help young people escape the limitations that hem them in. The dominant theme of LaVaughn's life is saving for college. Ever since she mentioned to her widowed mother that she would like to go to college, her mother—a strong, forceful woman—has held LaVaughn to that dream, opening a savings account and making sure that LaVaughn does not let any distractions keep her from earning good grades. Not many jobs other than babysitting are available to a fourteen-year-old, but caring for seventeen-year-old Jolly's two children seems likely to derail her plans, though Jolly's difficult life is a cautionary tale that, at one specific point, hardens LaVaughn's motivation. Her desire for a college education, she notes, came in fifth grade when she saw a video at school that showed beautiful grounds, well-equipped science labs, dormitory life, and a good job afterward, all these images in places where no gangs have painted gang symbols on the walls.

LaVaughn's father was killed by a gang's stray bullet; since then she and her mother have been a self-sufficient family. LaVaughn has her reservations about babysitting for Jolly, seeing the tiny, dirty apartment and knowing what her mother would think of it and of Jolly, but three-year-old Jeremy and his infant sister, Jilly, tug at her heartstrings, so she begins the job, only to find herself doing much more than babysitting: she cleans, she comforts, she toilet trains, she buys Jeremy shoes, and she finds herself staying overnight when Jolly gets home late, supporting Jolly when she is sexually harassed, and babysitting free when Jolly loses her job for refusing her boss's advances.

Jolly's life is a mess, as LaVaughn's mother is fond of reminding her, but it is easier to understand Jolly when her history comes out. In and out of foster homes, Jolly has lived in boxes with other homeless kids, and her two pregnancies were against her will. She has had little schooling, limiting her chances for getting another job. She lives in fear of welfare, not only because she is proud but also because she is convinced that any authorities she contacts will take her children from her. LaVaughn is tempted, out of sympathy and growing friendship with Jolly, to withdraw some of her savings to help Jolly, but in a moment of stunning clarity she sees that she cannot risk her future, in a decision that a teacher suggests may indicate that she herself is exploiting Jolly, along with nearly everyone else Jolly has ever known. LaVaughn does, however, convince Jolly to visit her self-esteem class and later to return to school in a program for teen mothers. Through the ups and downs of their time together—LaVaughn's sympathy, Jolly's envy of LaVaughn's home life, their anger and impatience with each other, their shared love of the children—LaVaughn eventually decides that it is not important to figure out who is exploiting whom. They have become friends, and they need each other; LaVaughn needs Jeremy and Jilly like she needs vitamins.

As Jolly becomes more self-sufficient, learns job skills and life skills, and her self-esteem increases, their friendship gets onto a more even keel, but it is cemented most firmly by the near-disaster that certifies Jolly's new ability to take hold of her life. When Jilly chokes on a toy, Jolly's knowledge of CPR, acquired in a required swimming class, enables her to save her child, and her true quality as a survivor and a mother as strong and fierce as LaVaughn's own mother emerges. The novel is a powerful story of survival, illustrating the saw "if life gives you lemons, make lemonade." LaVaughn repeatedly plants lemon seeds for Jeremy, and Jolly resents her attempts to convince him that they will indeed sprout after repeated disappointments. It is only after LaVaughn has stopped babysitting for Jolly that a lemon plant finally does emerge, emblem of the patience and persistence it takes to overcome the kind of challenges these young women face.

ADDITIONAL READING RECOMMENDATIONS

Hoops, 1983, and *Slam!* 1996, by Walter Dean Myers
Tex by S. E. Hinton, 1989
Send No Blessings by Phyllis Reynolds Naylor, 1990
Journey of the Sparrows by Fran Leeper Buss and Daisy Cubias, 1991
Lyddie, 1991, and *Jip: His Story*, 1998, by Katherine Paterson (both discussed in History Is about Young Adults, Too)

Sisters/Hermanas by Gary Paulsen, 1993

Striking Out, 1993, *Farm Team*, 1995, and *Hard Ball*, 1998, by Will Weaver

Don't You Dare Read This, Mrs. Dunphrey by Margaret Peterson Haddix, 1996

I Hadn't Meant to Tell You This, 1994 (discussed in Abuse, Sexual Violence, and Healing);
        Lena, 1998; and *Miracle's Boys*, 2000, by Jacqueline Woodson

When Kambia Elaine Flew in from Neptune by Lori Aurelia Williams, 2000

Black Mirror by Nancy Werlin, 2001

A Step from Heaven by An Na, 2002

Pregnancy, Parenthood, Abortion

My Darling, My Hamburger by Paul Zindel (1969)
Gingerbread by Rachel Cohn (2002)
Get It While It's Hot. Or Not by Valerie Hobbs (1996)
The First Part Last by Angela Johnson (2003)

Despite declining teen pregnancy rates, the United States has the highest rate among developed countries of births to teen mothers. By far the great majority of these pregnancies are unplanned. Teen parents face enormous physical, emotional, social, and economic challenges. Factors that contribute to young adults' independence in other areas enable them to choose to participate in sexual activity, though often on the spur of the moment and less informed than they might be. The range of choices for a pregnant teen is limited: having an abortion, giving the baby up for adoption, keeping the baby.

Even before *Roe v. Wade* legalized abortion, young women sought abortions, and this theme has appeared in a number of young adult novels, sometimes as a secondary issue (as in Robert Lipsyte's *The Summer Boy*, discussed in Chapter 20: Jobs: Assuming Adult Responsibilities, and Chris Crutcher's *Staying Fat for Sarah Byrnes*, discussed in Chapter 6: Beauty's Meaning). In novels discussed here, pregnant teens choose abortion or adoption—but they may end up keeping the babies they thought they could send to homes with adult parents.

Teens faced with these adult decisions and responsibilities may yearn for an earlier innocence or the opportunity to stay children just a little longer. Their choices, at best are bittersweet, and teen pregnancy remains a theme largely of loss in young adult fiction.

My Darling, My Hamburger (1969), by Paul Zindel, depicts the pressure on young women to engage in sex in an era when information on birth control was difficult to come by and abortion was illegal. The "hamburger" of the title comes from the health teacher's advice to senior girls on how to handle the pressure to have sex when they are out on dates—they should suggest going to get a hamburger. The health teacher assumes the only issue is a boy's getting too excited for self-control. Unfortunately, the tensions in Liz's life are more complex: she and Sean love each other; she has her own desires to rein in; her mother and stepfather's efforts to control her behavior inspire her to rebel; and in a hiatus in her relationship with Sean she dates an older guy with a reputation for having gotten several girls pregnant. Rod, consequently, knows of an abortionist, so he is the person she turns to when she realizes she is pregnant. Abortion is not her first choice. Sean wants to marry Liz, and for one brief night, she envisions her dreams coming true. But when he tries to find a way to tell his hard-drinking father he is engaged, his father's cynical attitude toward girls who get pregnant leads Sean to believe his parents will never condone his marrying Liz. Instead, he comes up with the money for the abortion, to which Rod takes her, accompanied by her best friend, Maggie.

Long-suffering Maggie has allowed most of her social life to be manipulated by Liz. She begins dating Sean's friend Dennis at Liz's urging, but then, just when they have come to like each other, Liz asks Maggie at short notice to accompany her to the abortionist, and Maggie breaks her date with Dennis for the prom, unable to explain to him why. (It is their greater freedom on prom night that has made it the logical date for the abortion.)

Later, when Liz admits she is still bleeding profusely just before Rod drops her off at home, it is Maggie who alerts her family, only to lose Liz's friendship. When the novel ends with their high school graduation, the occasion brings home Maggie's unhappiness as she recognizes how little any of them have known what they were getting into in the morass of dating. With this recognition, however, Maggie shows that she has grown more than any of the other characters. Liz is immured, allowed to receive a diploma but not to walk with her classmates, and the school is buzzing with gossip. Sean's feelings are revealed only in a cryptically allusive short story that earns him an A+ in English class and the teacher's congratulations on his imagination. The story thinly disguises the nature of the choice he has made and suggests he and Liz are victims, though he does show some awareness of his responsibility.

Interspersed with the third-person narrative, which usually reveals Maggie's point of view, are notes written by the girls and Sean's creative writing pieces, along with official announcements of the major senior social events. These texts create a fuller picture of school life and the teens' relationships.

In the final analysis, the characters seem very young, too young to handle the challenges of sexual intimacy. Their relationships with their parents are too superficial for real communication, and each of the main characters feels the weight of parental expectations. There is clearly no room for a pregnancy in their lives, and under the circumstances, abortion seems like the best choice, though the emotional fallout from Liz's and Sean's actions leaves a somewhat bleak final impression.

A much more contemporary tale of abortion is told in Rachel Cohn's *Gingerbread* (2002), in which sexual activity is linked to family problems and insecurity about one's identity. The protagonist, Cyd Charisse, needs to put together the jigsaw pieces that have made her who she is, and she gets the opportunity with her first visit to her biological father after a series of rebellious exploits that give her stepfather, Sid, a reason for his fond nickname for her—"Little Hellion." At sixteen, Cyd Charisse still carries a rag doll, named Gingerbread, with her everywhere, even with all her grownup knowledge of sex, drugs, and petty crime. Her memory of her father's buying the doll for her at the airport when she was five is bound up with a memory of foil-wrapped homemade gingerbread that he gave her. Between then and her visit at sixteen, she has had only one other contact with him, when she was at her New England prep school: she called him to ask his help in paying for an abortion. Now, after the death of her father's wife has made a relationship possible, her mother and Sid still might not have agreed to send her on a visit to New York City were she not driving them crazy, grounded in San Francisco.

Her grounding has nothing to do with the abortion—Sid and Nancy do not know about it. Instead, she has been caught staying overnight with her boyfriend, Shrimp, at the apartment he shares with his older brother, Wallace. Cyd has been on her best behavior up to this point, protecting her parents from most of the worldly knowledge she acquired at boarding school, where she got involved with Justin, whom her mother admires because he comes from a good Connecticut family. She was expelled because she was caught in flagrante delicto with him, but no one other than Justin and her dad knows about the abortion, and she has spared Sid and Nancy the details of Justin's drug deals and her sneaking out of school to shoplift munchies for him. Ironically, she notes, her mother gives her a box of condoms to make sure she will not get pregnant by Shrimp, who provides his own condoms and would not, she is sure, let her face an abortion clinic alone, as Justin did.

More recent shoplifting escapades have brought her a sentence of community service at a nursing home, where she has formed a real friendship with Sugar Pie. In addition to the constructive behavior enforced by her required community service, she has gotten decent grades, and she has started working at a coffee bar owned by Shrimp's brother, Wallace. Unfortunately, once she is grounded, the time away from Shrimp gives him a chance to think through their romance and tell her he thinks they need some time apart, a factor in her making life so miserable at home that her mother is happy to send her off to get to know her father, Frank. What they do not know about her misery is that she is grieving over the abortion as well, spending the day when her baby would have been due in inexplicable tears.

Cyd and her mother each thinks the other hates her, and it is not until Cyd is in New York that she acknowledges that she really could try harder with her mother. She is her stepfather's "pet," though. Shrimp and Sugar Pie have told her she is spoiled, something that her relationships with the family's housekeeper and driver certainly confirm, but, as Sugar Pie points out, her loving heart compensates for her faults. In many ways, though, CC is lost. She does not feel fully part of her family. She does not respect her mother's efforts to be accepted in a society life to which Sid's wealth has gained them entrée. Her nine-year-old and six-year-old stepsiblings look like their parents, but she looks like nobody in the family.

In New York, she finds uncanny likenesses between herself and her much older half brother, Danny, who owns a coffee shop with his life-partner, Aaron. He explains the family dynamics: their father's bad marriage and womanizing, his mother's Catholic objection to divorce, the friendship between their father and Sid (who is Danny's godfather as well as CC's stepfather) from their days as college roommates. She learns that her mother, a twenty-year-old model from Minnesota dreaming of a dance career when she became pregnant, considered an abortion. Her half sister, Lisbeth, is reluctant to meet her and, when she does, casts aspersions on CC's and her mother's character—of course, this is understandable, when she catches CC making out with their father's driver. But even Lisbeth eventually makes an effort that leads to CC's better understanding of her place in her biological family. The differences in their lives are underscored poignantly in a comparison between the contents of Lisbeth's briefcase with those of CC's backpack—all of the teen's emotional baggage is symbolized in the objects she carries.

Cyd has an ongoing fantasy about starting a commune somewhere warm, beautiful, and exotic so that she can live only with people she likes, not the people who happen to be her family. The fantasy allows her to escape the hurt she often feels. It is clear that her brashness is her defense against pain. Cyd Charisse is still a child emotionally, and an abandoned child at that. The doll Gingerbread bears mute witness to

CC's need for her father. Her time in New York City, meeting the family she has never known, allows her to let go of some of her past and make a fresh start in life. It is, surprisingly, Lisbeth who finally makes all the connections for Cyd, when she gives her a dress of their grandmother's. Grandma Molly, it seems, dealt in liquor during Prohibition, married five times, and was, in general, a character. CC also finds closure when she encounters Justin in New York and pointblank tells him what a jerk he is for leaving her on her own with the abortion. The episode, however, brings on a major bout of depression that she sleeps her way through, but it ends with a call from her mother, who has come to New York to collect her—and reconnect with her. As CC finally tells her mother about the abortion, she has a moment of insight into the challenges her mother faced, without help from her parents and learns that she was given her distinctive name, after the famous dancer, so that, if she were adopted, her mother could find her some day. She appreciates her mother's inability to give her up and discovers, not surprisingly, that she really does fit into her family—she is glad to know her biological family but finds them boring.

Get It While It's Hot. Or Not (1996), by Valerie Hobbs, has lost little of its timeliness over the past decade. Today's young people may know more about the transmission of HIV than their counterparts of a decade ago, but campaigns against sex education and condom dispensation are if anything more widespread. The title of this novel is the subtitle of an article that protagonist Megan Lane writes for the school newspaper; the article's full title is "Teen Sex: Get It While It's Hot. Or Not." Megan has been impelled to write the article by several factors shaping her life and school experience: her best friend Kit's pregnancy, her own efforts to keep her boyfriend in line because she is sure she is not ready for sex, and the intrusion on school grounds of community protesters, the Citizens for Responsible Schools, who have picketed the building, chanting "No Condoms on Campus!" In the course of writing the article, Megan learns how little her classmates know about birth control, pregnancy, and AIDS.

When Kit is consigned to bed rest for the last two months of her pregnancy, Megan and their other best friends, Mia and Elaine, create a schedule to spend some time with Kit daily, leaving her alone very little. Kit's mother runs a bar and spends her time at home sleeping, sometimes helped to sleep by overindulging in alcohol herself, and Kit's has struggled with depression and drug use in the past. Her friends want to ensure she will not succumb to depression again, isolated at home. To stave off boredom as well as depression, the girls watch rented movies with Kit, make tea for her, bring food, and even clean house. Kit plans to give the baby to a couple who cannot conceive, who spend more and more time with Kit, bringing her gifts. Megan, Mia, and Elaine must deal with their own attitudes toward motherhood as well as adjust to dramatic emotional and personality changes in Kit. Is she "selling" her baby for leather boots and a shot at college?

Meantime, the three have lives of their own that seem increasingly different from the life Kit is living, giving particular poignancy to their eighth-grade vow to be "friends to the end." The pregnancy has highlighted for them the challenges of dating, especially of making decisions about sex. Their concerns are heightened by the knowledge that the baby's father is HIV-positive. Whether Kit and the baby are, too, is still uncertain when Kit is rushed to the hospital for a premature delivery. Fearing for Kit's life, her friends find themselves considering whether they may all too soon be "friends to the end." The challenges of the situation remake Kit's decision for her, as the prospective adoptive parents bail out, fearing to adopt an HIV-positive infant, and once she holds the baby girl in her arms, she cannot part with her. Kit's mother rises to the occasion, changing her life to become a more responsible parent and grandparent. The baby's father, too, rises to the occasion, selling his sports car and turning over the money to Kit.

Megan, however, gets herself suspended for distributing her article after the principal has declined to permit its publication in the school newspaper. It becomes clear that her interpretation of the students' "right to know" the statistics of teen sex, pregnancy, and STDs is not the same as her lawyer father's. It is only afterward that she considers the implications for the newspaper sponsor, a new teacher and single mother who cannot afford to lose her job, and the principal, who faces negative publicity in the community.

A somewhat anticlimactic final chapter emphasizes the freedom that Megan, Mia, and Elaine still enjoy, when they attend the prom. They have made the choices that have allowed them the enjoyment and liberty of "normal" high school experience. This novel raises the very good question, though, of how uninformed teens can make good choices about sex.

Angela Johnson's *The First Part Last* (2003) highlights some of the dangers in a teen pregnancy as well as showing the dramatic transformation fatherhood can work on a sixteen-year-old's life. Bobby is in his last year of high school when his girlfriend Nia's pregnancy ends in her suffering irreversible brain damage and Bobby decides to raise his baby himself. He wants to be a man, a good man, and he believes that being a family man is the best way to accomplish this. Now much older and wiser than when he carelessly started this pregnancy, Bobby reflects that life would work so much better if one started out with knowledge, even wisdom, and then progressively lost it to end in innocence like his baby's.

The novel is structured around alternating "now" and "then" chapters through which Bobby tells the story of baby Feather's first few months of life and the earlier story of Nia's pregnancy, bringing the narratives together with a present-time visit to Nia in a permanent-care facility and the medical emergency that ended in her "persistent vegetative state." Only one chapter is in Nia's voice, and that is her inner voice as she floats away from the bleeding during an apparently peaceful late-pregnancy nap. This structure slowly reveals the reason that Bobby has ended up with sole responsibility for his child and illustrates the ways in which this responsibility has matured him, as well as chronicling his occasional lapse from responsibility.

Bobby's family life, as well as his love for the now-lost Nia, plays an important part in his decision to keep Feather. His father, divorced from his mother, and his brother, the single father of six-year-old twins, are nurturers who are committed to child-rearing. It is his father rather than his mother that Bobby can go to for comfort, and his brother can give him good advice about making a life that includes both his baby and an education. Both his parents are disappointed in him when learning of the pregnancy, having given him plenty of information as well as birth control to prevent such an eventuality, but they also take the situation in stride more comfortably than Nia's parents, who are in favor of giving the baby up for adoption, Nia's preferred course. Bobby's mother, with whom he lives, is particularly severe with him, absolutely refusing to share responsibility for Feather, and when he indulges his desire just to be a teenager for a day, Bobby realizes that living with his father—a decision his mother has made for him—will probably work out better, but then chooses living in a small town in Ohio near his brother in the hope that this will give him better opportunities in the long run.

Unlike his longtime friends, who can still drop everything to play ball or pursue a girl at a party, Bobby must make adult decisions. His growing up does not come all at once, but he is well on his way to a man's life by the time the novel ends. Perhaps as important as the day-to-day challenges of feeding, changing, and bathing his baby, regardless of how tired he is, is his ability to confront the question of what it means to be a man, and a good man, embodied for him in the question asked by the old man known as "Just Frank," a man who loses his life protecting a girl who is assaulted on the street. The most important factor in his maturation, however, is Feather herself, whose clear eyes accept him as her father and make him feel old in contrast to her newness. Her gaze inspires him with the desire not to let her down.

ADDITIONAL READING RECOMMENDATIONS

Mr. and Mrs. Bo Jo Jones by Ann Head, 1967
Don't Look and It Won't Hurt by Richard Peck, 1972
If Beale Street Could Talk by James Baldwin, 1974 (discussed in Guilty or Innocent?)
The Summer Boy by Robert Lipsyte, 1982 (discussed in Jobs: Assuming Adult
        Responsibility)
Sex Education by Jenny Davis, 1988
Effie's House by Morse Hamilton, 1990
A Couple of Kooks and Other Stories about Love by Cynthia Rylant, 1990
Dear Nobody by Berlie Doherty, 1991
The Dear One by Jacqueline Woodson, 1991
Like Sisters on the Homefront by Rita Williams-Garcia, 1995
Don't Think Twice by Ruth Pennebaker, 1996
Losing Louisa by Judith Caseley, 1998
Borrowed Light by Anna Fienberg, 2000
Hanging On to Max by Margaret Bechard, 2002

Religion and Spiritual Life

Bless Me, Ultima by Rudolfo Anaya (1972)
Armageddon Summer by Jane Yolen and Bruce Coville (1995)
True Believer by Virginia Euwer Wolff (2001)
Buddha Boy by Kathe Koja (2003)

Religion has played an increasingly prominent role in public affairs in recent years, its importance highlighted in armed conflicts around the globe, debates over who is legally entitled to marry in the United States, and controversies over teaching evolution in the public schools. Americans are people of faith, whether active churchgoers or not, and they are a multicultural people. Thus, they demonstrate a wide range of attitudes and practices associated with religious belief.

Adolescence is a period of questioning and challenging the values one has grown up with, as well as a period of adopting beliefs on one's own. Thus religious matters can easily divide families. Young people with strong religious convictions, or with a strong commitment to humanistic and scientific knowledge, may find that adolescence brings out their differences from friends in ways that childhood experiences did not. The most obvious reason for added pressure on their values is their developing sexual awareness, but greater independence, along with peer pressure, is another factor, making the teen's moral choices more problematic than in younger years. Protagonists of the novels discussed here have reason to deeply question their attitudes toward religion, arriving at a variety of answers.

The modern classic of Chicano literature *Bless Me, Ultima* (1972), by Rudolfo Anaya, is a coming-of-age novel, or bildungsroman, that starts in the young protagonist Tony's preschool days and chronicles his relationship with the elderly *curandera* Ultima. Tony (Antonio) is preoccupied with matters of faith. He wants to understand God's will, to keep from sinning, and to know how to obtain God's forgiveness if he should sin. He sees sin around him—he worries about his father's involvement as a vigilante in pursuit of a soldier who goes over the edge and kills the town's sheriff; he worries about his brothers' involvement with the town's prostitutes and the spiritual emptiness that accompanies them home from military service in World War II; he ponders the relationship between Ultima's magical healing and Christianity and the relationship between the old gods of the area and his own Raman Catholicism. He lives on the cusp of two worlds in several senses—between a magical spiritual belief system and Catholicism, a Spanish-speaking and an English-speaking world, his father's family's *vaquero* (cowboy) life of the *llano* (plain) and their association with the ever-restless seas through the surname Márez and the farming life of his mother's family in the river valley, which is lived in accordance with the cycles of the moon whose name (Luna) they bear. Through dreams and mystical experiences, as well as witnessing several violent episodes and healings, along with a dawning awareness of fertility and sexuality, Tony comes to an understanding of life that transcends the cultural divisions of his life.

Tony's religious training and questions pervade the novel. His mother is the staunch representative of Catholicism: she prays over every challenge as well as to give thanks, and she repeatedly expresses her hope that he will become a priest. Tony not only considers such questions but plays the role of a priest at several points: he hears the dying Lupito's partial petition for absolution and prays the Act of Contrition for him; he hears the dying Narciso's final confession in the shelter of a snow-covered tree; at his friends' instigation, he plays priest and hears their confessions, and later he prays the Act of Contrition for the unrepentant drowned Florence; he hears his older brothers' pleas for absolution in his dreams, and those whose death he has witnessed tell him that they live only in his dreams. In turn, Ultima blesses him in many ways—literally, as an elder and spiritual person and by sharing her wisdom with him; and through her example as well as her words, she conveys her sense of the harmony and goodness that pervade and unite creation, binding him to the natural elements. During his association with Ultima, he comes to recognize that the owl who accompanies her is her soul, a spirit of freedom and her bond with nature embodied.

Tony understands the restlessness, wildness, and freedom of his father's people, descended from the conquistadors who crossed the sea and who still embody the sea's restless change. His elder brothers, who similarly have gone overseas but have come back emptied rather than as conquering heroes, have inherited that restlessness and wildness. They lose their capacity for tempering that wildness to a dream of prosperity and property, their father's dream, and with their departure, he is left bereft of his old dream of taking the family to California for a new start. Tony's parents have established their household on the border between two ways of life, on the far side of the river from town, on the edge of the plain where they can feel the wind blow. Tony's mother's family, in contrast to his father's people and his brothers, are a sedate, peaceful clan who grow things in the well-watered river valley, planting and caring for their livestock according to the lunar cycle, and bringing forth an abundant harvest. Both ways of life are rich and productive. Both ways of life are perpetuated through change, the natural change of growth.

Only Ultima, who delivered Tony, knows what direction his life will take. She has buried the afterbirth in a place unknown to either family. The Lunas, his mother's family, would like to claim Tony for themselves, to plow his afterbirth into their land and fertilize it anew, in accord with the most ancient rituals of moon worship. Birth, like death, is accompanied with blood, blood that flows back into the land. Tony's father's family, the sea-people, would burn the afterbirth and scatter the ashes across the ocean of the plain. Both ways of life are productive, though different from each other. Violence and sterility, in contrast, come from lawlessness, the disruption of order. The novel's victims are victims of evil—the evil of war that takes a man's soul or makes him crazy, the evil of drink, the evil of witchcraft that attempts to manipulate the spiritual world to wreak harm on others. Ultima has the power to cure many ills, including those caused by evildoers, but a price is exacted from the balance of nature, and in the final analysis, order is restored with deaths.

It is Tony's task to accept change, to learn that death is as much a part of the cycle of life as birth, and to know that, just as he is part of the past, linked to the past, the past is a part of him, as he carries his dreams of the physically and spiritually dead with him into his future life. He most embodies the past in his acceptance of the river god, the Golden Carp that only a few who revere the ancient traditions ever see. The carp is associated with the indigenous inhabitants of the land. It is in learning about this god that Tony realizes that the town is surrounded by water. Water plays an important and ambiguous role in the novel, bringing life and fertility to the farms even when it carries off the blood of a dying man, washing and absolving individuals, ultimately reclaiming the solitary unbeliever, Florence, ironically and sadly just at the point when Tony and Cico are prepared to offer him the older river god in place of the faith he has been unable to accept. The voice of the river is, after Florence's death, sad. Tony feels the river's presence as a constant companion throughout the novel; at first he fears it, but later he recognizes its testimony to the interconnectedness of life.

As Ultima's death approaches, Tony develops a better understanding of his unique role in straddling the various elements of his culture. He has seen the limits of his Christian faith in bringing consolation to those whose lives have been marred by circumstances beyond their control. He has judged for himself the goodness of the old woman who has been feared and hated as a witch by some of the community, and he has received her blessing. It is fitting that he, as the representative of the unified cultures, should bury the owl associated with her and scatter her store of healing herbs, burying the past, on the verge of building his own future, his own dream, his own bridge.

Armageddon Summer (1995), by Jane Yolen and Bruce Coville, takes a sympathetic look at what it feels like to be in a compound erected by a religious cult with gun-toting cult members on the inside and local police, the FBI, the media, and onlookers outside. The story evolves through alternating narratives by Marina and Jed, with occasional interjections of excerpts from the sermons of the cult leader Reverend Beelson, FBI memos, transcripts of radio shows, and other relevant texts. Marina is the oldest child and only daughter in a family that is breaking apart, and it is her mother who takes Marina and her brothers to the mountaintop retreat where 144 Believers will await the imminent fiery Armageddon that will purge the world of its sinning population, to be followed by a new life begun by the saved. Marina is a Believer, that is, a Christian in Reverend Beelson's Church of the Believers, though once on the mountain, she has some doubts, and she does not want to be separated from her father, who loves his family. Jed, on the other hand, is a thoroughgoing skeptic, but he accompanies his father, who is alight with faith for the first time since Jed's mother left with another man, for the sole purpose of caring for him and protecting him, a decision Jed has come to with his older sister, a college student enrolled in a summer program.

In the mountaintop camp, the two teens share their perceptions and growing concerns, avoiding Marina's mother's watchful eye on potential sin. (She has apparently not thought about the implications of the 144 saved's future of repopulating the world, though several of the men have.) Marina must take over for her mother, who seems to have abandoned her responsibilities for the children, and so Marina needs someone to lean on. When a fiery confrontation and crisis come, the two teens play heroic roles in protecting the camp's small children and a couple of injured adults. They come through their parents' departure from normality as mature but not unscathed young people, with a healthy, romantic friendship forged in fire. Responsibility for others and duty to parents predominate in their motivation.

Much of the novel moves quickly and dramatically. Yolen and Coville's greatest achievements are the briefly rendered portraits of a number of good but deluded people and their depiction of the frenzy that can erupt when an emotionally charged situation explodes with a spark of violence.

"Make lemonade" may seem like easy advice in Virginia Euwer Wolff's novel by the same name discussed in Chapter 24: Poverty's Challenges. It is too simple for the complex issues that LaVaughn at age fifteen explores in Virginia Euwer Wolff's *True Believer* (2001), a novel dominated by her efforts to understand why things happen as they do. This novel gives a fuller picture of LaVaughn's experience: her mother starts a new, more demanding job and begins dating Lester; her friends Myrtle and Annie grow away from her in their commitment to an evangelical youth group; her heart is given entirely to her handsome but elusive neighbor Jody and for the first time she understands the temptation of sex; she faces serious academic challenges in college-prep biology and an intensive remedial grammar class; and she discovers the path her educational dream is taking her on when she begins working at the children's hospital and decides she will be a nurse.

LaVaughn begins to question God's existence and the purpose of things that happen in the world when her closest friends are drawn into a judgmental religious group whose focus not only seems to be on keeping teens chaste but preaching hellfire as the destiny of anyone who does not adopt their creed. Their contact with outsiders is limited; they become intolerant; they use every encounter as an occasion for proselytizing; and they condemn the scientific knowledge LaVaughn is learning in her biology class. As she thinks about religion, LaVaughn questions what kind of God would allow her father's death and the sorrow that it has brought to her mother. She asks her lab partner Patrick why he still wears the cross the nuns gave him (he is not Catholic but stayed with them between foster homes); she asks a friend in her grammar class whether she attends church, whether she is a believer; she asks her mother about church, only to discover something she never knew—her mother relies on her relationship with God to keep her going, even though they have not attended church since her father's death. And then, on impulse, she walks into a church one day and asks the minister whether a gay person or a woman who has had an abortion might attend his church. LaVaughn begins to articulate her own beliefs as she discovers that religious people can be more tolerant than Annie and Myrtle have led her to believe, finds out that God is a support when no other support exists, and trusts her joy in the wonders of nature.

Her sorest trial comes from falling in love with Jody, the attractive boy downstairs who dominates LaVaughn's thoughts. She and Jody were friends as small children, when their mothers were close friends, before his mother took him to a more expensive community, hoping to give him a better life than the one promised in the projects, after his best friend Victor got into drugs and was killed. When they are forced by limited finances to return, Jody is dedicated to earning an education through a scholarship as a competitive swimmer, and he breezes in and out of LaVaughn's life, smelling of chlorine, calling her "buddy." LaVaughn passionately wants to be more than a buddy to Jody, and she cherishes their casual conversations, working up the nerve to ask him to a dance, on a date that ends with a disappointing kiss that she initiates. She struggles to understand why he does not like her more until she discovers the truth about Jody—that he is gay. When her dreams come crashing down, it takes all her inner strength to overcome her desolation and, finally, to appreciate his friendship rather than mourn what cannot be.

Two other romances, one transient, one promising to last longer, contrast with LaVaughn's. Her mother accepts a new job and soon is dating Lester, and LaVaughn feels his presence as an invasion and thinks more about the death of the father she barely remembers. From the outset, LaVaughn sees more clearly than her mother does that Lester is getting more out of the relationship than he is giving, eating good home cooking on a regular basis. When he begins planning to buy a shabby house in a better neighborhood, LaVaughn fears her life will be totally rearranged for her—until Lester reveals his unworthiness by his attitude toward money. If her mother's heart is broken, she does not show it, though she irons everything within reach and tells LaVaughn about the dream in which LaVaughn's father teasingly suggested that her involvement with Lester was "pretty dumb." Jolly, LaVaughn's employer and friend in *Make Lemonade*, falls in love as well, and for once it looks as if she has made a choice that will be good and healthy for her, as LaVaughn observes when Jolly brings him to LaVaughn's sixteenth birthday party.

LaVaughn's yearnings are revealed not only through her dreams of having a boyfriend of her own but through her painting a tree around the cracks in her bedroom ceiling. This vision of her bedroom as a refuge in nature gives her security in the midst of daily challenges when life gets complicated. The tree, with its nest of baby birds, represents growth and the natural cycle of life. As an artistic production, it draws Jody's admiration and paves the way for their reconciliation as friends when he buys her an expensive book about Michelangelo for her birthday, noting that Michelangelo also painted on the ceiling. Knowing that Jody's savings for college are just as precious to him as her savings account is to her, she realizes how important his friendship is to her.

As important as her burning desire for education is to her, one of the major challenges LaVaughn faces comes from the way that it alienates her from other students. As she pursues her goal more openly, her friendships change. She begins to suspect she will be able to confide more in her classmate Ronelle, who broke up with a boyfriend as her vocabulary expanded. She takes pride in Patrick's high score on the citywide Scientific Aptitude Test and is touched by his birthday gift of a bouquet complete with hand-lettered labels carrying each flower's scientific name.

LaVaughn comes close to letting her disappointed romantic dreams interfere with her goal, but when her grades are dropping she finds out how many people are in her corner: the guidance counselor and teachers keep reiterating how important it is for the bright students in her school to survive and to succeed in the world, and they come through with specific suggestions to help her shape her goals. After working at the children's hospital, reflecting on the children's hopes, fears, and life prospects, LaVaughn realizes that she wants to become a nurse, and she is nudged into a summer science program designed to develop her ability to be competitive in college science curricula where her classmates will come from better schools than hers. As she considers what she believes in, LaVaughn affirms that she believes in possibilities, her belief shaped by a faith in people, the desire to heal and help others, and the knowledge that will enable her to fulfill her desire.

Buddha Boy (2003), by Kathe Koja, is one of the rare novels that deals with Buddhism—and perhaps even rarer, the novel is about religion lived rather than questioned. Justin learns the meaning of karma during the period in which he comes to know Jinsen (whose birth name is Michael Martin), called "Buddha boy" by the students determined to ostracize and harass him at their prisonlike upper-middle-class high school. From day one, Justin is cautious about getting to know this weirdo, who wears ill-fitting thrift store clothes and has shaved his head, carries a begging bowl around the school cafeteria, and wears a benign smile, or at least a calm expression, no matter what indignities his peers subject him to. And they do subject him to indignities far worse than name-calling—dropping trash in his bowl or throwing things at him, destroying his extraordinary artwork, and beating him up. Jinsen's refusal either to retaliate or to break down increases the fury of the school bullies, well-heeled kids who, ironically, win school awards for leadership. Though cautious, Justin is drawn to Jinsen and becomes his friend, learning a little about Buddhism through conversations but more through observing Jinsen's way of living in the world. The bullies' actions eventually catch up with them, and they are disgraced—their own unhappiness is manifested; Jinsen's patience pays off in a chance to attend a fine arts school—his happiness is justified. Justin learns that karma means that actions have consequences, but he nudges karma along a bit: his telling school authorities about the harassment results in the bullies' punishment, and his friendship with Jinsen enables him to step in to prevent Jinsen's taking matters into his own hands when he is finally on the verge of seeking revenge. What Justin has learned about karma is evident in the novel's ending, which equates understanding the future with clearly seeing oneself.

Seeing is an important concept in this novel—along with mindfulness. On one level, both Justin and Jinsen are artists, and their ability is manifested in the attention they give to the thing they are depicting as they work. The ways in which they share the quality of mindfulness is illustrated in the last drawing in Jinsen's sketchbook, one of Justin at work in art class. Another practitioner of seeing is Justin's father, an artist, who has taught his son some of the same lessons Justin sees demonstrated in Jinsen's attitudes and actions. Justin realizes from the outset that his father would like Jinsen, and he begins thinking about inviting him to spend spring break at his father's home. The shared interest in art forms the basis for their friendship, even when Justin is uncomfortable about becoming friends, experiencing a discomfort exacerbated by his other friends' absolute unwillingness to associate with the school's new pariah. And Justin sees the bullies (who are also the school leaders) clearly, despite their popularity among their peers and the approval they seek and earn from adults, which blinds the adults around them to their cruelty. Justin, true to his name, has a just nature, and he burns with anger at the unfairness of his peers' treatment of his new friend. At the same time, he lacks the courage to intervene; and he is also baffled by Jinsen's refusal to fight back in any way.

It is inevitable that Justin should question Jinsen about his beliefs. His curiosity about his friend's way of life has many dimensions, but it is Buddhism that is the most novel factor in Jinsen's lifestyle. Justin himself is not sure what to think about religion: his family used to attend church, but it is his father who is the believer, and since the divorce, Justin has not attended. He has difficulty understanding the answers he gets—Jinsen tells him that all beings are gods within, even those who are persecuting him, an assertion that Justin finds harder to accept than Jinsen's discipline—but Jinsen's openness and acceptance of all expressions of religion continue to draw him.

Jinsen is, however, reserved when it comes to sharing personal information. Gradually, Justin discovers that Jinsen's parents are dead and that he lives with his great-aunt, whose health is fragile. Not until Justin sees her reaction to Jinsen's bruises, after he's been beaten, does he learn the fuller story: that Jinsen enjoyed physical fighting and went from school to school, always expelled for fighting, until he gave it up after his parents were killed in an accident caused by a drunken driver. The way out of grief was shown to him by a Buddhist, who also taught him to express himself through art, and Jinsen vowed to his mentor and to his dead mother that he would not fight again. It was this teacher who gave him his new spiritual name, which reminds him that he is an expression of God in the world. Justin's understanding of his friend is significantly increased by the sharing of this information; he sees Jinsen's need for a mother in his response to Justin's mother. And when the destruction of Jinsen's work reaches its climax, his understanding helps him see in Jinsen's eyes the danger of his losing himself and fighting after his beautiful banner, the work on which his acceptance at the art school is riding, is destroyed.

Justin grows immensely through knowing Jinsen. He takes a step away from letting peer opinion limit his own actions; he gains the courage to face (but not to fight) the group who make Jinsen's life hell; he publicizes his peers' destructive behavior when he hangs Jinsen's ruined banner in a place of honor. Ultimately, he lets go of his friend as Jinsen prepares to attend art school, accepting his personal loss that accompanies his friend's personal gain—all part of karma.

ADDITIONAL READING RECOMMENDATIONS

The Drowning of Stephan Jones by Bette Greene, 1991 (reissue)
Asylum for Nightface by Bruce Brooks, 1996
Leaving Fishers by Margaret Peterson Haddix, 1997
The Revelation of Saint Bruce by Tres Seymour, 1998
Ordinary Miracles by Stephanie Tolan, 1999
The Boy in the Burning House by Tim Wynne-Jones, 2001
Counting Stars by David Almond, 2002

School Days

The Chocolate War by Robert Cormier (1974)
Probably Still Nick Swansen by Virginia Euwer Wolff (1988)
Nothing But the Truth: A Documentary Novel by Avi (1991)
Big Mouth and Ugly Girl by Joyce Carol Oates (2002)

School is the context in which the majority of teens' interactions with others occur. School is the site for meetings with friends, developing dating relationships, and participating in sports and other activities. It can provide intellectual stimulation, though it as often produces boredom. Relationships with teachers, coaches, and other mentors can affect the direction a young person takes in life, in every department from academics to career choices to personal values to artistic endeavors to athletics. Hence, school is the site of at least some scenes in many novels, though the degree to which school relationships influence plot outcomes varies significantly. In the novels discussed here, the social environment provided by the school is a major factor in the plot.

The Chocolate War (1974), by Robert Cormier, dramatizes the price of resisting the peer pressure that is omnipresent in school cultures. Jerry Renault is a freshman at Trinity, a Catholic day school, and his desires are uncomplicated and typical: to touch a girl's breast, to impress the football coach. Illustrating his efforts to accomplish the latter, the first chapter foreshadows the fate of those who "dare disturb the universe." (Jerry has hung a poster of a beach sign with the quotation from Eliot's "The Love Song of J. Alfred Prufrock" in his locker.) The first sentence is memorable and brutal, and the chapter explores the impact of resounding physical punishment on the body, as Jerry is hit again and again on the football practice field—punished but part of a team, with hope of success despite the pain. By the end of the novel, the pain has become meaningless and overwhelming—punishment for those who dare to step outside the official and unofficial cultural norms. Jerry has learned the price of disturbing the universe in this bleak novel, where evil wins.

The irony is that Jerry did not set out to buck the system. His refusal to sell fifty boxes of chocolates to raise money for the school is initially dictated by the school's secret organization, the Vigils, a group of upperclassmen who terrorize younger students by requiring them to complete "assignments" meant to disrupt the school's routine. The Vigils' most powerful member is Archie, the assigner, and Archie's manipulation of others through applying pressure at their weakest spots justifies his association with Satan, the "arch"-fiend. The evil that he perpetrates is highlighted in the second chapter, in which the shadow of the football goalposts is described by Archie's errand-boy, Obie, as being "like empty crucifixes," even though Obie ironically distances himself from this perception immediately after uttering it.

An unholy alliance occurs between the Vigils and Brother Leon, in charge of the school while the headmaster is seriously ill, as Brother Leon enlists the Vigils' help in promoting the chocolate sale. At first, Archie is lackadaisical about the sale, but when Jerry's assignment has ended and he decides on his own to resist participating in the fund-raiser, Archie uses the Vigils' organization to promote the sale, isolating Jerry and destroying the quiet wave of admiration for his stand on principle that has swept through the school, threatening to challenge both Brother Leon's petty tyranny and the secret organization's power over other students' actions. Brother Leon enjoys singling out students in the classroom for false accusations of cheating and manipulating them into spying for him by threatening them with arbitrary Fs, and his corruption is signaled by his rancid breath. Jerry's friend Goober identifies the source of his own unease in the school's atmosphere as "Evil," though when Jerry asks him to repeat what he has said, he backs off from his perception.

The Chocolate War portrays a courageous but futile stand for personal integrity in a world where institutional power is petty, vindictive, corrupt, and personal and the masses are complicit in the corruption through their conformity. The climactic scene of brutality enacts a gladiatorial scene in which the sole champion of the good is beaten bloody and unconscious by a tool of the secret organization. As an object-lesson in the dangers of unquestioning submission to authority and the power of the mob, *The Chocolate War* is compelling. The point of view shifts from chapter to chapter, showing the reader how each individual is caught up in forces that all too soon seem beyond any one individual's control.

Facing school can be a challenge for any teen, especially when everybody knows that a date ended in disaster, but Nick Swansen musters the courage to persist in Virginia Euwer Wolff's 1988 novel, *Probably Still Nick Swansen*. Nick copes with a number of challenges besides dating and doing his schoolwork: he spends each day in the special education classroom, Room 19, not knowing just what his learning problem is but knowing that he has a lot of questions about life, yet he is often unable to find the words he needs to frame his questions. Nick's challenges come mostly from limited verbal skills—finding the words, reading the words—and he has to come to terms with the fact that most of the answers he works out for himself have a "probably" in them.

Nick does know a lot of things—more or less. What he knows the most about is amphibians. He has little difficulty retaining a substantial body of knowledge about them, even many technical terms. He knows what to do when he is planning to go to the prom: buy tickets and a corsage (and work the extra hours at the greenhouse to earn the money for them), learn to dance, rent a tux. He does not know what to do when he looks at all the parts of the tux, but his father, remembering his own first experience with a tux, offers to help. Nick knows some basics of driving a car, but there is still a lot he does not know, as he discovers when he takes his dog Patsy to the vet in an emergency. Since he does not yet have a license, this lands him in trouble with his parents after he hits a trash can and is picked up by the police. His parents seem to overlook what Nick does know in this situation—he knows he should bind his arm after Patsy has bitten him; he knows he should muzzle Patsy so he can move her; and he knows the way to the vet's office. And there are things his parents do not know, like who left Patsy out in the yard to be hit by the car in the first place—it was not Nick.

Like any other teenager, Nick keeps a lot from his parents. He has found that it is not difficult to keep them happy most of the time. But it is not necessary for him to share his concerns and worries with them, like his nightmares about his sister Diane's drowning at age ten. Instead, he talks to Diane about his worries—understanding what a girl means, not making a fool of himself at the prom, believing the vet when he says Patsy will be fine after surgery. Still, he wonders whether Diane has stayed at age ten in death, though she would have been nineteen now, a knowledgeable older sister, had she lived: perhaps in death she has no more answers to his questions as a teenager than he has. But even as a little kid, Diane knew how to word the questions she wanted answers to, a knowledge that Nick lacks.

Nick has a lot of questions for Diane from the point when Shana holds his hand secretly while a group photo is taken to celebrate her "going up" to regular classes, to the night of the dance, when she stands him up, leaving him to wander around outside, freezing and feeling like a "drooler" that no girl would want to date. His efforts to cope with humiliation include staying out of school for several days, when he makes his first attempt at drinking alcohol and consequently experiences his first hangover. In the aftermath of the driving episode and his parents' anger, Nick realizes how sad it would be for his parents to lose their remaining child, an insight that helps him tolerate some of their invasions into his privacy. And they do, after all, appreciate that it takes more courage than ever to return to school after the fiasco with Shana, a courage that is quietly acknowledged by his teacher and a classmate.

Nick's reconciliation with Shana, when she explains the sequence of minor disasters that led to her not having a dress to wear, leads to conversations about some more fundamental issues. He explains how Diane died, though he does not talk about the sense of responsibility he has borne for not having recognized that she was drowning and gotten help from his parents sooner, and Shana points out to Nick the significance of his interest in amphibians: had Diane been an amphibian, she would have survived. Shana also gives a label to the kind of brain function that they share as well as naming his special ability: both have minimal brain dysfunction, and Nick is a savant.

Nick's reflection on how his brain functions brings him some kind of resolution. He realizes it was not stupid of him to ask Shana to the dance; he does know about plants and amphibians; he was not at fault in Diane's death; Patsy will be okay; his father will teach him to drive. He will have to accept a "probably" in most of the answers he finds for himself—just like other kids.

Nothing But the Truth: A Documentary Novel (1991), by Avi, gives the reader new insight into the politics of schools. Philip Malloy likes to kid around, but he just cannot get a laugh out of his no-nonsense English teacher, Miss Narwin, who has been teaching for twenty-one years, so he is convinced that she dislikes him. When he loses his copy of *Call of the Wild* and cannot finish reading it, she does not appreciate the humor of his flippant answer to an essay question on the test. The D in English that is the outcome makes him ineligible to try out for track. As if this were not punishment enough, when homeroom assignments are changed midyear, Philip gets Miss Narwin. Is any of this Philip's fault? Of course not! Every consequence he has faced comes from her dislike of him, not his own actions—or so he convinces himself. Unfortunately, he succeeds in convincing others as well. Philip's campaign to cause Miss Narwin mild annoyance rapidly escalates from the day he begins humming along with "The Star-Spangled Banner" in homeroom, instead of giving it the respectful, silent attention that school policy requires until Philip has attracted nationwide media attention for his defense of his First Amendment rights, in the process affecting several other lives around him.

Each short chapter of the novel is a document—a memo, a letter, a diary excerpt, the transcript of a conversation, an excerpt from a politician's speech, a newspaper article. These documents trace the conflict from Philip's initial attempt to make Miss Narwin laugh through his family's involvement when he is suspended, through his father's bringing in a candidate for the school board, through Miss Narwin's dismissal, to Philip's enrollment in a private school, where he finally acknowledges that he does not even know the words to the national anthem. The original incident has been changed beyond recognition much like the game of gossip, in which one person whispers a message to another, who in turn whispers it to another, and so forth. Philip has misrepresented his violation of school policy to his parents as Miss Narwin's dislike of him in order to excuse his poor schoolwork and its consequences for his sports participation, and each person involved has misunderstood and then misrepresented the episode enough that by the time talk radio picks it up, the story is that an elderly teacher is denying a boy his right to show his patriotism by singing the national anthem in school.

This is a story of petty malice and avoidance of responsibility. It is clear to most, if not all, members of the school community itself that Miss Narwin is a strict but fair teacher and that Philip is just causing trouble. Early inattention to the details of the situation and the need for good public relations in order to obtain needed funding for all the school's programs make members of the administration unwillingly complicit in the blackening of a good teacher's name that has served a politician well in getting him votes. The teacher's career is ruined, and Philip ultimately finds himself in a conservative school that welcomes him but one in which he does not really want to be when events have spun out of control. It is a pessimistic novel, but one that clearly makes the point that our failure to take responsibility for ourselves can have consequences far beyond those we dreamed of, illustrating clearly that our lives are interconnected with one another's in larger and larger communities.

In these post–Columbine High School days, it is not a good idea to joke about school violence, as Matt Donaghy learns the hard way in *Big Mouth and Ugly Girl* (2002) by Joyce Carol Oates. Matt comes to identify himself as "Big Mouth" after his brush with authorities who have overreacted to a report of his threat to blow up the school and massacre the students, a comment that was clearly a joke. Ursula Riggs, a tall and solidly built athlete and individualist, identifies herself as "Ugly Girl." An unlikely friendship between them buds and flowers after Ursula has cleared Matt's name, going to the principal to set the record straight as to the comment that she overheard.

Matt comes to see himself as more of a bigmouth than a class clown when he realizes how far-ranging are the results of his poor joke. The principal has acted swiftly to report the incident to the police, and Matt undergoes hours of questioning that lead him to understand how prisoners can admit to committing a crime they did not in fact commit; he is also suspended for three days while school authorities conduct a thorough investigation. After his suspension ends early, on the basis of Ursula's testimony, he finds that once a suspect, always a suspect—or at least it appears so in the weeks following the incident, when his friends dissociate themselves from him, advised to do so by their parents. Indeed, they dissociated themselves from him from the moment he was marched out of study hall by the police. The only email he receives the first evening is from Ursula, whom he has known from elementary school but with whom he has never been friends. In the wake of his vindication, he learns that his threat might almost as well have been serious. He has become a pariah, and he becomes bitter at first, then despondent, resigning his office as class vice president and leaving the newspaper staff. His isolation is deepened when his parents decide to sue the school for damages, and his situation is exacerbated by outright hostility on the part of some senior jocks who first assault him on the street and later take his dog. Through the course of this ordeal, he is pulled back from a despair that very nearly ends in suicide by a new friendship with Ursula.

Ursula is an independent young woman who pays little attention to what other people think of her. The oldest daughter of a corporate CEO, living in the most expensive home in the community, she acts assertively, on principle rather than out of any desire for approval, and she prompts her friend Eveann's mother to allow Eveann to add her testimony to Ursula's, when the mother's first reaction has been to tell her daughter not to get involved. Ursula is emotionally a loner, especially after she quits the basketball team, even though she is the captain and consistent high scorer, because she believes the coach and her teammates blame her for a loss to a tough team in a game in which she was tripped and sustained an injury, a situation that threatened her confidence when she went to the foul line, resulting in her missing the free throws. She is five ten and a half; she dresses in masculine clothes that cover her big body, afraid of exposure since she left the swim team in self-consciousness some years earlier; she confronts her peers with an aggressive stare; and she ignores any comments made about her. Her Ugly Girl persona is moody, almost bipolar with her heady "fiery red" moods and her black depressions. She has a more conventional personality, however, that she identifies with as simply Ursula. As Ursula, she is a good student, especially in biology and art. Ursula, however, is much more vulnerable than Ugly Girl.

As Ursula, she becomes involved with the isolated Matt when she keeps him from committing suicide. Both are given to solitary rambles, Matt with his dog—who often seems like his only friend at this point in his life. And while her spotting him on the verge of a plunge from high rocks is fortuitous, it is a credible coincidence. This face-to-face contact results in their exchanging much more email and spending more time together. Their growing friendship is facilitated by their honesty and their intelligence. One element of their mutual understanding is that each is an older sibling, who cares about and feels responsible for the younger sibling. Their relationship is cemented when Matt's dog is stolen, making the family frantic. Ursula wields power the way she has learned to from her CEO father, exerting the right kind of pressure to resolve the situation and win the dog's release.

In the aftermath of this confrontation and the closeness it brings, Matt and Ursula move from friendship to a couple relationship. They are ready to admit their vulnerability with each other and form an alliance without worrying about what other people think. Strong and secure in themselves, instead of defensive, each has the opportunity to be reintegrated into former activities and the school community as a whole.

ADDITIONAL READING RECOMMENDATIONS

The Day They Came to Arrest the Book by Nat Hentoff, 1982

Running Loose, 1983 (discussed in Teammates); Staying Fat for Sarah Byrnes, 1993 (discussed in Beauty's Meaning); and Whale Talk, 2001 (discussed in Accepting Difference), by Chris Crutcher

Have a Heart, Cupid Delaney by Ellen Leroe, 1986

Daniel and Esther by Patrick Raymond, 1990

One of the Boys by Scott Johnson, 1992 (discussed in Insiders and Outsiders)

Out of Control by Norma Fox Mazer, 1993

Where Do I Go from Here? by Valerie Wilson Wesley, 1993

The Night Room by E. M. Goldman, 1995

Under the Mermaid Angel by Martha Moore, 1995

How I Changed My Life by Todd Strasser, 1995

Don't You Dare Read This, Mrs. Dunphrey by Margaret Peterson Haddix, 1996

Get It While It's Hot. Or Not by Valerie Hobbs, 1996 (discussed in Pregnancy, Parenthood, Abortion)

Slam! by Walter Dean Myers, 1996

Rats Saw God, 1996, and *Slave Day*, 1997 (discussed in Accepting Difference), by Rob Thomas

The Schernoff Discoveries by Gary Paulsen, 1997

Speak, 1999 (discussed in Breaking Silence, Speaking Out), and *Catalyst*, 2002 (discussed in Friends Forever?), by Laurie Halse Andersen

The Year They Burned the Books by Nancy Garden, 1999

Breaking Rank by Kristen D. Randle, 1999

What's in a Name? by Ellen Wittlinger, 2000

You Don't Know Me by David Klass, 2001 (discussed in Abuse, Sexual Violence, and Healing)

Three Days Off by Susie Morgenstern, 2001

True Believer by Virginia Euwer Wolff, 2001 (discussed in Religion and Spiritual Life)

Tribes by Arthur Slade, 2002

Buddha Boy by Kathe Koja, 2003 (discussed in Religion and Spiritual Life)

Sexual Identity, Sexual Desire

Forever by Judy Blume (1975)
The Alice series by Phyllis Reynolds Naylor (1985–2006)
The Boy in the Moon by Ron Koertge (1990)
Emily Good as Gold by Susan Goldman Rubin (1993)
Breaking Boxes by A. M. Jenkins (1997)
Whistle Me Home by Barbara Wersba (1997)

The defining characteristic of adolescence is sexual maturation, and learning to handle sexual attraction—to know when to act, with whom to act, and how far to go—is a dominant concern throughout the period of young adulthood. Young people must cope with the pressures of their own bodies, peer pressure, the sometimes conflicting demands of love and desire, families' expectations, religious dicta, and the self-imposed pressures of the life choices they face immediately after high school in making decisions about sexual activity. The challenges of dating are discussed in Chapter 9; the problems brought by unplanned pregnancy, in Chapter 25; and the wounds inflicted by sexual assault, in Chapter 1. This chapter focuses on novels that revolve around how teens cope with self-knowledge about their sexual identity and with sexual desire.

Since its publication in 1975, Judy Blume's *Forever* has been well-known among teens for its explicit treatment of sexual relations; it is a virtual how-to manual for teens, covering the progression of Katherine and Michael's relationship from first attraction through progressively more intimate exploration of each other's bodies to the end of their relationship. Explicit information about seeking birth control at a clinic is included as Katherine moves toward her decision to have intercourse with Michael. As they fall in love during their senior year of high school, each thinks the relationship is "forever," but in the summer following graduation, as they go their separate ways to summer camp jobs, Katherine discovers she is attracted to someone else, ending their romance and, against her will, hurting Michael, making the point that a romance formed at so young an age is not necessarily forever.

Though nearly all the novel's suspense is focused on whether Katherine and Michael will consummate their sexual attraction, Katherine's relationships with her parents, her younger sister, and her grandparents are delineated, focusing almost entirely on their different ideas of whether Katherine is too young to be seriously involved. Two friends' experiences contrast with the course of Katherine's relationship. Her friend Erica tries vainly for months to help Michael's friend Artie determine whether he is gay by attempting to seduce him; the unhappy aftermath is Artie's unsuccessful suicide attempt. Their sexually active friend Sybil becomes pregnant, has the baby, and gives her up for adoption, determining that in future she will take precautions to prevent pregnancy. The strength of this novel has long been held to be its honesty and its nonjudgmental attitude toward young women's sexual desires and emotions.

Phyllis Reynolds Naylor's Alice series (1985–2006) meets the same needs for today's curious girls. Like most series, the novels deal more with incident than character development, preserving continuity of situation and a fairly stable group of characters, primarily Alice and her best friends, along with Alice's family members. The focus is consistently on Alice's curiosity about and experiences with dating and romance, along with growing knowledge about her body and sexual awareness. With a widowed father and a brother seven years older who is in no hurry to settle into a permanent relationship, Alice has plenty of dating situations to explore. She is unabashedly curious and willing to talk about nearly anything that she finds out about—yeast infections or her knowledge that the assistant manager at her father's store is carrying a torch for him—in a series of situations that facilitate frank discussion of matters of real concern. Of course, she sometimes embarrasses her brother and father, and she feels the lack of an older woman to whom she can address her most intimate questions, but she feels comfortable enough with a cousin a few years older than her brother to ask her for information on the rare occasions they are together. While this is a single-parent household, it is an honest, healthy, functional family where many issues may be addressed openly.

Naylor builds on several recurring themes throughout the series. Because Alice does not remember her mother, she often experiences a longing for motherly love. She is concerned with stability in relationships, as it plays out in her father's romance with one of her teachers, in her older brother's dating relationships, in her friendships and early romance, and in her friend Pamela's parents' relationship. Like any normal middle schooler, Alice has some embarrassing moments to live down, and she has to come to terms with her body. She learns a great deal from sharing nearly everything with her closest friends, and friendship's ups and downs is an important ongoing theme.

Alice and her friends face the challenges of growth and change in family relationships and changes in friendships and dating over time, but through their experiences they acquire tolerant and psychologically healthy attitudes. They work and participate in cocurricular experiences at school. Their school is multiracial, and, though the core group of best friends is white, their larger circle of friends includes a black friend, and they confront racism as junior counselors at a summer camp. Two of their friends are a lesbian couple, for the most part accepted in their group. They do not tolerate exploitation or abuse of women or younger kids, and they take action when they experience it: for instance, Alice writes an article for the school newspaper exposing episodes of hazing that raises student and administration awareness, resulting in new rules. Ultimately, however, the books are probably best known for providing clear, honest information about sexuality in response to teen girls' natural curiosity about it.

Ron Koertge's *The Boy in the Moon* (1990) explores some of the challenges that dating and sex bring through the story of three friends whose relationship undergoes a change when one of them spends the summer before their senior year in California, leaving the other two together. Without their acknowledging it, Nick and Frieda's relationship has undergone a change. Nick thinks of himself as "the boy in the moon" because acne has roughened his face, and he is sure that no girl could be attracted to him. Frieda, too, is self-conscious about her appearance, hiding her big-breasted body in loose sweats. When their friend Kevin returns, sporting punky hair, stylish clothes, muscles, and an attitude that women are there for the taking, his sharpened vision brings their budding romance into the open. When they do acknowledge it and begin to act on their feelings, the transition is fraught with their fear of making a wrong move or destroying the cherished friendship. Their first sexual encounter is awkward and intensifies the ambivalence of their emotional state, but ultimately it brings them closer, their awareness of this deepening intensity heightened by the imminence of separation as each follows the educational course already determined. All three are working their way through establishing life goals against the backdrop of their parents' choices, and their English teacher is requiring a major paper addressing the question "who am I?" Both Nick and Kevin take good, hard looks at their parents' relationships, while Frieda reflects on her mother's choice to run off at sixteen, leaving her to be passed around the family as an infant, now in the home of an independent single aunt.

Kevin's summer transformation seems less than positive at first. He looks good, having spent much of his time at the pool or the gym while staying with his mother in Los Angeles, as well as having discovered California style, and he buys a car with his summer earnings, then gets a date with the hottest local girl. He tells Nick and Frieda about his own sexual initiation, since they all have long since promised to share what they learn, but it is not until he has had time to settle back into his old self that he admits his experience was largely due to alcohol consumption. Kevin's desire to be cool is at least partly attributable to his need to distance himself from his father, a reformed drinker and revivalist preacher, whose first appearance in the novel is as a picketer against the town's "harlots." Kevin is in danger of following in his father's presalvation footsteps when he drinks to ease his pain and anger. What keeps him living there, instead of staying in California, is his younger brother, Hugh, whom his father will not allow to go to their mother, even though Hugh misses her very much. Ultimately, their father takes off with a whore whom he rescued from sin and took into his home, displacing Kevin from his own bedroom to the sofa. His abandonment of Hugh finally convinces Kevin to pack up his little brother and head to L.A. before his father repents and returns home.

Nick's relationship with his parents is shown through a series of funny scenes. His mother is a poet, his father the police chief, and they inhabit separate bedrooms, making it obvious to Nick when they share bedroom time for sex and leading him to speculate, at one point, whether they are drifting toward a breakup. His father gives him periodic embarrassing lectures on safe sex, encouraging him to keep a stock of condoms, well before Nick actually needs them, and he constantly hopes that Nick will build impressive muscles like his—and now Kevin's. Nick cannot help feeling that he disappoints his dad at moments when their differences become especially apparent. When he accompanies his mother to a reading of her poetry, he begins to worry over her poem "Dear Superman," which suggests that some of the romance wears off with middle age, and her friend suggests that all of her new work shows a concern with independence. Until Nick is satisfied that this does not foreshadow a divorce, he is uneasy, especially in light of the way that Kevin has changed over the summer. Actually, given Frieda's feminism, this part of his mother's personality makes Frieda's attractiveness to Nick even more understandable, and his nervousness about impending changes is realistic, given the way life will change for him and his peers at the end of their senior year. Ultimately, this is a novel about change and about the value of the less-than-perfect, embodied in Nick's mother's poem "The Burden of Narrative," about the perfect fairy-tale hero whose choices are bound by a predictable plot. Nick accepts his own imperfections, claiming that he has arrived safely from the moon, aided in his journey by his friends.

Susan Goldman Rubin tells a gentle story in *Emily Good as Gold* (1993) of a retarded thirteen-year-old, Emily Gold, who must cope with developing awareness of her sexuality. Emily tries to get correct information about sex after learning that babies—which she loves, looking forward to having her own baby some day—come from behaviors that she has been taught she must never do, like undressing in front of someone of the opposite sex. Her need for understanding is intensified by her adored older brother's marriage and her new sister-in-law's pregnancy, events that coincide with her recognition of two things: her parents are trying to keep her baby-ish in their decrees about clothes and makeup, and she feels a special closeness to a boy at school. As she begins to push against restrictions, other boys' interest in her helps her come to an intuitive understanding of which relationships with boys feel right and which feel wrong, an understanding that she has been unable to come to intellectually.

Emily finds it difficult to understand some of the changes in her relationships with her family, as all the attention focuses on the pregnancy and then her new niece. She feels excluded when family members lower their voices and have conversations about her in other rooms. She picks up bits of what is said and is distressed by the concern she hears that she will not be able to take care of herself. What puzzles her is that at school she and the other students are being taught to take care of themselves—to do laundry, to cook, to write letters. But at the same time, she is terrified by the idea of getting lost, and when the baby cries while her sister-in-law is taking a shower, Emily discovers how hard it can be to be grown up enough to care for a baby. Her parents' concerns for her future well-being should they predecease her is obvious, but her brother's love for Emily and his new wife's readiness to love her as she is are reassuring. Emily's mother is more understanding than her father of her desire to wear stylish clothes and makeup so she will look like other girls that she knows are her age, but they do not allow her to wear the kinds of clothes she is beginning to want or any makeup at all.

Emily's love for babies makes her father uneasy, and he is not his usual pleasant self when her friend Donny shows up at their home on Emily's fourteenth birthday with a gift for her. (Donny functions at a higher level than Emily and has been getting around by himself on buses for two years.) Mr. Gold fears for his daughter's innocence and his fierce protectiveness create a few days of alienation, but when he recognizes that Emily really can be trusted to know when to say no to boys who invite her to climb into a car with them, he recognizes that his wish to keep her safe simply will not keep her a child forever, and he reevaluates her friend Donny's worth.

The challenges of growing up mentally handicapped are sensitively portrayed in this novel, but at the same time, Emily's struggle to be "good as gold" in the midst of the physical and emotional changes of sexual maturation is the struggle many young people face, writ large. The family's love and support are unwavering, even when they don't understand what is going on inside Emily's thoughts.

Breaking Boxes (1997), by A. M. Jenkins, depicts the challenges faced by almost-sixteen-year-old Charlie when word gets around that his twenty-four-year-old brother Trent is gay. Trent has been Charlie's guardian since their mother drank herself to death; they have not seen their father since Charlie was born. The two of them have encountered homophobia before, but it is particularly difficult for Charlie to face, and for Trent to witness, when Charlie finds himself opening up and developing a new, close friendship with the popular Brandon. Through Brandon, Charlie has gained acceptance in a school where most of the kids have a lot more money than he has, though he has had little interest in achieving such status. This results in a significant change in his life at school after Brandon recoils in horror at Charlie's revelation of Trent's sexual orientation and subsequently passes the information along to others. Apparently believing that sexual orientation runs in families, students who have previously accepted Charlie question his sexual identity, but the quiet girl whose virginity Charlie took impulsively at a party steps forward as a witness to his heterosexuality. The ringleader of the group, however, in pain and humiliation at the discovery—he has carried a torch for this girl for some time—continues to goad Charlie until Charlie gives in to the urge to pound him into submission, in an action that paves the way for Charlie's coming to terms with his fear of getting emotionally close to others.

Brandon and Charlie's friendship has begun with a fight early in the school year, a fight instigated by Brandon's friend Luke. When both of them end up in on-campus suspension for three days, and Brandon begins offering Charlie rides home in his Corvette, Charlie discovers, much to his surprise, that he feels comfortable with Brandon, and the comfort rapidly grows into real friendship, something he has missed since his friend Nick moved away. Brandon clearly needs something that he finds in the time he spends with Charlie—they play street hockey and shoot baskets, enjoying athletic exercise outside of organized team sports, and Brandon finds out there are more ways to have fun than to drink.

They talk about a lot of things—family structure and expectations, abstract ideas, sex and dating. Brandon is unhappy at home, where his parents expect perfection and give him lots of things that he feels are for show, not really for him. Charlie reveals little about himself because his memories of his mother's drinking and abusiveness are painful, and he is cautious about risking negative reactions to Trent's homosexuality. Brandon likes and accepts Trent, not suspecting he is gay, and he becomes openly close to both brothers. When an awkward misunderstanding makes it necessary for Charlie to share the information about Trent, Brandon feels he has been betrayed, and his reaction makes Charlie feel equally betrayed.

This crisis leads Charlie to vent his frustrated anger on Trent, but he cannot stay angry with his wonderful, supportive older brother, so the pain of his customary isolation and caution have no outlet until Luke and the other kids provide him one through fighting. Trent has explained that much of the homophobia expressed by Charlie's peers derives from their insecurity about their own sexuality: until they have had sex themselves, they fear their virginity may mean they are not really heterosexual, and hence they boast of imagined conquests. Charlie, in contrast, does not boast; he has had sexual relationships and is secure about his sexual orientation, though he lacks the tenderness and consideration that would make sexual encounters more meaningful.

Charlie fears being hurt, and he avoids opening up emotionally to either girls or other guys because of, first, his childhood with a mother to whose home he could not bring friends and, second, his experience of being threatened with violence by homophobic neighbors. As the principal notes, Charlie is quick to react to verbal abuse by fighting. In many ways, he does not care what others think of him—he listens to uncool country music, in contrast with Brandon, who turns down the radio in order to make a better impression on a pretty girl. Charlie is proud, however; his first fight occurs when Luke taunts him about his shoes, and he is fierce in defending Trent.

His own experiences with alcohol and abuse make him reluctant to drink, even at parties, and he threatens the abusive father of a neighborhood six-year-old. The pathos of the little boy's situation haunts him, though he avoids the child's street after confronting the father, fearing that he has worsened the situation and comforting himself by remembering that small children learn early how to hide from trouble in their households. The child reminds him how his brother was a barrier between him and their mother's abusiveness, increasing his distress over the unfairness of misjudgments of who Trent is by those who do not know him at all.

Though Charlie does not like to confront feelings and he can act in callous ways, he is sensitive to others' pain. Charlie knows it was heartless of him to stop answering calls from the girl whom he dated and had sex with for several months, but he felt that he was caught in something more than he was ready for: Megan wanted their lovemaking to mean more to him than it did. When his talk with Katie at the party results in sex, he walks away from her without so much as asking whether she needs a ride home, and despite his enjoyment of their conversation about writing, he avoids her afterward. Brandon, in contrast, actively seeks the opportunity to lose his virginity but does not succeed. It seems that Charlie's emotional disengagement makes it easier for him.

It is this lack of feeling that Trent compares to living in a box. He and Brandon both take the position that caring about things, about people, makes a person vulnerable but also makes life worth living. Ultimately, Charlie must break the box around himself and admit that he does care about others. It is painful, but in doing so, he opens up to the possibility that others' care for him can sustain him through the pain of being vulnerable.

Whistle Me Home (1997), by Barbara Wersba, is the painful story of love between the heterosexual Noli (Noelle) and the homosexual TJ (Thomas Jerome). Their relationship develops over a period of six months following TJ's move to Sag Harbor from New York City, and months after Noli's discovery of TJ's sexual orientation and their explosive breakup, their hearts still ache with unrequited love, for it is clear to Noli that she cannot forswear her romantic attachment to be the straight girl hanging out with two gay guys, and TJ misses the love they shared as friends, apparently unable to understand why that cannot continue after her romantic dream has been shattered.

Noli and TJ are soul mates. They discover this on the first day of their acquaintance in school, when TJ chooses one of Gerard Manley Hopkins's poems to read aloud in English class, and the poem reaches right into Noli's inner being. They eat lunch together; he walks her home, whistling; they have dinner and go to a movie together that Friday; and from then on, they are inseparable. TJ's sophistication opens a new world for Noli—he knows about poetry and theater and art—and his beauty and athleticism make her the envy of every girl in school. From the outset, he praises her beauty, telling her she is a gamin, and assuages some of the pain she has felt in her mother's disapproval of her unwillingness to wear feminine clothing and makeup and to grow her hair. He is not afraid to express his feelings, moved to tears by the love shown to the dead in the old cemetery Noli has taken for granted, willing to say "I love you" to her. He is a vegetarian and does not drink or use profanity, and under his influence, Noli curbs her swearing.

Noli's use of alcohol is another matter, however; despite TJ's efforts to get her to stop drinking, her alcoholism is well established, and after their breakup, it becomes obvious to everyone. She drinks vodka regularly, in the mistaken conviction that it cannot be detected on her breath, feeling that she needs it to face her constant confrontations with her mother and later to cope with what she perceives as TJ's betrayal of her love and trust. There is a lot of anger in her home life. She blames her mother for the death of her poodle Alice, who got cancer at age five and was euthanized without Noli's knowledge at her mother's instigation. Her mother is a frustrated woman who pours her energy into housework, not having acquired enough education to develop other interests or get a good job and unable to have children after Noli. Noli cannot communicate her feelings and is unable to sympathize with her mother; she feels more sympathy with her father, but their conversations always stay on the surface of life.

Noli senses there are dark places in TJ's past, because he sometimes shows quick, unreasoning anger and he does not reveal much personal information though he shares his interests with her freely, even encouraging her to dress like him in an outward manifestation of their closeness. On their first day together, she tells him about her dog's death, and he promises to get her another dog, a promise he fulfills when he gives her Alice II early Christmas morning. With TJ, Noli opens up emotionally, telling him early in their relationship how she was sexually abused by a neighborhood teen when she was in elementary school. She admits that she felt dirty but also liked it to some extent. TJ clearly recognizes the feelings, naming the sense of uncleanness before she does, but Noli has difficulty interpreting his response beyond its element of ready sympathy. She also wonders why he does not kiss her, and when he does, she wonders why his kisses are not more passionate, though they are deeply tender, and why he makes no effort to touch her.

Noli's first real clue as to the reason for TJ's lack of passion comes when they go to New York for the day, and he is called by name by a flamboyant gay who takes Noli for a boy. When her parents' trip out of town gives them the opportunity for sexual intimacy, she arrives at the truth that TJ is gay when he fails to become aroused with her. Her need for sexual love from him is so great that she says ugly things, and from then on avoids him, though she spies on him in public places after she learns of his new friendship with the gorgeous and athletic Walker, who attends a nearby private school. This crisis, as well as Noli's desperate loneliness, gives her a reason to drink more, bringing her alcoholism to the attention of her parents and school authorities, who compel her to begin attending teen AA meetings. What makes her seriously consider sobriety at last, though, is her careless loss of her puppy when drunk.

Sobriety brings gradual transformation to Noli's life. She finds friendship with her AA sponsor, begins a dog-training class with her restored puppy, considers dating a boy she has met there, and makes strides toward reconciliation with her mother. It is not until she finally talks with TJ, however, that she feels in charge of her life again, able to care for herself, as shown in her recurring dream of being lost in the city, which, in the final chapter is resolved with her finding herself on a bus headed home. The structure of the novel emphasizes the transformation that Noli has undergone. Told in present tense, it begins with her observation of TJ and Walker nearly a year after her first meeting him, and in the next-to-last chapter, he confronts her on that day. Longingly, he asks whether they cannot still be friends, affirming again his love for her, but she asserts her need for a love that he cannot give her. Though this confrontation is painful and Noli fears she will love TJ hopelessly forever, it also bears witness to the beginning of healing for her.

ADDITIONAL READING RECOMMENDATIONS

I Never Loved Your Mind by Paul Zindel, 1970
The Man without a Face by Isabelle Holland, 1972

If Beale Street Could Talk by James Baldwin, 1974 (discussed in Guilty or Innocent?)

Dance on My Grave by Aidan Chambers, 1982

Annie on My Mind, 1982, and *Good Moon Rising*, 1996, by Nancy Garden (discussed in
        Dating's Challenges)

Running Loose by Chris Crutcher, 1983 (discussed in Teammates)

The Secret Diary of Adrian Mole, Aged 13¾ by Sue Townsend, 1986

The Arizona Kid by Ron Koertge, 1988

The Method by Paul Robert Walker, 1990

Out of Control by Erika Tamar, 1991

Damned Strong Love: The True Story of Willi G. and Stefan K. by Lutz Van Dijk, translated
        1995

Deliver Us from Evie, 1994, and *"Hello," I Lied*, 1997, by M. E. Kerr

Blue Coyote by Liza Ketchum, 1997

The House You Pass along the Way by Jacqueline Woodson, 1997

Hard Love, 1999 (discussed in Dating's Challenges), and *What's in a Name?* 2000, by Ellen
        Wittlinger

Empress of the World by Sara Ryan, 2001

Rainbow Boys by Alex Sanchez, 2001

Supernatural and Alien Beings: Confronting the Other

Interstellar Pig by William Sleator (1984)
Ender's Game by Orson Scott Card (1985)
Never Trust a Dead Man by Vivian Vande Velde (1999)
Companions of the Night by Vivian Vande Velde (1995)
Blood and Chocolate by Annette Curtis Klause (1999)

Stories about other intelligent creatures are the stuff of ancient myth and the most contemporary novels. Often, they emerge out of nightmares and people's worst fears. Such beings are likely to embody characteristics most would prefer to think of as inhuman, though the creatures imagined by humans may embody human characteristics, often magnified and, perhaps, amplified with other powers. Their magic may ensnare the human character, or it may be put to his or her service. When supernatural creatures are imagined as helpful, their abilities empower humans. The idea of other intelligent beings, whether hostile or helpful, is intriguing.

Fantasy is rife with magical creatures, often drawn from ancient legends and sacred texts. In fiction, dragons, wizards and witches, vampires, werewolves, and other such supernatural beings usually embody some recognizable, traditional features that have accompanied their history as literary characters or forces. Science fiction, on the other hand, draws on the present and the imagined future, inviting the reader to envision encounters with intelligent beings from other worlds. Either genre can be a powerful vehicle for social critique, enabling the reader to consider just what it means to be human through interaction with the nonhuman.

Interstellar Pig (1984), by William Sleator, draws the reader into a suspenseful story in which three glamorous but distinctly odd vacationers draw sixteen-year-old Barney into dangerous adventures and an apparently addictive, complex board game called Interstellar Pig. Barney and his parents are spending their second week in the historic New England beachfront home built by a nineteenth-century merchant captain when the other renters—an attractive young woman and two buff young men, all beautifully groomed and tanned—arrive for a week at the recently built cinder block cottage next door. The reader, undistracted by their attractiveness, is aware of their creepiness. Their use of language is funny, though the other vacationers and locals account for their malapropisms by assuming they are foreigners. They fascinate and even subtly hypnotize with their beauty, transforming Barney's parents' personalities, which are unattractively superficial or grasping at best.

The visitors exhibit obsessive curiosity about the house Barney's parents have rented. Barney has already ferreted out the ghost story associated with the house, a house that the new neighbors seem desperately anxious to gain access to. The Captain's brother apparently went mad, strangling the sole survivor of a shipwreck under the delusion that he was the devil, and spent the last twenty years of his life imprisoned in the bedroom Barney is sleeping in, speaking nothing but nonsense after being keelhauled for his crime.

Barney is as curious about his exotic neighbors as they are about his house, and he is quickly drawn into snooping and subterfuge to keep an eye on them as they draw near the solution of the mystery constructed out of the long-dead sailor's attempts to direct any investigator to a landmark on a nearby island. Barney sees the range of their moods, not always attractive, so that he begins to wonder about their ability to charm everyone. His speculations lead him to wonder what the reality beneath their appearance is, even before he discovers that they are aliens identified with the characters of the game they play. Sleator allows the reader to catch on just a bit ahead of Barney, when Barney fails to recognize where he has encountered his game character—in the pages of the Captain's narrative.

Once he overcomes his rational resistance to thinking of his neighbors as aliens, the suspense and action build rapidly. Barney proves himself—as representative of the human species—smarter than the universe's rulebook ranks him. Nonetheless, his former neighbors underestimate his victory as they streak away from Earth, because he has chosen not to kill when he could. One of the most interesting aspects of the tale is Barney's brief spell as part of the intelligent lichen that bear away the Piggy, the token whose capture indicates completion of the game. The reaction to his questions of the other cells in the organism suggest that individualism is an important characteristic of humans, and his neighbors have earlier suggested that young people are harder to fool than their elders. Ultimately, Barney remains unsure whether or not he has been duped by the Piggy, but he is content to clean up the mess and let the game go its way through the universe.

Ender's Game (1985), by Orson Scott Card, takes a more disturbing and serious look at encounters between humans and alien beings from another planet. From birth, children on Earth hear frightening references to "the buggers," the aliens who have been defeated in a first encounter but who are expected to initiate another conflict that may mean the end of human civilization. The sole aim of the military is to breed and train a commander who can defeat the buggers, a commander with the right combination of strategic and tactical skill, ruthlessness, and empathy. In a desperate effort to achieve their goal, with the aliens' space fleet actually on the way, they separate promising children from their families at a young age and begin their education and military training off-planet. Ender Wiggin, the commander on whom the survival of the human race depends, achieves victory at age eleven, commanding his fellow students in a war "game," which proves to be the actual assault on the aliens that culminates in the destruction of their home planet. The novel raises serious issues about the education of the gifted, the qualities needed for successful military leadership, and attitudes toward what is alien.

The education that Ender and his peers undergo is demanding, unsympathetic, and deceptive. The adults who select Ender and supervise his training know not only his intelligence and capabilities but also his psychological makeup. They present a strong rationale for his separation from his family, removing him from the dangerous malice of his brother, Peter, but also from his genuinely loving relationship with his sister, Valentine. Then, from the outset, they manipulate his relationships with other students, isolating him and continually challenging his ability to function well in each military unit to which he is assigned. Ender's personality predisposes him to collaborate with others. A brilliant military thinker himself, he shares his insights with other students, teaches them, and inspires their loyalty. His superiors disrupt these relationships, placing him in ever more difficult fighting situations. Ender, learning early that he can expect absolutely no help from adults, obliges them by toughening himself and meeting each challenge, including defending himself against physical attack. His success continues unabated, no matter what challenges they throw his way, but at the expense of happiness. Despite his ability to foster confidence and trust, Ender himself has no one to confide in or trust.

Ender can be ruthless when his survival is threatened, though he does not realize that in his calculated defense he has actually killed people, but he does not possess the hardness to knowingly send his forces to their deaths and obliterate his enemy. As the commander of the army that previously confronted the aliens tells him, no "decent person" can give himself wholeheartedly to warfare as if it were merely a game won with intellectual ability. He must believe he is simulating the battles in order to be successful. It is when he is exhausted by "training" under this commander that he apparently dreams his way into empathy with the enemy, an empathy that enables him to understand his the buggers' thinking so thoroughly that he can exploit their weaknesses. Ultimately, he realizes that the enemy race was communicating with him via his dreams. Ender's empathy has always been at the heart of his abilities as a commander; all the knowledge he has accumulated and the tactical skill he has developed would not be so effective were he not able to coolly assess the heart of an opponent's thinking and respond appropriately.

It is Ender's understanding of those he has destroyed that he takes with him after winning the war for humankind. This understanding is at the heart of Card's most effective sequels, *Speaker for the Dead* and *Ender's Shadow*. Ender's moral dilemmas are real; he does not want to be heartless, particularly because he fears being like his brother, Peter, who is not only brilliant but a monster, able to understand and exploit others' weaknesses and to dissemble to mask his real motives. Ender's fears and isolation bring him to a despair overcome only by timely messages from his sister, sent at the authorities' instigation. Ender accepts, though unwillingly, his supervisor's statement that his happiness is irrelevant because he is a tool, needed to preserve humanity.

The reader sees Ender's development primarily from his viewpoint, but conversations between often unnamed authorities responsible for his selection, supervision, and training head the chapters, presenting the motives and concerns of those who have selected Ender for this role. The problem-solving process that Ender goes through, as he meets challenge after challenge in his relationships with others and in the war games, is one of the most interesting elements of the novel.

Valentine and Peter make use of their intelligence, equal to Ender's, to influence Earth politics by posting carefully worded opinion pieces on the Internet, debating each other in preplanned interactions in a campaign that eerily suggests the blogs (Web logs) of today. Their wielding of power leads to a believable denouement, suggesting the kind of life that is possible to the brilliant child after he has defeated the aliens.

What is most disturbing is the inability of humans and buggers to communicate with each other. Each race attempts to exterminate the other because they cannot bridge the gulf between their vastly different natures. Thus, in the aftermath of the war, when Ender eventually understands how thoroughly the aliens have ultimately come to know him through their invasion of his thinking in the form of the dreams, Ender realizes that communication might, after all, have been achieved.

Some of Vivian Vande Velde's most entertaining novels place extraordinary happenings and beings into the most ordinary situations. *Companions of the Night* (1995) chronicles Kerry's suspenseful though brief adventures with a vampire whom she first encounters in a Laundromat. *Never Trust a Dead Man* (1999) is a humorous mystery set in a small village where a crime of passion is solved by the young man accused of murder with the help of the dead man himself, brought back from the dead by a witch who conveniently rescues the convicted killer from his punishment of being immured in the tomb with the victim. The witch, Elswyth, is wryly humorous and has a good heart, though she cuffs Selwyn, the condemned man, for stupidity and constantly gets the better of him in bargaining for years of his service in return for her aid in leaving the catacomb, calling up the murdered man's spirit, and creating disguises that will enable him to discreetly pursue the truth. In his initial fear of her, Selwyn moves at a crucial moment in the spell that calls back Farold so that he is resurrected in the body of a bat—most inconvenient since Farold is then nocturnal and Selwyn is not.

In the course of Selwyn's investigation into who stabbed Farold in his sleep with Selwyn's knife, stolen weeks before the murder, the innocent Selwyn learns a lot about the villagers' secret lives. Farold was not a very likable young man, he discovers; in addition to winning the hand of Selwyn's beloved, he has blackmailed some of his neighbors and been falsely accused of impregnating the tavernkeeper's daughter, and it does not take Selwyn long to generate a growing list of suspects. Farold is as irritating as a victim, and a bat, as he was as a living man, but Selwyn gradually develops compassion for him, especially as it becomes clear that few people liked him and that his betrothed rapidly transferred her affections to his elderly uncle, a much wealthier man than Farold. Selwyn is equally disillusioned by the pettiness and greed of the girl he thought he loved, and even though his name is cleared, there is little to tempt him to stay in the village, even when Elswyth releases him from his promised service and Farold offers to serve it for him.

Selwyn is honorable, though Elswyth's transformation into an attractive young woman undoubtedly makes his service more appealing. Farold survives an apparent second death, incarnated in a third postdeath body as a duck, and is in no hurry to return to the afterlife. Thus the novel ends in a companionable alliance among the three that underscores the predominant themes that appearances may well belie reality and that honesty and intelligence are more appealing qualities than personal attractiveness.

Companions of the Night is a darker novel. The vampire, Ethan, is brought bound and bleeding to the deserted Laundromat, where Kerry has ventured to retrieve her little brother's stuffed bear, by the owner and his confederates, a band of Christian vigilantes committed to rounding up vampires and exposing them to the sunlight that will destroy them. Kerry, seeing only a vulnerable and attractive young man held by a group of crazies, helps him escape, only to find the next day that her father and brother have been kidnapped by the vampire-hunters. Forced to accept Ethan as an ally in rescuing her family, Kerry finds herself coming to like him, even to trust him after a fashion, and finally to love him though she has the firmness to turn her back on his kind of life.

Ethan, who turns out to be really Michel, is truly alien, though sympathetic. Kerry finds it sensible never to trust what he says. He keeps firm control over her actions, physically restraining her when he deems it necessary, and she is under no illusions as to whether she is an equal partner in deciding how to track down her family members.

He often seems to read her mind, though it is likely that even an ordinary older youth could divine her thoughts in some situations, since she is just sixteen. Early in their partnership, she learns to recognize his look that suggests he is having an inward laugh at her expense over something that only another vampire would understand. Eventually she learns that her family is safe and that he has kept this knowledge from her so that she would stay committed to tracking down the remaining, and leading, vigilante.

Yet Ethan is likable, and as Kerry realizes that he truly will not harm her, she is intrigued and attracted in spite of herself. After sharing mortal danger at the moment of crisis, when each protects the other, Kerry acknowledges that she has fallen in love and is willing to imagine being a vampire herself. Ethan takes the surprising step of admitting to a sense of guilt and responsibility for another of his kind, an emotion that Kerry understands, because she has felt guilty and responsible for her family's involvement.

Kerry's decision is, ultimately, a very mature human choice. Unlike her mother, who left the family for a new romance, Kerry will stay with her family and will remain human. Though it is suggested the romance may continue in the future, and Ethan has admitted that he can make the choice to return to being human, the ending is realistic—and warmly friendly. The romance of otherness, even at the expense of normal humanity, has been acknowledged in the novel, but the characters' maturity is seen in their ability to avoid sudden, irrevocable decisions. This is a theme that is all too relevant to merely human relationships.

Most stories of human-alien interaction are told from the point of view of the human. In *Blood and Chocolate* (1999), Annette Curtis Klause presents the perspective of a teenage werewolf named Vivian, who lives in a Maryland suburb after her pack has been discovered and driven from a rural West Virginia community and who just wants to have friends like a normal teen. Above all, she wants to have a boyfriend, and she is drawn to the poet Aiden, a gentle youth who is intrigued by the supernatural and appears to be open to the knowledge of otherness that Vivian can share with him. Vivian is tired of some aspects of her pack life. She misses her father, who died in a fire set by outraged residents of their last community and is annoyed by her mother, who is running after a twenty-four-year-old male who seems likely to be the pack's next leader. At the same time she is tired of the antics of the five teen males who hang around her hoping to mate and who run wild, thus endangering the pack's existence by drawing attention with their attacks on dogs. The pack is leaderless until a midsummer all-out fight for dominance among the males, and part of her mother's jockeying for the powerful Gabriel's interest is, Vivian suspects, the desire to continue as the dominant female, a position from which she has been displaced by her husband's death.

At the same time as Vivian is annoyed by her pack's interactions with each other and the human community in which they live, she takes delight in her physical being. She loves her fur—her werewolf body—as much as she does her beautiful, healthy young woman's body. As wolf-kind, moreover, she has a fierce and unabashed sexuality that bowls over her human boyfriend. The closer they get, however, the closer comes the inevitable unmasking of her true identity, and though she convinces herself that he is open to who she truly and fully is, her revelation of her true otherness predictably sparks fear and loathing in Aiden. As Vivian works through her complicated feelings—partly simple hurt, partly jealousy of the merely human girl who replaces her in Aiden's affections, partly a deep loyalty to the pack and concern that she may have exposed them to danger—she also feels the pressure of Gabriel's desire.

After his victory in the Ordeal through which his leadership was established, she established herself as the pack's dominant female when she rushed to the defense of her mother. Gabriel is undoubtedly sexy and makes no secret of his interest in her, but it takes her fear and confusion following an attack by humans to fully bring out his tenderness and the understanding of her dual nature which, ultimately, is essential for her to mate successfully and happily.

In her hurt over Aiden's rejection, Vivian comforts herself with the soothing taste of chocolate. However, in the long run, she finds that she needs the taste of blood as well to experience the range of her emotional capacity. This is a story of a real outsider, barred by very biology from a normal life as a teen. It is also a story about self-acceptance, especially acceptance of conflicting parts of one's own nature. While the werewolves' rowdy personalities, blood-lust, and open sexuality may diminish their appeal for some readers, their regard for their own law and the loyalty of most of the pack to each other are qualities most human readers will respect.

ADDITIONAL READING RECOMMENDATIONS

Fade by Robert Cormier, 1988

Canyons by Gary Paulsen, 1990

The Promise, 1991; *Demons and Shadows: The Ghostly Best Stories of Robert Westall*, 1993; *In Camera and Other Stories*, 1993; *The Call and Other Stories*, 1993; *The Stones of Muncaster Cathedral*, 1993; and *Shades of Darkness: More of the Ghostly Best Stories of Robert Westall*, 1994, by Robert Westall

Night Terrors: Stories of Shadow and Substance edited by Lois Duncan, 1996

The Darkling by Charles Butler, 1998

The Haunting by Joan Lowery Nixon, 1998

Kit's Wilderness by David Almond, 2000 (discussed in Older People's Impact on Our Lives)

Fire Bringer, 2000, and *The Sight*, 2002, by David Clement-Davies

Being Dead by Vivian Vande Velde, 2001

Waifs and Strays (stories) by Charles DeLint, 2002

Alchemy by Margaret Mahy, 2003

Survival

The Cay by Theodore Taylor (1969)
Hatchet by Gary Paulsen (1987)
Brian's Winter by Gary Paulsen (1996)
Far North by Will Hobbs (1996)
Backwater by Joan Bauer (1999)

A conflict that drives the plot of many literary works is man versus nature. The classic novel exploring this theme is *The Old Man and the Sea,* long a staple of the high school English curriculum. Some of the most suspenseful adventure stories successfully integrate this theme with other conflicts, such as Richard Connell's "The Most Dangerous Game" (1924), a story as popular with students as it is with teachers, and Robb White's 1972 novel *Deathwatch.* The idea of proving oneself in a struggle against external forces is not a new one in Western culture, though the opportunities for doing so have dwindled in contemporary society. Extreme conditions, it is believed, bring out humans' true toughness and intelligence. The novels discussed here include middle school classics as well as more recent works that require young people to live by their wits in challenging locales remote from society. In most of the texts, the added dimension of struggle against societal attitudes, one's own prejudices, and family pressures give depth and poignancy to the effort simply to stay alive.

Theodore Taylor's 1969 novel, *The Cay,* is set in the Caribbean during World War II. It chronicles the American boy Phillip's survival under the care and tutelage of an elderly West Indian ship's hand, Timothy, with the companionship of the cook's cat, on an uncharted cay after the Germans have torpedoed the ship on which Phillip and his mother are returning to the United States. As the ship sinks, Phillip suffers a head injury that renders him unconscious for several hours, and he wakes to find himself drifting on a raft with the authoritative black man, no longer in the safe and privileged position he had on Curacao, in a situation that rapidly worsens as he becomes blind and then is shipwrecked for several months on the uninhabited island. What might be an adventure for a healthy boy under the protection of a man with much practical knowledge and wisdom becomes a nightmare with his handicap, but Phillip gradually adjusts to his blindness and masters the skills that Timothy is anxious to teach him, because he knows that his age and the dangers of their situation may bring his death, leaving Phillip on his own. Phillip's success in adjusting to his disability and his ability to outgrow racial prejudice dramatically transform him.

Phillip naturally reacts to his situation with fear, and his fear turns to helpless anger. From the outset he resents Timothy's apparent stinginess with their small keg of freshwater, lulled by the old man's assurances that they will certainly be rescued soon, empty assurances that he voices to keep Phillip calm in the early stages of their desperate plight. He is also angered by Timothy's decision to land on the uninhabited cay, especially when he learns of Timothy's suspicion that it is located within a nearly unnavigable stretch of coral reefs where they are unlikely to be rescued unless they can attract the attention of an aircraft. Gradually, he comes to recognize that Timothy does not always communicate his realistic appraisal of their prospects for rescue and even survival, and he begins to recognize how dire their situation is. As Phillip comes to terms with his blindness, he at first takes for granted Timothy's care for him and resists taking on any responsibility for creating and maintaining their shelter when they first arrive on the island. He must also come to terms with his prejudice against blacks, instilled in him by his mother. Their interdependence, however, gradually convinces Phillip that a difference in skin color, even a difference in cultural background and life experience, is superficial compared to the needs they share: to catch and wisely use rainwater, create and maintain shelter, gather all the food the tiny island and sheltered fishing area furnish, and prepare a signal fire that may be lit quickly should they hear an airplane. By the time they meet the most severe test of their ability to survive, early in the hurricane season, Phillip and Timothy have developed a mutual affection that makes the old man's death in the storm more deeply felt.

As Phillip faces the necessity of surviving on his own, he more fully appreciates what Timothy has taught him, and he learns how carefully he must tend to his own survival, by always placing his few tools where he can find them and by exercising caution in all his actions. He also has to use his own ingenuity to improve his signal fire, an effort that pays off when he succeeds in attracting an aircraft and ultimately is rescued.

In the aftermath of Phillip's ordeal, he lives differently on Curacao, as does his mother, once the family's priorities have been reordered by the crisis of his long separation from them. His mother has decided it is more important to stay with his father throughout the war than to feel safer on the North American mainland, and Phillip is able to appreciate fully the restoration of his sight through a series of operations. Not surprisingly, he finds that he no longer shares the interests of his peers but rather wants to get to know the West Indian black community, hoping one day to find his island again and pay tribute to the man who saved his life.

In *Hatchet* (1987), Gary Paulsen has created a modern classic. If a teen reads only one novel with a survival theme, this should probably be the one. What makes this story of a thirteen-year-old stranded alone in the Canadian wilderness so powerful? Brian discovers both the fragility and the richness of life in this straightforward tale of man versus nature. *Hatchet* contrasts several key aspects of contemporary life with a life lived off the land. When Brian takes stock of his situation after crash-landing the plane, he finds he has only his new hatchet and the clothes on his back. These resources from the life he has always known, along with ripe berries, fish, turtle eggs, and small game, are enough to sustain him until rescue finally comes. Through his experience, Brian learns what it means to be entirely dependent on his surroundings and his own abilities. Food is always his top priority. Creating safe shelter and becoming skilled at fire-starting are other high priorities, concerns that most readers rarely have to consider.

In the early days of his solitude, Brian sometimes gives way to discouragement, even trying to will himself to suicide at one point, but when he concludes that discouragement and self-pity are a waste of time, he develops a new standard of discipline that he hadn't suspected he was capable of. Food, thought, action—this is his sequence for each endeavor: he feeds the body (including the brain), figures out how to do something, and only then does he act. Brian must take care of himself, because careless action may result in a broken bone or blindness, which in turn probably means death. Alertness is important, and it is only when Brian allows himself to daydream or gets too anxious to take care that he is surprised by large, dangerous animals; he also learns new respect for the smaller ones. Fortunately, his senses are sharpened as he learns to live in his environment. He relies on all his senses, and he learns to fully focus his attention. After his bout with despair, Brian displays the tenacity that can save him from any number of dangers, including severe weather.

Throughout this process, we see glimpses of Brian's normal life, including the circumstance—his parents' divorce—that put him into this situation. The requirements of living off the land demand constant focus, so Brian finds it difficult to continue brooding on his mother's affair and his separation from his father. What Brian does recall from his old life are scraps of useful knowledge from science classes and his reading. He sometimes draws the contrast between the availability of food in contemporary urban society and the effort it takes to obtain an adequate supply in the wild. His least useful memory is his recollection of meals, a mental self-indulgence that quickly floods his mouth with saliva and distracts him from concentrating on the steady effort he must make to live in the wilderness. Having learned the necessary lessons, he is rescued.

Sequels indicate Paulsen's continuing fascination with the topic, as well as enthusiastic reader response. The most successful is *Brian's Winter* (1996), which forgoes the final rescue of *Hatchet* in favor of continued wilderness existence and further learning about survival, now in the cold of winter. The plot unfolds through incidents that allow Brian to recollect and build on the hunting and animal lore he has absorbed in the past. He re-creates the simple technologies he has learned about, making a heavy bow, chipping arrowheads from flint, creating winter garments from the hides of rabbits and a moose, making snowshoes.

In this novel, Brian's mistakes play a less important role in his learning process. His character has been formed by the summer's episodes so that now he reflects and plans his actions carefully. He does learn new things, because his world is a different one in the winter. Moreover, he reflects on the necessities of killing animals for his own survival—he does not like to see them die slowly, and it bothers him to kill an animal that is unconscious of his presence. He has a mystical side, creating a simple shrine for a special arrow and placing a doe's head in a tree, thanking her for giving him her meat.

Most important, Brian assumes a more equal footing with the human being who effects his "rescue." The Cree trapper whom Brian meets is living in the wild at this season with his family by choice and does not know of Brian's celebrity status as a missing person. Before leaving the wilderness in a supply plane, Brian shares his knowledge, and he is somewhat reluctant to leave, though his new friend assures him that he will be able to return to the waiting wilderness when he wants to.

Far North (1996), by Will Hobbs, is a thrilling, fast-paced book. Gabe Rogers, a fifteen-year-old Texan, starts boarding school in Yellowknife, Northwest Territories, Canada, to be nearer his father, who is working on an oil-drilling rig. Gabe's roommate Raymond is a Dene from a tiny village accessible by road only in the winter, when the ground and river are frozen and provide a firm surface for motor vehicles. Raymond seems suited to the English-speaking school, bringing a hockey stick and electric guitar to school, but in late October, when Gabe's father arranges some sight-seeing by air, Gabe discovers the bush pilot has been engaged to fly Raymond back home, along with his great-uncle, an elderly Athabascan speaker who has recently been released from the hospital. When the plane's engine fails, the plane and pilot are swept away on the Nahanni River a hundred miles from Raymond's village, and their chance of rescue seems slim since their pilot departed from the flight plan on file. Though Raymond's great-uncle speaks almost no English and Raymond almost no Athabascan, the uncle teaches them important survival skills before he dies on his last solitary hunting trip, and they learn to respect his knowledge, as well as the wild and fiercely cold world they are left in and the value of friendship in a mutually dependent situation.

This is a classic man-versus-nature novel that embodies a critique of the ways contemporary Western society has lured Native Americans away from intimate knowledge of the land. The wealth the boys need to survive winter in the wild is, fortunately, still available to them, in the remnants of the culture preserved in an elder's memory, though much is lost to them due to divergence from the native language. Early in their ordeal, Raymond jettisons his prized electric guitar; much later he tells Gabe he would like to learn to play the fiddle when they make it to his village. His great-uncle makes a small drum after finishing necessities like snowshoes, and he beats it as he recites the stories that are Raymond's heritage, even though Raymond knows only a few of the words. The drum is important enough to warrant repair after it is ravaged by a wolverine that invades the cabin they have found, and it is one of the few things they carry in their final, near-hopeless trek toward Raymond's village after he has broken his ankle in a fall.

Underscoring the man-versus-nature theme, the man and the two boys have a remarkably conflict-free relationship, even when disastrous mistakes are made. No time is wasted in regrets or recriminations; the three are united in the struggle to stay alive in the fearsome cold. It is impossible to read this exciting book without sharing the characters', and author's, awe at the beautiful light, the mountains, the rivers, and the snow, and gaining some understanding of humans' place in the ecosystem. This is an optimistic book that conveys the message that age-old knowledge can still be tapped into to save humans from their cultural excesses and reintegrate them spiritually as well as physically into the natural world. The characteristics that the characters embody, or learn—patience, persistence, courage—convey in a quiet, subtle way the lesson that maturity consists in responsibility to others and care in how one performs a task.

In a woman-versus-nature novel enlivened with a woman-versus-human subtheme, Joan Bauer's *Backwater* (1999) is about survival on two levels: survival of quiet, solitary introverts in an aggressively clannish, argumentative family and survival of grave injury in a wilderness environment. About one-third of the novel sets up the family situation: Josephine, the aunt of the protagonist Ivy, is dismissed by the family as crazy; the family has a passionate devotion to the law as a career and consequently they expect Ivy to abandon her love of and fascination with history to become a lawyer. Ivy's two-year Breedlove family history project is in danger of being eclipsed by a video family history, that Fiona (her aunt by marriage) is filming during a Christmas gathering at the remote family homestead. An elderly neighbor's comment about Josephine's visit to family graves sends Ivy on a quest to find and interview her aunt, who is living like a hermit near the summit of a mountain. Enter the comic figure of Mountain Mama, a wilderness guide with a yen to write a bestselling all-encompassing guide to surviving life—*One Mountain at a Time*. She is willing to take Ivy up the mountain in late December, and after Ivy talks her father into granting permission (Daniel Webster Breedlove is not one to be easily talked into anything that was not his idea first), the two women head up the mountain in a challenging hike. Not surprisingly, Ivy's interview with her aunt gives her new insight into her family and, because she too enjoys some solitude, gives her courage to hold out against her father's pressure to become something she is not. The two older women's approach to survival is just as courageous and honest as the men's, which is grounded in competitive public debate.

The second element of survival takes precedence when a storm brings down a tree on Josephine's cabin, caving in the roof and breaking her leg. Because Mountain Mama has been banished so the two Breedlove women can be alone, Ivy must decide what to do when Josephine's leg shows signs of internal bleeding. She strikes out across a frozen lake, pulling Josephine on a sled, guided by Josephine's pet wolf whom Ivy feared and distrusted on first acquaintance. Their journey is exciting but brief. Malachi the wolf leads them safely across the fragile ice, and they get help at a ranger station.

The role of animals is prominent throughout the novel. Josephine's odd life has been characterized by her ability to attract birds, and Malachi is devoted to her as well. Her mountain hideaway is her personal bird sanctuary, complete with a "hospital" for injured birds. Indeed, the hospital is only a small part of her "municipality" of Backwater, of which Josephine is the self-proclaimed mayor. She has claimed and transformed the identity the Breedlove family has scornfully attributed to others as being "stuck in the backwater." The birds, like Josephine, are wild and free, and Ivy comes to have a strong sense of accomplishment when she can feed a shy chickadee from her hand. A memory that she has formerly thought of as a dream resurfaces with new shape and clarity when her aunt tells her that the two of them fed birds on a hilltop the day of her mother's funeral. In addition to feeding wild creatures, Josephine is an artist: she carves wooden figures of family members, catching personality in striking ways. In her figure of a boy fisherman, she shows Ivy a side of her father she has never known. Through recapturing this memory of feeding the birds and sharing Josephine's visualization of the family, Ivy finds a role model for preserving her own identity while keeping the support of the family that she relies on. And Ivy's appearance on Josephine's doorstep helps Josephine reconnect with the family she loves despite her need for solitude.

ADDITIONAL READING RECOMMENDATIONS

Deathwatch by Robb White, 1972

Dogsong, 1985, and *Haymeadow* 1992, by Gary Paulsen (both discussed in Animals and the Environment)

Onion Tears by Diana Kidd, 1991

Death Walk by Walt Morey, 1991

Sweet Friday Island by Theodore Taylor, 1994

Between a Rock and a Hard Place by Alden R. Carter, 1995

Flash Fire by Caroline B. Cooney, 1995

Free Fall by Joyce Sweeney, 1996

Whichaway by Glendon and Kathryn Swarthout, 1997

The Grounding of Group 6 by Julian F. Thompson, 1997

The Wild Kid by Harry Mazer, 1998

When Eagles Fall by Mary Casanova, 2002

Teammates

Running Loose by Chris Crutcher (1983)
Wrestling Sturbridge by Rich Wallace (1996)
There's a Girl in My Hammerlock by Jerry Spinelli (1991)
If It Doesn't Kill You by Margaret Bechard (1999)
Roughnecks by Thomas Cochran (1997)

The number of teens participating in sports has been growing over the past thirty years, and team sports play an important role in school life and social relationships. While women's participation has shown substantial growth, the majority of novels focusing on sports have featured men's team sports. A notable exception is New Zealand swimmer and writer Tessa Duder's novels featuring women's competitive swimming, *In Lane Three, Alex Archer* (1989) and *Alex in Rome* (1992). Sports form a part of the social landscape, however, in many novels with other predominant themes. The novels discussed here address a range of issues against the backdrop of team sports.

Chris Crutcher's honest novels have been threatened with banning for their controversial subject matter, and his 1983 *Running Loose* was among the one hundred most challenged books of the 1990s. Protagonist Louie Banks challenges religious and authority figures—the school principal and football coach are petty tyrants and, in the coach's case a liar—and discusses his budding sexual relationship as well as frequent masturbation. The action occurs over the period of Louie's senior year, a period of intense questioning and anger on his part as he comes to terms with, first, physical intimidation based on racism, then anguish over his girlfriend Becky's death in a car accident, and finally the ill will of school authorities who want to punish his outraged reactions to hypocrisy. Throughout this year of challenges, Louie also discovers the strength of the support from his family, his oldest friends, his employer Dakota, Becky's father, and the track coach. He learns to cope through the discipline of running and, occasionally, through recognition of the natural beauty around him in mountainous western Idaho.

What he expected to be a wonderful senior year goes sour early when football is ruined for him from the time the coach begins urging the team to take out Washington, a rival team's new black quarterback—advice he knows the intolerant Boomer will be glad to act on. When Boomer deliberately injures Washington and the ref fails to penalize the team, Louie quits the team in his first confrontation with school authorities, a confrontation in which the coach blatantly lies about his role in instigating Boomer's rough hit. This is when Louie discovers that he is sustained by the support of the people who matter to him: his chair-of-the-school-board father, his mother and sister; Dakota, the wise old owner of the bar that Louie cleans; his best friend, the football star Carter; and Becky. His deepening relationship with Becky is the most important part of his life at this juncture, and they come close to sexual union. The real tenderness and love in the relationship is shown as they reach the decision not to have sex.

The emotional intensity of this moment makes Becky's sudden death all the more shocking, to the reader as well as to Louie. Though the novel is told as a conversational first-person narrative that occasionally addresses the reader as "you," in Louie's foreshadowing of the end of their relationship, he says only that Becky has "gone away." The whole town grieves, but Becky's death precipitates Louie's intense and extensive questioning, as he realizes there is simply no way to bargain with God—Becky is gone, no matter what he does. His anger is exacerbated by the huge funeral staged by Becky's mother. The East Coast minister who did not know Becky has the misfortune (the hypocrisy, in Louie's view) to utter the cliché that God works in mysterious ways, provoking Louie's disruptive outburst. Even Boomer, who has long scorned Louie as a "wussy," can display empathy for the extremity of Louie's grief, as he and Carter ease Louie out of the church.

Louie finds emotional lifelines from several older mentors, as well as in his family's concern. He grows closer to Becky's father in their shared pain—and shared opinion of the big funeral that only Louie expressed openly. Dakota teaches the rule of the life game—that we die and we do not know why—illustrating the blandness of an existence without rules through several games of checkers without rules. Finally, the track coach, expressing regret that as assistant football coach he did not speak out against the coach's racism, offers Louie a way to work through his feelings when he pressures the principal to allow Louie to run the mile and two-mile for the team. Running track gives Louie the opportunity not only to run off some of his grief and pain but also to discover Washington's respect both for his earlier action and for the heart he shows in his running.

By the end of the school year, Louie is "running loose" rather than running wild, feeling the pain but able to deal with it, and running for himself rather than for his school or in competition with anyone, except when he runs all out against Washington. He continues to resent the principal's self-important hypocrisy, and he is angry at survivors' ability to twist a dead person's life and achievements to illustrate their own beliefs or purposes, as was done at Becky's funeral. He will continue to express that anger and resentment but in a much more controlled way than he did earlier.

Wrestling Sturbridge (1996), by Rich Wallace, explores the dimensions of competition in the story of a Sturbridge High School senior's last wrestling season on a team that has good prospects for being number one in the state. Ben, who tells his own story, is "odd man out"—wrestling at 135 pounds, with his three close friends all better wrestlers at 130, 135, and 140. His need to prove himself competitive with his best friend Al (at 135) is as strong as his teammates' need to prove themselves against other teams. Ben's knowledge that this is the last season they will be together, with all the ambivalence this entails, combines with his desire to get out of his dead small town to produce a malaise that ends only with his last wrestle-off of the season, with Al. Ben feels enormous anger and frustration—he is "wrestling Sturbridge"—but he bottles it up until his new girlfriend, Kim, helps him put Sturbridge wrestling and relationships in perspective, allowing him to move on with his life.

The challenge of relationships that date back to elementary school is that old tensions slumber; the benefit of such relationships is the solid friendships that can develop. When there is nowhere to go in Sturbridge, or Smalltown anywhere, teens cruise, over and over and over again on a weekend night, or they drink at parties held where parents are out of town. Perhaps the biggest challenge to teens living in a very small town is that there is nothing to do but step into the roles the adults currently play. The former high school wrestlers run the booster club and attend the high school matches wearing old letter jackets, constant reminders that there is no place to go. Young men turn into their fathers—and this is something that Ben does not want to do, though he gets along with his father well enough. As he accompanies his dad on the occasional petty burglarizing expedition, breaking into nearby summer homes and stealing minor useful objects, and speculates as to whether his mother has slept with his friend's father, Ben assesses the likelihood of his three good friends' turning out just like their dads. Though he yearns to escape, he has not applied to any colleges.

Another potential trap is early marriage or fatherhood. Over the course of the season, Ben discovers that he loves Kim, even though he has had his eye on a mysterious twenty-year-old, but he remembers his father's advice that he should not marry the first girl he falls in love with. Nearly all his energy has been channeled into wrestling, and he has none to spare for dating relationships. Wrestling gives him a way to express intimacy—to touch others without the challenges of being involved emotionally with them. Ben bottles up his anger as well, rarely expressing it. Only after he has finally voiced his desire to best Al does he begin to acknowledge and cope with his love for Kim.

Ben particularly resents his small community's judgmental nature. He is irritated by the disapproval of many kinds of behavior he hears at his Protestant church, his irritation exacerbated by two things: a run-in over kids' sports with his minister that resulted in Ben's punching him and his grandmother's sour expectation of transgressions by him and others. He opposes hypocrisy and prejudice wherever he encounters them. Ben is at his most relaxed when he works with kids, coaching soccer or introducing them to wrestling, open emotionally where there is no threat of deeper involvement, able to express affection through shared physical activity.

Much of Ben's thinking is revealed through the lists he makes—or reads in the state's wrestling newsletter—that head up each chapter. These are usually two-part lists, contrasting bests and worsts or likes and dislikes, knowledge with speculation, and so forth. His narrative voice is often understated, but the tension that drives him in wrestling season comes through, along with his longing for a "bigger pond" than the one he has inhabited his whole young life.

Jerry Spinelli's novels focus on younger protagonists, and the tone is often laugh-out-loud funny. *There's a Girl in My Hammerlock* (1991), the story of eighth-grader Maisie Potter's wrestling season, explores the serious issue of gender discrimination in school sports, but it provides plenty of entertainment at the same time, largely due to the irrepressible Maisie's flamboyant personality and wry observations. The novel is framed as a letter to the editor from Maisie—in thirty-four chapters—because the local newspaper has published a number of articles and letters to the editor calling attention to Maisie's bold move in working for her place on Lenape Valley Junior High's wrestling team. The newspaper's report on the team's first match of the season featured a photo of Maisie and a teammate warming up, captioned "There's a girl in my hammerlock" and suggesting the surprise of opposing teams and the community at Maisie's presence on the mats.

Maisie is a middle child in a family that, for the most part, supports her choice to wrestle instead of play girls' basketball. The exception is her older brother, who shares the attitude of most of the school: girls belong on girls' teams, and there is something freaky about her trying out for wrestling, even though she won the trophy as the school's Outstanding Female Athlete of Seventh Grade. Her parents learn of her decision only when the coach requests a conference, attended also by the principal, but they rise to the occasion admirably, defending Maisie's right to go out for a boys' team when the school has no girls' team for the sport. Maisie's mother's support is underscored by her successfully completing a plumbing job in the bathroom just as Maisie is announcing her decision to quit the team, and her father's support is crystallized in his response to a father who calls their home to threaten taking his son off the team if Maisie stays. Her feisty little sister, P. K., cheers her on from the beginning, a fan—with Maisie—of Washerwoman, a wrestler on Saturday morning TV.

Coach Cappelli resists Maisie's presence at first, but he pushes her hard, and when she keeps coming back, he grants her the respect she has earned. Her teammates are, for the most part, harder to convince. It takes a formal "nutcracker" challenge—a five-minute confrontation with one after the other in succession—to win their respect. And once she has won it, she wins the first of several interscholastic matches through opponents' forfeits. When opponents begin wrestling her, and she is quickly pinned, she must cope with her fans from her school when they cheer her opponents. Maisie has chosen a long, lonely course, but one that reveals her friends' and community's mettle as well as Maisie's own. She loses her best friend but gains the solid friendship of her former teammate on the girls' basketball team. Suspected at first of wrestling only to be near the first guy she has ever been seriously attracted to, Maisie has to figure out whether Eric is really the only reason she is wrestling, a motivation that could not withstand the challenges she continues to face throughout the season.

Maisie proves her own courage in rescuing P. K.'s friend Tank from injury or death in the path of a snowplow without a moment's hesitation, even though she herself ends up packed into the snow and unconscious. The precipitating incident bears yet more testimony to Maisie's atypical gender behaviors. She has chosen a hooded rat as a pet—with feminine sympathy rescuing it from being sold as a snake's snack—and then yelled at Tank for letting her pet escape, unintentionally driving him out into the snow. She takes advantage of her extraordinary running speed to overtake Tank before disaster strikes, and her heroism seals her coach's and classmates' approval. This novel is ultimately about winning respect—the challenge that many teens face in sports, whatever the specific sport or context.

In *If It Doesn't Kill You* (1999), Margaret Bechard confronts another kind of prejudice in a story that shows the dual impact on a fifteen-year-old of a family's football tradition and a father's coming out as gay. Ben, a fullback and defensive end on his school's freshman team, is expected to go right to varsity football in his sophomore year because of his size and power. Ben is a big guy, whose father was a star quarterback at his high school and whose grandfather coached the team for many years, and Ben's prowess is accepted even expected from upperclassmen, who anticipate he will be their teammate next year, from members of the community, and from his grandmother. Ben, however, often feels unsure of himself, even as he recognizes that his size makes him seem more self-assured and older than he is, yet his fears of embarrassing himself while driving, drinking, or dating cause him as much concern as they would any freshman. His insecurity is exacerbated by his father's recent announcement that he can no longer live a lie and his subsequent move to share a house with Keith, a gay man. Ben, living with his mother, is hurt and angry with his father for breaking up the family, but worse, he does not know much about homosexuality—and at first does not want to know any more—and he worries about whether it runs in families and whether a person can change suddenly from straight to gay or can be gay without realizing it. His father's midlife crisis has come at a point when Ben is feeling particularly vulnerable, on the verge of attending high school beginning to date.

Ben is, above all, a nice guy—sensible and reliable. His thorough immersion in football culture sometimes makes him uncomfortable. For example, his friend's father reminisces about playing football with Ben's father, coached by his grandfather; he compliments Ben after games without acknowledging his own son's effort. As Ben is accepted by upperclassmen on the football team, he is often pummeled and pushed around by them in a spirit of camaraderie, and he knows that his classmates envy him, not realizing how much some of this camaraderie can hurt! He is not even sure he wants to play football throughout high school, but that possibility does not occur to anyone around him, especially his grandmother, widow of the legendary coach, who, when she visits, cheerily repeats many of his grandfather's maxims, chief among them, "If it doesn't kill you, it makes you stronger."

His grandmother's visit forces Ben to see his father, something he's been avoiding, though he has avoided confrontation as much as he has avoided his father. He is skilled at manipulating his father, telling him on the phone that yes, it would be nice to do this or that and then coming up with an excuse not to go when the day for the planned activity arrives. He even takes pleasure in getting at him this way. However, his grandmother does not know why her son's marriage has broken up, having been told only that he is having a midlife crisis, and she plans that Ben, his father, and she will attend a home varsity game. Her reaction to the truth, told to her at the game, helps Ben acknowledge and begin to cope with his own feelings.

At the same time, Ben's friendship with his new neighbor Chynna—Gail, until she arrived in a new town and could create a new, cooler image for herself—takes him into situations that expand his horizons. Chynna talks him into going downtown with her so she can have her navel pierced, prompting him to worry about his position as her bodyguard; while they are downtown, they run into Ben's father and his friend. It is Chynna, as well as Kyle, the junior she wants to date, who gets Ben to a party that proves to be mostly disastrous. He wanders around uncomfortably, carrying a warm beer that he doesn't want to drink, and about the time he finally gets into conversation with a girl he really likes, Chynna shows up drunk and upset, insisting that he must drive her home in her parents' car. These experiences help him begin to learn his way around high school social expectations, but it is his driving disaster as they leave the party that allows him an insight into the personality of his father's partner. Stuck in the mud, Ben must accept help from Keith, and he discovers that Keith can be a pretty decent guy.

As his social life begins to develop, Ben learns that many things, not just his parents' marriage, are not what they seem. At the party, he discovers that Kyle and his former girlfriend are meeting there to renegotiate their relationship, even though Kyle has invited Chynna. He learns from the girlfriend's friend that Kyle and the former girlfriend are virgins, committed to saving themselves for each other; this contradicts the boasting he has heard among the team members when they hang out together at school. He discovers that the girl he is interested in knowing better has brought a stash of sodas to the party so she and some others will not have to drink beer. He learns that Chynna is really plain old Gail, and she has deliberately started rumors about her exploits at her former school and changed her way of dressing and behaving to reinvent herself.

As he is drawn into some contact with his father and his father's friends, he learns that his father knew in high school that he was gay, and this helps allay some of

Ben's concerns about himself. He has to challenge some of the stereotypes he has held: even though his father has come out, he is not especially sensitive nor does he dress better than he did in the past nor does he talk about feelings, and his father's friend who pulls the car out of the mud is good with cars. After his father comes out to his grandmother, she stays with them for several days, cooking the kind of meals he has seen in classic TV shows and serving them at the properly set table, but he notes with irony that the family for whom she cooks is not a Nick at Nite family. One of the interests that Ben has long shared with his father is knowledge of old films and TV shows. His fondness for pop culture enables him to connect with people of different ages and backgrounds when they discover a shared interest.

In another novel of football tradition, *Roughnecks* (1997), Thomas Cochran takes the reader through the tension of big-day jitters in the first-person, present-tense narrative of senior Travis Cody as he anticipates the last game of his high school career, the game for the state championship against his hometown's fiercest rivals. Travis lives in a Louisiana town dominated by its football tradition, and he has two reputations to live up to, besides his teammates' and town's expectations of his own performance—his older brother Glen's and his father's. The end of high school football as "Roughnecks" is the end of athletic and educational possibilities for many of the high school players, most of whom will go to work on the oil rigs as "roughnecks," and this gives the game added poignancy. For Travis, moreover, the game is a test he must pass to redeem a past mistake, a moment of letting up that cost his school an earlier game against the same team. Feelings about the game are so intense that Travis has been getting anonymous phone calls from one drunken fan who abuses him for his failure, largely because, as Travis learns, the fan lost a bet on the earlier game. He spends his day psyching himself for the coming contest, focusing particularly on the star linebacker he will face, reflecting on the past, treasuring his friendships with teammates, and looking forward to the physical well-being he hopes to enjoy when he isn't facing the routine severe poundings of practices and weekly games. It is the most important game of Travis's life, and the subject of the novel is his coping with the meaning of this day and the passage of time, rather than the game itself.

Travis's Pawpaw has filled the place of male role model since his father's death in an accident many years earlier, and it is Pawpaw who has passed along a strong sense of family and community history in the physically demanding environment of the now-dying oilfields. Football is a natural expression of the roughnecks' fighting nature. Travis's memories of Pawpaw, now that he too has died, are for the most part pleasant, though he shies away from remembering the debilitating pain his grandfather went through during the final months, when he lost his anchor in time and confused Travis with his father. Travis's empathetic nature shows not only in his feelings about his grandfather and his appreciation of his mother's failure to remarry so that she may focus on caring for him and his brother, but also in his avoidance of hunting.

When Travis was twelve, Pawpaw reflected that time brought only a series of endings, a fatalistic view for a boy to accept, but as Travis has grown older, he has begun to understand Pawpaw's observation in the context of his own life. The clock that governs each football game is an important symbol of time's inexorable nature. Travis fantasizes about freezing time, and that is essentially what the novel does, capturing the doubts, hopes, and fears, the exciting anticipation of the last game. The novel stops short of depicting the end of Travis's high school sports career, thus leaving unanswered the question of whether Travis realizes his hope of being on a college team.

Coach Crews has encouraged the Roughnecks to touch the sign that reads "Sacrifice" every time they go through the door it is tacked to, and Travis has recently found himself thinking about how much he has sacrificed over the years. Sacrifice for football is the norm in a town in which each boy born in the hospital receives a tiny football, and boys play football from the time they can get their hands around a ball. It is not until his high school career is ending that Travis stops to wonder why he is expected to make the sacrifices he has made; that he and every other player will do so unquestioningly is simply expected in Oil Camp. He does not want to live in the past once his high school career is over, as so many of the town's football fans and boosters seem to do. Travis dreams of college, though he does not yet know how he will get there—by the sacrifice of a couple of years of working in the oil fields, most likely, unless the coach who sent him a letter likes what he sees at this championship game.

Along with sacrifice, practice, and seemingly endless reviews of game tapes—that freeze time in their own way—Travis believes in his rituals, despite his English teacher's dismissal of them. He makes his rounds on the big day—to the gym, to his job, to his girlfriend's home—before the day's pep rally and pregame activities take over his time. Despite the exhilaration of this day, Travis again dreams of freezing time in a ride on a new motorcycle with his girlfriend Nita on an endless beautiful afternoon. There is unrealized promise yet in his relationship with her—and her perfume, significantly, is Eternity.

ADDITIONAL READING RECOMMENDATIONS

The Football Rebels by Jackson Stolz, 1960

Vision Quest by Terry Davis, 1979

A Passing Season by Richard Blessing, 1982

Stotan! 1986; *Athletic Shorts: Six Short Stories*, 1989; and *Whale Talk*, 2001 (discussed in
       Accepting Difference), by Chris Crutcher

Forward Pass, 1989, and *Backfield Package*, 1992, by Thomas J. Dygard

Winners and Losers by Stephen Hoffius, 1993

Striking Out, 1993; *Farm Team*, 1995; and *Hard Ball*, 1998, by Will Weaver

Shadow Boxer, 1993; *Iceman*, 1994; and *Slot Machine*, 1995, by Chris Lynch

Twelve Days in August by Liza Ketchum Murrow, 1993

Necessary Roughness by Marie G. Lee, 1996 (discussed in Insiders and Outsiders)

Slam! by Walter Dean Myers, 1996

Tangerine by Edward Bloor, 1997 (discussed in Animals and the Environment)

Damage by A. M. Jenkins, 2001 (discussed in Emotional Problems Confronted)

Painting the Black, 1997, and *High Heat*, 2003, by Carl Deuker

Players by Joyce Sweeney, 2000

Home of the Braves by David Klass, 2002

Shakespeare Bats Cleanup by Ron Koertge, 2003

War's Impact

My Brother Sam Is Dead by James Lincoln Collier and
   Christopher Collier (1975)
Soldier's Heart by Gary Paulsen (1998)
No Man's Land by Susan Campbell Bartoletti (1999)
The Dreams of Mairhe Mehan by Jennifer Armstrong (1996)
The Last Mission by Harry Mazer (1979)
The Man from the Other Side by Uri Orlev (1989; translated
   by Hillel Halkin, 1991)
I Had Seen Castles by Cynthia Rylant (1993)
Sonny's War by Valerie Hobbs (2002)

Warfare is one of the most adult experiences that young adults can encounter. The average age of the U.S. soldier in Vietnam was nineteen—it was a war fought by young people. Historically, youths have lied about their ages in order to sign up, or sometimes about their gender. In defending the homeland from direct attack, young people and old alike may be impressed into service in spite of themselves. And the young are never exempt from a war that is fought on their home territory. Divided loyalties may even separate friends and family, as happens in civil wars.

   Beyond fulfilling a sense of responsibility to one's country or one's loved ones, though, young people, especially young men, seem prone to believe that war promises excitement. Swept up in war fervor, young people fear that the war will be over before they come of age, and their dreams of glory will go unfulfilled. It is also a dramatic crucible, in which boys generally pass to manhood, no matter how realistic or unrealistic their expectations upon enlistment—or they die trying. The near universality of this sentiment in a period when Americans feel threatened is perhaps best represented in the classic *Red Badge of Courage*, as timely now as ever. The older, sadder, and wiser tone achieved by the protagonists of the following novels conveys a realism acquired through the testing period they have survived.

American Revolution

   James Lincoln Collier and Christopher Collier's novel *My Brother Sam Is Dead* (1975) is a now a classic in young adult literature. The novel reflects the period of its writing, the end of the Vietnam conflict, as much as it does the period of its narrative. The story of Sam's stint in the Continental Army, ending ironically in his execution by that same army for "stealing" his own family's cows, is told by his younger brother, Tim, fifty years later, a consistently questioning narrative that ends by asking whether the issues that divided the colonists from their British government might not have been resolved by some means other than war. As he reflects on the events that shaped his boyhood, Tim notes the conflicting views of the War for Independence among his Connecticut neighbors, the impact of war on the community's economy and trust in one another as neighbors, its effects on his family's safety and livelihood, and the degeneration of character that accompanies disregard for law. This family story becomes a metaphor for the Revolution itself as it relates the tragedy of family division in any era dominated by a controversial war.

The story stretches over several years. When Sam comes home in Continental Army uniform early in 1775, having left Yale to get the family's musket, he quarrels with his father, a Loyalist; Tim wavers between his father's and his brother's views, observing the behavior of the adults who seem more interested in commandeering cattle than in serving more noble principles; he accompanies his father on a forty-mile early winter trip that is interrupted by confrontations with cattle thieves masquerading as Patriots and ends in his father's disappearance on the return trip (not until much later do Tim and his mother learn he has died on a prison ship); he witnesses a raid by British soldiers in which an innocent friend Tim's own age is imprisoned and the slave of a Patriot neighbor is killed; Sam returns with the army and, in an effort to protect the family's few remaining cattle, is captured by his own army's patrol and accused of stealing cattle; Sam is tried and executed by firing squad. Tim becomes a man, not by fighting and killing but by taking responsibility for his household, and his maturing through necessity suggests that performing a soldier's tasks does not confer true maturity; indeed, he observes that Sam, when he reenlists, does so not out of a sense of duty but out of a love of excitement.

From the outset, Tim recognizes his father's anguish over the falling out with Sam; the family members have courage, but they have pride too and are unwilling to retreat from their political convictions in order to assure each other of their love, reflecting the generational conflicts of the Vietnam era as well. Tim's mother is embittered by her husband's imprisonment and her son's choice of duty to the army over duty to his family, as life for noncombatants gradually worsens. Neither army embodies virtue or nobility as each helps itself to their goods, shortsightedly depriving them of the means to produce food for later consumption by troops and citizenry alike. As the war progresses, the values of honesty, integrity, and trustworthiness seem dispensable, leaving all citizens at the mercy of increasingly ruffian-like soldiers. It is an effort to stop such behavior with summary justice that results in Sam's execution. Bound to make an example of someone, the commanding officer turns a deaf ear to the pleas of Sam's mother and brother, even though his apparent act of stealing was actually an effort to keep family livestock from being stolen by others. The outcome of the war, for the Meeker family, is disintegration, pain, and ruin, despite the high-minded goals framed so beautifully in the rhetoric of the Revolution's leaders.

The American Civil War

The Civil War has furnished material for many a writer. A crucible in the forging of our nation, it is recent enough to be peopled by understandable characters but remote enough to be largely free of the passions that inspired the conflict. A range of perspectives on the war is represented in the following novels.

Soldier's Heart (1998), by Gary Paulsen, is the fictionalized account of a young Minnesota soldier's experience in the Union Army. Charley Goddard volunteered at age fifteen and saw action throughout the war; the novel recounts Charley's story from his volunteering to his being wounded at Gettysburg in 1863, and then in an epilogue in June 1867 shows the aftereffects of the war—Charley is an old man at twenty-one and contemplating suicide. In a foreword to the narrative, Paulsen gives a brief history of the identification of post–traumatic stress disorder, called variously over the years "battle fatigue," "shell shock," and "soldier's heart." Charley, like many young men before and since, expects the war to be short and imagines it as an adventure and a shortcut to manhood, lives with fear but finds the requisite strength to face it, comes to see the war more or less as a job to finish, and ultimately is horrified by the sights he sees, the acts he finds himself capable of committing, and the numbed grieving he experiences when comrades are cut down. The book is exceptional in representing the long-range emotional impact of Charley's experience.

Inevitably, the reader asks whether any cause is worth the waste of human life and human potential that war brings, foreseeing Charley's end as a casualty of war even though he survived the actual battles. Paulsen tells the story in a spare, straightforward prose that embodies the numbing emotional detachment that Charley imposes on himself much of the time as he faces enemy guns and bayonets over and over. Even when he experiences battle rage, reporting a sense of joy in killing, the language is understated. Some readers may be surprised that he regrets the slaughter of horses more than he does men, but Charley points out that the men are out to kill him whereas the horses are not. Still, as he becomes a seasoned veteran, Charley feels something like sympathy for the soldiers he faces, especially after the historically accurate episode of trading goods during nighttime guard duty on the perimeter. During his first battle, the first Battle of Bull Run (Manassas), Charley prays in desperation, but this is the last time he mentions God. After the war, when he draws back from suicide at the novel's end, he watches the river rather than reflecting on any religious or philosophical meaning in his existence. This is a moving story, despite its understatement, that naturally suggests itself as a bridge to the classic *Red Badge of Courage*.

Many of the same concerns are expressed in Susan Campbell Bartoletti's *No Man's Land* (1999), a novel of a fourteen-year-old Georgia soldier's early war experiences. The protagonist, Thrasher Magee, and his comrades in the Okefinokee (later spelled Okefenokee) Rifles are fictional characters, but the company's actions in Virginia in 1862—in Stonewall Jackson's Shenandoah Valley campaign and then at Gaines' Mill near Richmond—are accurately reported, as Bartoletti makes clear in a note "to the reader" and a useful bibliography of sources. Thrasher signs up because he has let his father down in a confrontation with alligators and feels he must prove himself a man. He does this when his regiment is assigned burial detail, makes a weary march across Virginia, and engages in a battle that costs Thrasher his arm.

Bartoletti brings together several elements of Civil War history in the imagined story: the young enlistee who avoids lying by placing a scrap of paper with "18" on it in his boot so that he may truthfully say he is "standing over eighteen"; the young woman soldier who hides her identity to fight like a man; the kindness of soldiers who return enemy wounded to their comrades under a flag of truce rather than leave the wounded to die on the battlefield; the trading of coffee for tobacco and the sharing of food. She also imagines a baseball game played by soldiers from the opposing armies during such a truce, a scene for which there is no historical source but which seems quite possible, given the documented exchanges and even fellowship among ordinary foot soldiers. What seemed simple and straightforward when he enlisted—a war of a few months' duration against a despicable foe bent on depriving Southerners of their rights (which specific rights remain hazy in Thrasher's mind) that will bring glory and honor in a change that will be immediately visible to his family—becomes much more complicated as Thrasher gets to know more about his fellow Confederates in arms as well as his foes. On both sides, their motives are complex, and their behaviors sometimes unpredictable.

Homesickness is a recurring theme. Thrasher's thoughts often turn to his mother's cooking and his dog's companionship, and he finds that others, too, speak of their loved ones often and pass along letters to their families for mailing in the event of their death in battle. Thrasher discovers honor in his fellow soldiers and his foes, but it is manifested in ways he could not have predicted. Perhaps the most surprising instance of this comes in the transformation of his irrepressible friend Baylor, whom even the loyal Thrasher has accused of being undependable because of his disregard for rules and regulations. Baylor searches diligently for Thrasher on the battlefield, takes him to the hospital tents, and comforts their comrade Tim as she dies, acknowledging her womanhood in quiet grief, without comment on their discovery of her gender. He admits to having sat with a Yankee as he died, giving him water and then adopting the soldier's sorrowing puppy; and he forgoes the opportunity to go home on furlough after the battle, quietly picking up his responsibility as a soldier.

The no-man's-land is the area designated for the baseball game, a game that ends in a tie when the Georgia troops are called by bugle back to camp. The game follows on sharing and trading supplies as well as sharing prayers for a dying Confederate soldier in the presence of soldiers from both burial parties. It is in the temporary no-man's-land that Thrasher must come to terms with the humanity of his foes, and his recognition of their humanity certifies his manhood more fully than any act of violence could.

In *The Dreams of Mairhe Mehan* (1996), Jennifer Armstrong poetically depicts the in-between status of Irish immigrants during the Civil War, with its impact on their sense of identity. Mairhe's mother is dead, and her father has not worked for a year, drinking and dreaming aloud of Ireland; her brother Mike is a bricklayer working on the new capitol dome. Mairhe herself works in a bar in Washington's Irish slum and makes lace at home to eke out their meager income in Washington's Irish slum as 1863 begins. Mairhe has the Irish second sight, dreaming her brother's fate as it unfolds after Mike announces his allegiance to the United States and his commitment to the implementation of emancipation by enlisting in the Union Army, a sudden move that tips the elder Mehan's shaky grasp on reality into a state of confusion. Both men reach their own goals, Mairhe herself is left desolate and fragmented by the war, though she clings to the strength of her dreaming.

After Mike's enlistment in the fight for equality among men, their father is thrust upon the charity of the parish, and Mairhe must live with her employers. Her family life shattered, unable to contact Mike because they are both illiterate, Mairhe is determined to get her brother back. She enlists the help of Walt Whitman to approach the authorities in an effort that proves fruitless: a recently passed law makes new immigrants subject to the draft, and it will cost Mairhe a whopping four hundred dollars to get his release. Resolutely, Mairhe makes yards and yards of lace, ultimately more than seventy dollars' worth at ten cents a yard, but before she can earn the needed sum, Mike is killed at Gettysburg. Since all her weaving of webs and dreams has failed to earn Mike's release, Mairhe turns the money over to her father for his return to Ireland.

Despite the men's actions, which she sees as foolhardy, Mairhe has thought of her lace-making as a means of connecting them all. She weaves a web to hold the family together, a net to rescue them from drowning in homesickness and war. However, her lace-making also entangles her in a web she cannot escape. After Mike's death, she perceives her balls of lace as cannonballs and rids herself of them by selling them to seamstresses, who, unlike her menfolks, recognize that she has "put [her] heart into" making the lace; when she sells it, her heart is numb. Overwhelmed by the war's carnage, she ultimately sees the lace as useful only in the production of winding sheets or bandages.

Mairhe is trapped in the immigrant's in-between state, with memories of her land of birth but no real allegiance to it, not yet committed to the land where she lives. In this state, only her sense of family, embodied in Mike, can give her stability, but even as she works toward his release, she knows that he would not want it, that he has chosen battle like his Celtic forebears and heroes, and she rails against men's need to hurt and kill one another. The emerging egg shape of the capitol dome, being built by the Irish, seems to be hatching broken men, wounded soldiers. Her dreams of Mike are connected to his life: the morning she awakes without having dreamed of him, she knows he is dead before she sees his name on the casualty list. The novel ends on a sad note as she makes it possible for her father to leave her, her only hope in nursing the wounded and helping the republic's egg to hatch.

Images and stories are skillfully interwoven with the narrative. The war is likened to a fight between two brothers, both of whom want their father's legacy. An engagement in Virginia is woven into the account of the Saint Patrick's Day celebration at Shinny's, likening the battle to a dance or celebration. Lincoln's efforts to convince his generals to destroy the Confederate army are portrayed as a solitary dance, a hornpipe. The novel has a dreamlike quality, with Mairhe's narrative of her own experience alternating with third-person narratives of Mike's experiences, Lincoln's experiences, and the life of the bustling capital city. With Whitman, in April 1863, Mairhe smells lilacs in a moment that reminds the reader of Whitman's poem about Lincoln after his April 1865 assassination, "When Lilacs Last in the Dooryard Bloomed." The sadness of this novel makes a more hopeful sequel desirable, and *Mairhe Mehan Awake* (1997) shows her restoration to love and her integration into American life after the war.

World War II

In *The Last Mission* (1979), Harry Mazer tells a straightforward story of an underage sergeant in the U.S. Army Air Forces in the latter days of World War II. Jack Raab, a Jew from the Bronx, signs up at age fifteen, using his brother's birth certificate (the older Irving has heart problems), because he is anxious to fight Hitler. To prevent his family from interfering with his plan, he leaves a note claiming that he is off to see the country, and then, fearing they will betray him to the authorities, he fails to contact them again until he is back in the United States after Allied victory in Europe. Motivated early in his military career by boyish dreams of glory, he rapidly discovers that he has chosen a lonely life, cut off as he is from his family. Full friendship and romance are also limited as he hides behind falsehoods with his fellow soldiers and the only girl he meets before leaving the States. The imagined glory is replaced with the realities of bombing runs over German and German-occupied Europe in a life dominated by nervous tension and the physical discomforts of the bombing runs themselves. His crew's last mission to Pilsen, Czechoslovakia, ends with the plane's being hit. Jack is the only survivor. He is captured by German troops who all too soon must abandon the prisoners in the face of the Allied advance, and during his brief time on the ground Jack sees firsthand what the bombing raids have wrought.

Jack's sobering experiences have made him ready for home, and he admits to his age at the risk of court martial. After he is reunited with his family, comes clean with the girl he has been corresponding with, and confesses his lies to his best friend's family, he finally returns to high school, though the only people he can really find mutual understanding with are other vets. Each of the novel's four parts begins with a quotation. The first three are lyrics from American songs of the period that celebrate patriotism or acknowledge the importance of prayer in the lives of fliers. The last is a German proverb that succinctly sums up the lesson that Jack takes from his experience, that war is not a glorious adventure for heroes: "At the end of a war there are three armies. The army of the wounded, the army of the dead, and the army of the mourners" (147). The novel's greatest strengths are its historical accuracy and its portrayal of young men's enthusiasm for war followed by loss of innocence. It has a strong autobiographical element, closely following Mazer's own World War II experiences as a seventeen-year-old on a bombing crew, including being shot down over Pilsen in an episode that only he survived; his dedication of the book to the members of his group in the Eighth Air Force—living and dead—underscores its emotional impact.

Uri Orlev also draws on personal experience to describe life in the Warsaw Ghetto before and during the uprising against the Germans in *The Man from the Other Side* (1989, translated by Hillel Halkin in 1991). The protagonist, Marek, overcomes the anti-Semitism he has unquestioningly absorbed from his culture when he learns the truth of his father's birth and comes to know a young Jewish man who, after escaping the ghetto, returns to join the Jews' fight against the German occupiers. As he is drawn into the arena of wartime conflict beyond his family circle, Marek comes to terms with the stepfather whom he has resented.

At fourteen, Marek is drawn into his stepfather Antony's smuggling operation, carrying food through the sewer system into the Jewish ghetto and, sometimes, carrying out infants. Antony has no use for Jews—he is in business for the profit—but he turns much of his profit over to the Polish resistance. Though Marek resents his stepfather, he does not question his politics or prejudices, nor does he resist being influenced by a couple of older teens to shake down an escaping Jew. However, when Marek's mother discovers his share of the money and demands an explanation, he receives a shock as he learns that his father, who died under torture in prison without betraying his Communist comrades when Marek was four years old, was Jewish. Marek must now reconcile himself to the picture of his father as Jewish, Communist (an ideology to which Marek is opposed), and a courageous believer in equality.

Already troubled by his robbery of the Jewish man, Marek soon finds himself in a position to redeem himself by helping another escapee from the ghetto. Marek finds shelter for Pan Jozek, a former medical student, with his maternal grandparents. Although his grandmother is strongly anti-Semitic (Marek now understands her opposition to his parents' marriage and the lingering tension between his mother and grandmother), she passes messages for the Polish underground and keeps a low profile at home. Once she has been convinced to take Pan Jozek in, she rapidly becomes fond of him, and Marek's grandfather, who is senile, improves in his company.

Having entered into a network of conspirators who are willing to risk hiding Jews for money, Marek discovers it is larger than he had suspected; the tavern where he works part-time is also a haven for Jews, and the tavernkeeper, Pan Korek, turns the proceeds of this sideline over to the Polish resistance. Working in the tavern, Marek hears news and rumors, and after becoming personally involved in hiding Jews, he becomes more sensitive to the political currents running through his city. When the Jews rise up against the Germans just after Passover, Jozek is anxious to return and support his community. Marek draws on his knowledge of the city's sewer system to lead Jozek back, but he is trapped there himself when a portion of his route caves in after an explosion. He is sure that Antony will be able to find him, knowing all of the ways to navigate the network of sewers, and he takes part in the Jewish uprising, seeing his friend Jozek killed, before helping his stepfather conduct a group of Jews out of the ghetto.

It is a dangerous escapade, and Antony is wounded by German soldiers when they emerge from a manhole outside of the ghetto, but Marek is able to get his stepfather home. After this brush with capture, Antony obtains permission for the family to live with a relative outside of the city, and it is then, after the danger they have shared, that Marek finally allows Antony to adopt him. Seeing the suffering of the Jews and recognizing the hard-heartedness and greed of many of his neighbors, as well as of some of the ghetto residents, Marek doubts God's existence, as did many people who witnessed the horrors of the Holocaust and the war, but reflecting on his experience many years later, he proclaims his belief. The story of the Warsaw Ghetto's uprising is tragic, and any novelistic treatment of this historic drama is gripping. Though Marek discovers that he shares a heritage of prejudice and loses friends, even loses his faith for a time, this is ultimately a life-affirming story, one that ends in acceptance of human nature and acknowledges the presence of the good side by side with the bad.

I Had Seen Castles (1993), by Cynthia Rylant, is an elegy for lost youth and lost innocence that questions the necessity of war. Seventeen-year-old John Dante reacts to Pearl Harbor as most of his contemporaries do, eager to volunteer for the military and fight against the Axis armies. The focus of this novel is the period of waiting for a teen whose parents will not grant him permission to enlist before finishing school and reaching his eighteenth birthday. It depicts the patriotic fervor and emotional tensions generated by the beginning of the war, shown largely through John's brief romance with Ginny and his observation of his beautiful sister's relationships with the young men, on the verge of leaving for war, who crave the love of a woman.

The nostalgic first-person narrative mourns a time of life and a way of life that can never be recaptured by those who have lost boyhood friends and comrades and have participated in the destruction of others' lives and homes, shown most vividly through John's war experience when he witnesses the carnage wrought in a peaceful sheep pasture that lies below a castle in Italy. The epigraph, from Rainer Marie Rilke, likens the heart to a tower standing alone bearing witness to pain. Early on, John identifies himself as a retired literature professor, now living in Toronto after twenty years in France. He is seeking a life of solitude, one he hopes will bring him some measure of peace. His childhood life in Pittsburgh, even his emotional connection to his family, has been totally destroyed for him by World War II. From this privileged position of later knowledge, he tells of his involvement with Ginny, a young woman who challenges his readiness to fight as well as the United States' readiness to declare war, remembering her as the only person from his past with whom he has retained a sense of connection, despite fifty years of silence between them.

John meets Ginny early in 1942, as the country is mobilizing fully for the war effort. Ginny is new to the city and comes from a working-class background, unlike John, whose family is educated and middle class. His father, a scientist, is recruited into development of the atomic bomb, while Ginny's father has come to Pittsburgh to take a factory job producing war materials, appreciating the economic opportunity the war has offered. Everyone is affected by the war, everyone is caught up in it one way or another, and everyone talks about the war. With her background and values, along with her individualism and outspoken honesty, Ginny questions John's assumptions about military might and a man's duty. Despite their differences, their mutual attraction draws them together, overcoming their differences. John's love-making with Ginny is the only area of adult experience he knows when he goes to war at age eighteen, and he regards her certainty that he will live to be old as a prophecy, whose magic sustains him later when the dangers of the war threaten him with loss of life or loss of will to go on.

In contrast to his sister, Diane, who becomes engaged to several young men and bears a child to one who dies, John creates no lasting bond with Ginny. Once at war, he finds himself unable to answer her letters because he needs to believe in the nobility of the cause he has enlisted in, and her letters remind him too powerfully of her antiwar position. The act of love has not made them one, but it makes Ginny unforgettable to John, though he cannot find her again after the war.

Lives are shattered by war, and there is no turning back, John asserts, no recapturing the innocent joy that those who have not witnessed war can find in life. His experience has altered him forever, and he no longer can share his mother's and sister's sentiments, nor can he live in America, which has not suffered the ravages of war and does not know how horrible it is. Fifty years later, John observes, with understated irony, that those countries that were enemies in the 1930s and 1940s have become allies in the 1990s. Despite the horrors of war that he touches on very lightly, he knows that young men will continue to go to war. He has long since forgiven Ginny her opposition to war, and in this quiet retrospective, he declares his continued love for her.

Vietnam

In *Sonny's War* (2002), Valerie Hobbs traces the development of fourteen-year-old Cory's opposition to the Vietnam War during 1967–68, while her brother, Sonny, is in the army, as well as the change wrought in Sonny by his war experience, as seen by Cory. Neither teen has thought much about the war's causes or justification, absorbed as they are in family life and adjusting to the small town where their parents have recently opened a restaurant. The army seems like a ticket out of the California mountain town in which they sometimes feel trapped. After their father's unexpected death virtually on the eve of Sonny's departure, Sonny is motivated largely by a need to prove himself in a way that would have made his father proud. Although their mother asserts that he was proud of both of his children, Sonny is not convinced. His life in Ojala revolves around cars: he works in a local garage, and, like his peers, he races on the mountain roads, vying for the status earned by the most reckless driver with the fastest car. This competition, fueled further by Sonny's rivalry with the current champ, Jason, for the favors of Jason's girlfriend, is the private war he is engaged in before leaving for the army, but this small personal contest is thoroughly eclipsed by his Vietnam experiences.

Before leaving for war, Sonny has strong family ties. Cory adores her older brother. She is a part of his social life: she rides along when he is cruising, curses the police officer who arrests him for speeding, witnesses the illegal races, attends the parties he attends, and knows his friends who leave for war with him, Goose the drinker and carefree Luis. She takes nearly as much pride in Sonny's red Ford as he does, and he has taught her to drive it before he leaves it in her care. Sonny is close to his mother too. He has stepped into the role of man of the family, arranging his father's funeral and shouldering responsibility for its expense. He seems to have a clear vision about his life while his mother struggles to figure out whether she can continue to run the restaurant without her husband. However, Sonny's apparent clarity as he leaves for the army, congratulated as a hero even by the police officer who recently arrested him, dissolves when he confronts the actuality of the war.

The progress of Sonny's disillusionment with the war, as he moves from seeing it as a way out and a testing ground, is shown briefly in his letters to his mother and sister but more fully in Cory's own growing political awareness sparked by her new history teacher's activism. Cory develops a serious crush on twenty-three-year-old Lawrence, but his teaching has an impact on her thinking that outlasts her infatuation. Lawrence assigns newspaper reading and initiates classroom debates that require research; he talks seriously with students about the war; he starts a daily silent protest against the war outside the cafeteria during lunch—where he is gradually joined by other teachers and a few students—and he starts a school debate club. Cory's reading of Sonny's letters becomes more sophisticated with her knowledge of the war and the growing antiwar movement. Their mother remains comparatively innocent; for instance, she interprets Sonny's "getting out more" as welcome action rather than dangerous missions.

Lawrence's political activities and long hair get him fired, despite Cory's vigorous defense of his teaching to Sam, a school board member who is also her mother's devoted admirer. When Cory seeks him out at a weekend peace rally at the nearby university, her feelings for Lawrence change as she witnesses him instigate violence. She feels lucky to have come through her adventure without being arrested or hurt, either at the rally or in illegally driving her brother's car. The episode leaves her confused, as she recalls Lawrence's commitment to peace and his preaching nonviolence in the classroom and then contrasts it with his actions: does this mean that Lawrence is not a good person after all? A later phone conversation destroys the love she thought she felt when he denies his involvement in the crime she saw him commit.

Sonny is still the most important male in her life, and she and her mother worry through his reports of being wounded, especially after his friend Goose comes home in a wheelchair and Luis comes home in a body bag. When Sonny does arrive, he is emotionally distant and haunted. Though he no longer cares about racing, Jason is spoiling for a decisive run, and Sonny agrees to it in a moment when he is ready to throw his life away, an attitude that Cory only understands after she is out of the car, waiting to observe the contest. It is Jason who crashes, however, but after it is clear that he will survive, Sonny wraps up life in Ojala, at least for the present, by acting as Jason's best man in a hospital wedding, selling the Ford to settle the debt for his father's funeral and headstone, and heading out on a directionless hitchhiking trip to try to come to terms with what he has seen and what he has done, not at all convinced that he can be a good person after having killed people. Sonny's war with himself is in its earliest stages. In only one area has Sonny reached resolution: Cory and her mother can prove his father was proud of him, having discovered a wealth of personal notes and observations scattered through the cookbook he kept during his years of restaurant cooking.

While Sonny's changes may have scarred him for life, Cory and her mother have grown significantly in his absence. Her mother has learned how to cook, made changes in the restaurant, and begun to develop a life for herself. Cory is significantly more mature at fifteen than she was at fourteen: she has come to terms with her father's death, accepted changes in her mother, and begun working as a waitress, as well as driving legally with a learner's permit, and she has adopted an antiwar position that proves more than a manifestation of Lawrence's influence. Sonny's emotional pain and permanent limp have sealed her opinion that he should have gone to Canada to begin with, rather than to the army. She has become aware of the relationships among family dynamics, social forces, and international policies that shape individual lives.

ADDITIONAL READING RECOMMENDATIONS

Africa

AK by Peter Dickinson, 1990; U.S. edition, 1992

American Civil War

Across Five Aprils by Irene Hunt, 1964
Which Way Freedom? 1986; *Out from This Place*, 1988; and *The Heart Calls Home*, 1999,
        by Joyce Hansen

Cambodia

The Clay Marble by Minfong Ho, 1991

Fictional War

The Forty-third War by Louise Moeri, 1989

Gulf War

Hometown by Marsha Qualey, 1995
Gulf by Robert Westall, 1996

Japan

The Samurai's Tale, 1984; *The Boy and the Samurai*, 1991; and *The Revenge of the Forty-
        Seven Samurai*, 1995, by Erik Haugaard

Latin America

Journey of the Sparrows by Fran Leeper Buss and Daisy Cubias, 1991
Before We Were Free by Julia Alvarez, 2002
Tree Girl by Ben Mikaelsen, 2004

Vietnam

Fallen Angels by Walter Dean Myers, 1988
Song of the Buffalo Boy by Sherry Garland, 1992
Stand Tall by Joan Bauer, 2002
Island Boyz: Short Stories by Graham Salisbury, 2002
Our Time on the River by Don Brown, 2003

World War II

Blitzcat, 1989; *The Kingdom by the Sea*, 1991; and *The Promise*, 1991, by Robert Westall
Shadow of the Wall, 1990, and *But Can the Phoenix Sing?* 1992, by Christa Laird
Code Name Kris, 1990; *After the War*, 1996; *The Garden*, 1997; and *Greater Than Angels*,
    1998, by Carol Matas
Along the Tracks by Tamar Bergman, 1991
Tug of War by Joan Lingard, 1991
Alex, Who Won His War by Chester Aaron, 1991
Molly Donnelly by Jean Thesman, 1993
The Boys from St. Petri by Bjarne Reuter, translated by Anthea Bell, 1994
Spying on Miss Muller by Eve Bunting, 1995
The Lady with the Hat by Uri Orlev, 1995
The Final Journey by Gudrun Pausewang, translated by Patricia Crampton, 1996
Stones in Water by Donna Jo Napoli, 1997
Two Suns in the Sky by Miriam Bat-Ami, 1999
Good Night, Maman by Norma Fox Mazer, 1999
Soldier Boys by Dean Hughes, 2001
Slap Your Sides by M. E. Kerr, 2001

Yugoslavia

Smiling for Strangers by Gaye Hicyilmaz, 1998

Appendix: Additional Themes and Topics

African Americans

America by E. R. Frank
The Buffalo Tree by Adam Rapp
The Cay by Theodore Taylor
The Contender by Robert Lipsyte
Dancing on the Edge by Han Nolan
The First Part Last by Angela Johnson
From the Notebooks of Melanin Sun by Jacqueline Woodson
The Glory Field by Walter Dean Myers
A Hero Ain't Nothin' but a Sandwich by Alice Childress
Humming Whispers by Angela Johnson
If Beale Street Could Talk by James Baldwin
Jip: His Story by Katherine Paterson
Like Sisters on the Homefront by Rita Williams-Garcia
Monster by Walter Dean Myers
Necessary Roughness by Marie G. Lee
Running Loose by Chris Crutcher
Seedfolks by Paul Fleischman
Shayla's Double Brown Baby Blues by Lori Aurelia Williams
Slave Day by Rob Thomas
Tangerine by Edward Bloor
Toning the Sweep by Angela Johnson
True Believer by Virginia Euwer Wolff
Whale Talk by Chris Crutcher
A White Romance by Virginia Hamilton

American Indians

Beardance by Will Hobbs
Bearstone by Will Hobbs
Dogsong by Gary Paulsen
The Facts Speak for Themselves by Brock Cole
Far North by Will Hobbs
Go and Come Back by Joan Abelove (South America)
Walk Two Moons by Sharon Creech

Art, Music, Theater, and Writing as Means of Expression

The Arthur trilogy by Kevin Crossley-Holland
The Body of Christopher Creed by Carol Plum-Ucci
The Book of the Banshee by Anne Fine
Buddha Boy by Kathe Koja
Dance on My Grave by Aidan Chambers
Dancing on the Edge by Han Nolan
Fat Kid Rules the World by K. L. Going
From the Notebooks of Melanin Sun by Jacqueline Woodson
Good Moon Rising by Nancy Garden
Hard Love by Ellen Wittlinger
Homeless Bird by Gloria Whelan
The House on Mango Street by Sandra Cisneros
Humming Whispers by Angela Johnson
If Beale Street Could Talk by James Baldwin
I Was a Teenage Fairy by Francesca Lia Block
Izzy, Willy-Nilly by Cynthia Voigt
Jacob Have I Loved by Katherine Paterson
Kit's Wilderness by David Almond
Like Sisters on the Homefront by Rita Williams-Garcia
Lombardo's Law by Ellen Wittlinger
Monster by Walter Dean Myers
Of Sound Mind by Jean Ferris
The Other Side of Silence by Margaret Mahy
Seek by Paul Fleischmann
Shizuko's Daughter by Kyoko Mori
The Sisterhood of the Traveling Pants by Ann Brashares
Smack by Melvin Burgess
Speak by Laurie Halse Anderson
Stoner & Spaz by Ron Koertge
Straydog by Kathe Koja
A Time for Dancing by Davida Wills Hurwin
24 Hours by Margaret Mahy
The Watcher by James Howe
When She Was Good by Norma Fox Mazer
Whirligig by Paul Fleischmann
You Don't Know Me by David Klass

Asian Americans

Necessary Roughness by Marie G. Lee
Seedfolks by Paul Fleischmann

Australia/New Zealand

Letters from the Inside by John Marsden
The Other Side of Silence by Margaret Mahy
24 Hours by Margaret Mahy

Chicano/Latino Culture

Bless Me, Ultima by Rudolfo Anaya
Buried Onions by Gary Soto
Hard Love by Ellen Wittlinger
The House on Mango Street by Sandra Cisneros
The Sisterhood of the Traveling Pants by Ann Brashares
Slave Day by Rob Thomas
Tangerine by Edward Bloor
Whirligig by Paul Fleischmann

Disabilities

Are You Alone on Purpose? by Nancy Werlin
God of Beer by Garret Keizer
Of Sound Mind by Jean Ferris
Whale Talk by Chris Crutcher

England

The Arthur trilogy by Kevin Crossley-Holland
The Book of the Banshee by Anne Fine
Catherine, Called Birdy by Karen Cushman
Dance on My Grave by Aidan Chambers
Eva by Peter Dickinson
Kit's Wilderness by David Almond
The Midwife's Apprentice by Karen Cushman
Smack by Melvin Burgess

Gays and Lesbians

Breaking Boxes by A. M. Jenkins
Dance on My Grave by Aidan Chambers
God of Beer by Garret Keizer
Good Moon Rising by Nancy Garden
Happy Endings Are All Alike by Sandra Scoppettone
Hard Love by Ellen Wittlinger
If It Doesn't Kill You by Margaret Bechard

I Was a Teenage Fairy by Francesca Lia Block
Whistle Me Home by Barbara Wersba

Immigrants

The Dreams of Mairhe Mehan by Jennifer Armstrong
Mairhe Mehan Awake by Jennifer Armstrong
Seedfolks by Paul Fleischman

India

Homeless Bird by Gloria Whelan

Japan

Shizuko's Daughter by Kyoko Mori
The Spring Tone by Kazumi Yumoto

Jewish Experience

Are You Alone on Purpose? by Nancy Werlin
Chernowitz! by Fran Arrick
The Man from the Other Side by Uri Orlev
One Fat Summer by Robert Lipsyte
Seek by Paul Fleischmann
The Summer Boy by Robert Lipsyte

Medicine, Healing, Hospitalization, Dying

Are You Alone on Purpose? by Nancy Werlin
Backwater by Joan Bauer
Bless Me, Ultima by Rudolfo Anaya
The Borning Room by Paul Fleischmann
The Bumblebee Flies Anyway by Robert Cormier
Catalyst by Laurie Haltz Anderson
The Facts Speak for Themselves by Brock Cole
The First Part Last by Angela Johnson
Freak the Mighty by Rodman Philbrick
Get It While It's Hot. Or Not by Valerie Hobbs
Go and Come Back by Joan Abelove
Good Moon Rising by Nancy Garden
Homeless Bird by Gloria Whelan
Hope Was Here by Joan Bauer
Izzy, Willy-Nilly by Cynthia Voigt
Jacob Have I Loved by Katherine Paterson
Like Sisters on the Homefront by Rita Williams-Garcia
The Midwife's Apprentice by Karen Cushman
My Darling, My Hamburger by Paul Zindel
Of Sound Mind by Jean Ferris
The Outsiders by S. E. Hinton

Phoenix Rising by Karen Hesse
Rules of the Road by Joan Bauer
The Sisterhood of the Traveling Pants by Ann Brashares
The Spring Tone by Kazumi Yumoto
Staying Fat for Sarah Byrnes by Chris Crutcher
A Time for Dancing by Davida Wills Hurwin
Walk Two Moons by Sharon Creech
Winning by Robin Brancato

Selected Bibliography
of Secondary Sources

General

Agnew, Kate, and Geoff Fox. *Children at War: From the First World War to the Gulf*. New York: Continuum, 2001.

Beacham's Guide to Literature for Young Adults. Washington, DC: Beacham, 2002.

Berger, Laura Standley, ed. *Twentieth-Century Young Adult Writers*. Detroit: St. James Press, 1994.

Brown, Joanne, and Nancy St. Clair. *Declarations of Independence: Empowered Girls in Young Adult Literature, 1990–2001*. Scarecrow Studies in Young Adult Literature. Lanham, MD: Scarecrow Press, 2002.

Cai, Mingshui. *Multicultural Literature for Children and Young Adults: Reflections on Critical Issues*. Westport, CT: Greenwood Press, 2002.

Contemporary Authors Online. Thomson Gale, 2005.

Crew, Hilary S. *Is It Really Mommie Dearest? Daughter-Mother Narratives in Young Adult Fiction*. Lanham, MD: Scarecrow Press, 2000.

Egoff, Sheila, et al., eds. *Only Connect: Readings on Children's Literature*. New York: Oxford UP, 1996.

Hipple, Ted, ed. *Writers for Young Adults*. 3 vols. New York: Charles Scribner's Sons, 1997.

———. *Writers for Young Adults*. Supplement 1. New York: Charles Scribner's Sons, 2000.

Hogan, Walter. *Humor in Young Adult Literature: A Time to Laugh*. Scarecrow Studies in Young Adult Literature. Lanham, MD: Scarecrow Press, 2005.

Hunt, Peter, and Millicent Lenz. *Alternative Worlds in Fantasy Fiction*. New York: Continuum, 2001.

Karolides, Nicholas J., ed. *Censored Books, II: Critical Viewpoints, 1985–2000*. Lanham, MD: Scarecrow Press, 2002.

Lehr, Susan, ed. *Beauty, Brains, and Brawn: The Construction of Gender in Children's Literature*. Portsmouth, NH: Heinemann, 2001. (of interest to educators)

MacRae, Cathi Dunn. *Presenting Young Adult Fantasy Fiction*. Twayne's United States Authors Series (Young Adult Authors). New York: Twayne, 1998.

Manlove, C. N. *From Alice to Harry Potter: Children's Fantasy in England*. Christchurch, New Zealand: Cybereditions, 2003.

Marcus, Leonard S., ed. *Author Talk: Conversations with Judy Blume, Bruce Brooks, Karen Cushman, Russell Freedman, Lee Bennett Hopkins, James Howe, Johanna Hurwitz, E. L. Konigsburg, Lois Lowry, Ann M. Martin, Nicholasa Mohr, Gary Paulsen, Jon Scieszka, Seymour Simon, and Laurence Yep*. New York: Simon and Schuster, 2000.

Molin, Paulette F. *American Indian Themes in Young Adult Literature*. Scarecrow Studies in Young Adult Literature. Lanham, MD: Scarecrow Press, 2005.

Moore, John Noell. *Interpreting Young Adult Literature: Literary Theory in the Secondary Classroom*. Portsmouth, NH: Boynton/Cook, 1997. (of interest to educators)

Nelson, Emmanuel S., ed. *Contemporary African American Novelists: A Bio-Bibliographical Critical Sourcebook*. Westport, CT: Greenwood, 1999.

Novels for Students. 22 vols. Detroit: Thomson Gale, 1999–2005.

Pendergast, Tom, and Sara Pendergast, eds. *St. James Guide to Young Adult Writers*. 2nd ed. Detroit: St. James Press.

Smith, Karen Patricia. *African American Voices in Young Adult Literature: Tradition, Transition, Transformation*. Scarecrow Studies in Young Adult Literature. Lanham, MD: Scarecrow Press, 2001.

Zitlow, Connie S., ed. *Lost Masterworks of Young Adult Literature*. Scarecrow Studies in Young Adult Literature. Lanham, MD: Scarecrow Press, 2002.

Lloyd Alexander

May, Jill P. *Lloyd Alexander*. Twayne's United States Authors Series. New York: Twayne, 1997.

Rudolfo Anaya

Adams, Robert M. "Bless Me, Ultima." *New York Review of Books* 34 (March 26, 1987): 33(2).

Bruce-Novoa, Juan. "Learning to Read (and/in) Rudolfo Anaya's *Bless Me, Ultima*." *Teaching American Ethnic Literatures: Nineteen Essays*. Edited by John R. Maitino and David R. Peck. Albuquerque: U of New Mexico P, 1996. 179–91. (of interest to educators)

Candelaria, Cordelia. "Problems and Promise in Anaya's *Llano*." *American Book Review* 5.6 (Sept.–Oct. 1983): 18–19.

Dick, Bruce, and Silvio Sirias, eds. *Conversations with Rudolfo Anaya*. Jackson: UP of Mississippi, 1998.

Fernandez Olmos, Margarita. *Rudolfo A. Anaya: A Critical Companion*. Westport, CT: Greenwood Press, 1999.

Godina, Heriberto, and Rachelle McCoy. "Emic and Etic Perspectives on Chicana and Chicano Multicultural Literature." *Journal of Adolescent and Adult Literacy* 44.2 (Oct. 2000): 172–79. (of interest to educators)

Kanoza, Theresa M. "The Golden Carp and Moby-Dick: Rudolfo Anaya's Multi-Culturalism." *MELUS* 24.2 (summer 1999): 159–71.

Klein, Dianne. "Coming of Age in Novels by Rudolfo Anaya and Sandra Cisneros." *English Journal* 81.5 (Sept. 1992): 21–26. (of interest to educators)

"Rudolfo A(lfonso) Anaya." *Contemporary Literary Criticism*. Vol. 23. Edited by Sharon R. Gunton. Detroit: Gale Research, 1983. 22–27.

"Rudolfo Anaya." *Contemporary Literary Criticism*. Vol. 148. Edited by Jeffrey W. Hunter. Detroit: Gale Research, 2002. 1–64.

Avi

Bloom, Susan P., and Cathryn M. Mercier. *Presenting Avi*. Twayne's United States Authors Series (Young Adult Authors). New York: Twayne, 1997.

Francesca Lia Block

Susina, Jan. "The Rebirth of the Postmodern Flaneur: Notes on the Postmodern Landscape of Francesca Lia Block's Weetzie Bat." *Marvels & Tales* 16.2 (Oct. 2002): 188–201.

Judy Blume

Weidt, Maryann N. *Presenting Judy Blume*. Twayne United States Authors Series (Young Adult Authors). New York: Twayne, 1990.
Younger, Beth. "Pleasure, Pain, and the Power of Being Thin: Female Sexuality in Young Adult Literature." *NWSA Journal* 15.2 (summer 2003): 45–56.

Orson Scott Card

Christine, Doyle. "Orson Scott Card's Ender and Bean: The Exceptional Child as Hero." *Children's Literature in Education* 35.4 (Dec. 2004): 301–17. (of interest to educators)
Tyson, Edith S. *Orson Scott Card: Writer of the Terrible Choice*. Scarecrow Studies in Young Adult Literature. Lanham, MD: Scarecrow Press, 2003.

Alice Childress

Gebhard, Ann O. "The Emerging Self: Young-Adult and Classic Novels of the Black Experience." *English Journal* 82.5 (Sept. 1993): 50–54. (of interest to educators)

Sandra Cisneros

Cruz, Felicia J. "On the 'Simplicity' of Sandra Cisneros's 'House on Mango Street.'" *Modern Fiction Studies* 47.4 (winter 2001): 910–42.
Doyle, Jacqueline. "More Room of Her Own: Sandra Cisneros's 'The House on Mango Street.'" *MELUS* 19.4 (winter 1994): 6–35.
Klein, Dianne. "Coming of Age in Novels by Rudolfo Anaya and Sandra Cisneros." *English Journal* 81.5 (Sept. 1992): 21–26. (of interest to educators)
Petty, Leslie. "The 'Dual'-ing Images of la Malinche and la Virgen de Guadalupe in Cisneros's *The House on Mango Street*." *MELUS* 25.2 (summer 2000): 119–33.
"Sandra Cisneros." *Contemporary Literary Criticism*. Vol. 118. Edited by Jeffrey W. Hunter and Timothy J. White. Detroit: Gale Research, 1999. 169–220.
"Sandra Cisneros." *Contemporary Literary Criticism*. Vol. 193. Edited by Tom Burns and Jeffrey W. Hunter. Detroit: Gale Research, 1999. 1–136.

Robert Cormier

Campbell, Patricia J. *Presenting Robert Cormier*. Twayne's United States Authors Series (Young Adult Authors). New York: Twayne, 1985.
Silvey, Anita. "An Interview with Robert Cormier." *Horn Book Magazine* 61 (March–April 1985): 145–55.
———. "An Interview with Robert Cormier. (Part 2)." *Horn Book Magazine* 61 (May–June 1985): 289–96.

Kevin Crossley-Holland

Baker, Deirdre F. "Poetry in Prose." *Horn Book Magazine* 81.3 (May–June 2005): 271–79.

Chris Crutcher

Bushman, John H., and Kay Parks Bushman. "Coping with Harsh Realities: The Novels of Chris Crutcher." *English Journal* 81.3 (March 1992): 82–84. (of interest to educators)

Crutcher, Chris. *King of the Mild Frontier: An Ill-Advised Autobiography*. New York: Greenwillow, 2003.

Davis, Terry. "A Healing Vision." *English Journal* 85.3 (March 1996): 36–41. (of interest to educators)

———. *Presenting Chris Crutcher*. Twayne's United States Authors Series (Young Adult Authors). New York: Twayne, 1997.

McDonnell, Christine. "New Voices, New Visions: Chris Crutcher." *Horn Book Magazine* 64.3 (May–June 1988): 332–35.

Soublis, Theoni, and Erik Winkler. "Transcending Bias through Reader-Response Theory." *English Journal* 94.2 (Nov. 2004): 12–25. (of interest to educators)

Peter Dickinson

Cameron, Eleanor. "A Discussion of Peter Dickinson's 'Eva.'" *Horn Book Magazine* 70.3 (May–June 1994): 291–96.

Carter, Betty. "A Second Look: 'Eva.'" *Horn Book Magazine* 77.5 (Sept. 2001): 541–48.

Karen Hesse

Oliphaunt-Ingham, Rosemary. *Karen Hesse*. Scarecrow Studies in Young Adult Literature. Lanham, MD: Scarecrow Press, 2005.

S. E. Hinton

Daly, Jay. *Presenting S. E. Hinton*. Twayne's United States Authors Series (Young Adult Authors). New York: Twayne, 1989.

Will Hobbs

Hobbs, Will. "Survival Micro and Macro." *Horn Book Magazine* 72.2 (March–April 1996): 174–77.

M. E. Kerr

Nilsen, Alleen Pace. *Presenting M. E. Kerr*. Twayne's United States Authors Series (Young Adult Authors). New York: Twayne, 1986.

Robert Lipsyte

Cart, Michael. *Presenting Robert Lipsyte*. Twayne's United States Authors Series (Young Adult Authors). New York: Twayne, 1995.

Harry Mazer

Reed, Arthea J. S. *Presenting Harry Mazer*. Twayne's United States Authors Series (Young Adult Authors). New York: Twayne, 1996.

Norma Fox Mazer

Holtze, Sally Holmes. *Presenting Norma Fox Mazer*. Twayne's United States Authors Series (Young Adult Authors). New York: Twayne, 1989.

Reed, Arthea J. S. *Norma Fox Mazer: A Writer's World*. Lanham, MD: Scarecrow Press, 2000.

Walter Dean Myers

Bishop, Rudine Sims. *Presenting Walter Dean Myers*. Twayne's United States Authors Series (Young Adult Authors). New York: Twayne, 1991.

Myers, Walter Dean. *Bad Boy: A Memoir*. New York: HarperCollins, 2001.

Phyllis Reynolds Naylor

Stover, Lois Thomas. *Presenting Phyllis Reynolds Naylor*. Twayne's United States Authors Series (Young Adult Authors). New York: Twayne, 1997.

Zibby Oneal

Bloom, Susan P., and Cathryn M. Mercier. *Presenting Zibby Oneal*. Twayne's United States Authors Series (Young Adult Authors). New York: Twayne, 1991.

Katherine Paterson

"Katherine Paterson: *Jacob Have I Loved*." In *Literature and Its Times: Profiles of 300 Notable Literary Works and the Historical Events That Influenced Them*. Vol. 4: *World War II to the Affluent Fifties (1940–1950s)*. Edited by Joyce Moss and George Wilson. Detroit: Gale Research, 1997.

Schmidt, Gary D. *Katherine Paterson*. Twayne's United States Authors Series. New York: Twayne, 1994.

Smedman, M. Sarah, and Joel D. Chaston, eds. *Bridges for the Young: The Fiction of Katherine Paterson*. Scarecrow Studies in Young Adult Literature. Lanham, MD: Scarecrow Press, 2003.

Gary Paulsen

Salvner, Gary M. *Presenting Gary Paulsen*. Twayne's United States Authors Series (Young Adult Authors). New York: Twayne, 1996.

Richard Peck

Gallo, Donald R. *Presenting Richard Peck*. Twayne's United States Authors Series (Young Adult Authors). New York: Twayne, 1993.

Philip Pullman

Hunt, Peter, and Millicent Lenz. *Alternative Worlds in Fantasy Fiction*. New York: Continuum, 2001.

Loy, David R., and Linda Goodhew. *The Dharma of Dragons and Daemons: Buddhist Themes in Modern Fantasy*. Boston, MA: Wisdom, 2004.

Pullman, Philip. "The Republic of Heaven." *Horn Book Magazine* 77.6 (Nov.–Dec. 2001): 655.

Wood, Naomi. "(Em)Bracing Icy Mothers: Ideology, Identity, and Environment in Children's Fantasy." In *Wild Things: Children's Culture and Ecocriticism*. Edited by Sidney I. Dobrin and Kenneth B. Kidd. Detroit: Wayne State UP, 2004. 198–214.

Cynthia Voigt

Reid, Suzanne Elizabeth. *Presenting Cynthia Voigt*. Twayne's United States Authors Series (Young Adult Authors). New York: Twayne, 1995.

Paul Zindel

Clarke, Loretta. "The Pigman: A Novel of Adolescence." *English Journal* 61 (1972): 1163–69, 1175. (of interest to educators)

Forman, Jack Jacob. *Presenting Paul Zindel*. Twayne's United States Authors Series (Young Adult Authors). New York: Twayne, 1988.

Index

About the Author

ALICE TRUPE is Director of the Writing Center and Associate Professor of English at Bridgewater College, in Virginia. Her wide-ranging interests include Shakespeare, nineteenth-century novels, poetry, and American history.